Interpretive Lenses in Sociology

Series editors: **Thomas DeGloma**, Hunter College, City University of New York, and **Julie B. Wiest**, West Chester University of Pennsylvania

---

The *Interpretive Lenses in Sociology* series provides a unique forum for scholars using a wide range of interpretive perspectives to explore their approaches to uncovering the deep meanings underlying human actions, events and experiences.

Forthcoming in the series

Interpreting Subcultures
Sense-Making from Insider and Outsider Perspectives
Editor **J. Patrick Williams**

Out now in the series:

Interpretive Sociology and the Semiotic Imagination
Editors **Andrea Cossu** and **Jorge Fontdevila**

Interpreting the Body
Between Meaning and Materiality
Editors **Anne Marie Champagne** and **Asia Friedman**

Interpreting Religion
Making Sense of Religious Lives
Editors **Erin Johnston** and **Vikash Singh**

Find out more at
bristoluniversitypress.co.uk/interpretive-lenses-in-sociology

International advisory board:

Jeffrey C. Alexander, Yale University, US
Marni A. Brown, Georgia Gwinnett College, US
Giuseppina Cersosimo, University of Salerno, Italy
Lynn S. Chancer, Hunter College, City University of New York, US
Erica Chito-Childs, Hunter College, City University of New York, US
Manase Kudzai Chiweshe, University of Zimbabwe, Zimbabwe
Jean-François Côté, University of Montreal, Canada
Emma Engdahl, University of Gothenburg, Sweden
Veikko Eranti, University of Helsinki, Finland
Emily Fairchild, New College of Florida, US
Gary Alan Fine, Northwestern University, US
Stacey Hannem, Wilfrid Laurier University, Canada
Titus Hjelm, University of Helsinki, Finland
Annemarie Jutel, Victoria University of Wellington, New Zealand
Carol Kidron, University of Haifa, Israel
Krzysztof T. Konecki, University of Lodz, Poland
Joseph A. Kotarba, Texas State University, US
Donileen Loseke, University of South Florida, US
Eeva Luhtakallio, University of Helsinki, Finland
Lisa McCormick, The University of Edinburgh, Scotland
Neil McLaughlin, McMaster University, Canada
Beth Montemurro, Pennsylvania State University, Abington, US
Kylie Parrotta, California Polytechnic State University, US
Laura Robinson, Santa Clara University, US
Andrea Salvini, University of Pisa, Italy
Susie Scott, University of Sussex, UK
Cristine G. Severo, Federal University of Santa Catarina, Brazil
Xiaoli Tian, University of Hong Kong, Hong Kong
Vilna Bashi Treitler, Northwestern University, US
Hector Vera, National Autonomous University of Mexico, Mexico
Gad Yair, The Hebrew University of Jerusalem, Israel
J. Patrick Williams, Nanyang Technological University, Singapore
Eviatar Zerubavel, Rutgers University, US

Find out more at
bristoluniversitypress.co.uk/interpretive-lenses-in-sociology

INTERPRETING CONTENTIOUS MEMORY

Countermemories and Social Conflicts over the Past

Edited by
Thomas DeGloma and Janet Jacobs

First published in Great Britain in 2025 by

Bristol University Press
University of Bristol
1-9 Old Park Hill
Bristol
BS2 8BB
UK
t: +44 (0)117 374 6645
e: bup-info@bristol.ac.uk

Details of international sales and distribution partners are available at bristoluniversitypress.co.uk

© Bristol University Press 2025

British Library Cataloguing in Publication Data
A catalogue record for this book is available from the British Library

ISBN 978-1-5292-1866-4 hardcover
ISBN 978-1-5292-1867-1 paperback
ISBN 978-1-5292-1868-8 ePub
ISBN 978-1-5292-1869-5 ePdf

The right of Thomas DeGloma and Janet Jacobs to be identified as editors of this work has been asserted by them in accordance with the Copyright, Designs and Patents Act 1988.

All rights reserved: no part of this publication may be reproduced, stored in a retrieval system, or transmitted in any form or by any means, electronic, mechanical, photocopying, recording, or otherwise without the prior permission of Bristol University Press.

Every reasonable effort has been made to obtain permission to reproduce copyrighted material. If, however, anyone knows of an oversight, please contact the publisher.

The statements and opinions contained within this publication are solely those of the editors and contributors and not of the University of Bristol or Bristol University Press. The University of Bristol and Bristol University Press disclaim responsibility for any injury to persons or property resulting from any material published in this publication.

Bristol University Press works to counter discrimination on grounds of gender, race, disability, age and sexuality.

Cover design: blu inc, Bristol
Front cover image: iStock/oorka (chain) and Unsplash/Jan Kopřiva (background)

Contents

Series Editors' Preface: Interpretive Lenses in Sociology – On the Multidimensional Foundations of Meaning in Social Life *Thomas DeGloma and Julie B. Wiest*		vii
Notes on Contributors		xii
Acknowledgments		xvii
1	Introduction: Interpreting Contentious Memories and Conflicts over the Past *Thomas DeGloma and Janet Jacobs*	1
PART I	**Interpreting Memories in the Social Dynamics of Contention**	
2	On the Social Distribution of Soldiers' Memories: Normalization, Trauma, and Morality *Edna Lomsky-Feder*	29
3	Feminist Approaches to Studying Memory and Mass Atrocity *Nicole Fox*	49
4	Mobilizing Memories: Remembrance as a Social Movement Tool in the Vieques Anti-Military Movement (1999–2004) *Roberto Vélez-Vélez*	69
5	The Ballot of Donald and Hillary: Hateful Memories of Celebrity Leaders *Gary Alan Fine, Christopher Robertson, and Cal Abbo*	89
PART II	**Racism, Exclusion, and Mnemonic Conflict**	
6	Building a Case for Citizenship: Countermemory Work among Deported Veterans *Sofya Aptekar*	113
7	Commemorations as Transformative Events: Collective Memory, Temporality, and Social Change *Claire Whitlinger*	134

8	Contentious Pasts, Contentious Futures: Race, Memory, and Politics in Montgomery's Legacy Museum *Amy Sodaro*	154

PART III Genocide, Memory, and the Historicizing of Trauma

9	Remembrance and Historicization: Transformation of Individual and Collective Memory Processes in the Federal Republic of Germany *Werner Bohleber*	177
10	Enlisting Lived Memory: From Traumatic Silence to Authentic Witnessing *Carol A. Kidron*	197
11	Changing Memories of the Shoah in Post-Communist Countries: New Memories and Conflicts *Selma Leydesdorff*	217
12	How Difficult Pasts Complicate the Present: Comparative Analysis of the Genocides in Western Armenia and Rwanda *Jacob Caponi and Fatma Müge Göçek*	236
13	Conclusion: Memory and the Social Dynamics of Conflict and Contention: Interpretive Lenses for New Cases and Controversies *Janet Jacobs and Thomas DeGloma*	258
Index		266

Series Editors' Preface: Interpretive Lenses in Sociology – On the Multidimensional Foundations of Meaning in Social Life[1]

Sociology is an interpretive endeavor. Whatever the approach taken to study and explain an aspect of social life – qualitative or quantitative, micro or macro – sociologists work to interpret their data to reveal previously unseen, or to clarify previously misunderstood, social forces. However, within the broad field of sociology, and under the purview of its kindred disciplines, there are many scholars who work to unpack the deep structures and processes that underlie the *meanings* of social life. These interpretive scholars focus on the ways that social meanings constitute the core structures of self and identity, the ways that individuals negotiate meanings to define their shared situations, and the collective meanings that bind people together into communities while also setting any given group or context apart from others. From this perspective, meaning underscores social mindsets and personal orientations in the world, as well as the solidarities and divisions that define the dynamics and mark the boundaries of our social standpoints and relationships. Furthermore, such scholars are concerned not only with how the individuals and groups they study actively make and remake the definitions that are central to their lives, as well as how those understandings influence their behaviors, but also how they seek to impact the world with their meaning-making processes. In this regard, meaning is of paramount significance to both the extraordinary moments and the routine circumstances of our lives.[2]

In their efforts to illuminate the deep social foundations of meaning, and to detail the very real social, political, and moral consequences that stem from the ways people define and know the world around them, interpretive scholars explore the semiotic significance of social actions and interactions, narratives and discourses, experiences and events. In contrast to those who take a positivist or realist perspective and see the world – or, more precisely, argue that the world can be known – in a more direct or literal light,³ they use various approaches and draw on different interpretive traditions to decipher their cases in order to better understand the deep social, cultural, and psychic foundations of the phenomena they study. From such interpretive perspectives, a fundamental part of any social phenomenon is not directly evident or visible. Rather, the core foundations of meaning underlying the cases scholars study need to be unpacked, analyzed, and interpreted – and then rearticulated – to comprehend their deeper essences.⁴ And they do this work of interpretation from various angles and perspectives, using different "lenses." It is with such interpretive lenses, in sociology and beyond, that we concern ourselves here. How do the people we study make sense of the world? How do they cooperate with others to construct shared understandings, and how do such actors define their situations for various audiences? Furthermore, how do scholars understand their sense-making processes and interpret their actions and experiences? How do they get at the deep social forces, culture structures, and relationships underlying the topics and themes they study?⁵ Finally, how do their interpretations allow scholars to construct new and powerful explanations of social phenomena? How do they "possess explanatory torque" with regard to various topics of widespread significance (Reed, 2011, p 11; see also Garland, 2006, pp 437–438)?

This is the perspective from which we organized a unique conference, *The Roots and Branches of Interpretive Sociology: Cultural, Pragmatist, and Psychosocial Approaches*, in Philadelphia, Pennsylvania, in August 2018. From this endeavor, we learned that many scholars were excited by our call to bring them to the table to discuss their interpretive lenses with one another. Many almost intuitively grasped the distinctions we made among traditions and camps in the field (the cultural, the pragmatist/interactionist, the psychosocial, and others) that could be gathered under the umbrella of a broader "interpretive" agenda in sociology. And why not? We make such distinctions between different camps, with their various theoretical and methodological traditions, when we teach. This is how we organize many of our journals, our professional societies and their sections, and other scholarly institutions. We also often use such categories to explain our scholarly identities. In line with these distinctions, qualitative interpretation has developed simultaneously along different paths and among a field of factional communities, and the proponents of these different camps make various claims to distinguish their respective approaches from others.

However, despite the fact that we use such distinctions to delineate our disciplinary field, they rarely sync neatly with the work scholars actually do when they interpret the cases, communities, and issues they study. Rather, in their practices of social research and in their acts of interpretation, scholars combine and integrate elements of different traditions and programs in various ways that help them to focus on and make sense of their experiences as scholars. In other words, the process of interpretation comes alive in the practice of research and, more particularly, in research situations that demand a range of theoretical and methodological tools to illuminate and articulate the social foundations of meaning central to the case at hand.[6] Thus, over the course of their work, scholars develop interpretive lenses that help them find answers to the questions that drive them. While this may not come as a surprise to many readers, we rarely interrogate or compare the nuances of these lenses explicitly.

The purpose of this series is to interrogate, explore, and demonstrate the various interpretive lenses that scholars use when they engage their areas of interest, their cases, and their research situations. Each volume is centered on a substantive topic (for example, religion, the body, or contentious memories) or a particular interpretive-analytic method (for example, semiotics or narrative analysis). The editors of each volume feature the work of scholars who approach their central topic using different interpretive lenses that are particularly relevant to that area of focus. They have asked each author to explicitly illustrate and reflect on two dimensions of interpretation in their work, and to explore the connections between them. First, they asked authors to address how the individuals and communities they study assign meanings and achieve shared understandings with regard to the core topic of their volume. In doing so, authors address the social and cultural forces at play in shaping how people understand their identities, experiences, and situations, as well as how they frame their accounts, motivations, and purposes while acting, communicating, and performing in the world. Second, volume editors asked contributing authors to explicitly reflect on their interpretive processes and approaches to unpacking the meanings of the social phenomena they study. Some authors present new material while others provide a reflexive overview of their research to date, but all illustrate and discuss the work of interpretation and the central significance of meaning. Such conscious reflection on our interpretive traditions and lenses – on how they shape our analytic foci (in terms of what cases we explore, at what levels of analysis, and with regard to which social actors) and the ways we find meaning in our cases – can illuminate under-recognized or unspoken choices we make in our work. Furthermore, it can expose blind spots and suggest new frameworks for dialogue among scholars. This reflexive dimension, along with the diversity of lenses featured together in each volume, is what makes this series unique. In this vein, and to these ends, we hope the volumes of this series will present arrays of interpretive lenses that readers can use while working to make sense of their own cases and to develop new perspectives of their own. In the process, we also hope to advance the dialogue about interpretation and meaning in the social sciences.

In this volume, Thomas DeGloma and Janet Jacobs present a collection of essays that explore the morally and politically charged phenomenon of "contentious memory." With an overarching emphasis on the ways that actors promote countermemories as they confront dominant and entrenched views of the past, this collection highlights different theoretical and methodological traditions scholars use to explore a variety of cases that show how the past is commonly a focal point of social conflict. Approaching a breadth of topics from a range of interpretive perspectives, the chapters in this book offer numerous insights that the editors tie together in the volume's introduction, which also offers a cogent and compelling overview of the various issues and dimensions of analysis associated with mnemonic conflict and contentious memory. With this important work, DeGloma and Jacobs show how and why disputes over the past are central to the broad and developing area of social memory studies, as well as to many other areas of sociological concern and study.

The contributors to this volume are all memory scholars in their own right, but, as the editors point out, "they are also variously known by the ways their research makes other contributions – as psychoanalytic social theorists, anthropologists, historians, immigration scholars, race scholars, ethnographers, gender theorists, social movement researchers, and more." These scholars apply various combinations of analytic perspectives to unpack the complexities of conflict and contention with regard to social memory and history, with many calling direct attention to the frictions between personal or autobiographical memories, on the one hand, and more public and collective memories, commemorations, and memorials, on the other hand. In the process, they call attention to consequential issues such as war, genocide, military occupation, electoral conflict, immigration and deportation, race and racism, trauma and its transmission, and various political conflicts over history. All the while, these authors have worked to illustrate and reflect on their particular interpretive lenses, considering not only what their cases illustrate, but also how they have come to know and understand this – how the people they study build the meanings of the past and how they, as scholars, create their own meanings and frameworks for comprehending the social dynamics of memory. All of these chapters, therefore, offer readers various tools that can be used to study new cases focused on unresolved, difficult, and problematic past events, episodes, and experiences. We are thrilled to feature this important book as part of our *Interpretive Lenses in Sociology* series.

Thomas DeGloma
Hunter College and the Graduate Center, CUNY
Julie B. Wiest
West Chester University of Pennsylvania

Notes

1. An extended series introduction is available for open access download at www.bristoluniversitypress.co.uk/interpretive-lenses-in-sociology. Shorter and slightly modified versions appear as prefaces to the different volumes of this series.
2. On the centrality of meaning in interpretive social analysis, see Reed's (2011) important work on interpretation and knowledge, especially his discussions of the "interpretive epistemic mode" (pp 89–121) and the "normative epistemic mode" (pp 67–88).
3. See Reed (2011), especially on the "realist semiotic and the illusion of noninterpretation" (p 52).
4. Indeed, this is what Clifford Geertz (1973) meant when he called for "thick description" in ethnographic analysis.
5. Alfred Schütz (1967 [1932], pp 205–206; 1970, p 273) recognized the layers of interpretation we point to here when he argued, "The thought objects constructed by the social scientist ... have to be founded upon the thought objects constructed by the common-sense thinking of [people], living their daily life within their social world. Thus, the constructs of the social sciences are, so to speak, constructs of the second degree, namely constructs of the constructs made by the actors on the social scene." Geertz (1973, p 9) made a similar distinction when he argued "that what we call our data are really our own constructions of other people's constructions." Also see Reed (2017, pp 29–31) on "interpreting interpretations." Such a distinction informs the fundamental premises of psychoanalysis, as the analyst is always in the business of interpreting interpretations and unpacking layers of symbolism.
6. See also Tavory and Timmermans (2014), who advocate engaging the process of research and interpretation armed with "multiple theoretical perspectives" (p 35).

References

Garland, D. (2006) "Concepts of Culture in the Sociology of Punishment," *Theoretical Criminology* 10(4): 419–447.

Geertz, C. (1973) "Thick Description: Toward an Interpretive Theory of Culture," in *The Interpretation of Cultures*, New York: Basic Books, pp 3–30.

Reed, I.A. (2011) *Interpretation and Social Knowledge: On the Use of Theory in the Human Sciences*, Chicago: University of Chicago Press.

Reed, I.A. (2017) "On the Very Idea of Cultural Sociology," in C.E. Benzecry, M. Krause, and I.A. Reed (eds) *Social Theory Now*, Chicago: University of Chicago Press, pp 18–41.

Schütz, A. (1967 [1932]) *The Phenomenology of the Social World*, Evanston, IL: Northwestern University Press.

Schütz, A. (1970) *On Phenomenology and Social Relations*, Chicago: University of Chicago Press.

Tavory, I. and Timmermans. S. (2014) *Abductive Analysis: Theorizing Qualitative Research*, Chicago: University of Chicago Press.

Notes on Contributors

Cal Abbo is a Detroit-based journalist with the *Chaldean News*, where he is a writer, content editor, and design contributor. His work focuses on community engagement and Chaldean history. Cal received his B.A. in Sociology with a minor in journalism from Hillsdale College.

Sofya Aptekar is Associate Professor of urban studies at the City University of New York School of Labor and Urban Studies. She writes about the US immigration system, military and imperialism, urban public space, and alternatives to capitalism. Aptekar is the author of *Green Card Soldier: Between Immigrant and Security Threat* (MIT Press) and *The Road to Citizenship: What Naturalization Means for Immigrants and the United States* (Rutgers University Press).

Werner Bohleber is a psychoanalyst in private practice in Frankfurt, Germany and former President of the German Psychoanalytic Association. From 1997 to 2017 he was main editor of the journal *PSYCHE*. In 2007 he received the Mary S. Sigourney Award, an international award recognizing outstanding contributions to psychoanalysis. His research subjects and main publication themes are late adolescence and young adulthood; psychoanalytic theory; history of psychoanalysis in Germany; transgenerational consequences of the Nazi period and the war on the second and third generation; nationalism, xenophobia and anti-Semitism; trauma; terrorism. His most recent book in English is *Destructiveness, Intersubjectivity, and Trauma: The Identity Crisis of Modern Psychoanalysis* (Karnac).

Jacob Caponi is a PhD student at the University of Michigan. His research interests are in societal responses to violence, and particularly overlapping systems of oppression that interact at times of atrocities. His current project, supported by the US National Science Foundation, examines the relationship between law, medicine, and human rights in Rwanda.

Thomas DeGloma is Associate Professor of Sociology at Hunter College and the Graduate Center of the City University of New York. He specializes in the areas of culture, cognition, memory, symbolic interaction, and sociological theory. His research interests also include the sociology of time, knowledge, autobiography, identity, and trauma. He is the author of *Seeing the Light: The Social Logic of Personal Discovery* (University of Chicago Press) and *Anonymous: The Performance of Hidden Identities* (University of Chicago Press), along with articles published in *Social Psychology Quarterly*, *Sociological Forum*, *Symbolic Interaction*, the *American Journal of Cultural Sociology*, and in various edited volumes. DeGloma has served as President of the Society for the Study of Symbolic Interaction (2017–18) and Secretary of the Eastern Sociological Society (2016–19).

Gary Alan Fine is the James E. Johnson Professor of Sociology at Northwestern University. He received his PhD in Social Psychology from Harvard University. He is known as an ethnographer, a sociologist of culture, and a social theorist with a focus on the dynamics of interaction. Among his many ethnographic projects are studies of Little League baseball, fantasy role-playing games, restaurant kitchens, art schools, meteorology offices, competitive chess, and senior citizen activism. His most recent books are *The Hinge: Civil Society, Group Cultures, and the Power of Commitment* (University of Chicago Press); *Group Life: An Invitation to Local Sociology* (Polity); and *Fair Share: Senior Activists, Tiny Publics, and the Culture of Resistance* (University of Chicago Press).

Nicole Fox is Assistant Professor of Criminal Justice at California State University Sacramento. Her research centers on how racial and ethnic contention impacts communities, with a focus on how remembrances of adversity shape social change and collective memory. Her 2021 book *After Genocide: Memory and Reconciliation in Rwanda* (University of Wisconsin Press) analyses how memorials to past atrocity impact community development and reconciliation for survivors of genocide and genocidal rape. Her work has been supported by the Harry Frank Guggenheim Foundation, the National Science Foundation, Andrew Mellon Foundation, Prevention Innovation Research Center, and the American Sociological Society's Fund for the Advancement of the Discipline, among other sources.

Fatma Müge Göçek is Professor of Sociology at the University of Michigan. Her research focuses on the comparative analysis of history, politics, and gender in the first and third worlds. She critically analyses the impact of processes such as development, nationalism, religious movements, and collective violence on minorities. She is the author of *Denial of Violence: Ottoman Past, Turkish Present, and Collective Violence against the Armenians, 1789–2009* (Oxford University Press) and is currently working on a theory book, constructing social theory from the vantage point of minorities.

Janet Jacobs is Professor of Distinction in Women and Gender Studies at the University of Colorado Boulder. Her research focuses on ethnic and religious violence, gender, mass trauma, and collective memory. She is author of numerous books and journal articles, including *Divine Disenchantment: Deconverting from New Religions* (Indiana University Press), *Victimized Daughters: Incest and the Development of the Female Self* (Routledge), *Hidden Heritage: The Legacy of the Crypto-Jews* (University of California Press), *Memorializing the Holocaust: Gender, Genocide and Collective Memory* (I.B. Tauris), and *The Holocaust Across Generations: Trauma and Its Inheritance Among Descendants of Survivors* (New York University Press). She is editor of *Religion, Society and Psychoanalysis* and *William James: The Struggle for Life*. Her articles have been published in *Signs: A Journal of Women in Culture and Society*, the *Journal for the Scientific Study of Religion*, *Gender and Society*, and *Memory Studies*. Her current work is on genocide and collective memory in Bosnia-Herzegovina.

Carol A. Kidron is Associate Professor in the Department of Sociology and Anthropology at the University of Haifa. Kidron has undertaken comparative ethnographic work with Holocaust descendants in Israel and children of Cambodian genocide survivors in Cambodia and Canada. She has focused on the interface between private and public Holocaust and Genocide memory work, aiming primarily to reconceptualize trauma descendant lived memory of difficult pasts as silent intersubjective embodied and emotive presence. Beyond her interest in personal and collective Holocaust and Genocide commemoration, Kidron's more recent research examines the globalization of discourses on justice and reconciliation, victimhood, and memory in post-conflict societies. Her present field work in Cambodia explores processes of localization and friction in local-global encounters and the multi-layered responses to hegemonically imposed memorialization, organic forms of genocide commemoration, and atrocity tourism.

Selma Leydesdorff is Emeritus Professor of Oral History and Culture at the University of Amsterdam. She has published extensively on both Jewish history and oral history. Her dissertation, *We Lived with Dignity,* was published in a German and an English translation. She is one of the principal editors of the *Memory and Narrative Series* (Routledge) and has published extensively on the Holocaust and on surviving genocide and trauma. Leydesdorff has supervised several international projects and is best known for her work on women surviving the genocide of Srebrenica, which was translated in English and Bosnian. For the last ten years she has worked on the history of Sobibor and has interviewed survivors and co-plaintiffs around the Demjanjuk trial. The collection is stored in the United States Holocaust Memorial Museum in Washington DC. In 2017 she published a biography of Alexandr Pechersky, the leader of the uprising in Sobibor in 1943 dealing with Nazism and the persecution of Jews in the communist world.

Edna Lomsky-Feder is Full Professor at the Department of Sociology and Anthropology and at the School of Education, the Hebrew University of Jerusalem. Her research interests include memory and nationalism, war and military from a cultural perspective, young adults and transition to adulthood, immigration and identity and personal narratives.

Christopher Robertson is a doctoral candidate in the Department of Sociology at Northwestern University, where he is a Mellon Cluster Fellow in Comparative-Historical Social Science and affiliate of the Science in Human Culture Program. His research sits at the intersection of education, religious belief, knowledge making, and right-wing politics. Christopher's dissertation is a comparative-organizational ethnography of two conservative liberal arts colleges, one that emphasizes the "Western Tradition" and the other evangelical witness. He received his BA in Sociology from the University of Texas at Austin.

Amy Sodaro is Associate Professor of Sociology at the Borough of Manhattan Community College, City University of New York. Her research focuses on museums, memory, and commemoration. She is author of *Exhibiting Atrocity: Memorial Museums and the Politics of Past Violence* (Rutgers University Press) and co-editor of *Museums and Sites of Persuasion: Memory, Politics and Human Rights* (Routledge) and *Memory and the Future: Transnational Politics, Ethics and Culture* (Palgrave Macmillan). Her current research focuses on memory, slavery, and race in new US museums.

Roberto Vélez-Vélez is Associate Professor of sociology and affiliated faculty for Latin American, Caribbean and Latinx Studies at State University of New York-New Paltz. His research areas include social movements, memory studies, culture, and Latin American Studies. He has published on the anti-military movement in Vieques, Puerto Rico, the intersection between memory, identity and politics, and US-Latin American political dynamics. More recently, Vélez-Vélez has been collaborating on an NSF-funded ethnographic project that examines the post-hurricane community recovery response through the formation, reach, and impact of *Centros de Apoyo Mutuo* in the aftermath of hurricane María in Puerto Rico.

Claire Whitlinger is Associate Professor of Sociology at Furman University in Greenville, South Carolina. Her research examines the causes and consequences of commemorating difficult pasts, investigating the relationship between social identities, collective memory, and social change. She is the creator and co-founder of Furman's Intergroup Dialogue Program and the 2019 recipient of Furman University's Meritorious Diversity & Inclusion Award for faculty. Her research has been featured in *Sociological Forum, Mobilization*, and PBS's *American Experience*, and her book, *Between Remembrance and Repair: Commemorating Racial Violence in Philadelphia, Mississippi*, was published in 2020 by the University of North Carolina Press.

Acknowledgments

We are grateful to all the people who worked to make this book a reality in the midst of the global COVID-19 pandemic and the various political crises that have shaped the past few years. As scholars, we feel that the crises we face, past and present, demand our attention and prompt us to develop new lenses with which to understand the world and guide meaningful action. We humbly and respectfully hope this book contributes in this regard. We would like to thank Victoria Pittman, Anna Richardson, Shannon Kneis, Bahar Celik Muller, Dawn Preston, and all the wonderful editors and production staff at Bristol University Press for their work, consistent support, and guidance. We would also like to thank our anonymous reviewers who, at various stages, provided invaluable feedback. We owe a special word of appreciation to Max Papadantonakis for his careful proofing and formatting work and to Katie Holstein Mercer and Ian Whalen for their helpful contributions. Finally, as we look to the future of this project, we are grateful for the work of memory scholars and activists of the past who have paved the way for our own modest contributions.

1

Introduction: Interpreting Contentious Memories and Conflicts over the Past

Thomas DeGloma and Janet Jacobs

On June 27, 2015, ten days after white supremacist Dylan Roof shot and killed nine people attending a bible study group at the Emanuel African Methodist Episcopal Church in Charleston, South Carolina, Bree Newsome Bass, a 30-year-old Black woman, climbed a flagpole at the South Carolina statehouse in Columbia and removed the Confederate flag – a historic symbol that, at the time, had flown there for over 50 years.[1] For some, including many South Carolina state officials at the time, the Confederate flag stands as a symbol of pride in the history of southern culture and values, one that distinguishes southern states from their northern counterparts.[2] However, for many others it is one of the most recognizable symbols of slavery, oppression, and white supremacy in the US. Reflecting on her actions, Newsome Bass later stated that when she learned of the Charleston Church shooting, "all the ghosts of the past seemed to be rising" (Edwards, 2015). From her perspective, the contemporary shooting was not an isolated act of racist hate, but one connected to a long chain of events – an ongoing system of violence with deep roots. By targeting this flag, she linked the contemporary fight against systemic racism and violence against Black people in America to unresolved issues and events in US history and collective memory. Her protest was as much a confrontation focused on that past and its legacy as it was an expression of outrage spurred by a current tragedy. Similar confrontations focused on Confederate memorials, iconography, and symbols have occurred in the wake of contemporary acts of police violence, including the 2020 murder of George Floyd, linking this current and ongoing issue to the history of US slavery and racism (Ortiz and Diaz, 2020; Logan, 2021).[3]

To more fully grasp the meaning of Newsome Bass's 2015 protest at the South Carolina statehouse, we must delve even deeper to further unpack and interpret the *subversive semiotics* and the multiple layers of *contentious memory* that underlie the act itself. Newsome Bass was not protesting a static symbol, but one that, in its contemporary context, became meaningful as an act of commemoration, and one that therefore expresses a contemporary social standpoint associated with a particular orientation to the past. State authorities in South Carolina first raised the Confederate flag at the State House in 1961 to commemorate the 100th anniversary of the *beginning* of the Civil War which ignited with the Battle of Fort Sumter just outside of Charleston (see Worland, 2015). In other words, the flag was first raised over the seat of government in South Carolina to mark the initiation and birthplace of a war of secession fought to defend the system of slavery. Furthermore, 1961 was also the year of the Freedom Rides, when the US Civil Rights Movement was gaining steam, achieving unprecedented national attention along with growing support from white Northerners. Thus, the flag Newsome Bass removed was mobilized in its commemorative symbolism to oppose efforts to overthrow Jim Crow segregation in the South and achieve civil rights and racial equality. In 1861 *and* in 1961, the flag represented the defiance of white Southerners in the face of efforts to advance Black liberation and expand democracy. Moreover, it was actively and intentionally situated as a symbol of government in the state of South Carolina, flown at the State House and thereby linked to the meaning of political power, authority, and the boundaries of democratic representation.[4] In short, white supremacist actors have always used this flag to advance the causes of racist oppression. Building on the argument that we must explore "what monuments are intended to *do* for and within a body politic" (Murphy, 2021: p 1144), we also need to interpret *what people do* with various symbols of the past. Such a perspective allows us to consider how the past, in whatever form it is mobilized (as flag, monument, memorial, textbook, or testimony, for example) becomes meaningful in contemporary performances which are situated in complex and pluralistic social environments.[5]

In this vein, and just as importantly, we should also interpret the meaning of Newsome Bass's actions as a response to the violent massacre perpetrated by Dylan Roof ten days prior, which was itself steeped in the contentions of history and memory. The two events exist in semiotic opposition, as a contemporary expression of deeply entrenched dynamics of power and as dueling orientations to both past and present. Roof targeted one of the oldest Black churches in the country. With a history dating to the early 19th century, the Emanuel African Methodist Episcopal Church (Emanuel A.M.E.) is an iconic center of work to achieve Black liberation and civil rights in the US. Commonly referred to as "Mother Emanuel," the original place of worship in South Carolina was burnt down by a mob of whites in

1822, after one of its founders was executed for organizing a slave rebellion, forcing members to meet in secret for decades, until well after the end of the Civil War (Weisman, 2015). The church also served as an organizing center for the Civil Rights Movement in the 20th century, standing in symbolic opposition to the forces that raised the Confederate flag over the South Carolina statehouse in 1961 (Reverend Martin Luther King, Jr. spoke at Emanuel A.M.E. in 1962). Thus, the church is well known for "its legacy of rebellion" against the institutions of racism (Weisman, 2015), making Roof's attack deeply meaningful in a historic sense. While Roof's act of violent terrorism evoked the history and memory of slavery and white supremacy, Newsome Bass's actions ten days later, which in her words she conducted "in the name of Jesus … against … hatred, oppression, and violence,"[6] evoked the history and memory of southern Christian Black resistance. Together, the two actions – Roof's followed by Newsome Bass's – expressed counter-positions with regard to the history and collective memory of slavery in the US.

This book is focused on exploring the ways that scholars interpret contentious memories and social conflicts over the past. How can we understand disputes over the meanings and consequences of past events, prior experiences, and historical episodes? How can scholars better grasp the meanings of contemporary actions, especially those steeped in contention, conflict, and dynamics of power, by exploring their mnemonic or historically oriented characteristics? Our subject matter includes explicit disputes over the past – what scholars have referred to as "mnemonic battles" (Zerubavel, 2003; DeGloma, 2015; see also Irwin-Zarecka, 1994: pp 67–84) – but also other types of political clashes and unresolved moral issues that involve parties that act with different visions of the past and different ideas about its relevance to present concerns and issues. In many cases, memory and the meanings of the past are deeply embedded in contentious social relationships, especially relations of power, and power is enacted in ways that rely on "a wide variety of *mnemonic products and practices*" (Olick, 2016: p 43; see also Olick and Robbins, 1998; Rigney, 2008). Thus, the social analysis of memory often "goes to the heart of many of the issues at the forefront of contemporary political debate and struggle" (Radstone, 2008: p 32), as well as many of our deepest moral and existential concerns. Discussing various topics, themes, and cases rooted in different parts of the word and situated at different levels of analysis, from intrafamilial dynamics to international relations, the contributors to this volume show us how interpreting contentious memories is central to their work. In the process, they elucidate the ways that contemporary social conflicts and other forms of unrest, upheaval, and confrontation commonly involve memory work. That is, parties to contemporary social disputes and confrontations, and those who are positioned differently relative to entrenched relations of power, often mobilize different and competing versions of the past as they make their claims in the present and pursue their future-oriented objectives (DeGloma, 2014a: pp 67–68; Szpunar, 2021). Thus, with this book we are broadly concerned with the ways that past events, experiences, and circumstances remain contentious in the present, and how various actors experience and mobilize particular visions of the past as they navigate difficult social circumstances and, sometimes, engage in open social conflict.

Contentious memories and conflicts over the past take a variety of forms and manifest at various levels of social life, and we are especially interested in the ways these different levels interact. From an intrapersonal psychoanalytic perspective, contentious memories manifest as unresolved inner conflicts that create a powerful impetus to repression and form a core foundation of personal suffering – pain or anguish that often impacts social relationships from the interpersonal to the broadly collective. On another level, contentious memories manifest when actors use personal testimony and autobiographical stories to dispute mainstream meanings. Expressing a tension between "forms of public and private remembering and forgetting" (Barnier and Hoskins, 2018: p 388), they share their personal life memories to (re)define socially relevant events and issues of the past. In addition, mnemonic contention and conflict also take form as heated debates or drawn-out clashes between different communities, from small groups and movements to large religious and political camps, including nations, that stand opposed over the meaning and impact of political events and episodes in history. Such groups compete to establish the proper version of both personal and collective memory, as when, for example, actors in different camps struggle to determine how nations ought to relate to their difficult pasts (Olick, 2003a, 2016; Saito, 2006; Simko, 2015; Badilla and Aguilara, 2021). In each case, and at each level, the past is very much alive and unresolved; it intrudes on the present to define current issues and relationships in important ways.

With these different levels of social life in mind, we hope this book contributes to a more integrated and comprehensive exploration of the foundations and dynamics of contentious memory and mnemonic conflict. But beyond studying memory for memory's sake, we also hope to demonstrate a variety of ways that scholars integrate the analysis of contentious memory into the study of social conflict and contention more broadly, enhancing our understanding of social inequalities and power relations of all types. To this end, we are primarily focused on elucidating different "interpretive lenses" (DeGloma and Wiest, 2022) that scholars use to explore the manifold social dimensions and manifestations of contentious memory and conflict rooted in the past. In line with the aims of the series in which this book is published, we have asked the contributors to this volume "to illustrate their interpretive processes and reflect on them so that the diversity of interpretive lenses in" the study of contentious memories and mnemonic conflict "can be made more explicit" (DeGloma and Wiest, 2022: p 4). In response to our prompts, each author offers their version of analytic reflection by carefully illustrating how they come to grasp the meanings of contentious memory in their research. Some authors provide a more personally reflexive approach while others have focused more on unpacking the nuances of their methodological and theoretical contributions. However, all the authors illustrate the strengths of their interpretive vision and thereby provide a model that readers can use to understand contentious memories and conflicts over the past.

In developing this volume, we intentionally chose to include a diverse collection of scholars who approach the issue of contentious memory from different angles and perspectives as they work to make sense of their cases. We thus embrace the eclecticism of this collection, and we hope this aspect of the project will encourage readers to think more about how different scholars view contentious memories from different angles, and how various interpretive lenses can contribute to a more holistic (though multifaceted) study of mnemonic conflict. We also hope this aspect of the project will inspire readers to combine different approaches and to see connections between different levels of analysis and different themes. Memory is a core dimension of social conflict and fundamental to durable relations of power. It must be explicitly engaged and interpreted for a clear and comprehensive account of the ways that conflict and power dynamics play out over time, take dramatic form, and involve *meaning* at the most fundamental level. We have asked the contributors to this volume to show us how they do this work of interpretation – how they understand the ways that contentious memory is central to the cases they study, and how they uncover the ways that the people they study come to understand the past in the midst of their contentious situations and relationships.

The social foundations of contentious memory

The social analysis of memory has developed around complementary concerns with *mnemonic solidarity* and *mnemonic contention* – with the harmonies and the divisions that define our social relationships with regard to the past. On the one hand, building on the seminal ideas of Maurice Halbwachs ([1950] 1980, 1992), many scholars have worked to elucidate the social forces underlying shared memories (Schwartz, 1982, 1996) and collective mnemonic practices (Olick and Robbins, 1998; Rigney, 2008), along with the ways that sharing a vison of the past creates and reinforces bonds of social solidarity and collective identity in the present. Taking such a perspective, scholars explore the ways that memory manifests as a collective phenomenon that resides at the level of groups and communities (both small and large), as commonly held (aggregated) visions of past events and scenarios that matter for both personal identity and social affiliation (see Olick, 1999a), or as processes of "collaborative remembering" in social relationships (see Meade et al, eds, 2018; see also Fivush, Hayden, and Reese, 1996; Fivush, 2011). With this emphasis on the shared character of memory, scholars have also shown how our seemingly personal accounts and autobiographical reflections are shaped by social forces and cohere around norms rooted in the communities to which we belong (Prager, 1998; Vinitzky-Seroussi, 1998; DeGloma, 2014a; DeGloma and Johnston, 2019). Thus, social memory scholars explore and interpret the various ways that actors – both individuals and groups – cooperate to define the past and its relevance to present and future concerns, whether via collective rituals and team performances of various types, or by institutionalizing particular visions of the past with museums, memorials, monuments, and educational curricula, for example. In the process, such actors express and reinforce the bonds of social solidarity that unite moral and political communities and shape the social identities they share.

However, on the other hand, memory scholars have simultaneously been concerned with *contentious memories* and conflicts over the past. In this regard, scholars have explored how the meanings of past events and experiences create turbulence and motivate conflict and contention in the present, and the ways that disputes and tensions between contentious agents (from individuals to nations) commonly involve explicit references to, and disagreements over, both the meaning and significance of past events and occurrences. Such disputes and controversies typically occur when the members of different mnemonic communities (Zerubavel, 2003) have competing frames of memory (Irwin-Zarecka, 1994) with which they define broadly relevant issues and events of the past and connect them to present circumstances. In this sense, the past is contested terrain, and history and memory exist as disputed narratives. Such memory conflicts manifest at different levels of human experience, from the psychological to the broadly social and cultural, and they occur with regard to various politically and morally charged topics and subject matters. Moreover, such contentious memories and mnemonic disputes often take form according to different entrenched relations of power. They can thereby give us insight into broadly relevant social dynamics regarding, for example, race, sex and gender, ethnicity and nationality, religion, and much more. In fact, many of the most salient moral and political conflicts of our current era, along with the most fundamental relations of power in the world, involve disputes over how we ought to understand events and experiences of the past. Put plainly, memory is central to social conflict and contention.

From a holistic perspective, these two frameworks – one that stresses harmony and solidarity and the other that stresses conflict and contention – complement one another and help us to see how mnemonic norms and solidarities form in the midst of contentions over past events and issues. As mnemonic communities establish shared normative visions of the past, they actively express and perform their particular visions in contentious relation to different groups that have alternative perspectives on the meanings of history or the significance of past occurrences to their present concerns (Irwin-Zarecka, 1994: pp 67–85). That is, they pit their social orientation to the past against other standpoints; their mnemonic solidarity takes form in the face of contention. In this regard, "shared memories can be effective markers of social differentiation" (Olick, 2016: p 43; see also Halbwachs, 1992, per Olick's discussion), history and memory are rarely undisputed, and our late modern cultural and political milieu is defined by its increasingly fragmented character (Gubrium and Holstein, 2000; Vinitzky-Seroussi, 2002; Olick, 2003b; DeGloma, 2014a, 2015), marked by a proliferation of communities with different standpoints from which the past takes on meaning and significance. Moreover, we are increasingly aware that there are different versions of the past – different interpretations which can be contentious and even quite openly controversial. In this fragmented social arena, different actors make use of various "means of symbolic production" (Alexander, 2004a: p 532; 2017: p 79; see also Olick and Robbins, 1998: p 122; Vinitzky-Seroussi, 2002: pp 32, 46–47; Mast, 2012) as they perform their version of, and their orientation to, the past in different settings (see also Rigney, 2008). Thus, "the commemorative field, as a whole, remains dynamic over time" (Steidl, 2013: p 750) and the collective mnemonic practices of different groups take form and become meaningful in relation to, and in communication with, one another in ways that express and reflect the social contours of the evolving cultural and political climate (see also Rigney, 2008: p 92; DeGloma, 2015; Olick 2016). In such a social milieu, "controversy ... may be the most important motor in keeping memory alive" (Rigney, 2008: p 94). If we might say that memory in our modern era is marked by "crisis" (see Olick, 2016: pp 17–20; see also Simko, 2015; Olick and Teichler, 2021, and the December 2021 special issue of *Memory Studies*), then that crisis manifests as contention and conflict over the past in an increasingly fractionalized social and cultural environment, where little is widely agreed upon, *mnemonic authority* is consistently challenged, and memory itself is often "in flux" (Olick, 2003b: p 7; see also Rigney, 2008; Steidl, 2013).

Most broadly, scholars who study contentious memories are interested in exploring how groups – from families to nations – remember and commemorate difficult pasts (Wagner-Pacifici and Schwartz, 1991; Vinitzky-Seroussi, 2002; Conway, 2010; Steidl, 2013; Simko, 2015, 2020; Whitlinger, 2020). Such scholars explore the social and political dynamics involved when agents remember issues and events that remain deeply troubling, or in some cases shameful (Giesen, 2004; Olick, 2007), on personal, social, and cultural levels. Many hone in on the ways that mnemonic entrepreneurs or "agents of memory" (Vinitzky-Seroussi, 2002. See also Irwin-Zarecka 1994: p 67; Armstrong and Crage, 2006; Conway, 2010; Ghoshal, 2013; Whitlinger, 2020), who are often morally or politically motivated, advance countermemories (Foucault, 1997: p 160; Zerubavel, 1995; DeGloma, 2015; Whitlinger, 2020; Logan, 2021) as they work to accomplish various goals and shift relations of power in the present. Countermemories are inherently subversive insofar as agents who advance these alternative perspectives present challenges to official or otherwise dominant versions of the past, mainstream historical narratives, and established frameworks for personal memory – the dominant and default visions of the past which often represent the interests of powerful groups and express hegemonic worldviews (cf. Bodnar, 1992: p 13; Olick and Robbins, 1998: p 127; Polletta, 2003; Badilla and Aguilara, 2021).

Countermemories typically express "the views of marginalized individuals or groups within the society" (Zerubavel, 1995: p 11; see also Rigney, 2008: p 94). They can, and often do inhere in broadly relevant social relations marked by inequalities and power imbalances, such as those that revolve around gender (Jacobs, 2010, 2016, 2017; Bonnes and Jacobs, 2017; Fox, 2021), for example. In such cases, countermemories can remain subdued or repressed, private rather than public, which challenges researchers to carefully draw them out (see Fox, this volume). When actors give voice to countermemories, they then become subversive agents who make claims "for a more accurate representation of history" (Zerubavel, 1995: p 10), often sparking a more open contest or public battle between groups – subversive and dominant – that have conflicting perspectives on the past. In such cases, "the official mnemonic record" of various events and historical periods, "as well as the nature of their consequences, is highly disputed in the public conflicts between ... oppositionally situated camps" (DeGloma, 2015: p 161).[7]

As DeGloma (2015) has discussed elsewhere, disputes over the past manifest with regard to three principal dimensions: as conflicts over the *existence* of some past event or episode, as contests to define the *nature* of the past and especially its moral character, and as heated debates over the ongoing *significance* or current relevance of the past. Moreover, each of these ideal typical forms or dimensions of mnemonic dispute can manifest simultaneously at the level of autobiographical memory and personal testimony, on the one hand, and collective memory and shared history, on the other hand. In fact, the personal memories of individuals and the collective memories of the groups to which they belong often follow similar patterns and reinforce one another (DeGloma, 2015: p 180; see also Kidron, 2003: p 537; Olick, 2016: p 43), thereby strengthening group solidarity in the midst of conflict with others. From this perspective, we should not view "autobiographical and collective memory ... as separate and distinct phenomena, but as interrelated modes of engaging [a] multifaceted and contentious discursive field" (DeGloma, 2015: p 160).

When agents dispute the existence of the past, one camp openly remembers or commemorates some past event, experience, or historical episode while another camp denies that that it happened at all. Such conflicts call our analytic attention to the "opposing logics of *mnemonic discovery* and *mnemonic denial*" (DeGloma, 2015: p 167) and to the tension that can exist between acts of remembering (which are often explicit, marked, and "overt") and forgetting (which are often, by their nature, "unacknowledged," "unmarked," and tacit) (see Connerton, 2008: pp 61, 63, 67; see also Ricoeur, 2004: pp 443–456; see Vinitzky-Seroussi and Teeger, 2019 on the complex issue of silence).[8] These disputes often occur when some agent, whether an individual or group, claims to break some established silence or recall something officially forgotten, and their claims are then opposed by those who seek to preserve the official or established record of the past. In such cases, the subversive mnemonic agents often claim that "forgetting has had … debilitating consequences" and remembering will remedy a problem (Polletta, 2003: p 215). Disputes over the existence of the past center on a range of different topics and concerns, from interpersonal issues that occur within families and small groups to mass atrocities and other events of international significance. They call our attention to the ways that social forces and interests shape *mnemonic selectivity*, and how a social *structure of historical attention* defines every story or claim about the past. From the perceptive of those on one side of this dispute, they are replacing silence and denial with missing pieces of history, along with the social recognition of forgotten voices. From the contrasting perspective, claims to discover new truths are actually false claims that amount to "misremembering" (Prager, 1998; see also Davis, 2005a, 2005b; DeGloma, 2007, 2015).

In other scenarios, competing camps do not dispute the fact that the past event or episode at hand existed, nor do they deny its significance, but they fundamentally disagree on its moral character and meaning (see DeGloma, 2015: pp 170–175). As subversive actors work to (re)define particular events, experiences, and characters of the past with their stories and performances, they advance understandings of the past that conflict with established perspectives. Such battles over the nature of the past occur at both autobiographical and collective levels (between individuals and communities) with regard to a diverse variety of cases and topics, such as the September 11 terrorist attacks in the US (Simko, 2015: pp 174–195), the founding of the state of Israel (see Abu-Lughod and Sa'di, 2007), the Cuban revolution (Bustamante, 2021), or with regard to the moral character and reputations of historical figures (Jansen, 2007; Ghoshal, 2013: pp 338–341; see also Fine, 2001, 2019 on reputation management in relation to collective memory). In many cases, individuals use personal reflections, mobilizing autobiographical memory in the form of testimony, to contest or remake the dominant collective meaning associated with a particular event or situation. In other cases, dueling communities commemorate the same past event differently, with each group using the same event to draw different conclusions and justify different courses of action. In some cases, for example, one group mourns what the other celebrates; one honors what the other condemns.

Finally, some mnemonic battles take form as disputes between camps with different ideas about the ongoing significance of the past event, episode, or situation of concern. As one camp argues for the ongoing or continual relevance of the past, building causal links between past circumstances and present conditions, another works to sever the past from the present, using logics of historical and mnemonic closure (vs. connection), distance (vs. proximity), and, most basically, discontinuity (vs. continuity) through time (see DeGloma, 2015: pp 176–180; cf. Teeger and Vinitzky-Seroussi, 2007; Crage, 2008; Simko, 2020; Sodaro, this volume). Those who stress continuities between the past and the present often recognize similarities across time, using mechanisms such as historical analogy (Khong, 1992; Zerubavel, 2003) and memorial genre (Wagner-Pacifici and Schwartz, 1991; Olick, 1999b; Smith, 2005) to link the present to its roots and precedents. Those who stress discontinuity between past and present often emphasize temporal distinction and the particularity of the present to justify "moving on" from past circumstances and previous periods at both personal and collective levels. Moreover, some disputes can revolve around different perspectives with regard to *how* an individual or group moves on – whether or not they have artificially severed the difficult past from the present or sufficiently and thoroughly remembered, interpreted, and processed it (see Olick 2003b, 2016; Simko, 2020; Bohleber, this volume). These disputes over the significance of the past call our scholarly attention to the ways that memory is inseparable from the inherently social structure of time, and to the ways that temporality (including narrative emplotment) is central to collective and autobiographical memory and the disputes that form at both levels.

These three principal dimensions of mnemonic battle are often interrelated in various real-world cases. To illustrate the point, we can consider the topic of trauma, our modern conception of which involves both psychological and cultural dimensions (see especially Alexander, 2004b). Our contemporary trauma paradigm arose via the efforts of Holocaust survivors, war veterans, feminist activists, and others in the 1960s, 1970s, and 1980s to tell their personal stories in public venues, and to link psychological suffering to social causes in the process (see Lifton, [1973] 2005; Herman, 2000, 1992 for early articulations of this psychosocial perspective). This paradigm was deeply influenced by psychoanalytic notions that the past exists as repressed painful memories which motivate action in the present (DeGloma, 2014b). If we are interested in liberation from this pain and its hold on us, such mnemonic agents claimed, our task is to give voice to the past by recognizing it, defining its nature, and understanding its consequences. From this perspective, forgetting is "something to overcome" (Eichhorn, 2019: p 14) and remembering is "a struggle against forgetting" (Ricoeur, 2004: p 413).[9] This fundamentally psychosocial issue linked the psyche and memories of personal experiences to interactive relationships and inherently collective events and issues, sparking an emergent "ethic of autobiographical storytelling" that took root in the 1970s and 1980s (DeGloma, 2015: pp 160–163). Personal memories of the Holocaust, war, interpersonal violence, childhood abuse, and more became central to new public challenges to redefine these events on a broader social level, and thereby to challenge various entrenched relations of power (see also Alexander, 2004b; Davis, 2005a; DeGloma, 2007, 2014b). Thus, some form of unresolved or volatile past is central to what we know and experience as trauma. Moreover, it is precisely because of its profound yet unresolved character that a traumatic past is often one that is contentious or contested on some level, whether the tension is between individual and collective memories, private and public memories, or between groups with different claims to interpret the exact meaning of the traumatic past and its significance to present concerns and future-oriented actions (see Eyerman, 2001; Alexander et al, 2004; Olick, 2007; Simko, 2015).

Interpretive approaches to the contested past

The contributors to this book are rooted in various areas of study and scholarly orientation. Some are known as memory studies scholars, but they are also variously known by the ways their research makes other contributions – as psychoanalytic social theorists, anthropologists, historians, immigration scholars, race scholars, ethnographers, gender theorists, social movement researchers, and more. Some highlight the interplay of social forces and psychological states, or the ways that individuals process broadly relevant traumatic experiences in socially meaningful ways. Using a psychosocial lens, they focus on the ways that personal memories and psychological states are inseparably linked to collective memories and broadly relevant social issues, as well as on the social impact of the deep structures and processes of personal memory. In addition, many contributors illuminate the ways that individuals use personal testimonies and shared autobiographical memories to challenge official or default collective memories and histories, either by directly confronting the dominant meanings of past events, by using their life stories to illustrate the ongoing impact of the past, or by introducing new information that, they claim, has been forgotten, ignored, or otherwise marginalized by powerful forces who advance the more mainstream versions of history. In such cases, the meanings of the self and identity are emplotted and performed as a way of engaging in mnemonic conflict. Moreover, a number of contributors illustrate the ways that meso-level communities and movements form to raise silenced or otherwise subordinated perspectives on past events and experiences, mounting public challenges to entrenched memorial frameworks, established historical narratives, and other dominant ways of representing and expressing the meanings of the past, becoming a collective counterforce of memory and history, and ultimately of social meaning, in their own right. And some elucidate deep collective fissures and fragmented societal and international landscapes that show how the past fuels broad collective dynamics of power and contention, which are sometimes expressed in memorial sites and museums and at times manifest as open hostilities and social conflicts. Many contributors address more than one of these different dimensions of contentious memory, and we have asked them to do so with some degree of reflexivity with regard to their approaches – to show us how they focus their "analytic attention" in ways that allow them "to see certain social structures, processes, and forces while [consequentially and inevitably] backgrounding or ignoring others" (DeGloma and Wiest, 2022: p 4).

In this vein, the primary purpose of this volume is to explore various "interpretive lenses" that scholars use to analyze contentious memory, broadly conceived, with regard to a variety of topics, themes, and cases – to illustrate the ways scholars engage contentious memories from different analytic standpoints, using different interpretive paradigms including various cultural, interactionist, and psychosocial perspectives. As such, this book is not an exhaustive exploration or comprehensive overview of topics and cases in the study of contentious memory, nor is it an attempt to summarize the state of social memory studies with regard to the analysis of social conflict and contention, power, or trauma.[10] Instead, our primary focus is on illustrating how different scholars "work to unpack the deep structures and processes that underlie the *meanings*" (DeGloma and Wiest, 2022: p 1) of contentious memories, and the ways that conflict over the past is central to more general disputes over the meaning and consequences of various morally and politically salient events, issues, and experiences. To this end, we have asked the contributors to the volume to explicitly reflect on and illustrate how they come to understand the ways that the people they study make the meanings of the contentious past and engage in different forms of mnemonic conflict. We have asked them to explore how they grasp the "interpretive struggles" (Simko, 2015: p 10) that are central to their cases, along with the social contours of contentious memories and mnemonic conflicts, and how their various interpretive lenses allow them to explain important questions in new and illuminating ways.

In line with these objectives, we are concerned with elucidating both the meanings of contentious memories and the various tools that scholars use to make sense of them. Some contributors to this volume present new data and new case studies while others reflect on years of research and analysis. However, they all focus on unpacking their interpretive processes and illustrating how they study and understand the phenomena and meanings of contentious memory. Thus, while each contributor focuses on a particular case or topic, they also offer general models and broadly relevant interpretive lenses that can be used and adapted well beyond their particular cases. We hope that readers approach this volume with attention to both the particular and generalizable contributions of each chapter, and apply versions of the various lenses outlined here as they explore new cases, topics, and themes related to contentious memory and mnemonic conflict.

Overview of the book

We have divided this book into three parts. In Part I, we present four chapters that each illustrate a different approach to the interpretation and analysis of memory as a core feature of contentious social dynamics. Each of the chapters in this section addresses a different subject matter, and the authors have different perspectives on the significance of memory to the cases they explore and illuminate. Thus, this opening section shows how analytically diverse the study of contentious memories and mnemonic conflict can be, and how central memory is to a variety of otherwise different cases and circumstances in the world.

First, Edna Lomsky-Feder presents a reflexive engagement with her growing body of research on Israeli war veterans, reinterpreting and expanding her studies of the memories of soldiers who fought in the *Yom Kippur* War of 1973 and those who more recently served in the occupied territories and Gaza, as well as veterans of the 1948 War of Independence. Thus, Lomsky-Feder presents us with an analytic framework that addresses memory across different generations of combat veterans in Israel, considering "how the interrelationship between personal and national memory changes in different historical-cultural contexts," and with regard to shifting social meanings associated with war, trauma, and resilience in each historical and generational period, along with evolving discourses of honor and heroism. Unpacking multiple layers of interpretation in her discussion, Lomksy-Feder shows how her interpretive and analytic perspective, along with the responses of her interviewees and the broader social reception of her work, were all shaped in significant ways by the changing cultural and political context in Israel. Such a reflective interpretation not only helps us to better understand the connections and tensions between personal and collective memories, as well as personal testimony and national culture, but also how such tensions shape scholarly lenses and claims.

Following Lomsky-Feder, Nicole Fox presents an illuminating and multipronged feminist approach to memory, genocide, and mass atrocity.

Reflecting on a decade of intensive ethnographic study and interviews focused on the memorialization of the 1994 Genocide in Rwanda, Fox explores "the gendered dynamics of commemoration and collective memory" to better understand how the violence of mass atrocity "is remembered through a gendered lens," and what the consequences of gendered memory are for our vision of the past. Centrally, Fox shows how the marginalization of women's voices creates dominant commemorative frameworks that obscure women's experiences during genocide. Furthermore, she argues that these processes of ignoring or otherwise excluding the memories of women contribute to inequalities and power dynamics of the present era. In the process, Fox outlines the dimensions of "a feminist interpretive lens" and feminist methodologies that can help to remedy this problem, bringing important gendered experiences and dynamics to our attention, including the centrality of sexual and gender-based violence in mass atrocities. Her analysis, and the feminist interpretive lens Fox outlines, is relevant well beyond the commemoration of the genocide in Rwanda. Indeed, Fox offers us an analytic perspective that will be useful for scholars studying autobiographical and collective memories with regard to wars, atrocities, disasters, and social conflicts of many types and in many contexts.

Addressing a very different case, Roberto Vélez-Vélez shows us how the memories of individuals living in Vieques, Puerto Rico formed a core part of social movement efforts to stop US military bombing drills and close the US Navy base on the island. In particular, individuals' recollections of military presence throughout their lives were central to the ways the anti-military movement was able to define military presence as an unjust occupation and as consistently harmful to local interests over time, despite becoming an increasingly "normal" part of their lives. Even though the 1999 death of David Sanes, a civilian employee at the base, "triggered a mass mobilization to stop the bombing in the island, end the military presence, and close the naval station," the personal memories of community members and movement participants served to define the problem of the base and its bombing tests as something that extended well beyond Sanes's death. For Vélez-Vélez, "this was an exercise in personal remembrance as a way of making and conveying collective memory." In other words, Vélez-Vélez shows us how people use local and personal memories to shape the broader collective mnemonic record with regard to a highly contentious issue, one that ultimately received international attention. For Vélez-Vélez, meaning is central, and we should understand "movement organizers and activists" to be "simultaneously political actors and mnemonic agents" who use personal memories to ascribe meaning to highly contentious collective events and issues.

Wrapping up our introductory section of the book, Gary Alan Fine, Christopher Robertson, and Cal Abbo give us a very unique and thought-provoking analysis of the ways that "hateful memories" fuel the conflicts surrounding high profile political contests and disputes. Building on prior work analyzing the candidacies of Richard Nixon and Bill Clinton (Fine and Eisenberg, 2002), along with Fine's (2001, 2019) general theory of "difficult reputations," the authors detail the ways that contentious reputations fueled the heated and often hateful 2016 presidential battle between Hillary Rodham Clinton and Donald J. Trump. The authors show how political agents on both sides of this dispute drew on and defined contentious reputations as fodder for their political attacks. For Fine, Robertson, and Abbo, such reputations are best understood as *collective memories* of *personal pasts*, or shared perspectives on the biographies (personal histories) of the controversial political leaders that are rooted in oppositional communities. Thus, they show us how personal histories and reputations are infused into democratic politics in ways that can create "intense emotional energy." Moreover, "partisan ties" can be "bound by reputation" and "controversial figures with irredeemable reputations (for some) can deepen and widen existing fissures among a citizenry." This is indeed a unique and fruitful perspective on the social analysis of contentious memories, and one that has obvious applications and timely relevance for a variety of cases. For these authors, shared memories of personal pasts (which are public or collective reputational narratives) are central to the character work that polarizes political contests into battles in which self-defined saviors emerge to defeat evil menacing villains.

In Part II of this book, we present three chapters that show how contentious memories and countermemories are central to issues of race, racism, and xenophobic exclusion.

First, Sofya Aptekar carefully illustrates how veterans of the US armed services who have been deported to Mexico engage in autobiographical memory work to focus attention on their military service as an essential part of their present identities. Drawing on interviews and ethnographic fieldwork, along with various materials and social media activity associated with the "Deported Veterans Support Houses" (a support and advocacy network), Aptekar uses a "transborder" lens to address the ways that such deported veterans engage in shared memory work to challenge dominant views about the nation, immigration, military service, and belonging more generally. Such individuals, Aptekar shows, construct and mobilize their personal memories to challenge dominant cultural norms, working to "open up a future of return" by engaging in a "shared countermemory project with which [they] establish their claims of belonging in the United States." In the process, they use various materials, including photographs of themselves from their service days, US flags, and military uniforms and regalia to make "dramatic claims on US citizenship." This involves a performative and "embodied construction of the past" where "mnemonics of the body link the present to the past." For Aptekar, this case also exposes how social tensions and inequalities, along with experiences of belonging and betrayal, can mark the distinction between different aspects of personal memory and identity. Thus, according to Aptekar, memory studies needs greater focus on transborder and immigration issues, but just as importantly immigration scholars must pay more attention to memory at various levels of analysis.

In Chapter 7, Claire Whitlinger carefully details her comparison of the 1989 (25th) and 2004 (40th) commemorations of the infamous murders of three civil rights workers – James Chaney, Andrew Goodman, and Michael Schwerner – in Philadelphia, Mississippi in order to show how she came to understand "the causes and consequences of commemorating racial violence." Reflecting on years of ethnographic and archival research along with interviews of key organizers and others central to the commemorative process, Whitlinger presents us with an interpretive lens that spans multiple levels of analysis – micro, meso, and macro – while comparing commemorative events (ceremonies), processes, *and* outcomes over historical time. While the 1989 commemoration had little effect, the 2004 commemoration led to important changes including the criminal prosecution of Edgar Ray Killen (the mastermind behind the murders), landmark legislation establishing civil rights education in Mississippi schools, and the Mississippi Truth Project aimed at acknowledging the past for the purposes of repair and reconciliation. Whitlinger's research focuses on accounting for this discrepancy of transformative outcome, and she has developed a complex and multifaceted analytic lens to address this question. Creatively combining different theoretical frames, she is interested in how "memory movements raise awareness of marginalized pasts, or marginalized interpretations of the past, by their very existence" and how "commemoration functions *as* protest" that addresses, in her case, ongoing issues related to the divisions of race and racism. While analyzing the collective commemoration of a silenced, marginalized, and contentious past, Whitlinger ultimately finds her interpretive key in the local interactive processes and relationships that were cultivated during the planning of commemorative activities.

In Chapter 8, Amy Sodaro gives us an important and striking analysis of two recently established commemorative institutions, The Legacy Museum: From Slavery to Mass Incarceration and the affiliated National Memorial to Peace and Justice, located a few blocks apart in Montgomery, Alabama. While most memorial museums in the US "adhere to hegemonic American narratives of US innocence" while advancing "ideals of democracy and freedom," Sodaro argues, The Legacy Museum differs in many ways, especially the way it traces a continuous thread between the past era of US slavery and the present situation of institutionalized racism, most specifically the racism of the US criminal justice system. Sodaro also interprets the ways that the museum communicates "the burden of responsibility" to its visitors, especially its white visitors, which stems directly from its perspective that past violence and atrocity is not contained in the past; the past is not divorced from the present (cf. Teeger and Vinitsky-Seroussi, 2007), but rather social conflict and contention, oppression and victimization, as well as resistance and countermemory, reach from the past into the present as the ills of racism may change form but remain unresolved and unrepaired. With a keen sensitivity to symbolism and an astute cultural interpretive lens, Sodaro details the ways this message of social and historical continuity is conveyed via the form and structure of museum design and facilitated by advanced technologies, all of which serves to bridge the past and present through various forms of personal testimony and promote necessary social change.

Part III of this volume shifts to focus on genocide, and on the historicization of collective traumas and the personal injuries that stem from mass atrocities. In this section, we feature the work of a psychoanalyst, an anthropologist, a historian, and a pair of sociologists. Each of them focuses on the issues related to genocide and memory in a different way, using different interpretive lenses to frame different arguments about the ways we relate to such horrors of history – the ways we define them and the ways we find meaning in moving beyond them.

First, Werner Bohleber, former President of the German Psychoanalytic Association, applies a psychosocial interpretive lens to history and to individual and collective memory with regard to the deep and ongoing legacies of the Holocaust in Germany. For Germans, according to Bohleber, the history of the Holocaust has always been contentious on a number of levels and we need psychoanalysis to grasp exactly why and how this consciousness with regard to the past has evolved over time. Furthermore, he shows us how the memory of the Holocaust was not only traumatic for survivors, but also presented profound difficulties for German society at large. At both levels, "feelings of fear, guilt, and shame" motivated a range of defensive responses and other psychosocial mechanisms that kept the past from being effectively processed. From this perspective, Bohleber focuses predominantly on how the national memory of the Holocaust and the Nazi era more generally evolved for descendants of the perpetrators and bystanders among the German population. He tackles deep questions associated with "the processing of traumatic catastrophes ... over several generations," recognizing that those who were complicit in perpetrating violence claimed their own victimization (stemming from the war) as a defense against recognizing their own crimes (see both Kidron and Leydesdorff, this volume, for related discussions). Bohleber sees this victim mentality as being fundamentally similar to the ways the Nazis created a sense of popular community and cultivated a sense of purpose among large segments of the German population. After the war, this same German population sought sympathy and closure, cutting themselves off from any responsibility for the Nazi atrocities "through a collective victim identity fixated on oneself." Advancing this psychosocial lens, Bohleber argues that open social discourse and acknowledgment of the past are necessary if "the shattered understanding of the self and the world can be regenerated" (cf. Giesen, 2004; Olick, 2016). By shedding light on processes of defensiveness and integration, denial and acceptance, avoidance and recognition, and stagnation and transcendence, a psychosocial lens, according the Bohleber, can help Germans to continually accept a shameful past, reject mythic notions of a pure and good national identity that are built on a denial of the past, and look for new humanistic visions of progressive national identity.

Taking a very different perspective on the evolving collective memory of the Holocaust, Carol Kidron unpacks how social forces rooted in both therapeutic and ethnonational logics have shaped and mobilized survivor identities and the memories of the second and third generation descendants of survivors in Israel. In the process, Kidron critically engages with her own scholarship, interrogating her interpretive lens and positionality as it evolved over the course of her research. Reflecting on her research at different stages in her scholarly career, Kidron is fundamentally interested in how descendants learned, through established and institutionalized group processes, "to constitute themselves as carriers of Holocaust memory." Simultaneously analyzing her case at multiple levels of analysis with attention to the connections between them, she addresses micro-dynamic processes institutionalized in meso-level settings shaped by, and mobilized to advance, macro-level notions of collective identity through suffering that serve ethnonationalist objectives. In Kidron's understanding, second and third generation descendants assumed the social responsibility for Holocaust survivor memory and a burden of voice, taking on a testimonial standpoint that comes with psychological consequences. They are given a "mnemonic-moral mission" and "must carry the weight of contemporality and fulfil the role of carriers of Holocaust memory not only as inevitable psychic familial process but as moral obligation to all those who died." Overtime, Kidron began to see that descendants lived the presence of the Holocaust and were often quite resilient (rather than defeated by trauma). Through her work, and with her evolving interpretive perspective, Kidron is able to more clearly see how survivors and their families experience public commemorations as distinct and separate from their personal memories and domestic forms of commemoration. Ultimately, Kidron documents her interpretive evolution to understanding the complex layers and multiple forces that, in combination, shape the social phenomenon of descendant memory and identity.

Both Kidron and Bohleber are interested in family as a locus and carrier of memory. For Bohleber, who focuses on perpetrators and bystanders among the German population, "family memory forms a filter through which contents of the collective memory are absorbed, manipulated, or excluded." Families provide a buffer against realizing the guilt associated with one's complicity in the past. For Kidron, who focuses on victims, the family is a space of more authentic lived memory, where distortions of the victim identity may be contradicted by genuine expressions of the past in individual lives. Both see the family as situated within, and in some ways against, cultural and collective memories and normative perspectives on the socially shared past.

Taking an altogether different tack, Selma Leydesdorff then examines "the 'new' histories in the post-communist world, where the surge of commemorative work that highlights the World War II-era victimization of citizens by communist forces is driven by agents with nationalist ideologies and agendas competing with the memories of the Shoah" (cf. Olick, 2003a: p 270; Olick, 2016). Leydesdorff uses a broadly comparative and historically oriented lens, analyzing several cases throughout Europe (including Russia, Poland, Hungary, the Czech Republic, and the Baltic States of Estonia, Latvia, and Lithuania) to illustrate broadly relevant patterns of mnemonic contention. Throughout her chapter, she combines her analysis of the collective politics of these mnemonic contentions with personal reflection and a keen sensitivity to the ways that personal testimony can conflict with dominant versions of history. In each case she addresses, the debates and controversies regarding how the past ought to be represented are often highly polarized, hindering any possibility of "a pluralist attitude where the past can be contradictory." These forces not only shape the dominant visions of history, but also determine the parameters of socially acceptable personal testimony. At stake, according to Leydesdorff, is "the freedom" of both academic history and popular collective memory, along with the curricula of formal education, all of which are shaped by powerful political forces that do not tolerate a plurality of views about the past. Moreover, at the core of this inter- and multinational mnemonic battle is a politics of victimhood. Taking a strongly compassionate and humanistic perspective, critically incisive while simultaneously embracing the complexities of violence, perpetration, and victimization, she shows how a more rigid and partisan politics of victimization is often used to obscure the contradictions and nuances of history, and to keep us from seeing how actors who identify as victims can also be complicit in, and even perpetrate, other acts of mass violence and atrocity.

Finally, Jacob Caponi and Fatma Müge Göçek present a richly comparative and historical analysis of genocides across time and context, using a set of common themes to compare the 1915 Armenian Genocide with the 1994 Genocide in Rwanda against the Tutsi. They explore several dimensions, including the very conceptualization of genocide, the agency of the actors involved, and the processes of post-genocidal narration, revealing patterns that apply to both cases despite their otherwise significant differences. In the process, Caponi and Göçek show us "how contentious memory is integral throughout the process of genocide" and "does not evolve only in the aftermath of genocide, but contention" is rooted in the relations of the violence as it unfolds, and in the ways we understand the events at hand from the start. In other words, we must understand the dynamic power relations that shape social processes of genocide through time, from its origins through its aftermath, if we are to understand how the definitions of genocide are always controversial and contested. As they explore each of their two cases, Caponi and Göçek advance a concept of agency that not only involves power in terms of the ways actors shape the experiences of genocidal events, but also links this manifestation of power to the abilities of actors to define reality and create knowledge of those events. As with Leydesdorff's chapter, Caponi and Göçek challenge the neat binaries of perpetrator and victim that we use to define genocide, advancing a more nuanced analytic vision. Such an analytic perspective is necessary, they argue, if we are to understand the historical layers and complex relations that underlie mnemonic conflicts and contention with regard to genocides and mass atrocities.

Notes

[1] As of this writing, video of Newsome Bass's protest can be viewed at www.youtube.com/watch?v=LYgbwbmsHfw. Retrieved June 23, 2022.

[2] Indeed, some passionately and even militantly defend the public display of Confederate symbols and memorials, as when white nationalists rallied in defense of a statue of Confederate General Robert E. Lee in 2017 in Charlottesville, Virginia. This public conflict over a memorial achieved widespread attention in part due to the fact that white supremacist rally attendee, James Alex Fields Jr, drove his car into a crowd of peaceful counter-protestors, killing Heather Heyer and wounding many others. See Olick and Teichler (2021).

[3] While our opening discussion is focused on a US-based case, there are many examples from different places around the world in which activists connect current issues to contentious memories and unresolved controversies rooted in the past. For example, Badilla and Aguilera (2021) discuss the ways that activists engaged in performative confrontations with colonial monuments in Chile while protesting contemporary neo-liberal policies in a general uprising sparked by a subway fare increase in Santiago, connecting "colonial memories with recent memories through repertoires of decolonial demonumentalization" (p 1227). Taking another example, one that touches on some of the themes discussed by Selma Leydesdorff in this volume, Řehořová (2021) discusses a contemporary controversy over the statue of a Soviet military leader in the Czech Republic. The controversy, Řehořová shows, is as much about contemporary Czech-Russian relations and international conflicts across Europe as it is about the meaning of the past.

[4] State officials removed the flag from government property on July 10, 2015, 13 days after Newsome Bass's protest, in response to a wave of local and national pressure.

[5] For a similar perspective on the act of "mobilizing memory," see Altinay et al, eds, 2019. See especially Hirsch, 2019: p 2. See also Logan, 2021: pp 1174–1175 on this point.

[6] See Newsome Bass's remarks [online] www.youtube.com/watch?v=LYgbwbmsHfw Retrieved June 29, 2022. See also Nelson (2015).

7   Different groups – from social movements to ethnic and racial communities, from neighborhoods to nations – vary in their "mnemonic capacity," which refers to their ability to successfully "create commemorative vehicles" and to establish and preserve their particular vision of the past (Armstrong and Crage, 2006: p 726; Ghoshal, 2013). In some cases, memory activists successfully institutionalize new commemorative rituals and establish resilient stories that ground broader challenges to mainstream meanings with regard to morally and politically salient issues (Armstrong and Crage, 2006). However, official actors may in time embrace the memory of a subversive past, normalizing or institutionalizing challenges to power in ways that assimilate and liquidate those challenges, leading to a situation of "persistent tensions" between subversive actors pushing for social change and those who use the memories of social change for more official or institutional reasons, creating ongoing "battles over the legacy of protest" and social change itself (Polletta, 2003: pp 206, 220).

8   Collective remembering and forgetting always stand in tension with one another. Indeed, there are many potentially memorable events that are not remembered in any socially meaningful way (see Spillman, 1998; Armstrong and Crage, 2006). Likewise, there are many harmful and atrocious occurrences that never amount to collectively commemorated cultural traumas (Alexander, 2004a).

9   In this sense, psychoanalysis and trauma psychology provide discursive foundations for the deep seated cultural phenomenon that Paul Ricoeur (2004: p 417) refers to as "the idea of reversible forgetting, even ... the idea of the unforgettable" (see also pp 444–448 on "blocked memory").

10 The field of social memory studies, and within it the study of mnemonic conflict, is incredibly diverse. It is both multidisciplinary and interdisciplinary in character (see Olick, 2007; Meade et al, 2018; Barnier and Hoskins, 2018). The interdisciplinary journal *Memory Studies* serves as a central forum for the diverse array of scholarship in this field.

References

Abu-Lughod, L. and Sa'di, A.H. (2007) "Introduction: The Claims of Memory," in A.H. Sa'di and L. Abu-Lughod (eds) *Nakba: Palestine, 1948, and the Claims of Memory*, New York: Columbia University Press, pp 1–24.

Alexander, J.C. (2004a) "Cultural Pragmatics: Social Performance between Ritual and Strategy," *Sociological Theory* 22(4): 527–573.

Alexander, J.C. (2004b) "Toward a Theory of Cultural Trauma," in J.C. Alexander, R. Eyerman, B. Giesen, N.J. Smelser, and P. Sztompka (eds) *Cultural Trauma and Collective Identity*. Berkeley: University of California Press, pp 1–30.

Alexander, J.C. (2017) *The Drama of Social Life*, Cambridge: Polity Press.

Alexander, J.C., Eyerman, R., Giesen, B., Smelser, N.J., and Sztompka, P. (eds) (2004) *Cultural Trauma and Collective Identity*, Berkeley, CA: University of California Press.

Altinay, A.G., Contreras, M.J., Hirsch, M., Howard, J., Karaca, B., and Solomon, A. (2019) *Women Mobilizing Memory*, New York: Columbia University Press.

Armstrong, E.A. and Crage, S.M. (2006) "Movements and Memory: The Making of the Stonewall Myth," *American Sociological Review* 71(5): 724–751.

Badilla, M. and Aguilara, C. (2021) "The 2019–2020 Chilean Anti-neoliberal Uprising: A Catalyst for Decolonial De-monumentalization," *Memory Studies* 14(6): 1226–1240.

Barnier, A.J. and Hoskins, A. (2018) "Is There Memory in the Head, in the Wild?," *Memory Studies* 11(4): 386–390.

Bodnar, J. (1992) *Remaking America: Public Memory, Commemoration, and Patriotism in the Twentieth Century*, Princeton, NJ: Princeton University Press.

Bonnes, S. and Jacobs, J. (2017) "Gendered Representations of Apartheid: The Women's Jail Museum at Constitution Hill," *Museum and Society* 15: 153–170.

Bustamante, M.J. (2021) *Cuban Memory Wars: Retrospective Politics in Revolution and Exile*, Chapel Hill, NC: University of North Carolina Press.

Connerton, P. (2008) "Seven Types of Forgetting," *Memory Studies* 1(1): 59–71.

Conway, B. (2010) *Commemoration and Bloody Sunday: Pathways of Memory*, Hampshire: Palgrave Macmillan.

Crage, S.M. (2008) "Negotiating the Relevance of the Past: Refugee Aid Policymaking in Berlin," Paper presented at the annual meeting of the American Sociological Association, Boston, MA.

Davis, J.E. (2005a) *Accounts of Innocence: Sexual Abuse, Trauma, and the Self*, Chicago, IL: University of Chicago Press.

Davis, J E. (2005b) "Victim Narratives and Victim Selves: False Memory Syndrome and the Power of Accounts," *Social Problems* 52: 529–548.

DeGloma, T. (2007) "The Social Logic of 'False Memories': Symbolic Awakenings and Symbolic Worlds in Survivor and Retractor Narratives," *Symbolic Interaction* 30: 543–565.

DeGloma, T. (2014a) *Seeing the Light: The Social Logic of Personal Discovery*, Chicago, IL: University of Chicago Press.

DeGloma, T. (2014b) "The Unconscious in Cultural Dispute: On the Ethics of Psychosocial Discovery," in L. Chancer and J. Andrews (eds) *The Unhappy Divorce of Sociology and Psychoanalysis: Diverse Perspectives on the Psychosocial*, Basingstoke: Palgrave Macmillan, pp 77–97.

DeGloma, T. (2015) "The Strategies of Mnemonic Battle: On the Alignment of Autobiographical and Collective Memories in Conflicts over the Past," *American Journal of Cultural Sociology* 3(1): 156–190.

DeGloma, T. and Johnston, E.F. (2019) "Cognitive Migrations: A Cultural and Cognitive Sociology of Personal Transformation," in W.H. Brekhus and G. Ignatow (eds) *Oxford Handbook of Cognitive Sociology*, Oxford: Oxford University Press, pp 623–642.

DeGloma, T. and Wiest, J.B. (2022) "On the Multidimensional Foundations of Meanings in Social Life: An Invitation to the series Interpretive Lenses in Sociology," Available from: https://bristoluniversitypress.co.uk/asset/11003/de-gloma-wiest-series-editors-article.pdf [Retrieved February 7, 2023].

Eichhorn, K. (2019) *The End of Forgetting: Growing Up with Social Media*, Cambridge, MA: Harvard University Press.

Edwards, B. (2015) "Bree Newsome Opens Up about Taking Down Confederate Flag on SC Statehouse Grounds," *The Root*, [online] June 30, Available from: www.theroot.com/bree-newsome-opens-up-about-taking-down-confederate-fla-1790860347 [Retrieved August 7, 2022].

Eyerman, R. (2001) *Cultural Trauma: Slavery and the Formation of African American Identity*, Cambridge: Cambridge University Press.

Fine, G.A. (2001) *Difficult Reputations: Collective Memories of the Evil, Inept, and Controversial*, Chicago, IL: University of Chicago Press.

Fine, G.A. (2019) "Moral Cultures, Reputation Work, and the Politics of Scandal," *Annual Review of Sociology* 45: 247–264.

Fine, G.A. and Eisenberg, E. (2002) "Tricky Dick and Slick Willie: Despised Presidents and Generational Imprinting," *American Behavioral Scientist* 46: 553–565.

Fivush, R. (2011) "The Development of Autobiographical Memory," *Annual Review of Psychology* 62(1): 559–582.

Fivush, R., Haden, C., and Reese, E. (1996) "Remembering, Recounting, and Reminiscing: The Development of Autobiographical Memory in Social Context," in D.C. Rubin (ed) *Remembering Our Past: Studies in Autobiographical Memory*, New York: Cambridge University Press, pp 341–358.

Foucault, M. (1977) *Language, Counter-Memory, Practice: Selected Essays and Interviews*, Ithaca, NY: Cornell University Press.

Fox, N. (2021) *After Genocide: Memory and Reconciliation in Rwanda*, Madison: University of Wisconsin Press.

Ghoshal, R.A. (2013) "Transforming Collective Memory: Mnemonic Opportunity Structures and the Outcomes of Racial Violence Memory Movements," *Theory and Society* 42(4): 329–350.

Giesen, B. (2004) "The Trauma of Perpetrators: The Holocaust as the Traumatic Reference of German National Identity," in J.C. Alexander, R. Eyerman, B. Giesen, N.J. Smelser, and P. Sztompka (eds) *Cultural Trauma and Collective Identity*, Berkeley: University of California Press, pp 112–154.

Gubrium, J.F. and J.A. Holstein (2000) "The Self in a World of Going Concerns," *Symbolic Interaction* 23: 95–115.

Halbwachs, M. ([1950] 1980) *The Collective Memory*, New York: Harper and Row.

Halbwachs, M. (1992) "The Social Frameworks of Memory," in L.A. Coser (ed) *On Collective Memory*, Chicago: University of Chicago Press, pp 37–189.

Herman, J.L. ([1981] 2000) *Father–Daughter Incest*, Cambridge, MA: Harvard University Press.

Herman, J.L. (1992) *Trauma and Recovery: The Aftermath of Violence – from Domestic Abuse to Political Terror*, New York: Basic Books.

Hirsch, M. (2019) "Introduction: Practicing Feminism, Practicing Memory," in A.G. Altinay, M.J. Contreras, M. Hirsch, J. Howard, B. Karaca, and A. Solomon (eds) *Women Mobilizing Memory*, New York: Columbia University Press, pp 1–23.

Irwin-Zarecka, I. (1994) *Frames of Remembrance: The Dynamics of Collective Memory*, New Brunswick, NJ: Transaction Publishers.

Jacobs, J. (2010) *Memorializing the Holocaust: Gender, Genocide and Collective Memory*, London: I.B. Tauris.

Jacobs, J. (2016) *The Holocaust Across Generations: Trauma and its Inheritance Among Descendants of Survivors*, New York: New York University Press.

Jacobs, J. (2017) "The Memorial at Srebrenica: Gender and the Social Meanings of Collective Memory in Bosnia-Herzegovina," *Memory Studies* 10(4): 423–239.

Jansen, R.S. (2007) "Resurrection and Appropriation: Reputational Trajectories, Memory Work, and the Political Use of Historical Figures," *American Journal of Sociology* 112(4): 953–1007.

Khong, Y.F. (1992) *Analogies at War: Korea, Munich, Dien Bien Phu, and the Vietnam Decisions of 1965*. Princeton, NJ: Princeton University Press.

Kidron, C.A. (2003) "Surviving a Distant Past: A Case Study of the Cultural Construction of Trauma Descendant Identity," *Ethos* 31(4): 513–544.

Lifton, R.J. ([1973] 2005) *Home from the War: Learning from Vietnam Veterans*, New York: Other Press.

Logan, K. (2021) "'History is Illuminating': Public Memory Crises and Collectives in Richmond, Virginia," *Memory Studies* 14(6): 1173–1184.

Mast, J.L. (2012) *The Performative Presidency: Crisis and Resurrection during the Clinton Years*, Cambridge, MA: Cambridge University Press.

Meade, M.L., Harris, C.B., Van Bergen, P., Sutton, J., and Barnier, A.J. (eds) (2018) *Collaborative Remembering: Theories, Research, and Applications*, Oxford: Oxford University Press.

Murphy, K.M. (2021) "Fear and Loathing in Monuments: Rethinking the Politics and Practices of Monumentality and Monumentalization," *Memory Studies* 14(6): 1143–1158.

Nelson, L. (2015) "Watch Bree Newsome Climb a 30-Foot Flagpole to Take Down South Carolina's Confederate Flag," *Vox*, [online] June 27, Available from: www.vox.com/2015/6/27/8856969/bree-newsome-confederate-flag [Retrieved August 7, 2022].

Olick, J.K. (1999a) "Collective Memory: The Two Cultures," *Sociological Theory* 17(3): 333–348.

Olick, J.K. (1999b) "Genre Memories and Memory Genres: A Dialogical Analysis of May 8th, 1945 Commemorations in the Federal Republic of Germany," *American Sociological Review* 64(3): 381–402.

Olick, J.K. (2003a) "What Does It Mean to Normalize the Past? Official Memory in German Politics since 1989," in J.K. Olick (ed) *States of Memory: Continuities, Conflicts, and Transformations in National Retrospection*, Durham, NC: Duke University Press, pp 259–288.

Olick, J.K. (2003b) "Introduction," in J.K. Olick (ed) *States of Memory: Continuities, Conflicts, and Transformations in National Retrospection*, Durham, NC: Duke University Press, pp 1–16.

Olick, J.K. (2007) *The Politics of Regret: On Collective Memory and Historical Responsibility*, New York: Routledge.

Olick, J.K. (2016) *The Sins of the Fathers: Germany, Memory, Method*, Chicago, IL: University of Chicago Press.

Olick, J.K. and Robbins, J. (1998) "Social Memory Studies: From 'Collective Memory' to the Historical Sociology of Mnemonic Practices," *Annual Review of Sociology* 24: 105–140.

Olick, J.K. and Teichler, H. (2021) "Memory and Crisis: An Introduction," *Memory Studies* 14(6): 1135–1142.

Ortiz, A. and Diaz, J. (2020) "George Floyd Protests Reignite Debate over Confederate Statues," *New York Times*, [online] June 3, Available from: www.nytimes.com/2020/06/03/us/confederate-statues-george-floyd.html [Retrieved August 7, 2022].

Polletta, F. (2003) "Legacies and Liabilities of an Insurgent Past: Remembering Martin Luther King Jr. on the House and Senate Floor," in J.K. Olick (ed) *States of Memory: Continuities, Conflicts, and Transformations in National Retrospection*, Durham, NC: Duke University Press, pp 193–226.

Prager, J. (1998) *Presenting the Past: Psychoanalysis and the Sociology of Misremembering*, Cambridge, MA: Harvard University Press.

Radstone, S. (2008) "Memory Studies: For and Against," *Memory Studies* 1(1): 31–39.

Řehořová, I. (2021) "Visual Symbols, Democracy and Memory: The Monument of Ivan Stepanovich Konev and the Memory of Communism in the Czech Republic," *Memory Studies* 14(6): 1241–1254.

Ricoeur, P. (2004) *Memory, History, Forgetting*, Chicago, IL: University of Chicago Press.

Rigney, A. (2008) "Divided Pasts: A Premature Memorial and the Dynamics of Collective Remembrance," *Memory Studies* 1(1): 89–97.

Saito, H. (2006) "Reiterated Commemoration: Hiroshima as National Trauma," *Sociological Theory* 24(4): 353–376.

Schwartz, B. (1982) "The Social Context of Commemoration: A Study in Collective Memory," *Social Forces* 61(2): 374–402.

Schwartz, B. (1996) "Memory as a Cultural System: Abraham Lincoln in World War II," *American Sociological Review* 61(5): 908–927.

Simko, C. (2015) *The Politics of Consolation: Memory and the Meaning of September 11*, Oxford: Oxford University Press.

Simko, C. (2020) "Marking Time in Memorials and Museums of Terror: Temporality and Cultural Trauma," *Sociological Theory* 38(1): 51–77.

Smith, P. (2005) *Why War? The Cultural Logic of Iraq, the Gulf War, and Suez*, Chicago, IL: University of Chicago Press.

Spillman, L. (1998) "When Do Collective Memories Last? Founding Moments in the United States and Australia," *Social Science History* 22(4): 445–477.

Steidl, C.R. (2013) "Remembering May 4, 1970: Integrating the Commemorative Field at Kent State," *American Sociological Review* 78(5): 749–772.

Szpunar, P.M. (2021) "Memory Politics in the Future Tense: Exceptionalism, Race, and Insurrection in America," *Memory Studies* 14(6): 1272–1284.

Teeger, C. and Vinitzky-Seroussi, V. (2007) "Controlling for Consensus: Commemorating Apartheid in South Africa," *Symbolic Interaction* 30(1): 57–78.

Vinitzky-Seroussi, V. (1998) *After Pomp and Circumstance: High School Reunion as an Autobiographical Occasion*, Chicago, IL: University of Chicago Press.

Vinitzky-Seroussi, V. (2002) "Commemorating a Difficult Past: Yitzhak Rabin's Memorials," *American Sociological Review* 67(1): 30–51.

Vinitzky-Seroussi, V. and Teeger, C. (2019) "Silence and Collective Memory," in W.H. Brekhus and G. Ignatow (eds) *The Oxford Handbook of Cognitive Sociology*, New York: Oxford University Press, pp 663–673.

Wagner-Pacifici, R. and Schwartz, B. (1991) "The Vietnam Veterans Memorial: Commemorating a Difficult Past," *American Journal of Sociology* 97(2): 376–420.

Weisman, J. (2015) "Killings Add Painful Page to Storied History of Charleston Church," *New York Times*, [online] June 18, Available from: www.nytimes.com/2015/06/19/us/charleston-killings-evoke-history-of-violence-against-black-churches.html [Retrieved August 7, 2022].

Whitlinger, C. (2020) *Between Remembrance and Repair: Commemorating Racial Violence in Philadelphia, Mississippi*, Chapel Hill, NC: University of North Carolina Press.

Worland, J. (2015) "This Is Why South Carolina Raised the Confederate Flag in the First Place," *Time*, [online] June 22, Available from: https://time.com/3930464/south-carolina-confederate-flag-1962/ [Retrieved August 7, 2022].

Zerubavel, E. (2003) *Time Maps: Collective Memory and the Social Shape of the Past*, Chicago, IL: University of Chicago Press.

Zerubavel, Y. (1995) *Recovered Roots: Collective Memory and the Making of Israeli National Tradition*, Chicago, IL: University of Chicago Press.

PART I

Interpreting Memories in the Social Dynamics of Contention

2

On the Social Distribution of Soldiers' Memories: Normalization, Trauma, and Morality

Edna Lomsky-Feder

Introduction

This chapter aims to address the interrelationship between personal and national recollections of war as reflected by the memories of different generations of combatants among Israeli society. This multi-generational observation offers the analysis a dynamic dimension and enables us to learn of how the interrelationship between personal and national memory changes in different historical-cultural contexts, and in accordance with the nature of the fighting. More particularly, the chapter aims to explore the cultural discourses that shape the field of memory within which the subjects remembering operate. That is, to identify the different discourses that grant meaning to the combat experience, track their changes over time, examine their interplay, and situate the mode through which they shape personal memories and are shaped by them.

I discuss these issues through a critical reading of my work, in light of further research on soldiers in the Israeli context. I present this reading in two phases: First, I engage in a close reflexive analysis of a study I conducted on the memories of soldiers who fought in the 1973 War – *The Yom Kippur War* – which is perceived as the most traumatic war among Israeli society's national memory. This analysis reveals blind spots in the original work that masked key processes in constructing personal memory. Second, I expand the discussion on the interplay between personal and collective memory by focusing the lens on the soldiers who served in the occupied territories and Gaza during the 2000s.

This two-pronged reading indicates how the discourse of trauma becomes central in the memory field among Israeli society. In more detail: the analysis exposes various manifestations of trauma discourse over time, examining the interrelationship between this discourse and others (the heroic, critical, and resilience) that grant meaning to memories of the war; and addressing the means through which Israeli society seeks to monitor the threatening implications of traumatic interpretation through the design of what I call "normalized trauma."

Prior to delving into the discussion, it is important to stress here that the study deals only with the Jewish-Israeli national and personal memories of the war and not with the memories of the Palestinian-Israelis. The Palestinians and the Jews are two distinct national mnemonic communities which recall the wars in a different and even opposing manner. Thus, for example, while the 1948 War is the heroic War of Independence for the Jews, it is the *Nakba* (catastrophe) for the Palestinians. The mnemonics of these communities are opposed, yet represent the complementary versions of the same historical event. Each of these two mnemonic communities are entrenched within their own collective memories as part of a process of constructing their own national identity and symbolic boundaries. There is hardly any negotiation or common public discourse between Palestinian-Israelis and Jewish-Israelis over the memory of the wars.

The story behind the study

In my book *As if There Was No War*, published in 1998, I addressed the reciprocal relations between personal and collective memory through analyzing the life stories of soldiers from the *Yom Kippur* War, which is deemed a national trauma among Israeli memory. The book revealed the cultural criteria that determined who was entitled to speak critically about the war and interpret the affair as a traumatic crisis on a personal level; and alternatively, who was required to normalize it – that is, to incorporate it into their life without identifying it as a transformative experience. The book's central claim is that social oversight with regard to the bounds of interpreting the war's influence is a device through which society ensures the normalization of military violence throughout the course of individuals' personal and social lives. Additionally, it is a cultural mechanism that affirms and preserves the power of the warrior ethos, which constitutes male-military hegemony among Israeli society.[1]

The book received relatively widespread attention, not only among academics, but also in the public sphere (articles in public media, reviews in literary supplements, letters from readers). Among the academic community, the work received attention as it sounded a new voice in war research – a field that had been dominated until then by works that addressed the macro-social level on the one hand (ranging from sociology to political science, economics, and history) – along with micro-level work on the other, such as psychological research focused on the individual (Ben-Ari et al, 2001). While this work investigated the individual, its insights were socio-cultural rather than psychological. This point of view aroused curiosity along with a great deal of unease among both macro- and micro-researchers.

Macro researchers have found it challenging to incorporate work that addresses life stories, not only because of its focus on the individual, but also because they believed that the narrative nature of the work raised doubts regarding its scientific legitimacy. From the perspective of many who study war and militarism from a macro-level, using individual stories as data does not allow for rigorous scientific analysis. As a narrative work, *As if There Was No War* was one of the first studies that researched Israeli militarism within an interpretive paradigm. This paradigm challenged the positivist model that had previously dominated the sociology of war, and thus provoked opposition among scholars from this school. Alongside paradigmatic differences in mode of analysis, the reservations of these macro-focused scholars also seem to have been an expression of a gender conflict: the interpretive paradigm is perceived as "feminine" in nature (see Oakley, 1981 for example) while this mode of interpretive analysis was predominantly conducted by women researchers. The entry of such interpretive work into the sociology of war thus threatened the male hegemony that dominated this field of study, and it largely remains on the fringes of the field's research corpus to this day (see Ben-Eliezer's, 2017 review, for example).

Micro-researchers – practically all of whom are also psychologists – were also critical of my work in *As if There Was No War*, and their opposition, which was sometimes abrasive, spilled over into the public arena. Many argued that it is difficult to accept the position that the meanings of personal war memories – whether traumatic or normalized – are a product of social construction and not necessarily a derivative of psychological processes. The fact that I did not first deem the combatants suffering subjects, but rather examined the ways in which they normalize the war in their lives, was perceived by them as an alienating position. The idea that some combatants normalize the war infuriates them, especially since the research addresses those who fought in the Yom Kippur War, a war publicly defined in traumatic terms.

The trauma discourse that permeated the Israeli public at that time was among the central cultural sources that shaped the perception of the Israeli soldier as a suffering subject (Bilu and Witztum, 2000). Psychologists who bore this discourse perceived themselves, with a great sense of justice, to be "breaking the silence" around the emotional price that soldiers pay, a price that was silenced over the years by powerful normative social forces. It is thus not surprising that many of these psychologists perceived my work to be in complete defiance of their position. For them it sounded "like a new incarnation of denying the heavy mental and social price of wars in Israel" (Berman, 1999: p 58).

Opposition to this work thus stemmed from conceptual disagreements, both intradisciplinary and interdisciplinary, yet not from them exclusively. Today, with retrospective observation of such responses over time – especially those that slid into the public arena through academic discourse – these disputes seem to reflect a deeper state of mind among Israeli society at the time.

Opposition to the work may also be read as a fundamental difficulty accepting research that does not center the Israeli soldier as a victim, but rather as an agent of violence. This stance did not solely derive from the study's focus on the *Yom Kippur* War, which was perceived as particularly traumatic and difficult, but also from the threat to Israeli society's self-image as just, and to the image of its soldiers as moral. As such, the debate around *As if There Was No War* can be read as a manifestation of a mnemonic dispute or contentious memory with regard to the meanings of war and, by extension, the moral culpability of the state. This moral tension stems from the army's involvement in a war of choice (the Lebanon War) following the *Yom Kippur* War, which did not enjoy social consensus, and because the army was primarily engaged in the maintenance of occupied territories. Under these conditions, it is difficult to demonstrate the heroic and defensive aspects of combat, which are key to establishing the army's legitimacy. Public discourse relating to soldiers as victims masks the fact that the Israeli soldier in the occupied territories primarily acts as an agent of state violence against citizens living under occupation. Thus, research indicating the social significance of trauma discourse and its role in normalizing Israeli militarism aroused resistance.

Next I will demonstrate how this social context not only shaped the responses to my work, but also the manner in which interviewees shared their memories, and the manner in which I analyzed the memories as a researcher.

Close reflexive analysis: silences and managing emotions

Throughout my research I hardly encountered any resistance from interviewees who spoke with me of the 1973 War. The opposite is true, in that interviewees expressed great interest in sharing their experiences, even if they often implied that I would have a hard time fully understanding their experiences as a woman (Lomsky-Feder, 1996). Though I took this openness for granted, with time it grows clearer as a phenomenon that was quite distinct – especially in light of the publication of works addressing other generations of combatants, which indicate that the interviewees found it challenging to discuss their war-related experiences.

Research that addresses combatants from the 1948 War – the heroic independent war – shows that they primarily addressed the war among themselves in gatherings of combatants, yet did not often share their experiences with strangers to war, including family members. When speaking publicly about war-related experiences, veterans did so in a restrained manner. They were cautious of expressing emotions and instead projected an image that matched the ethos of the warrior willing to sacrifice his life and control his emotions. Many argued that there was no place in the public sphere to express emotions such as fear, anger, or pain over loss, and that moral hesitation and criticism should not be exposed. They also did not directly address death, and to the extent that they did relate to it, macabre humor was used. As far as most of these veterans were concerned, emotional preoccupation with war was a weakness of sorts, and those who expressed emotions were perceived as "whining" (Spector-Mersel, 2008; Ben-Ze'ev, 2011). Their emotional restraint shines a different and unique light on *Yom Kippur* combatants. A study comparing the latter to their fathers' generation of soldiers demonstrates that *Yom Kippur* War veterans expressed many more conflicted feelings regarding the war, and are more reflexive regarding its impact on their lives. Moreover, they did not perceive expression of emotions as a weakness, but rather predominantly as a privilege reserved for those who epitomized the warrior ethos (Lomsky-Feder, 2004; Ben Ze'ev and Lomsky-Feder, 2009).

Difficulty speaking about combat experiences also arises in research on soldiers serving in the occupied territories. Agam and Tubin's work (2009) based on interviews with (male) combat officers on their military service, for example, indicates that interviewees primarily addressed issues of promotion in the military hierarchy and the educational significance of commanding soldiers. They refrained from speaking of combat experience throughout their service, and did not discuss the military violence to which they were exposed in any sense. Devorah Manekin's work (Manekin, 2014), wherein she also interviewed men in combat roles, is even more interesting for our case: she directly investigated the way men speak about the military violence to which they were exposed throughout their service in the occupied territories and identifies various practices through which they mask it. Among them is what she deems a "concealment" practice, through which interviewees avoid speaking of their combat experiences in the occupied territories, even with people to whom they are very close (including family, non-combatant friends, and spouses), and solely speak of them with fellow members of their military unit.

When *Yom Kippur* War combatants speak freely of their experiences through emotionally saturated descriptions, we should not take their personal recollections for granted. These descriptive accounts may be explained as a response to me as the researcher who initiated the interview on the subject, when in "real" life they have difficulty speaking of the war with people close to them. Nonetheless, it is important to stress that most of them did not report such difficulty (as seen in other generations of combatants). Moreover, *Yom Kippur* War veterans often engaged in the combatants' protest that broke out following the war, which was accompanied by personal testimonies of what occurred during the war. Thus, even if the interviewees' openness may be explained by the circumstances in which they recounted the war, I believe that the difference between the generations of combatants is more significant, and that the meaning of hiding behind speech and silence must be culturally understood.

The silence among the generation of combatants who served in 1948, and of soldiers who served in the occupied territories, has a completely different meaning. They are positioned in vastly different stances relative to the "warrior ethos": 1948 combatants, who are members of a canonical generation required to represent the warrior ethos, imposed silence upon themselves, which is an inherent element of this ethos and the accompanying code of masculinity. They feel compelled to quell their private voices, neutralize their emotions, and swallow their criticism (Ben-Ze'ev and Lomsky-Feder, 2009) as a way of performing and living up to the warrior ethos that framed their actions on a cultural level. In contrast, soldiers of the occupation sentence themselves to silence as they are unable to realize the celebrated heroic ethos according to which they were educated, and thus feel compelled to conceal their actions. Their silence expresses an emotion code of shame, rather than one of pride.

In the backdrop of both such silences, *Yom Kippur* combatants' voices grow clear. Unlike the 1948 generation, they have already been exposed to cultural and social processes, global and local, which have brought about changes in masculine imagery at large, and combatant imagery in particular. All interviewees were men, secular and highly educated – representing the social group from which Israeli society enlists most of its social elite. As such they are members of social groups that were exposed to, and greatly influenced by, the psychological discourse that permeated Israeli culture in the 1970s. This discourse that centers the individual who reflexively observes their mental distress has enabled these men to express their feelings and to speak of the prices of war, as combatants. As opposed to soldiers who served in the occupied territories, veterans of the *Yom Kippur* War – who participated in a war publicly deemed a war of necessity – generally met the demands of the warrior ethos and purity of arms; thus from their point of view, there is no reason to remain silent, nor any need to conceal.

The absence of moral considerations

This comparative intergenerational analysis not only reveals a difference in silence or discussion around war, but also a difference in the manner of speech and repertoire of emotions that arise in the soldiers' personal memories. The sentiments typically felt by 1973 combatants were primarily those of disappointment, anger, and accusation. Their voices were not those of aggressors but rather victims; the "other" who stood before them upon remembering the war was not the enemy against whom they fought, but rather the leadership that sent them to fight.

I attributed that repertoire of emotions to the public discourse that prevailed in the wake of the war, which focused on the failure and crisis of trust in leadership. The voices of the soldiers reflected this discourse and constituted one of the sources that shaped the traumatic collective memory of the *Yom Kippur* War. I argued that interviewees who did not sound a traumatized and critical voice were those who did not have the social legitimacy to sound such a voice (Lomsky-Feder, 1998, 2004). In this interpretative process, I largely disregarded other groups of combatants who fought in this war and did not accept its traumatic national meaning. Take, for example, religious Zionist combatants, for whom the war was perceived to be another component of the historical-mythical struggle of a nation's return to its land. Within this struggle, there is no space to give in to the difficult experiences of war or existential personal crises, such that they were thoroughly denied among their memories (Feige, 2017).

Moreover, my analysis focused on the emotions present in the texts, yet I was not sufficiently attentive to what was missing from them. I took for granted the absence of guilt, shame, and moral dilemmas – sensations that nearly always accompany killings in wars, however just they may be. This absence may be explained by the fact that the surprise attack in *Sinai* and the *Golan* Heights, the sense of emergency, the concrete danger of conquest of the *Galilee*, battles of survival in the *Golan* Heights and *Sinai* (against armies and not civilians or terrorists) – all the same elements of heroic wars of necessity – softened notions of moral responsibility for the aggressive aspects present in all acts of combat. This explanation was anchored in the unique nature of the *Yom Kippur* War. Yet it should be noted that the interviewees spoke of the war with the distance of time, and their memories were constructed also under the influence of the social context within which the story is told. Thus, the absence of the moral dilemmas and accompanying emotions should also be read within this context.

Interviews were conducted from the years 1987–90, just as activity in the occupied territories became particularly intense and challenging – in the backdrop of the outbreak of the First Intifada. During this period, a new type of soldier was formed, a soldier whose primary occupation involved policing civilians and combating terrorist cells. The nature of such a soldier's activity is very different from the ways that the interviewees described their roles and experiences in war stories, and represents a model of soldiering that is antithetical to the traditional soldiering represented by *Yom Kippur War* veterans. Activity in the occupied territories is not praiseworthy and is subject to ongoing criticism both at home and abroad. Such activity harms the self-image of soldiers as professional combatants and undermines the values of a defensive army, sacrifice, and the purity of arms that characterized the ethos of Israeli combatants (Ben-Ari, 1989; Grassiani, 2013).

In retrospect, it is clear that when interviewees emphasized the victim aspect in describing their combat experiences, they were responding – not necessarily consciously – to processes that eroded the warrior ethos, thus spurring a twofold interpretive and partially paradoxical process. On the one hand, they distinguished themselves from the soldiers serving in the occupied territories, thus preserving the moral impression of their war. On the other hand, they responded to the cultural discourse that seeks to strengthen Israeli society's sense of victimization at large (Gan, 2014), and that of soldiers in particular (Lomsky-Feder and Ben-Ari, 2010). This impression blurs the power relations between Palestinians and Israelis, thus enabling a perception of allegedly equitable and fairer combat.

By virtue of their self-perception and presentation as victims of the war, the interviewees engaged in nearly no moral deliberations with regard to their service as agents of violence. However, they expressed extremely sharp criticism of the military and political leadership's complacency. Although it is fundamentally political criticism and not moral criticism, it was sounded loudly and vigorously as a central part of defining their generational identity. As opposed to their parents' obedient generation (of 1948 combatants), they went against traditional leadership in seeking to absolve the ranks of both military and politics (Ben-Ze'ev and Lomsky-Feder, 2009). Indeed, following this war in 1977 a political upheaval occurred and the Labor Party lost its hold over the government.

The interviewees expanded on critical speech that was perceived by them – as well as by me – to be a self-evident right. Today, as time has elapsed, our complacency as a privileged group has grown clear. Children of *Yom Kippur* War combatants, who served in the occupied territories, feel less confident in sounding their critical voices, exercising more self-censorship instead (Bar-Tal, Halperin, and Oren, 2010), while increasingly exposed to therapeutic discourse and perceptions of war experiences in terms of trauma.

Expanding the scope: between trauma and resilience

As of the 1990s, the figure of the soldier in public discourse has been increasingly perceived and portrayed as mentally vulnerable and military service as potentially leading to traumatic experiences. Take, for example, two autobiographies of soldiers published in the early 2000s (Neumann, 2001; Spivak, 2001) that describe military service as characterized by suffering, crises, and depression. In an article devoted to both books, they are described as "documentation of trauma" (Bar-El, 2001). An outcome of this impression of the service experience is the growing importance of therapeutic models in contending with crises in the military as part of the concept of the therapeutic state (Nolan, 1998). This is expressed in the words of the IDF's (Israeli Defense Force) Chief Mental Health Officer, who says that "the IDF has transformed from a body that automatically discharges weak people, into an organization that reaches out for help and grants tears legitimacy" (Eilon, 2001). The Gulf War (in the early 1990s) and the terror attacks as part of the Palestinian uprisings in the occupied territories (1987–93, 2000–5) led to the expansion of trauma discourse for the entire civilian (Jewish) population (Plotkin Amrami, 2013; Freidman-Peleg, 2014). A clear expression of this trend is the establishment of NATAL (the Israel Trauma and Resiliency Center) in 1998, which aims to grant assistance to anyone suffering from the traumatic consequences of the Arab-Israeli conflict.

The media has been very influential in intensifying the traumatic discourse around the soldiers' memories. This impact is related to characteristics of Israeli society as an "interview society" (Atkinson and Silverman, 1997), in which the media offers platforms for confession and self-discovery in light of psychological models. Combatants are central guests on these confessional stages with trauma discourse among the chief models that grants meaning to their memories. War movies or TV series are major catalysts for featuring combatants' traumatic memories in the media, while social networks greatly intensify the process. A blaring example of this was the series "Valley of Tears," which aired on the public broadcasting channel from October to December of 2020 amid the coronavirus pandemic. The ten-episode series addressed the initial days of the *Yom Kippur* War, which are perceived as the most traumatic. The series' success was tremendous both in terms of ratings and its resonance among public discourse: articles were written about it, social networks erupted around it, and it remained on the public agenda for a considerable period of time. Concerning the matter at hand, a particularly interesting point was the arousal of traumatic memories as is evident in a headline from a daily newspaper:

> Through the time tunnel of Valley of Tears, the living room sometimes becomes a battlefield: a month after the series on the Yom Kippur War aired, outreach to NATAL leaped by 70%. On the other side of the line are combatants contending with the trauma, which is receiving unprecedented engagement. (Aderet, 2020)

Public reactions were so strong that following each episode, the TV channel broadcast a program that aimed to address and process the content that arose in the episode and to alleviate viewers' reactions. Furthermore, a radio program also broadcast live conversations with combatants. In parallel, NATAL launched a campaign to raise awareness around trauma victims. These intense reactions must also be understood in the backdrop of the public atmosphere amid the coronavirus pandemic. The past trauma around *Yom Kippur* resonated with present challenges – the surprise, future uncertainty, and deep disappointment with dysfunctional leadership. Moreover, as opposed to the coronavirus as a new and unfamiliar threat, coping with trauma around *Yom Kippur* channeled feelings of personal and collective helplessness in the face of a recognized national emergency around which Israeli society united.

An analysis of various venues of soldiers' memories since the new millennium indicates interesting processes regarding the trauma discourse. First, unlike *Yom Kippur* War combatants who hardly contended with moral dilemmas, younger combatants' memories were characterized by feelings of shame, remorse, and guilt arising around violent actions conducted during their service. These voices indicate what is referred to as "moral injury" (Frankfurt and Frazier, 2016), or the "trauma of the perpetrator" (Morag, 2013). Among these memories, the soldier's trauma lies in morally examining their actions as an agent of violence, yet the distinction between victim and victimizer is often blurred. The speakers are preoccupied with the impossible situations they have encountered as emissaries of the state, and perceive themselves as its victim. However, the critical voices are relatively rare among soldiers and are often part of a political act of resistance and criticism of the state. They primarily appear in testimonies that soldiers give to the organization Breaking the Silence (established in 2004), which documents the IDF's mode of operation as an occupying military (Shavit and Katriel, 2009; Lomsky-Feder and Sasson-Levy, 2018). Another channel is that of films – fiction and documentary – which expose the military violence in the occupied territories and the psychological implications for soldiers. Many of these films are of an autobiographical nature in that combatants recount and confess their actions (Duvdevani, 2010; Morag, 2013).

The second process involves the recognition of women's trauma, which lacked any expression until recent years. For example, in a book by Harel-Shalev and Daphna-Tekoah (2020) that addresses women combatants' memories, an entire chapter is devoted to this topic. In parallel, the media (newspapers and TV) issue more and more items on women who underwent traumatic experiences. Women's assumption of combat roles and their increasing participation in operational activities seems to have granted them the right to sound their pain and suffering. Although this voice is often used by those who oppose the inclusion of women in combat units as proof that they lack the proper mental resilience, the voice of traumatized women combatants is increasingly recognized in broader public discourse. This stands in contrast to the traumas of women in traditional roles, who are also exposed to difficult experiences such as sexual harassment, and do not receive social proper recognition (Rotem, 2018).

The third process involves the appearance of ever more traumatized voices in the public sphere, sounded by older combatants who had not previously granted such meaning to their combat experiences in public. This process is especially noticeable among the generation of veterans from the 1948 War, some of whom have broken the silence around their difficult experiences at an older age, including confessing to immoral actions in which they partook that have haunted them all their lives. Thus, for example, we witness a traumatic voice among the memories of combatants from the 1948 War, who recount their experiences in the 2000s as part of a documentation project at the Reut Museum, which addresses their war (Ben-Ze'ev and Lomsky-Feder, 2020). These voices may be explained by the fact that as 1948 combatants near the end of their lives, they wish to share what they have repressed in the past. Yet it seems that their breach of silence is also related to the contemporary cultural context that enables, and to a large extent even encourages, sharing the pain and price of war.

In contrast to the previous three processes, the fourth process indicates an erosion of the dominance of the trauma discourse and the growth of what Nitzan Rotem (2019) refers to as a "non-traumatic battle reaction." Rotem analyzed the book *Soldiers' Talk – Protective Edge* (Ben-Ari and Yogev, 2018), which consists of conversations, journal excerpts, letters, and poems, from *Nahal* Battalion combatants who fought in the operation in Gaza in 2014. She claims that the book's speakers are motivated by the strong sense that while nothing happened in the aftermath of the war, their lives did not return to the way they were. The trauma discourse does not help them interpret their experience and offer meaning. As one speaker says: "It seems to me that psychology explains to a person why they're not okay, when it's actually their reality that's not okay. The basic situation is illogical, the war itself ... assuming it's a round, that it will happen again" (Rotem, 2019: p 30).

According to Rotem, the linear and teleological conception of the traumatic-therapeutic model is incompatible with combatants' sense of cyclical time in being doomed to constant combat with no political solution on the horizon (Rotem, 2019, 2021). While the trauma discourse served their parents – the generation of *Yom Kippur* War combatants – in breaking free from the state, this is not the case for the Protective Edge combatants of Generation Y. In their case, this discourse inversely illustrates how the country has trapped them in a dead end of violent conflict. This local sense of time is integrated into more global notions of time that characterize members of this generation, who live in a sense of an ongoing present with no certain future (Leccardi, 2006).

In the face of establishing and naturalizing trauma discourse, and largely in response to these processes, resilience discourse that rests on positive psychology is growing. While trauma discourse posits hard sediments over time that are difficult to contend with and require therapeutic intervention, mental resilience discourse emphasizes an individual's capacity to swiftly recover from challenging experiences (Plotkin-Amrami and Brunner, 2017). The notion of resilience arrived in Israel in the 2000s as part of efforts to contend with security pressure at the time, and was used to facilitate the decline of the Israeli welfare state, as it sought to reduce its therapeutic responsibility to its citizens. Through the articulation and ascription of personal and communal capacities for resilience, the state shifts responsibility to citizens in coping with stressful situations, thereby neutralizing the political aspect that produced the challenging reality (Friedman-Peleg, 2014). Programs to increase national and civic resilience have been implemented, first and foremost, in communities located on lines of confrontation and in schools.

From civil society, the discourse of resilience migrated towards the army, and in this spirit, the army speaks of the need to develop "mental fitness" alongside physical fitness (Svetlitzky, 2016). The discourse of resilience indicates the process of individualization of the warrior ethos, which emphasizes professional capacities and personal responsibility over contribution and sacrifice for the country. The personal memories of soldiers in the 2000s are thus shaped in a cultural context that grants increasing space to the trauma discourse, while also demanding mental resilience. Within this duality, the veterans shape their personal memories and express their service experience as "normalized trauma."[2]

The normalized trauma

The tension between trauma discourse and resilience discourse is embodied in the activities of the organization *Resisim* (shrapnel in Hebrew), which was established in 2015 by discharged combatants who felt that the difficult experiences they underwent are silenced and lack social approval. The organization creates platforms and activities (such as alternative memorial ceremonies, publishing soldiers' stories on their website, and holding meetings among combatants) to voice difficult combat experiences, and their aim is presented on their website as such:

> Over the years, hundreds of thousands of Israelis have experienced combat directly or indirectly, and many bear an experience that ranges along the scope between a visible bodily injury and mental

injury. It lacks a name, and when there's no word for a certain feeling it's repressed and shoved aside to the point of completely suppressing discourse on the matter. The lack of an accurate concept, does not entail the lack of experiences and memories of those who came back alive. The *Resisim* Project invites everyone to come and share, to find the words to describe the same experience aloud, find identification and relief, and create a community together. The project seeks to shape Israeli society's collective memory, and guide a discourse of sharing and processing the personal and social impact of warfare.

There are two important points of relevance in this text: first, the concept of trauma is not explicitly mentioned, although the assumptions of trauma discourse lie in the text – service can cause long-term mental harm, yet it may be addressed upon processing the experience. Second, the organization also has social goals and a desire to influence, yet solely through sharing. The text is conciliatory and lacks any overtone of political criticism. Accordingly, a study that tracked the organization's activities describes how its activists make sure to emphasize that combatants who share their stories with *Resisim* are not post traumatic nor are they affiliated with the organization Breaking the Silence (Findler, 2020). They conduct clear boundary work among themselves and both groups of combatants who threaten their identity as "worthy" citizens: on the one hand, they distinguish themselves from soldiers defined by the medical establishment as suffering from post-traumatic stress disorder, as a key criterion for this diagnosis entails dysfunction in life. On the other hand, they distinguish themselves from soldiers who offer testimony to Breaking the Silence, which is perceived as a radical left-wing organization. Their voice is thus neither pathological nor political, but rather that of normalized trauma.

An example of normalized trauma is the hit song "*Resisim*" (the name of which is hard to believe is incidental) which was immensely successful in December 2020, and was later named song of the year on the public radio channel's Israeli annual Hebrew song chart. The hit was sung by a young musician named Raviv Kaner who participated in a reality show and was portrayed as a discharged soldier who fought in Gaza and copes successfully with post-traumatic stress disorder. In an article in a daily newspaper, the author explains the song's winning formula: "The text speaks (not entirely explicitly) of a soldier who experienced trauma while serving in a military operation. There's both militaristic heroism and vulnerability here, which is a combination that the Israeli ear really likes to hear" (Shalev, 2020).

This combination of heroism and vulnerability rests on the fact that Israeli culture is increasingly concerned with the personal cost of war and perceives soldiers as victims of violence (Levy, 2012), while also not tolerating political criticism that presents soldiers as agents of violence. Those who break the silence suffer from opposition and de-legitimization and are deemed traitors. Israeli society is expressing less and less tolerance for criticism and moral deliberation among soldiers (Weiss, 2011) while strengthening silencing mechanisms around military violence.

Silencing mechanisms

By "silencing mechanisms" I refer to the ways in which society seeks to reduce public discourse on military violence. These are mechanisms through which soldiers and civilians learn not to speak of military violence, especially not critically. The assumption is that silence is not a passive practice (conducted out of indifference or ignorance), but rather the product of active processes – cultural and social mechanisms that strengthen and support silence (Herzog and Lahad, 2006). Through analyzing the soldiers' voices, three central silencing mechanisms may be identified: monitoring the right to speak, authorizing violence, and sanctions against those who break the silence.

"Monitoring the right to speak" functions via construction of cultural criteria that define who has the right to speak about military violence. Such supervision enables the exclusion of most soldiers in the military from the circle of those "entitled to speak." In the context of the *Yom Kippur* War, this right was granted to those who participated in the major incidents identified with the traumatic memories of the war (Lomsky-Feder, 2004). This participation ensured two central authoritative sources for the speakers: the authority of "first hand" witnesses – namely, witnesses who saw and experienced the incidents themselves; and the authority attained by virtue of the suffering involved in direct participation in warfare. Reliance on such sources of authority is evident to date in reports from soldiers who serve in the occupied territories, who offer testimony to Breaking the Silence (Shavit and Katriel, 2009). Analysis of testimonies from women who broke silence indicates the degree to which these sources of authority are gendered. Even if some women were given the right to testify since they served in the "territories," their texts differed in nature from those of men since most of the women were not combatants. They thus expressed less confidence in their testimony – ranging from knowing to not-knowing about violence – and they do not perceive themselves as victims of the state (Lomsky-Feder and Sasson-Levy, 2018).

The second mechanism, "authorizing violence," inhibits moral deliberation by constructing a worldview according to which warfare is "fair." A central practice for shaping such a worldview that emerges from soldiers' memories is the implementation of the notion that soldiers are victims of military violence. The perception of victimhood rests on the trauma discourse that primarily addresses the price that the soldiers themselves pay, and blurs the distinction between the victim and victimizer. It is a discourse that incites the debate over combat from the social to the personal, from the code of ethics to individual suffering, and neutralizes the political and moral debate around the occupation (Lomsky-Feder and Ben-Ari, 2010; Friedman-Peleg, 2014). It is important to emphasize that trauma victim discourse is just one means of curbing moral dilemmas, alongside which other means exist, such as the adoption of legal and human rights discourses. Such discourses, which Ben-Ari calls "restraining discourses" (Ben-Ari, 2009), have permeated the military in various forms, and provide ethical, emotional, and legal backing to the military's actions in seeking to validate them.

The third "sanctions against those who break the silence" mechanism includes deterrents that teach soldiers that it is not in their interest to speak of military violence, as it leads to sanctions and punishments. There are several means of doing so: direct social oversight on behalf of fellow members of their unit demonstrates to soldiers that it is preferable for them to remain silent (Elitzur and Yishay-Krien, 2012; Lomsky-Feder and Sasson-Levy, 2018). Alternatively, soldiers' accumulated experiences teach them that silence will spare them of the need to explain and justify their actions to those who were not "there." Whoever has not engaged in combat in the occupied territories, they claim, cannot understand the complexity of the situation and the manner in which they acted (Manekin, 2014). Finally, the soldiers internalize the almost complete lack of tolerance for criticism of military violence at the macro-social level – a trend that has intensified over the years. The systematic attempt to delegitimize public criticism against military violence is most clearly illustrated by the top-down organized resistance to Breaking the Silence's operations, including banning its activities within the framework of the education system and the military.

The set of silencing mechanisms may be perceived as hoops that capture the subject being recalled, making it difficult not only to resist military violence, but also to properly see and address it emotionally, cognitively, and morally.

Discussion

This chapter addresses the interrelationship between personal and national memory, through deciphering and discussing the various cultural discourses that construct combatants' memories among Israeli society over time. In the analysis, special attention was paid to the various shifting manifestations of the trauma discourse that have become central to shaping Israeli war memory compared to other discourses: the heroic, critical, and resilience. On the basis of this analysis, I seek to formulate some general insights on how personal and national memories of war are intertwined.

First, creating a personal version of war remembrances entails an ongoing journey within a field of national memory which offers a scope of cultural discourses for the interpretation of private experiences. This field is not simply a rich fabric of meanings but also one that is internally ordered, stratified according to the social prestige that is attached to the different memories. Thus, the movement in this national memory field is socially constructed and the remembering subject is not free to choose any interpretation he/she wishes. His/her selections are guided by social-cultural criteria that distribute accessibility to the different models of memory (traumatic, normalizing or heroic) according to social entitlement. For example, as women increasingly assume combat roles, they have more social permission to interpret their service experience as traumatic, and voice those memories in the public sphere.

Second, the nature of the discourses and reciprocal relations between them vary among wars and generational units in a given war. Thus, for example, combatants' memories from the "good" 1948 War were predominantly shaped by a heroic discourse. In contrast, memories of *Yom Kippur* War combatants permeate new discourses: the critical and trauma discourses, which also shape the traumatic memory of this war. Nevertheless, *Yom Kippur* War combatants should not be perceived as one entity. In this manner, for example, religious combatants of the same generation are much more influenced by the historical-mythical discourse that leaves no room for trauma or criticism. The group's marginal social position at the time resulted in their personal memories failing to undermine the traumatic meaning constructed around this war.

The meaning of trauma also varies among generations of soldiers. For example, while for *Yom Kippur* War combatants, trauma originally emerged from them being victims of military violence, over the years another trauma emerged – namely, the trauma of the perpetrator (Morag, 2013). This interpretive schema grants meaning to the memories of soldiers engaged in policing operations in the occupied territories, and their memories primarily focus on them as agents, alongside victims, of violence.

Third, soldiers' memories are dynamic and influenced not only by the nature of the war and its collective memory, but also by the discourses that dominate the period from which the memories emerge. Accordingly, should we return to the 1948 combatants, we find that upon recalling the war approximately 50 years later, their memories are less heroic than those that emerged closer to the war. These memories are much more charged with difficult emotions, which befits the dominance of the trauma discourse at the time of later recall.

Fourth, the memory field shapes not only what combatants share of their personal memories, but also what is not shared. Thus, cultural and political forces particular to each period construct various silencing mechanisms to monitor and neutralize soldiers' critical voices and disturbing memories.

Finally, the discourses that shape the soldiers' memories are diverse and sometimes even contradictory. We thus witnessed the prominence of trauma discourse in the context of combatants from the 2000s who operated in the occupied territories and in Gaza, along with the significant presence of resilience discourse. All this takes place as the heroic discourse of the combat soldier remains dominant. The tension between the discourses and ongoing interpretive shift from heroism to resilience and vulnerability creates a new category of meaning for personal memories of war, which I refer to as normalized trauma.

The normalized trauma enables combatants to voice pain and suffering derived from combat experience, while also clearly distinguishing them from the pathological definition of post-traumatic stress disorder associated with those who failed to resume functioning properly following their service. Moreover, the emphasis on normalized trauma (opposite to the trauma of the perpetrator) centers the combatant as a victim of violence, masking the fact that the combatant is also a victimizer – an agent of violence primarily directed against civilians living under occupation. Thus, from the perspective of the remembering subject, normalized trauma allows one to soften moral dilemmas and permits participation in military violence, which also directly reflects Israeli society's capacity to maintain its self-image as a moral and just society in its national memory.

Notes

[1] The book was published in Hebrew, yet English articles were published on the basis of the work: Lomsky-Feder (1995; 1996; 2004).

[2] Similarly, Kidron et al (2019), who analyze the memories of second generation Holocaust survivors in Israel, indicate how they shift from resilience to trauma and define their voices as characterized by "resilient vulnerability."

References

Aderet, O. (2020) "Through the Time Tunnel of Valley of Tears, the Living Room Sometimes Becomes a Battlefield," *Ha'aretz*, November 11. (Hebrew)

Agam, I. and Tubin, D. (2009) "Combat Unit Officers and the Military Service – Identification and Disenchantment," *Social Issues in Israel* 7: 151–171. (Hebrew)

Atkinson, P. and Silverman D. (1997) "Kundera's Immorality: The Interview Society and the Invention of the Self," *Qualitative Inquiry* 3(3): 304–325.

Bar-El, T. (2001) "Everything Is Memory," *Ha'aretz*, July 27. (Hebrew)

Bar-Tal, D., Halperin, E., and Oren, N. (2010) "Socio-psychological Barriers to Peace Making: The Case of the Israeli Jewish Society," *Social Issues and Policy Review* 4(1): 63–109.

Ben-Ari, E. (1989) "Masks and Soldiering: The Israeli Army and the Palestinian Uprising," *Cultural Anthropology* 4(4): 372–387.

Ben-Ari, E. (2009) "Between Violence and Restraint: Human Rights, Humanitarian Consequences and the Israeli Military in the Al-Aqsa Intifada," in T. van Baarda and D. Verweij (eds) *The Moral Dimension of Asymmetrical Warfare: Counter-Terrorism, Democratic Values, and Military Ethics*, Amsterdam: Martinus Nijhoff Publishers, pp 231–246.

Ben-Ari, G. and Yogev T. (2018) *Soldiers' Talk – Protective Edge*, Hertzelia: The Library of Tarbut Movement. (Hebrew)

Ben-Ari, E., Rosenhek, Z., and Maman, M. (2001) "Introduction," in D. Maman, Z. Rosenhek, and E. Ben-Ari (eds) *War, Politics and Society in Israel: Theoretical and Comparative Perspectives*, New Brunswick, NJ: Transaction Publishers, pp 1–41.

Ben-Eliezer, U. (2017) "Sociology of 'No-War' in Israel," *Megamot* 41(2): 115–143. (Hebrew).

Ben-Ze'ev, E. (2011) *Remembering Palestine in 1948: Beyond National Narratives*, Cambridge: Cambridge University Press.

Ben-Ze'ev, E. and Lomsky-Feder, E. (2009) "The Canonical Generation: Trapped between Personal and National Memories," *Sociology* 43(6): 1–19.

Ben-Ze'ev, E. and Lomsky-Feder, E. (2020) "Remaking Generational Memory: Practices of De-canonization at Historical Museums," *International Journal of Heritage Studies* 26(11): 1077–1091.

Berman, E. (1999) "Mental Health: That of the Soldier or the Army?," *Sihot* 14(1): 57–58. (Hebrew)

Bilu, Y. and Witztum, E. (2000) "War-related Loss and Suffering in Israeli Society: A Historical Perspective," *Israel Studies* 5(2): 1–32.

Duvdevani, Sh. (2010) *First Person Camera*, Jerusalem: Keter. (Hebrew)

Eilon, A. (2001) "The Man Who Made You Mad," *Bamahane*, July 13. (Hebrew)

Elitzur, Y. and Yishai-Karin, N. (2012) "'How Can an Incident Occur?' Narrative Research on the Injustices of IDF Soldiers during the Intifada," in Y. Elitzur (ed) *The Blot of a Light Cloud: Israeli Soldiers, Army, and Society in the Intifada*, Tel Aviv: Hakibutz Hameuchad, pp 39–76. (Hebrew)

Feige, M. (2017) "*Yom Kippur* War in the Israeli National Memory: Crisis versus Continuity," in D. Ohana (ed) *Al Da'at Ha'makom: Israeli Realms of Memory*, Sde Boker: The Ben Gurion Research Institute for the Study of Israel and Zionism, pp 210–225. (Hebrew)

Findler, Y. (2020) "On Trauma and Violence: Therapeutic, Ethical, and Political Discourses of Veterans NGO in Israel and USA," Paper presented in workshop on *Legitimacy to Violence*, Tel Aviv: Open University. (Hebrew)

Frankfurt, Sh. and Frazier, P. (2016) "A Review of Research on Moral Injury in Combat Veterans," *Military Psychology* 28(5): 318–330.

Friedman-Peleg, K. (2014) *A Nation on the Couch*, Jerusalem: Magnes. (Hebrew)
Gan, A. (2014) *From Victimhood to Sovereignty: An Analysis of the Victimization Discourse in Israel*, Jerusalem: The Israel Democracy Institute (Hebrew)
Grassiani, E. (2013) *Soldiering Under Occupation: Processes of Numbing Among Israeli Soldiers in the Al-Aqsa Intifada*, New York: Berghahn Books.
Harel Shalev, A. and Daphna-Tekoah, Sh. (2020) *Breaking the Binaries in Security Studies: A Gendered Analysis of Women in Combat*, Oxford: Oxford University Press.
Herzog, H. and Lahad, L. (2006) "Introduction: Knowledge–silence–action and What's in Between," in H. Herzog and K. Lahad (eds) *Knowledge and Silence: On Mechanisms of Denial and Repression in Israeli Society*, Jerusalem and Tel Aviv: Van Leer Institute and Hakibutz Hameuchad, pp 7–22. (Hebrew).
Kidron, C.A., Kotliar, D., and Kirmayer, L.J. (2019) "Trauma as Badge of Honor: Phenomenological Experiences of Holocaust Descendant Resilient Vulnerability," *Social Science and Medicine* 239: 112524.
Leccardi, C. (2006) "Redefining the Future: Youthful Biographical Constructions in the 21 Century," *New Directions for Child and Adolescent Development* 113: 37–48.
Levy, Y. (2012) *Israel's Death Hierarchy: Causality Aversion in a Militarized Democracy*, New York: NYU Press.
Lomsky-Feder, E. (1995) "The Meaning of War through Veterans' Eyes: A Phenomenological Analysis of Life-stories," *International Sociology* 10(4): 463–482.
Lomsky-Feder, E. (1996) "A Woman Studies War: Stranger in a Man's World," *The Narrative Study of Lives* 4: 232–242.
Lomsky-Feder, E. (1998) *As If There Were No War: The Perception of War in the Life Stories of Israeli Men*, Jerusalem: Magnes. (Hebrew)
Lomsky-Feder, E. (2004) "Life Stories, War and Veterans: On the Social Distribution of Memories," *Ethos* 32(1): 1–28.
Lomsky-Feder, E. and Ben-Ari, E. (2010) "The Discourse of 'Psychology' and the 'Normalization' of War in Contemporary Israel," in G. Sheffer and O. Barák (eds) *Militarism and Israeli Society*, Bloomington, IN: Indiana University Press, pp 280–304.
Lomsky-Feder, E. and Sasson-Levy, O. (2018) *Women Soldiers and Citizenship in Israel: Gendered Encounters with the State*, London: Routledge.
Manekin, D. (2014) "Fighters' Discourse; How Soldiers Talk about Violence," Presentation in the conference: *Talking Peace – Doing War*, Paper presented in workshop, Truman Institution, Hebrew University, Jerusalem.
Morag, R. (2013) *Waltzing with Bashir: Perpetrator Trauma and Cinema*, London: I.B. Tauris.
Neumann, B. (2001) *Good Soldier*, Tel Aviv: Zmora-Bitan. (Hebrew)
Nolan, J.L. (1998) *The Therapeutic State: Justifying Government at Century's End*, New York: NYU Press.

Oakley, A. (1981) "Interviewing Women: A Contradiction in Terms?," in H. Roberts (ed) *Doing Feminist Research*, London: Routledge and Kegan Paul, pp 30–61.

Plotkin Amrami, G. (2013) "Between National Ideology and Western Therapy: On the Emergence of a New 'Culture of Trauma' Following the 2005 Forced Evacuation of Jewish Israeli Settlers," *Transcultural Psychiatry* 50(1): 47–63.

Plotkin Amrami, G. and Brunner, J. (2017) "Constructing the Resilient Subject in Israeli Classrooms: Professional Interventions, Culture and Politics in a Protracted Conflict," *Pedagogy, Culture & Society* 25(3): 417–430.

Rotem, N. (2018) "Suicide, Heroism and the Gender," in O. Sassaon-levy and E. Lomsky-Feder (eds) *Gender at the Base – Women, Men and Military Service in Israel*, Jerusalem: Van Leer and Hakibbutz Hameuchas, pp 203–230. (Hebrew)

Rotem, N. (2019) "How to Come Back from Never-Ending War," Unpublished paper. (Hebrew)

Rotem N. (2021) "We Encourage Post-traumatic Soldiers to Recover and to Go On – It Is a Problematic Message," *Ha'aretz*, August 6. (Hebrew)

Shalev, B. (2020) "What a Twist," *Ha'aretz*, December 27. (Hebrew)

Shavit, N. and Katriel, T. (2009) "We Have Decided to Speak Out: The Testimonial Project of Breaking the Silence as Counter-discourse," *Israel Studies in Language and Society* 2(2): 56–82.

Spector-Mersel, G. (2008) *Sabras Don't Age*, Jerusalem: Magnes. (Hebrew)

Spivak, O. (2001) *Whose Golani?*, Jerusalem: Scena. (Hebrew)

Svetlitzky, V. (2016) "The Missing Unit," *Maarchot* 468–469: 60–65. (Hebrew)

Weiss, E. (2011) "The Interrupted Sacrifice: Hegemony and Moral Crisis Among Israeli Conscientious Objectors," *American Ethnologist* 38(3): 576–588.

3

Feminist Approaches to Studying Memory and Mass Atrocity

Nicole Fox

In 1994, Andrea Dworkin published the *Ms. Magazine* article titled, "The unremembered: Searching for women at the Holocaust Memorial Museum." Dworkin (1994) had gone "to the United States Holocaust Memorial Museum with questions about women," only to find no answers because women and gender were not discussed in the museum or the respective archives. Since 1994, feminist scholars have examined the gendered dimensions of mass atrocity (Wolf, 1996; Sharlach, 1999; Jones, 2004; Brown, 2017), and the Holocaust in particular (Baumel-Schwartz, 1998; Ofer and Weitzman, 1998; Goldenberg and Shapiro, 2013), including patterns of victimology, misogynistic propaganda, gendered mobilization efforts, and sexual and gender-based violence (SGBV). Gendered dynamics also include the ways that previously established gender norms and division of labor shape victimization and perpetration experiences and their respective aftermath. Despite such discoveries, however, collective memory projects and memory studies have been slow to recognize gender as a central element of both atrocity and memory. Yet, doing so is imperative; understanding the gendered dynamics of commemoration and collective memory in general allows for interrogation of how a past wrought with state-sanctioned violence, extermination, and mass human rights violations is remembered through a gendered lens in particular. Social scientists have long argued that how we remember the past shapes present-day social relations, access to resources, and power/privilege (Graybill, 2001; Savelsberg and King, 2005; Hagopian, 2009). Thus, it follows that the marginalization of narratives that illuminate the gendered dynamics of commemoration, memorialization, and collective memory perpetuates present-day inequalities.

This chapter begins with an overview of how and why narratives that shape national collective memory of past atrocity neglect gender. This neglect is shocking given the sheer magnitude and ubiquity of SGBV documented in all recorded wars and mass atrocities. Importantly, such silences translate into contemporary inequalities as who a society remembers and values as a victim of a crime shapes who has access to resources such as education, financial support, and social capital. Next, I suggest ways for scholars to remedy this oversight in research on gender and case studies of contentious memory, and how to integrate a feminist lens in various stages of the research and writing process. This includes oversampling strategies, choosing subjects, qualitative data collection strategies, and approaches to analyzing data, including the analytical vitality of listening to the silences and gaps present in qualitative data. Last, I address the personal cost for the researcher who adopts a feminist interpretive lens when studying gender and memorialization in the context of mass atrocity and SGBV.

Past silences and contemporary inequalities

Creating a collective memory for a nation is a process marred by complex social relations, unequal power dynamics, and competing notions of what is best for the country. As scholars of collective memory and social scientists more broadly have shown, these mnemonic practices shape the trajectories of public policy, civic engagement, and collective identities (Zerubavel, 2003; Savelsberg and King, 2011). Societies often institutionally commemorate histories tarnished by atrocity to advance varied goals and purposes, including symbolic reparations, solidifying group identity, or supporting governmental regimes (Barkan and Karn, 2006; Sasson-Levy et al, 2011; Bezirgan-Tanış, 2019). Through commemoration processes and structures (such as memorials, commemorations, and monuments), the past is remembered, as well as forgotten, in a contested and stratifying dynamic involving a range of social actors who have access to varying levels of resources and social capital.

By creating a dominant collective memory, mnemonic entrepreneurs can assist in healing cultural trauma and repairing a divided community or nation (Lewis and Serbu, 1999; Coombes, 2003; Hawdon and Ryan, 2011; Fox, 2021). As discussed next, they can also institutionalize silences, gaps, and inequalities in that memory. A primary way in which memory projects are thought to "heal" is by acknowledging those who have suffered from atrocities and allowing their voices to be heard (Herman, 1997; Howard-Hassmann, 2004; Hayner, 2011). Testimony and autobiographical memories are prime examples of the link between collective and collected memories and are particularly important tools in the struggle for "mnemonic authority" (DeGloma, 2015: p 158). While those who possess power often silence those who occupy the lower end of the social order, mnemonic supremacy is never absolute; indeed, marginalized groups can create "counter-memories" that contest hegemonic narratives of the past (Cunningham et al, 2010; Whitlinger, 2015).

Scholars have inquired into whose memories are shared in spaces of official or dominant memory, documenting gendered silences within collective memories (Markwick, 2008; Seo, 2008) and memorials (Jacobs, 2010, 2017; Woodley, 2018). Such interrogations reveal how gender, or the gendered patterning of violence are often disregarded. Even when memorial spaces are curated in ways that do include narratives or information about SGBV, such as select national memorials in Rwanda which commemorate the 1994 Genocide, these narratives are not consistent, direct, or universally inclusive, for some national memorials rarely mention SGBV (Fox, 2019). In the case of Rwanda, the reasons stated for not including stories of SGBV stemmed from a desire to maintain (a perhaps misplaced sense of) gender-neutrality and equality while discussing genocide's victims and in efforts to avoid upsetting visitors or survivors (Fox, 2019).

Public stories of women's experiences during political violence (outside of genocide) expose similar patterns of silences, with women's voices mostly invisible outside legal testimony and international tribunals. For example, in South African efforts to develop an exhaustive archive of apartheid, Black women's experiences of violence are repeatedly ignored (McEwan, 2003). Silence was also present in the case of Somalia, where sexual violence was related in personal stories told by survivors of rape yet underplayed in national historical narratives (Declich, 2000). In these cases, both the collected memories (that is, accumulated individual accounts) and collective forms of memory (that is, memorials and commemorations)[1] appearing in national contexts marginalize women's experiences of violence. An absence of women's stories is no mere accident; rather, it is a form of institutional forgetting – an intentional and conscious effort to silence specific histories (Teeger and Vinitzky-Seroussi, 2007; Vinitzky-Seroussi and Teeger, 2010; Whitlinger, 2015; Bezirgan-Tanış, 2019).

These gendered gaps in collective memory projects have significant consequences, including devaluing women's place in the nation and delimiting their roles in the future (with regard to leadership opportunities, decision-making positions, economic prosperities, and governing posts that consider gender). For example, with regard to race and gender in South Africa, McEwan notes (2003: p 740): "if they [Black women] are denied a presence and agency in stories of national liberation, Black women's belonging and citizenship in South Africa is compromised in the process of nation building." Because collective memory demonstrates what a country values, when women are left out of those narratives, so is their imagined participation as citizens. Further, how a nation remembers mass violence and its associated gendered dimensions structures gender roles in its aftermath (Najmabadi, 1996; Yuval-Davis, 1997). In the case of Iran, Najmabadi (1996) argues that, had the stories of women's participation been written into a more inclusive gendered history, the gendered roles, expectations, and ideologies around modernity might have been expanded, leaving more room for women's participation in political, economic, and social life. In the case of mass rape of the Zo Hnahthlak people in the Myanmar region, memories of women's victimhood continue to influence present-day gender expectations with men encouraged to act as protectors because in the past they were unable to protect women from sexual violence (Chakraborty, 2010).

Integrating a feminist lens

In my own research I have drawn inspiration from feminist criminologists and sociologists who study collective memory and mass atrocity. Their work has guided my research over the past decade on memorialization in post-genocide Rwanda and the dynamics of rescue during the 1994 Genocide (Fox and Nyseth Brehm, 2018; Fox, 2019, 2021). In the pages that follow, I explore how feminist methodologies – particularly in terms of including women and stories of SGBV, having participants guide the research questions, the importance of trust, and analyzing silences – can aide in illuminating how gender shapes remembering mass atrocity. While I focus on particular cases of mass atrocity in this chapter, a feminist lens in analyzing contentious memory/memories is vital in a range of cases (collective, public, traumatic, autobiographical) as mnemonic practices, rituals, and outcomes are inherently intersectional. Memories of a contentious past are indeed contentious because of power relations, and a feminist intersectional approach demands the researcher to untangle such dynamics often illuminated in the built environment.

Such undertakings are challenging, and as a researcher who has spent the last decade speaking with people who have survived the worst of humanity (rape, death of their entire families, torture, war, destruction of their homes, attempted murder), in the final section of this chapter, I address the emotional labor of conducting such scholarship. This is not to suggest martyrdom for those who take on this task, but rather in line with feminist research methodologies, to write openly and honestly about positionality, emotions, and trauma (Reinharz, 1992; Burman et al, 2001; Simic, 2016). Research centering on social memories about contentious events (mass atrocity and sexual violence in particular) requires that researchers care for themselves as well as their research subjects. Overlooking the emotional labor and trauma involved in this research reinforces the anti-feminist notion of "objectivity" that underpins the idea that rigorous science is an enterprise devoid of humanity and emotion.

Including women and stories of sexual and gender-based violence

To risk stating the obvious, in order to have women and survivors of SGBV included in scholarship about contentious memory, researchers must specifically include women and survivors of SGBV as subjects of research. This means oversampling for women if conventional sampling methods do not yield this population. In my own work with Dr Hollie Nyseth, during our study of rescue behavior,[2] we had to evaluate the lack of women in the database of rescuers from which we drew for qualitative, in-depth interviews. Our sample began with interviewing those who were on a national vetted list of rescuers provided by a government sponsored survivor service organization (see Fox, Wise, and Nyseth Brehm, 2021 for more detailed description of the methodology utilized for this project). However, after our first set of interviews, we checked our sample demographics for representation, even though we were aware that specific demographics may shape a person's ability to rescue.[3] We quickly noted how few women were included in this national sample. When inquiring about research methods, we discovered that researchers who conducted this study only interviewed the head of the household, who were most often men, and women were only interviewed when they rescued alone (without a male partner) or if they were widowed and had rescued with their husband who was now deceased (that is, making them the head of the household). If a woman rescued with her husband, only her husband was interviewed, as her story was thought to be analytically insignificant, not yielding any additional information beyond that which was gleaned from her husband's interview.

Together, we began to integrate new questions into our initial survey to inquire if participants rescued with another person and, if so, their relationship to that person. If the participant was a married male and he said he rescued alone, though was married to a woman at the time of the rescue behavior, we inquired if his wife provided food, shelter, or childcare for the people he rescued. Often, male rescuers who initially said their female partners did not help, then answered that they did provide food, shelter, emotional support, or childcare for those they rescued. Such actions were not framed as rescuer behavior even when they were essential to the rescue's success. We then asked if we could interview their partner in a separate interview; a request often met with a response that there was no need as they rescued together, or that she did not know the details of the rescue.

Rescue behavior is only recently being commemorated in Rwanda's memorials and public memory campaigns. Given the contradictions we discovered with regard to the very conception of rescue work, in public remembrances where these social actors are recognized, mostly men speak of the heroic actions they took to save others, in some cases hundreds of innocent people. Such behavior is no doubt remarkable and deserving of public recognition, but so is the behavior conducted by women who saved others. In interviewing the wives of rescuers and oversampling for women rescuers we found that women rescued in particularly gendered ways, using gender norms and expectations to save others. This meant they breastfed the babies they saved along with their own, cooked for large groups of people hiding in their house or property, raised children as their own, and executed creative plans to save those under their watch (such as one woman who pretended she was in labor and the boys she was saving had to take her to the hospital). Through insisting that women were their own subjects in rescue, we also found that in some cases, women were the ones who convinced their husbands to rescue, that some rescued people their husbands never knew about (and still didn't), and that many women were essential to the rescue project that saved hundreds of lives. Without an explicit feminist intervention into the process of research, women's rescue work would have remained invisible.

Having participants guide research inquiries

As noted, scholars from an array of disciplines have inquired about the physicality of memorial spaces, the contested narratives that often surround them, and the political motivations behind them. However, these scholars rarely talk to people, including those whom these spaces ostensibly honor, leaving us to wonder *how* memorials matter to people. Through a case study of post-genocide Rwanda, in my recent book, I situate people at the center of analysis, documenting who is remembered and how (Fox, 2021). The general research question that guided me through my fieldwork focused on how memorials and the events held at these sites shape the collective memory of a nation and, in particular, survivors' lives.

After the genocide in Rwanda, women were vital to their nation's recovery. The country was majority female, with women filling all aspects of societal life, including the central care work for traumatized and/or orphaned children (Newbury and Baldwin, 2000), spearheading NGOs that served widows and single parents (Mukamana and Brysiewicz, 2008), and creating women's councils, initiatives, and development funds (Burnet, 2008; Berry, 2018). Yet, during the few months I spent observing memorials (before conducting interviews), I found that women were often not among the people featured at memorials, or in the public stories of survivorship. This was particularly jarring because since the 1994 Genocide, Rwanda has been lauded as a model for gender progress internationally as they lead the world with one of the highest percentages of women in its national legislature (if not the highest at times, surpassing Sweden in 2003) (Longman, 2006; Berry, 2014).

Such gender progress did not necessarily translate into making women's experiences of SGBV during the genocide central in memorials (Fox, 2019) or (in the form of testimony) at commemorations (Fox, 2021). Those curating these memory projects felt that stories of SGBV, a familiar experience for most women (and some male) survivors, were too traumatizing for the public. What their exclusion meant is that they were not part of the written and recorded history of commemoration and memorialization, as these memorials and events are quite literally the written history of what happened during those horrific spring months of 1994. Memorials and commemorations are highly attended spaces/events, by both the Rwandan population but also by international leaders, diplomats, and decision-makers. When stories of women's survival or the prevalence of sexual violence and its lasting impact are marginalized, such stories are literally written out of history. How, then, can future generations remember an event that is not commemorated? Collective memory is only possible by making social memories recognizable and relatable to those who witness and engage with such memories and narratives.

Observing who was not centered in collective memory processes and products allowed me to refocus my inquiry into why and how women are left out of public memorialization and what variables coalesce in these spaces to break such silences (Fox, 2019). My intellectual curiosity thus shifted to understanding how micro-level decisions impact macro-level narratives, analyzing decisions about whether to incorporate discussions of SGBV that occurred during the genocide into memorial tours and, if so, how. What I discovered is that some guides found unique ways to bring the experiences of women survivors into the larger narrative of past violence. However, breaking the silence around SGBV was not the case for all memorials. The spaces that focused on reconciliation often sacrificed the stories of rape during the genocide for ones that offer more inspiration and justification for practices of forgiveness.

When studying collective memory through qualitative methodologies such as interviewing, a feminist practice I adopted is to be guided by a broad research question that can be refocused over time to become more inclusive. As I interviewed women who ran NGOs that assisted widows, or guided visitors through memorial tours, their stories illuminated how inequality culminated over time. While they occupied positions of power on many levels, the lack of public narratives about their survival hindered some women's participation and belief in reconciliation practices and programs. Focusing on gender revealed the myriad ways that micro-social processes can both help and hinder reconciliation through efforts to remember. Ultimately, asking a range of questions about gender roles, expectations, and challenges allowed me to gain a broader understanding of how gender functioned on multiple fronts (the home, public, memorials, narrative dissemination).

Collective memory is interconnected to broader reconciliation processes and memorialization can be used as a mechanism of transitional justice,[4] often used in combination with other judicial initiatives (Barsalou and Baxter, 2007; Fox, 2021). When survivors of mass atrocity do not see themselves in the stories about violence or survival, it becomes more difficult for them to imagine themselves as valued citizens in a post-conflict nation. Feeling devalued has serious implications as their civic engagement and participation in reconciliation efforts are essential in building a future without violence. Their marginalization in the collective memory of the nation's difficult past, over time, can result in a decline in peaceful coexistence. Thus, commemorating the gendered experiences of violence (and survival), even when such testimonies ask for people to bear witness to SGBV, is essential for a more peaceful future.

The importance of trust

Before I started interviewing survivors in Rwanda, I attended and observed tours at the national memorials throughout the country. Three national memorials were included as field sites for my research and over several weeks I became familiar with the tour guides and learned how the memorial spaces operated in a variety of ways outside traditional memorialization. My first interview was with a village leader whom I had gotten to know through my time at one of the memorial sites for my book. She worked and served as a gatekeeper for the rest of the community. I first interviewed her in the fall, before commemorations took place, then again in winter, and then during the mourning months (April to July each year).

Interviewing participants more than one time was beneficial for two central reasons. First, mass atrocity, political violence, and war are all traumatic experiences that break trust: trust in institutions, in social order, and in humanity. Some participants were reasonably skeptical of a white woman from the United States who wanted to interview them. Memorial guides had often been interviewed several times and had frequently articulated their experiences to foreigners in a range of contexts. It was important to interview them multiple times to gather different data, and to get past the initial answers that they wanted me to know and the answers that they gave to foreigners who often "flew in and flew out after they got what they wanted."[5] Some participants in the more rural areas had never been interviewed and were unsure what I wanted to know from them. Spending time with them prior to interviewing and observing their work at the memorials in addition to interviewing them multiple times showed my investment in their narrative.

Second, trust and rapport were built by immersing myself in the communities and interviewing participants more than once. I was keenly aware I would always be an outsider, a foreigner with a US passport and access to a plethora of resources and privileges that were the result of colonialism and long histories of violence and oppression. As other scholars of Rwanda have noted (Jessee, 2012; Ingelaere, 2015), researchers immerse themselves in ways "to be Kinyarwandan," but clearly, no matter how many language lessons or trips to Rwanda I took, I was never going to become Rwandan. However, continuing to return to participants' communities and returning to Rwanda after going home time and again, showed some participants, women in particular, that I was dedicated to hearing their stories and how they might shift over time or with changes in their life circumstances.

With continued interviews came longer and more complex narratives about the aftermath of genocide, and of genocidal rape.[6] It often took two interviews and many weeks together for someone to disclose their survival of SGBV. No men disclosed to me, though scholars have demonstrated the gendered dynamics of violence that include SGBV against men (Ferrales, Nyseth Brehm, and McElrath, 2016). Like survivors of rape in contexts outside of war and genocide, the women with whom I spoke feel deep shame about the violence inflicted on them, telling few people (sometimes not even their partner if they had since remarried) and some travelling far distances to maintain their anonymity while seeking much-needed psychological and physical resources (Campbell et al, 2001; Tjaden and Thoennes, 2006; Lorenz et al, 2018).[7] The SGBV survivors who were known rape survivors in the community due to the public aspect of their assaults described feeling ostracized and even accused of "having sex with the enemy." This means that in building trust, and dedication to the sensitivity of the rape culture in which SGBV occurs, the researcher must do all they can to make it possible for survivors to feel safe to share their stories if they wish. However, some may choose to share their experiences through silences, rather than testimonies, which is also an important source of data and a powerful way to express the brutality of such violence.

Analyzing silences

We are living in a historical era in which memorials, rather than monuments, occupy the built environment as both sites of contention and tools to reckon with oppressive histories and regimes in their aftermath (Jinks, 2014; Simko, Cunningham, and Fox, 2020). Until recently, there was no major national memorial in the world that commemorated sexual violence (Sardina and Fox, 2021).[8] Even memorials dedicated to commemorating events that were marred by known "rape camps" and sexual violence to terrorize an entire population speak fairly little to the astounding prevalence of SGVB and its lasting legacy (Jacobs, 2017; Fox, 2019; Funk, Good, and Berry, 2020). The shocking absence of a memorial space dedicated to survivors of SGBV stands in stark contrast to its astonishing frequency both in times of peace and war (Barstow, 2000; Campbell and Wasco, 2005; Buss, 2009).

A commitment to seeing collective memory through a feminist lens looks for the absences and the silences in the built environment, asking who is not there and why. Of course, the quest to see what is not there is also dependent on understanding the nuances of a violent past in which memorials commemorate. Here, we are interconnected with the researchers who document the gendered experience of mass atrocity, political violence, and wars. Their research is vital to seeing contrasts, such as the approximate 350,000 rapes that occurred during the 100-day genocide in Rwanda, and the silences in commemoration testimonies about such crimes and victimization (Bijleveld, Morssinkhof, and Smeulers, 2009; Fox, 2019).

Silences also operate on the micro-level of collective memory research, specifically in the form of all that is not said during interviews and other forms of testimony. Qualitative data, evident in ethnography and in-depth interviews, includes what Lee Ann Fujii has called "meta-data." Fujii (2010) states that meta-data is:

> the spoken and unspoken expressions about people's interior thoughts and feelings, which they do not always articulate in their stories or responses to interview questions. Meta-data can take both spoken and unspoken forms. They include rumors, silences, and invented stories. Meta-data are as valuable as the testimonies themselves because they indicate how the current social and political landscape is shaping what people might say to a researcher. (p 231)

In my own research, meta-data took the form of untold stories, sentences not completed, and heavy, long pauses.

In the aftermath of mass atrocity, memories of violence often fall outside the limits of language. Scholars have noted how difficult it is to give physical pain, such as torture, and emotional pain such as grief and loss, descriptive language (Scarry, 1985; Malkki, 1995; Rosaldo, 2004). While talk therapy and safe spaces to debrief trauma can be positive for healing, narration without agency can retraumatize a survivor (Pals and McAdams, 2004; de Haene, Grietens, and Verschueren, 2010). Furthermore, trauma is a disorientating experience with long-term impacts, including the shattering of previous beliefs about the world and how it functions.[9] As Rajiva and Takševa (2020) explain of the challenges Bosnian genocidal rape survivors experience in describing the layers of victimization in the violence they endured:

> The event of rape itself stems from deeply entrenched transhistorical and transcultural attitudes rooted in misogyny and sexism that manifest themselves in particular social, political and local circumstances. In the

case of the war rapes of Bosnian women, in addition to this dimension, the rapes also stemmed from a political ideology of exclusionism and the ethno-nationalist rhetoric that unleashed and legitimized extreme sexual violence against the women of the "enemy" group. (p 9)

Given that narratives aim to create order, it may feel impossible to order a disorderly event that attacks one's identity from so many angles and an experience that provides no coherent meaning.

Individual silences may also reflect broader social silences. Because SGBV survivors are also survivors of the genocide, they are included in aspects of national commemoration but as scholars have noted: "their more individual experiences of the war and its survival, because it is related to an attack on their sexuality (a category of female identity historically and traditionally regulated through collective, public means), has prevented them from sharing in 'allowable' forms of collective memory" (Rajiva and Takševa, 2020: p 10). The silence about SGBV on the macro-level, often steeped in nationalist justifications made in post-conflict societies across the globe, also situates narratives of SGBV as a form of "political opposition" and resistance (Bezirgan-Tanış, 2019: p 338).

Yet, it is also true that survivors of SGBV may not want to be agents of counter-state resistance. For them, silence can be a safe and rational choice. In this case, a researcher can sit with them in the silence, and through time and trust, determine if they want to break the silence, breathe through it, sit with it, or move on from it.

Emotional labor

While it is not the norm in social science research to discuss the emotional toll of conducting qualitative research on violence, we know from the previous sections that public silences do not indicate private absence. Failing to acknowledge secondary/vicarious trauma (and the emotionality of certain methods and areas of inquiries) is detrimental to the researcher, participants, and the research design (Kleinman, 1991; Carpenter, 2012; Fox, 2021). Neglecting the emotional costs to the researcher can create situations in which research ethics are compromised, the researcher is unprepared, and undue harm is caused in situations where too much harm has already occurred. Ignoring emotions and pretending that such social science research cannot be rigorous if not objective is both gendered in its assumption and inaccurate. For as Connolly and Reilly (2007: p 505) note: "When the natural order of the world gets so radically disturbed ... [such as in the case of genocide, rape, mass atrocity, war] it becomes quickly apparent that these research interests cannot be explored in a distant, remote, objective manner [as with a conventional positivist approach]. They simply are too human – too real – too traumatic."

Researching victims of mass atrocity and SGBV is emotionally and physically trying.[10] Extended exposure to testimonies of violence, mass murder, and SGBV, at all stages of the research process (that is, interviewing trauma survivors, listening to transcripts and/or coding data about violence, torture, and rape), increases the researchers' risk for vicarious and/or secondary trauma, grueling emotions (anger, guilt, rage, despair), mental health challenges (anxiety and depression), and physical symptoms of illness (nausea, flu-like symptoms) (Campbell, 2002; Fontes, 2004; Wray et al, 2007; Coles and Mudaly, 2010; Coles et al, 2014; Fox, 2021). Rebecca Campbell (2002) explains what it is like to be a researcher who studies rape, "That means I think about rape for prolonged periods of time. I read about it, talk about it, write about it and bear witness to it" (p 1).

When I first read Rebecca Campbell's work on researching rape, I could relate. In the past decade there were just a handful of days that I did not think about rape, atrocity, or mass violence. When I was in Rwanda studying gender, genocide, and commemoration, I attended burials, memorial openings, religious ceremonies, and small and larger gatherings remembering genocidal violence on a very regular basis, especially during the mourning months. At these events, genocide survivors often experienced extreme trauma responses where they begin to scream and have a flashback to the genocidal violence they experienced decades ago (for more, see chapter four of Fox, 2021). I witnessed these flashbacks and heard stories of brutality that were beyond even the most disturbing dimensions of my imagination.

When this first occurred, I did not realize that I was experiencing my own secondary trauma. I was exhausted, but that seemed like a staple of fieldwork. However, even when I was not conducting fieldwork, I continued to hear screams (an experience which I describe in detail in my book) even when there were no survivors present or when I was not attending commemorations. A handful of stories I heard made me physically ill when I finished the interview, with one leading me to vomit on the side of the road after the interview had ended. Despite these alarming experiences, I was hesitant to slow down or stop my research. It felt unwarranted. I had not lived these experiences, I was only listening to them, and I believed in my role of bearing witness to the survivors who shared their stories with me. Yet, I could not stop hearing the screams of people who were reliving their traumatic experience during the genocide.[11]

Now, years later, though there are still stories that haunt me, I have found ways to mitigate the secondary trauma in ways that have allowed me to continue this line of work. Scholars have noted ways to lessen the vicarious trauma through being informed/prepared (Johnson and Clarke, 2003; Coles et al, 2014); ensuring an emotional support system, research management, such as taking breaks (Coles et al, 2014); and self-care practices, such as exercise (Connolly and Reilly, 2007; Dickson-Swift, James, and Liamputtong, 2008).[12] I would encourage each researcher to find and practice their own strategies that mitigate the very real costs of the emotional labor involved in conducting this research.

Conclusion

Researching collective memory and commemoration efforts in the aftermath of contentious violence and/or oppression inherently places the researcher in the dialectical process of memory-making. The researcher documents the narratives that are remembered and shared. The researcher also has the power to document those pieces of memory that are not remembered, either because they are intentionally forgotten or unintentionally marginalized in favor of a more hegemonic or digestible story for the public. Utilizing a feminist approach to studying contentious memory, and mass atrocity in particular, resists replicating the institutional silences and gaps described here. Such silencing stratifies already frayed communities. It disproportionately impacts those who were, and continue to be, on the lower end of the social order – those with less access to resources and social capital such as women, children, those in poverty and LGBTQ communities. Listening to silences is an integral part of data collection that lends to more dynamic and inclusive understandings of memory.

Exposing the stratifying impacts of contentious mnemonic processes gives researchers the opportunity to shed light on the broader patterns of inequality, including its repercussions. In grasping these nuances at play, especially in the case of mass atrocity, social science research can become better equipped to prevent such destruction in the future. For it is difficult to put forth policy or recommend resources to remedy that which we do not know. Feminist approaches to studying memory (methodologically and analytically) are a way forward in the aftermath of atrocity that leads to possibilities of a more inclusive, if not more multifaceted, future.

Notes

[1] Collected memories are understood as a process by which, while shaped by social structures, *individuals* remember, whereas collective memory is framed as an active and constructive process by which society remembers, which can be shaped and reshaped in lieu of the present (Olick and Robbins, 1998; Olick, 1999).

[2] We conceptualize rescue as a high risk, often collective action that occurs during periods of genocidal violence and in Rwanda comprised of Hutu who saved Tutsi, the group that were the primary ethnic target of extermination during the 1994 Genocide in Rwanda.

[3] Factors that shape a person's ability to rescue can include biographical availability, socialization, religion, and situational contexts. For more information on how social factors shape rescue see Fox and Nyseth Brehm (2018).

[4] According to the International Center for Transitional Justice, "Transitional justice refers to the ways countries emerging from periods of conflict and repression address large-scale

or systematic human rights violations so numerous and so serious that the normal justice system will not be able to provide an adequate response" (www.ictj.org/).
5   Stated by a participant in Kigali, Rwanda, October 2011.
6   Genocidal rape is rape that is part of a genocidal campaign aimed at exterminating a specific group or community in whole or in part. The International Criminal Tribunal of Rwanda (ICTR) prosecuted Jean Paul Akayesu in the first case where rape was considered an act of genocide. This case changed legal precedent, see Alvarez (1999); MacKinnon (2006); Fitzpatrick (2016).
7   For analysis on mental health care for Rwandan survivors of SGBV, see: Zraly, Rubin-Smith, and Betancourt (2011). Holly Porter's work on social harmony and justice after rape in Northern Uganda is also relevant: Porter (2017).
8   The first survivors' memorial opened in October 2020 in Minneapolis Minnesota. For more information on the Survivors Memorial, please visit www.survivors memorial.org/.
9   Researchers and practitioners across various disciplines have consistently documented the lasting, harmful effects of sexual violence on victims, their families, and communities. See: Dube et al (2005); Tjaden and Thoennes (2006); Ullman et al (2007).
10 Of course, ethical research also ensures that the participant is also not experiencing undue hardship because of the research being conducted, however that is the not the topic of this section. The World Health Organization has outlined ways to protect survivors of domestic violence from harm (WHO, 1997, 1999: p 13). For more information see: Finkelhor, Hotaling, and Yllo (1988); Fontes (1998); Ellsberg et al (2001).
11 As Coles et al (2014) note, it is not only the qualitative interview that can be problematic for researchers but that working with the data generated can be difficult, too. "Researcher saturation is described when triangulating qualitative data by doing observational studies, in-depth interviews, transcription, and coding ... Repeated exposure to text describing traumatic events such as coroners' files can be distressing, as can listening to and transcribing research interviews, coding data, and writing up reports" (p 100).
12 See: Gilbert (2001); Dickson-Swift (2008); Dickson-Swift et al (2009).

References

Alvarez, J.E. (1999) "Lessons from the Akayesu Judgment," *Journal of International & Comparative Law* 5(359): 359–370.

Barkan, E. and Karn, A. (eds) (2006) *Taking Wrongs Seriously: Apologies and Reconciliation*, Stanford, CA: Stanford University Press.

Barsalou, J. and Baxter, V. (2007) *The Urge to Remember: The Role of Memorials in Social Reconstruction and Transitional Justice*, Washington, DC: United States Institute for Peace.

Barstow, A.L. (2000) *War's Dirty Secret: Rape, Prostitution, and Other Crimes against Women*, Cleveland, OH: Pilgrim Press.

Baumel-Schwartz, J.T. (1998) *Double Jeopardy: Gender and the Holocaust, Parkes-Wiener Series on Jewish Studies*, Portland, OR: Vallentine Mitchell.

Berry, M. (2014) "When 'Bright Futures' Fade: Paradoxes of Women's Empowerment in Rwanda," *Signs: Journal of Women in Culture and Society* 41(1): 1–27.

Berry, M. (2018) *War, Women, and Power: From Violence to Mobilization in Rwanda and Bosnia-Herzegovina*, New York: Cambridge University Press.

Bezirgan-Tanış, B. (2019) "History-writing in Turkey through Securitization Discourses and Gendered Narratives," *European Journal of Women's Studies* 26(3): 329–344.

Bijleveld, C., Morssinkhof, A., and Smeulers, A. (2009) "Counting the countless: Rape Victimization during the Rwandan Genocide," *International Criminal Justice Review* 19(2): 208–224.

Brown, S. (2017) "Gender and the Genocide in Rwanda: Women as Rescuers and Perpetrators," in L. Sjoberg and C. Gentry (eds) *Routledge Studies in Gender and Security*, New York: Routledge.

Burman, M.J., Batchelor, S.A., Brown, J.A. and Brown, A. (2001) "Researching Girls and Violence – Facing the Dilemmas of Fieldwork," *The British Journal of Criminology* 41(3): 443–459.

Burnet, J.E. (2008) "Gender Balance and the Meanings of Women in Governance in Post-Genocide Rwanda," *African Affairs* 107(428): 361–386.

Buss, D.E. (2009) "Rethinking 'Rape as a Weapon of War,'" *Feminist Legal Studies* 17(2): 145–163.

Campbell, R. (2002) *Emotionally Involved: The Impact of Researching Rape*, London: Routledge.

Campbell, R. and Wasco, S.M. (2005) "Understanding Rape and Sexual Assault: 20 Years of Progress and Future Directions," *Journal of Interpersonal Violence* 20(127): 127–131.

Campbell, R., Wasco, S.M., Ahrens, C.E., Sefl, T., and Barnes, H.E. (2001) "Preventing the 'Second Rape': Rape Survivors' Experiences with Community Service Providers," *Journal of Interpersonal Violence* 16(12): 1239–1259.

Carpenter, R.C. (2012) "'You Talk of Terrible Things so Matter-of-factly in this Language of Science': Constructing Human Rights in the Academy," *Perspectives on Politics* 10(2): 363–383.

Chakraborty, A.S. (2010) "Memory of a Lost Past, Memory of Rape: Nostalgia, Trauma and the Construction of Collective Social Memory Among the Zo Hnahthlak," *Identity, Culture and Politics* 11(2): 87–104.

Coles, J. and Mudaly, N. (2010) "Staying Safe: Strategies for Qualitative Child Abuse Researchers," *Child Abuse Review* 19(1): 56–69.

Coles, J., Astbury, J., Dartnall, E., and Limjerwala, S. (2014) "A Qualitative Exploration of Researcher Trauma and Researchers' Responses to Investigating Sexual Violence," *Violence against Women* 20(1): 95–117.

Connolly, K. and Reilly, R.C. (2007) "Emergent Issues When Researching Trauma: A Confessional Tale," *Qualitative Inquiry* 13(4): 522–540.

Coombes, A. (2003) *History After Apartheid: Visual Culture and Public Memory in a Democratic South Africa*, Durham, NC: Duke University Press.

Cunningham, D., Nugent, C., and Slodden, C. (2010) "The Durability of Collective Memory: Reconciling the 'Greensboro Massacre,'" *Social Forces* 88(4): 1517–1542.

De Haene, L., Grietens, H., and Verschueren, K. (2010) "Holding Harm: Narrative Methods in Mental Health Research on Refugee Trauma," *Qualitative Health Research* 20(12): 1670.

Declich, F. (2000) "Fostering Ethnic Reinvention: Gender Impact of Forced Migration on Bantu Somali Refugees in Kenya," *Cahiers d'Études Africaines* 40(157): 25–53.

DeGloma, T. (2015) "The Strategies of Mnemonic Battle: On the Alignment of Autobiographical and Collective Memories in Conflicts over the Past," *American Journal of Cultural Sociology* 3(1): 156–190.

Dickson-Swift, V., James, E., and Liamputtong, P. (2008) *Undertaking Sensitive Research in the Health and Social Sciences: Managing Boundaries, Emotions and Risks*, Cambridge: Cambridge University Press.

Dickson-Swift, V., James, E., Kippen, S., and Liamputtong, P. (2009) "Researching Sensitive Topics: Qualitative Research as Emotional Work," *Qualitative Research* 9(1): 61–79.

Dube, S.R., Anda, R.F., Whitfield, C.L., Brown, D.W., Felitti, V.J., Dong, M., and Giles, W.H. (2005) "Long-term Consequences of Childhood Sexual Abuse by Gender of Victim," *American Journal of Preventative Medicine* 28(5): 430–438.

Dworkin, A. (1994) "The Unremembered: Searching for Women at the Holocaust Memorial Museum," *Ms. Magazine* 5(3).

Ellsberg, M., Heise, L., Peña, R., Agurto, S., and Winkvist, A. (2001) "Researching Domestic Violence against Women: Methodological and Ethical Considerations," *Studies in Family Planning* 32(1): 1–16.

Ferrales, G., Nyseth Brehm, H., and McElrath, S. (2016) "Gender-based Violence against Men and Boys in Darfur: The Gender-genocide Nexus," *Gender & Society* 30(4): 565–589.

Finkelhor, D., Hotaling G., and Yllo, K. (1988) *Stopping Family Violence: Research Priorities for the Coming Decade*, New York: Sage.

Fitzpatrick, B. (2016) *Tactical Rape in War and Conflict: International Recognition and Response*, Bristol: Bristol University Press.

Fontes, L.A. (1998) "Ethics in Family Violence Research: Cross-cultural Issues," *Family Relations* 47(1): 53–61.

Fontes, L. (2004) "Ethics in Violence against Women Research: The Sensitive, the Dangerous and the Overlooked," *Ethics & Behavior* 14(1): 141–174.

Fox, N. (2019) "Memory in Interactions: The Remembering and Forgetting of Gender-based Violence during Atrocity," *Signs* 45(1): 123–148.

Fox, N. (2021) *After Genocide: Memory and Reconciliation in Rwanda*, Madison, WI: University of Wisconsin Press.

Fox, N. and Nyseth Brehm, H. (2018) "'I Decided to Save Them': Factors That Shaped Participation in Rescue Efforts during the Genocide in Rwanda," *Social Forces* 96(4): 1625–1647.

Fox, N., Wise, J., and Nyseth Brehm, H. (2021) "Following Heavenly Orders: Heroic Deviance and the Denial of Responsibility in Narratives of Rescue," *Deviant Behaviour* 43(11): 1–21.

Fujii, L.A. (2010) "Shades of Truth and Lies: Interpreting Testimonies of War and Violence," *Journal of Peace Research* 47(2): 231–241.

Funk, J., Good, N., and Berry, M.E. (2020) *Healing and Peacebuilding after War: Transforming Trauma in and Herzegovina*, New York: Routledge.

Gilbert, K. (2001) "Collateral Damage? Indirect Exposure of Staff Members to the Emotions of Qualitative Research," in K. Gilbert (ed) *The Emotional Nature of Qualitative Research*, Boca Raton, FL: CRC Press, pp 147–161.

Goldenberg, M. and Shapiro, A. (2013) *Different Horrors, Same Hell: Gender and the Holocaust*, Seattle, WA: University of Washington Press.

Graybill, L. (2001) "The Contribution of the Truth and Reconciliation Commission Toward the Promotion of Women's Rights in South Africa," *Women's Studies International Forum* 24(1): 1–10.

Hagopian, P. (2009) *The Vietnam War in American Memory: Veterans, Memorials and the Politics of Healing*, Boston, MA: University of Massachusetts Press.

Hawdon, J. and Ryan, J. (2011) "Social Relations that Generate and Sustain Solidarity After a Mass Tragedy," *Social Forces* 89(4): 1363–1384.

Hayner, P.B. (2011) *Unspeakable Truths: Transitional Justice and the Challenge of Truth Commissions* (2nd edition), New York: Routledge.

Herman, J. (1997) *Trauma and Recovery: The Aftermath of Violence- from Domestic Abuse to Political Terror*, New York: Basic Books.

Howard-Hassmann, R.E. (2004) "Getting to Reparations: Japanese Americans and African Americans," *Social Forces* 83(2): 823–840.

Ingelaere, B. (2015) "Learning 'to Be' Kinyarwanda in Post-genocide Rwanda: Immersion, Iteration, and Reflexivity in Times of Transition," *Canadian Journal of Law and Society* 30(2): 277–292.

Jacobs, J. (2010) *Memorializing the Holocaust: Gender, Genocide and Collective Memory*, New York: I.B. Tauris.

Jacobs, J. (2017) "The Memorial at Srebrenica: Gender and the Social Meanings of Collective Memory in Bosnia-Herzegovina," *Memory Studies* 10(4): 423–439.

Jessee, E. (2012) "Conducting Fieldwork in Rwanda," *Canadian Journal of Development Studies* 33(2): 266–274.

Jinks, R. (2014) "Thinking Comparatively about Genocide Memorialization," *Journal of Genocide Research* 16(4): 423–440.

Johnson, B. and Macleod Clarke, J. (2003) "Collecting Sensitive Data: The Impact on Researchers," *Qualitative Health Research* 13(3): 421–434.

Jones, A. (2004) *Gendercide and Genocide*, Nashville, TN: Vanderbilt University Press.

Kleinman, S. (1991) "Fieldworkers' Feelings: What We Felt, Who We Are, How We Analyze," in W.B. Shaffir and R.A. Stebbins (eds) *Experiencing Fieldwork: An Inside View of Qualitative Research*, London: Sage, pp 184–195.

Lewis, M. and Serbu, J. (1999) "Commemorating the Ku Klux Klan," *Sociological Quarterly* 40(1): 139–158.

Longman, T. (2006) "Rwanda: Achieving Equality Or Serving an authoritarian State?," in G. Bauer and H.E. Britton (eds) *Women in African Parliaments*, London: Lynne Rienner Publishers, pp 190–214.

Lorenz, K., Ullman, S.E., Kirkner, A., Mandala, R., Vasquez, A.L., and Sigurvinsdottir, R. (2018) "Social Reactions to Sexual Assault Disclosure: A Qualitative Study of Informal Support Dyads," *Violence against Women* 24(12): 1497–1520.

MacKinnon, C.A. (2006) "Defining Rape Internationally: A Comment on Akayesu," *Columbia Journal of Transnational Law* 44: 940–958.

Malkki, L. (1995) *Purity and Exile: Violence, Memory, and National Cosmology Among Hutu Refugees in Tanzania*, Chicago, IL: Chicago University Press.

Markwick, R.D. (2008) "'A Sacred Duty': Red Army women Veterans Remembering the Great Fatherland War, 1941–1945," *Australian Journal of Politics and History* 54(3): 403–420.

McEwan, C. (2003) "Building a Postcolonial Archive? Gender, Collective Memory and Citizenship in Post-Apartheid South Africa," *Journal of Southern African Studies* 29(3): 739–757.

Mukamana, D. and Brysiewicz, P. (2008) "The Lived Experience of Genocide Rape Survivors in Rwanda," *Journal of Nursing Scholarship* 40(4): 379–384.

Najmabadi, A. (1996) "'Is Our Name Remembered?': Writing the History of Iranian Constitutionalism as if Women and Gender Mattered," *Iranian Studies* 29(1/2): 85–109.

Newbury, C. and Baldwin, H. (2000) *Aftermath: Women in Post-Genocide Rwanda*, New York: US Agency for International Development.

Ofer, D. and Weitzman, L.J. (1998) *Women in the Holocaust*, New Haven, CT: Yale University Press.

Olick, J. (1999) "Collective Memory: Two Cultures," *Sociological Theory* 17(3): 333–348.

Olick, J. and Robbins, J. (1998) "Social Memory Studies: From Collective Memory to the Historical Sociological of Mnemonic Practices," *Annual Review of Sociology* 24(1): 105–140.

Pals, J. and McAdams, D. (2004) "The Transformed Self: A Narrative Understanding of Posttraumatic Growth," *Psychological Inquiry* 15(1): 65–69.

Porter, H. (2017) *After Rape: Violence, Justice and Social Harmony in Uganda*, New York: Cambridge University Press.

Rajiva, M. and Takševa, T. (2020) "Thinking against Trauma Binaries: The Interdependence of Personal and Collective Trauma in the Narratives of Bosnian Women Rape Survivors," *Feminist Theory* 22(3): 405–427.

Reinharz, S.T. (1992) *Feminist Methods in Social Research*, New York: Oxford University Press.

Rosaldo, R. (2004) "Grief and Headhunter's Rage," in A.C.G.M. Robben (ed) *Death, Mourning, and Burial: A Cross-Cultural Reader*, Oxford: Blackwell Publishing, pp 156–166.

Sardina, A. and Fox, N. (2021) "America's First Memorial Honoring Survivors of Sexual Violence," *Journal of Interpersonal Violence* 37(17–18): 14914–14937.

Sasson-Levy, O., Levy, Y., and Lomsky-Feder, E. (2011) "Women Breaking the Silence: Military Service, Gender, and Antiwar Protest," *Gender & Society* 25(6): 740–763.

Savelsberg, J. and King, R. (2005) "Institutionalizing Collective Memories of Hate: Law and Law Enforcement in Germany and the United States," *American Journal of Sociology* 111(2): 579–616.

Savelsberg, J. and King, R. (2011) *American Memories: Atrocities and the Law*, New York: Russell Sage Foundation.

Scarry, E. (1985) *The Body in Pain: The Making and Unmaking of the World*, New York: Oxford University Press.

Seo, J. (2008) "Politics of Memory in Korea and China: Remembering the Comfort Women and the Nanjing Massacre," *New Political Science* 30(3): 369–392.

Sharlach, L. (1999) "Gender and Genocide in Rwanda: Women as Agents and Objects of Genocide," *Journal of Genocide Research* 1(3): 387–399.

Simic, O. (2016) "Feminist Research in Transitional Justice Studies: Navigating Silences and Disruptions in the Field," *Human Rights Review* 17(1): 95–113.

Simko, C., Cunningham, D., and Fox, N. (2020) "Contesting Commemorative Landscapes: Modes and Mechanisms in Contemporary Debates over Confederate Monuments," *Social Problems* 69(3): 591–611.

Teeger, C. and Vinitzky-Seroussi, V. (2007) "Controlling for Consensus: Commemorating Apartheid in South Africa," *Symbolic Interaction* 30(1): 57–78.

Tjaden, P.G. and Thoennes, N. (2006) *Extent, Nature, and Consequences of Rape Victimization: Findings from the National Violence against Women Survey*, Washington, DC: United States Department of Justice.

Ullman, S.E., Filipas, H.H., Townsend, S.M. and Starzynski, L.L. (2007) "Psychosocial Correlates of PTSD Symptom Severity in Sexual Assault Survivors," *Journal of Traumatic Stress* 20(5): 821–831.

Vinitzky-Seroussi, V. and Teeger, C. (2010) "Unpacking the Unspoken: Silence in Collective Memory and Forgetting," *Social Forces* 88(3): 1103–1122.

Whitlinger, C. (2015) "From Countermemory to Collective Memory: Acknowledging the 'Mississippi Burning' Murders," *Sociological Forum* 30(S1): 648–670.

WHO (1997) *Protocol for WHO Multi-Country Study on Women's Health and Domestic Violence*, Geneva: WHO.

WHO (1999) *Putting Women's Safety First: Ethical and Safety Recommendations for Research on Domestic Violence against Women*, Geneva: Global Program on Evidence for Health Policy, WHO.

Wolf, D. (ed) (1996) *Feminist Dilemmas in Fieldwork,* Boulder, CO: Westview Press.

Woodley, J. (2018) "'Ma Is in the Park': Memory, Identity, and the Bethune Memorial," *Journal of American Studies* 52(2): 474–502.

Wray, N., Markovic, M., and Manderson, L. (2007) "'Researcher Saturation': The Impact of Data Triangulation and Intensive Research Practices on the Researcher and Qualitative Research Process," *Qualitative Health Research* 17(10): 1392–1402.

Yuval-Davis, N. (1997) "Women, Citizenship and Difference," *Feminist Review* 57(1): 4–27.

Zerubavel, E. (2003) *Time Maps: Collective Memory and the Social Shape of the Past*, Chicago, IL: University of Chicago Press.

Zraly, M., Rubin-Smith, J., and Betancourt, T. (2011) "Primary Mental Health Care for Survivors of Collective Sexual Violence in Rwanda," *Global Public Health* 6(3): 257–270.

4

Mobilizing Memories: Remembrance as a Social Movement Tool in the Vieques Anti-Military Movement (1999–2004)

Roberto Vélez-Vélez

In 2004 the community of Vieques, Puerto Rico witnessed the last chapter of a struggle that unfolded over the previous 60 years – the official closing of the US Navy station and target range, Camp Garcia. The closing of the base came after an intensive five-year protest mobilization manifesting in a diversity of sectors across the archipelago of Puerto Rico. However, this mobilization was most prominently known via its local consolidation as the Vieques Movement. The Movement's claim for ending the military presence in the municipal island focused on three core issues – stopping all live ammunition practices (the regular occurrence of bombing), permanently closing the target range and military station, and returning the land to civilian control. The Vieques Movement deployed a multiplicity of protest tactics to challenge the military institution and sustain popular mobilization – civil disobedience, marches, picket lines, letter writing campaigns, as well as congressional lobbying. As the movement unfolded, activists also engaged in the more subtle process of articulating community members' experiences of the military presence, experiences centered on their perceptions of the past. This was more than a storytelling exercise focused on the impact of military presence; this was an exercise in personal remembrance as a way of making and conveying collective memory. Upon close examination, storytellers intended to re-present the military presence experience in a new light, one that casts the military base and military operations as a source of grievance, conflict, and trauma. How are the memories of residents' experiences with the military related to the narratives for mobilization activated by movement actors? What influence, if any, did this remembrance exercise over the mobilization against the military? In what ways, if any, were notions of the past challenged here?

In this chapter, I explore the Vieques Movement via local narratives of the military presence using an approach that elucidates the role of memory – and the links between personal and collective memory – in the social movement mobilization processes. I analyze embedded remembrance structures – *mnemonic signifiers* that serve as rich sources of meaning – for their activation capacity and significance to narratives of mobilization (Vélez-Vélez, 2013). The goal is that of approaching the mobilization process from the standpoint of memory and remembrance. In doing so, I trace how the narratives that social movement actors use as tools to achieve political mobilization are made significant via their allocation of meaning to the past.

Grounded on the perspective that mnemonic processes are always ongoing and involving continuous negotiations with the past and its meaning, I argue that we must pay attention to how remembrance, as a personal and collective process, serves to elicit those meanings that shape mobilization narratives. Instead of assuming that movement actors approach representations of the past as fixed frames to be mobilized, I examine the signifying power that personal experiences of historic events render to social movement processes. Focusing on the ways that personal memories connect to larger collective memories, and the role of both in infusing movement narratives with meaning, I build a bridge between the micro and macro dimensions of remembrance and collective action. Using a lens of mnemonic dynamics allows us to better appreciate the allocation of meaning to sources of grievance and, hence, the action-triggering effect for mobilization processes.

To illustrate, I first establish the link between memory and social movement narratives as a foundation for the empirical examination. Next, I present some background on the Vieques Movement. Then, I elucidate the mobilization process rooted in the setting for this analysis. Working retrospectively, I analyze the narratives used to recast the memories of the military presence, revealing them to be mnemonic structures that take on meaning under a new context of mobilization. I will conclude by highlighting how the action-triggering power of the emerging narratives of mobilization rests on the problematization of the past as a grievous and traumatic collective experience.

Narratives for mobilization

Social movement scholars have detailed the significance of narration and the relevance of storytelling practices to processes such as solidarity building, identity construction, and claims articulation (Fine, 1995, 2002; Johnston and Klandermans, 1995; Jasper, 1997; Kane, 1997; Benford, 2002; Davis, 2002; Polletta, 2002, 2005; Yates and Hunter, 2002; Eyerman, 2003). By recognizing that narratives are an analytical tool for mobilization, researchers have outlined the nuances of a distinctive cultural paradigm. However, in using a narrative approach, one can overlook significant issues. By interpreting social movement narratives as vehicles of meaning, scholars must recognize that they operate retrospectively. "[The] events earlier in time take their meaning and act as causes only because of how things turn out later ... in the future" (Davis, 2002: pp 11–12). This means that a narrative's explanatory power relies on emplotment or the rendition of past events, which can be seen as a form of social remembrance. In other words, a narrative for mobilization draws its potentiality for triggering action from its constitution of memories or representations of the past (Olick, Vinitzky-Seroussi, and Levy, 2011). This implies a link between those renditions of the past and the process of constructing meaning to mobilize action and make future-oriented change. Given that this is the case, then there is an analytic gap in models of narrative analysis if the subject of memory is not problematized or further developed (Davis, 2002; Polletta, 2003, 2005). If meaning allocation and interpretative power depends on the emplotment of past events, particularly when those renditions of the past are the result of social, cultural, and political dynamics, we must look at the remembrance process as central to the power of narrative to mobilize people. Thus, social movements can be approached as "mnemonic agents" in that they operate within the "arena of public memory" and with "collective memories as a strategic feature" of their work (Zamponi, 2013: p 2). Hence, I here propose a mnemonic dynamics approach to better observe and understand the mobilization effect of narratives in social movements (Vélez-Vélez, 2013).

The Vieques Movement

The establishment of a military station in Vieques, Puerto Rico was part of a strategic plan of expansion by the US on the eve of World War II. As the US sought to secure its interests and influence over the Caribbean Basin and the western hemisphere, naval outposts in the region proliferated (Meléndez, 1989; Barreto, 2001). Given the colonial relation of Puerto Rico to the US and its geographic position, the archipelago became a stronghold for the North Atlantic Treaty Organization (NATO) and the Atlantic Fleet Training Facilities (AFTF) (Garcia Muñiz, 1987; Melendez, 1989; Rodríguez Beruff, 1999; Paralitici, 2005). Though resistance to military presence in Vieques can be traced to the establishment of the naval station in the 1950s, the most prominent and organized efforts took place in the 1970s (McCaffrey, 2002). The movement organizations of the 1970s created the foundation, rhetorical and tactical, for other organized efforts to follow over the years. The anti-military movement reached a new effervescence in the spring of 1999, after David Sanes, a civilian security guard at the naval station, was killed by a missile that missed its target (Colombani, 1999). This event triggered a mass mobilization to stop the bombing in the island, end the military presence, and close the naval station. This mobilization held a sustained protest movement for five years that combined political actions like lobbying and legislation with direct actions like massive marches and acts of civil disobedience.

The death of David Sanes not only triggered the visibility of the movement but also served as a turning point regarding the articulation of mobilization narratives and the meaning of military presence on the island (Vélez-Vélez, 2013). Specifically, as local activists linked the death of David Sanes to the struggle to end the bombing and close the naval station, they discursively organized their moral and political claims around a bank of shared memories and experiences of the past. Before the tragedy of Sanes's death, the *Comité Pro-Rescate y Desarrollo de Vieques*[1] (CPRDV) had established a mobilization campaign named *4Ds*, which stood for demilitarization, decontamination, devolution, and development. The 4Ds represented a programmatic agenda for Vieques, one that instead of focusing solely on immediate issues established a scheme of gradual development that would, activists claimed at the time, lead to fundamental changes regarding military presence on the island. This sequence of stages consolidated into the 4Ds can be interpreted as a master narrative, a storyline to be followed, through which activists envisioned a desirable ending to the struggle (Benford, 2002: pp 54–55).

As a master narrative for mobilization, the 4Ds provide a beginning point, demilitarization, which entails the removal of the military from the island; but does not specify how this can be accomplished (Polletta, 2002). The lack of specificity on how to reach this stage gives the activists freedom to imagine (Davis, 2002: p 19), experiment, and activate their creativity (Polletta, 2002: p 37). This is what Francesca Polletta (2002) refers to as "present ambiguities," which entice an interpretative audience into solving or finding resolution to a problem (p 35). The 4Ds storyline provides an image of the future, sustainable development, an endpoint towards which people can project their current reality and imagine a new one, feeding the need to search for and mobilize to reach this new reality. The narrative plot structure, a clear timeline, combined with its ambiguous beginning, created expectation among activists who awaited a signal on their horizon. This pushed activists to examine and consider each event that appeared in terms of its potential as source for cognitive liberation of the wider population, and a tipping point on the path to social change and local self-determination. So, the unexpected and accidental death of David Sanes on April 19, 1999 became the needed spark for the movement to turn their master narrative into action. Movement activists then worked to guide the popular burst of emotion into a coherent claim for change (Fine, 2002; Polletta, 2005).

¡Ni una bomba más!: a narrative of change and challenge

The accidental death of David Sanes brought to the attention of those outside the island a glimpse into the realities that permeated life in Vieques with a military presence, specifically the impact of the bombing. The first outcry of the 1999 mobilization was that of *¡Ni una bomba más!* (Not one more bomb!), a slogan that took center stage in the popular discourse and throughout the news media and movement-related activities. The bombing became the epitome of the problems and concerns of the island's population, and the immediate target of the struggle. According to some residents, this process created a new sense of awareness, connecting the recent accident with their own safety. Edwin, a man in his sixties, retired teacher and longtime leader in the anti-military movement, stated: "[After the accident] a sense of indignation started to grow. Then the people claimed for the bombing to stop. Not one more bomb! That is one of the first claims of Viequenses: Stop the bombing now!"

The process triggered a conscious association between the bombing, the struggle, and the military presence, turning dormant memories and the accident of 1999 into evidence to counter any argument in favor of their continuation.

The end of the bombing became the central objective from 1999 to 2004, the period with the most intensive continuous protest action in the history of the movement (Barreto, 2001; McCaffrey, 2002). The issue of the bombing captured the imagination of people in and outside of the archipelago, drawing supporters in mass numbers to the municipal island from all corners of the globe. This global attention brought an opportunity to seriously challenge the military presence. For many activists this shift in focus was decisive for their success as they narrowed the claim into a fundamental maxim. According to Edwin, "everyone was aware that if the bombing was stopped, the Navy had no other reason to be here" In other words, the bombing was the most elemental connection between the military presence and the end of it; to force an end to the bombing was to remove the asset value of the island to the US Navy (Rodríguez Beruff, 1999).

A parallel process that emerged with global attention on the struggle in Vieques was a revisiting of the island's past as it related to the impact of military presence. To understand the bombing as a lived experience of the military presence, non-residents required contextualization within historical and political timelines (Vélez-Vélez, 2013). For locals, this meant they were to tell and retell their life stories, describe their lives, and produce images of their life experiences for those who did not share their references and perspectives. Sixty years of military presence left indelible marks on the life of three generations of Viequenses. The exercise of revisiting and retelling their pasts experiences, like all mnemonic practices, involved navigating present social dynamics, namely the "group settings" (Halbwachs, 1992: p 39) and the influence of our "particular social surroundings" (Zerubavel, 1996: p 286) on "the mediation between the past and the present" (Falasca-Zamponi, 2003: p 49). In other words, producing those memories about the military presence involved "an ongoing dialogue" (Olick, 2003: p 264), a negotiation and debate over the stories, events and plots that constitute that memory (Wagner-Pacifici, 1996; Olick and Robbins, 1998; Falasca-Zamponi, 2003). This social process of remembrance was critical in the articulation of the mobilization narratives of the campaign, for "memory is at the same time an outcome of protest and a tool in constructing new mobilizations" (Zamponi, 2013: p 3). It was this social exercise of remembering the military presence experience that established the meanings of the bombing, past and present, and spurred a new cognitive liberation which triggered action from the population. Examining these mnemonic dynamics, as well as the articulation of life experiences, not only reveals the conflicts, tensions, and negotiations that such processes involved, but also elucidates the meaning allocation processes that transformed the stories told by activists and locals into triggers of anti-military collective action in Vieques (Vélez-Vélez, 2013).

Analyzing remembrance of the military presence

Every interpretation of the past is set within its particular moment as a product of negotiation and transformation among those within a community whose members work to advance particular meanings that address their concerns (Zerubavel, 1995; Olick and Levy, 1997; Eyerman, 2003; Olick, 2003; Feindt et al, 2014). "Memory's salience at any given point in time ... depends not only on its meanings and their manipulations but ... on the complex trajectories memory forms over time" (Olick, 2003: p 8). This negotiated nature of the elements that comprise the narrative of the past creates a separation between those events or happenings that are excluded from the story, but also a distinction among those included. In the constellation of stories that local residents expressed in their shared accounts of growing and living on the island, three stories became prevalent when talking about the military experience: (i) those related to the expropriation of land after the military arrived on the island, (ii) those concerning the contact between the military and civilians, and (iii) those regarding the bombing itself. These stories represent key *mnemonic signifiers* that guide and structure locals' renditions of their collective experience as a framework that establishes context for, and meaning of, the movement's claims.

The term mnemonic signifier refers to "any socially relevant figuration of memory" (Feindt et al, 2014: p 31). I borrow this term to add that this figuration can carry the quality of activating meanings grounded in the collective memory and shared experiences of a community (Vélez-Vélez, 2013). While there are multiple events that can be identified as essential in these stories, not all of them are equally significant to the storyline. I suggest that the factor for this distinction is their centrality to the plot of the story. There are elements in the story that function as carriers of the plot, referred here as *primary signifiers*, while others provide texture or dimension to that story, *secondary signifiers*. The logic of their order – primary or secondary – in the remembrance analysis process serves to situate their properties as meaning carriers.[2]

Primary mnemonic signifiers carry more than just the story; they also carry meanings, symbolic values that serve to frame the story. So, signifiers of a primary order represent significant events that carry strong, shared resonance to the community members. For every primary signifier, there are a few other mnemonic signifiers that are considered of secondary order. The secondary mnemonic signifiers are those events or elements that provide certain texture or depth to the story while not providing significant change to the progression of the story. These secondary signifiers highlight certain aspects of the story, filling in the spaces between turning points of the narration. While the primary order signifiers can sustain the storyline independently, this is not the case for secondary order signifiers; the latter are dependent on the primary as they provide context.

Within the three main stories told by local residents about their experiences living with a military presence, each contained a mnemonic signifier of primary order: the expropriation of the land, contact with the soldiers, and the bombing of the island. Each one of these events represents a key segment of the island's history and carries a specific set of meanings concerning how islanders remember and make sense of the military presence in Vieques.

The expropriations: beginning of new realities

A series of evictions took place between 1941 to 1943 – popularly known as *las expropriaciones* (the expropriations) – targeting large sugar plantations owned by absentee landlords as well as small properties used by local owners and landless sharecroppers (McCaffrey, 2002). The expropriations are considered by residents a significant and defining event in the lives of Viequenses. This event simultaneously transformed their spatial reference and livelihood on the island.[3] Hence, it was a source of change, a turning point. While most scholars highlight the loss of jobs and the economy as the direct impact of this process (Ayala and Carro-Figueroa, 2005; Ayala and Bolivar, 2006; McCaffrey, 2006), Viequenses point to the loss of place and belonging. The erection of spatial constraints such as restricted-water zones, fences and gates, altered the geography of the island and the ways Viequenses related to it.

To no surprise, the expropriations have a central place in the local stories of Viequenses serving as a boundary marker, a divider in their life stories and in the island's history, between a period before and a period after. Edwin states: "The 1940s is when the first expropriations took place, around [19]40 [to 19]41. I was born in [19]44, which means, that I was born after the expropriations. Thus, I am post … I'm from the generation that was born after the expropriations."

Similarly, Mariano, a fisherman and leader in the fishing community, in his thirties at the time of the mobilization, comments:

> "Since I was born, the Navy has been in Vieques, because I was born in the 1970s and the Navy has been here since 1942. Thus, it's to say that I was born being part of the Navy … It's not the same for those who were here before their arrival [Navy], and then this thing was integrated into their lives. They didn't have it, and now they do. No. I was born with that Navy."

As a mnemonic signifier, the expropriations frame two versions of Vieques; one framed around the sugar industry heydays, thriving fishing and self-sustainability (before the expropriations); and the other framed around the lack of land, end of sugar production and spatial restrictions (after the expropriations).

The expropriations have also been articulated as a life-determining event, one that defines where people were born and belong. Elsa, a retired teacher in her late fifties and longtime activist comments:

> "Well, sadly, I was not born in Vieques, like many other Viequenses. When the Navy arrived to Vieques in the [1940s], my family was among those that suffered the expropriations. Back then, my grandparents had relatives in Luquillo,[4] so they moved to Luquillo … That's one of the reasons why me and my brother were born in Luquillo instead of Vieques."

Dolores, a woman protester in her sixties, reminisced: "My grandmother grew up in Playa Grande … She told me that my mother was born there [pointing to the fenced area of the base], she was born there and her mother was also born there in Playa Grande … She had a life of poverty but filled with happiness."

By interpreting their lives in the light of the expropriation experience, the event provided a pivot to ground their life stories. The articulation of the expropriations as a reference point of the self illustrates the strength of this event as a turning point of their stories, and a defining element of their experiences as they relate to previous generations and to the community more broadly. This contextualization is carried by establishing symbolic associations that might surface in the process of narrative construction, such as the relation between individuals and the land, the relative deprivation of the islanders from other Puerto Ricans, the artificial spatial isolation of the population, and their socio-economic underdevelopment. Through plotting the story of the expropriations, many of these issues were recognized, considered, and explained.

Local accounts illustrated the impact of the expropriations by relating this event with others. Two events that are bound to the expropriation experience are stories of relocation and migration. These secondary signifiers increase the capacity of residents to articulate other experiences as significant by tethering them to the expropriations. These two events provide more depth and complexity to the stories of the expropriation, enhancing the multidimensionality of this experience. Relocation stories illustrate the immediate internal consequence of the expropriations, while the stories of migration, temporary or permanent, also show the external reach and impact of the event. These signifiers, nonetheless, are very much charged with meaning, and it is in their context of complementing the expropriations stories that they move into secondary order.

Thus, in remembering the expropriations, Viequenses represented a starting point for new realities and the beginning of the islanders' life *with* the military in Vieques. This event is the boundary mark to the autobiographical stories of many Viequenses, setting their initial contact point with the military presence as one with visceral implications – loss, displacement, and permanence. The residents situate their eviction stories as a turning point, marking the beginning to a period of decline and giving shape to a shared narrative structure and timeline. Further, by establishing the genesis of the military presence in the expropriations, Viequenses are attributing a more complex context to the issue in present time. Instead of allowing immediate events, like the death of David Sanes and the bombing, to be main signifiers of the military experience, the timeline is expanded and the texture of this experience is problematized. By incorporating the expropriations through the remembering process, it gives nuance to Viequenses's claims; it underlines that to understand their claim for ending the military presence, those supporting them must also understand the breadth and depth of their grievance.

Soldiers versus civilians: the tangible presence

The expropriation of land gave way to the opening of a military station in Vieques, Camp Garcia; an extension of one of the largest military installations in the Caribbean, Roosevelt Roads Naval Base in Ceiba, Puerto Rico. This expansion and the incorporation of a target range in Vieques intensified the military presence on the island, the Atlantic and the Caribbean Basin (Ayala and Bolivar, 2006). The entrenchment of the Cold War also brought about a stronger military presence on the islands of Vieques and Culebra (McCaffrey, 2002). This growth in militarization was characterized by the introduction of large amounts of soldiers who took part in war games and exercises. As locals recalled, military personnel became a common sight in the civilian space during the periods of the late 1940s and throughout the 1950s. Thus, the insertion of soldiers in Vieques and the forced interactions with them became the second mnemonic signifier in the life stories of those living on the island.

As locals remember growing up in Vieques, their childhood interactions with soldiers provide intimate and concrete representations of the civilian population's contact with the military institution. In other words, the presence of soldiers on the island serves as a signifier which characterizes changes in the local setting and an alteration of social interactions within their social space. The soldiers are recalled as intruders, and the stories recount the introduction of a foreign subject into the sphere of everyday life. Again, Dolores recalls:

> "They landed at the beach, close to the malecón[5] in Esperanza ... They camped for twelve days, and then they marched [by the] thousands ... to Camp Garcia. They marched up the street, and through that road no one could pass. The cars, as few as they were, they had to park. No one could go up that street until they finished marching ... As a young girl, I looked at them with excitement, but now I see it as an abuse."

Most accounts featured the soldier as the vivid personification of the larger institution, the US Navy, and used the individual soldier to express the way the institution intrudes into different segments of their routines. The tangible nature of the soldier dispelled the notion of *the military* as an abstraction, giving body, face and physicality to that subject previously only alluded to.

Stories of soldiers and civilians interacting *within* the military space were presented as rare occurrences and glossed with cynicism, as they contrast with a larger set of images that take place within the civilian space. Raúl, a man in his sixties who has been active throughout the movement's history, recalls:

> "I remember when I was carried in a military truck, to go in and see the military base. Although at night there were fights with the soldiers [and civilians], they [the Navy] were in a constant public relations campaign. So, they took us into the base like today they take kids to

Disney World. I rode on a helicopter, they put us in their trucks, they fed us hamburgers, they brought us all sorts of things."

The incursion of soldiers into civilian spaces placed indigenous and foreign populations in direct contact, an occurrence that forced a large array of reactions and outcomes. The dominant accounts about soldier-civilian contact presented the public space as the main stage of frictions and clashes, suggesting conflict as the main interaction between these two actors. Edmundo, a maintenance worker in his sixties recalled: "[They] entered the church looking for young women, and everything ended up in riots. We defended Viequense citizens, their rights, and we fought with punches, rocks, kicks, and sticks ... These were the riots."

Likewise, Edwin states: "The situation in which I was growing in my neighborhood was that of watching the [street] fights ... I took part in those fights in my youth ... I saw their [soldier's] abuses ... If you were in a bar and they came in, you would have to flee, if not [he winces]."

Locals remember these interactions as epic stories where they and other locals were victims defending themselves against military agents who were presented as a foe or villain. This image of conflict has become common in portrayals of the past, one that reaffirms the sentiments of present circumstances. In these retrospective narratives, the Navy is an invading force and locals have been victimized from the beginning.

Though women have been present throughout the movement process, the mobilization in the 2000s situated women as cardinal actors and voices of resistance (McCaffrey, 2008; Vélez-Vélez, 2010). Women told another set of stories that cast the soldiers, and hence the institution they represented, as a physical threat. The interaction with soldiers, as remembered by women, highlights their sense of being dehumanized and objectified by these agents of the foreign military institution. Karen, an activist in her late fifties and member of a local women's organization recalls: "Here, we [women] stopped visiting the church, or going to the plaza, because they didn't care about the age of a woman, if they passed by, they tried to grab her."

Dolores recounts: "I remember seeing them along the houses, knocking on doors ... People locked their doors, and around a certain hour they would say, 'Let's get in, it is time to go to bed!,' especially to girls."

Likewise, Raúl remembers: "Our mothers liked the idea of the military, because they could work washing and ironing their uniforms, but at night they [the soldiers] got drunk and entered into peoples' houses where they knew young women lived."

The stories of the harassment experienced by female residents bolstered the image of the military forcibly imposing themselves and appropriating everything, be it land, water or bodies, which were all at the disposal of the soldier.

From the stories of riots to those of harassment, the mnemonic signifier of the soldier further contextualized, in a relational way, how the boundaries that separated these two spheres, civilian and military, were transgressed. Along with the soldiers, a secondary signifier that is articulated is that of a proliferation of prostitution which provides another contact point between the military and civilian spaces. This element is usually presented as a collateral effect of the soldiers' presence, one that is interpreted as an "erosion" of social codes of decency stemming from the concomitancy of sex work. Thus, while the signifiers of expropriations articulated imagery of spatial constraints, the soldier carries the idea of social encroachment; the transformation of their sociability.

Further, the military takes a physical form in the stories after this point. While before, the military was presented as an abstract force in the expropriation stories, the remembered character of the soldier suggests a direct contact point between the military and the civilian. The soldier embodies multiple attitudes attributed to the institution of the US Navy, becoming a personified focus of resentment, giving traction to current local claims of intrusion and hostility. The remembrance of the soldier also brings about the notion of a population under threat, one being physically harassed and forced to adopt new interactions and dynamics, images that are not lost in the activist claims of the 2000s. Hence, the urgency to remove the military presence is renewed; this is a claim that can be grounded in experiences of the past that were still vivid decades later.

The bombing: a living trauma

While memories of the expropriations defined the conditions of space, and those of the soldiers embodied altered sociability, the bombing is presented as *the* defining element of the military presence in the life of Viequenses. In its early days, military training in Vieques was focused on landing exercises and small artillery practice. That training exercises in Culebra and Vieques intensified in the 1960s in an assertion of US dominance over the region under the gaze of Cuba's new regime (Garcia Muñiz, 1987). In 1975, after an intensive protest campaign led by fishermen and prominent political figures in Culebra, the heavy artillery target range there was forced to close, ending the military presence in that island (Mullenneaux, 2000; McCaffrey, 2002). With the closing of Culebra's naval operations, training was relocated to Vieques, where a new target range was established, turning the island into the core feature of the Atlantic Fleet Training Facilities (Melendez, 1989; Rodríguez Beruff, 1999). This intensification of military exercises transformed the situation for most residents as they witnessed a new dimension of the military presence moving deeper into their lives; live bombings.

Under the context of the latest mobilization, locals raised the emergence of the bombing as a major mnemonic signifier, an element that embodies the deep indelible imprint of the military presence in the life of Viequenses. After the death of David Sanes, the bombing occupied a central place in the local narrative, providing a pivot for reflecting on the normalization of disruptive conditions while also accentuating how imperative ending the military presence was. In revisiting the memories of growing with the bombing and how this was disruptive to their lives, their claim of ¡Ni una bomba más! was strengthened by signifying more than this single incident and grounding it as the source of ongoing trauma.

Trauma is understood as a collective experience when it is constructed on the fabric of shared meanings and the remembrance practices of a mnemonic group (Sztompka, 2000; Langenohl, 2008). The characterization of the event as traumatic is the result of its articulation and construction, not the quality or nature of the event itself. Thus, events are not inherently traumatic but socially deemed as such by the attribution of moral significance in their rendition as part of a shared experience, a collective memory (Kidron, 2003).[6] However, not all individuals in the mnemonic community assume the traumatic experience in the same way or may share the interpretation of an event as traumatic. Moreover, certain traumatic events are integrated into the community's view of normalcy throughout generations by transforming its moral significance (Eyerman, 2001). We see this integration of the bombing into normalcy when considering the perspective of the youth in Vieques regarding the bombing and the military.

In describing the bombing, some youth in the island presented a story that was deprived of any allusion to fear or dread. Their depictions presented the bombing as an extension of a normal life within a space that is shared with a military installation. Carla, a young woman in her late teens, who turned activist in the last few years, states:

> "While in grade school, it did bother [me] at the beginning, the airplanes passing by at night, the bombing ... but I got used to it, and the classes ran normally, these were not interrupted because of the bombs ... Even my mom and I sat at the porch to look at the flares, these red lights in the sky ... it was normal ... Everyone seemed to live in peace with the Navy ... very normal."

Likewise, Jonathan, also about 20 and member of the same youth organization as Carla, recalls:

> "When you are ten, eleven years old, they talk to you about the pollution ... the bombing and the noise, and you do not look at it as a problem. Instead, we thought that it was something normal, not a

problem. ... As a kid I grew up with the bombing, the jets, and made it part of my daily life."

As a shared experienced, the bombing for these youth has transcended into their understanding of normal, free of contradictions or conflict with their expectations of normalcy. This naturalization of the bombing provides a point of conflict in the construction of a narrative that would spearhead a mobilization process to challenge the military presence, in particular, the bombing.

In the context of the mobilization post-David Sanes's death, however, the stories that dominated the discussion involved the articulation of normalcy as an oxymoron for describing Vieques's reality, a condition in total conflict with the routines of a place where bombing was a feature of everyday life. Claudio, former security guard at the base, retired and in his seventies states:

"I cannot describe a normal day prior to [the civil disobedience]. Because ... for you to say that you have a normal day, you would have to be out of the island. Not feeling the bombing, the roar of the machine guns up there, none of that ... Only by leaving the island you couldn't hear it ... So, if you left Vieques, you could have a normal day, but when you returned, Vieques was hell. This was hell."

These stories challenged the integration of the bombing into normalcy presented by younger generations by attributing the fear, dread, and threat we heard from the stories with the soldiers to the bombing itself. In doing this, the way the event is remembered and interpreted is problematized, suggesting a process of negotiation and reconstruction. Given that remembrance involves a reiteration of those signifiers that provide context, prominence, and meaning to the shared experiences, the bombing is recast as a signifier of trauma (Feindt et al, 2014: p 32).

When locals articulate the experience of growing up in Vieques, they present the bombing as intangible yet as interfering in their daily routines, especially via the sound of the bombs or the vibration from explosions. Residents stressed how their lives were interrupted or upset by the reverberation of the bombs or the gun fire, even miles away. Mariano claims: "With the explosions ... the windows rattled, and that was at a distance of miles ... really far. The houses shook with the detonations, the windows ... boom, boom ... you knew there was bombing over there."

Again, Elsa adds: "As a teacher, in many occasions the class was interrupted because of the jets and the bombing ... it did not allow students to focus, neither could we ... You could not even take a nap, because they were doing their bombing."

In these stories, the bombing slithers through the cracks of the quotidian, moving deeper into residents' lives. With this slippage of the bombing into the ordinary, it is more than sound that invades the spaces of civilians, but what it represents. This representation of the bombing constructs an image of the military as an omnipresent subject, a disembodied form that traverses Viequenses's public and private spaces alike, unchecked and unbounded. The mnemonic signifier of the bombing situates the military presence as an intractable force, one that shaped their sense of normalcy in permanent ways.

Above all, locals present the bombing as an intrusive force that transformed their view and their approach to everyday life. As the bombing gained terrain in the quotidian routines, this eroded the sense of security among residents. Those spaces previously conceived as safe from soldiers' intrusion was now made vulnerable by the pervasiveness of the bombing. The sense of threat created around this experience became a common denominator in the stories about the bombing. Laura, a community outreach worker in her thirties who moved to the island some years before the new mobilization started and now co-led a local women's organization, says: "I could see the lightning of the bombs as they exploded, because my house was towards the eastern area. I was there, thinking, I cannot handle this. I cannot deal with this, I'm scared ... I don't like this."

Similarly, Dolores added: "The most awful experience of my youth was the boom [the bombs]. ... All the time, while you sleep, play, in school ... there was the boom. ... But you play, the boom ... taking a shower, the boom [explosion] of the bombs ... sometimes one after the other, boom, boom, boom."

In the context of post-David Sanes's death, to retell the stories of fear and dread is to reveal the mindscape of a community that had been waiting and foreseeing a tragedy of this magnitude for years. These stories brought forth their awareness of the threat that the bombing represented to their lives and their community. As Karen states so clearly and succinctly, "The threat changed from, 'It is possible that one day a bomb can fall on us ...' to 'the bomb just fell on one of us ...'."

The stories of dread about the bombing further accentuate the emotional toll the recurrence of the bombing carved on the people and put into perspective the impact this experience had over the years. As locals articulated their memories of the bombing, they meant to illustrate how the military presence entered their everyday lives and affected their routines. Their stories illustrated the military as a transforming agent in the lives of Viequenses. Engaging these memories of the bombing as a collective experience of trauma makes the narrative to end the bombing into a direct cry for resolution with an ongoing trauma rooted in both past and present, but also an attempt to change their future. Thus, to end the bombing involved more than ending the military presence; it was a signifier of a possible resolution to a trauma that has been growing for 60 years.

Conclusion

How were these elements – the remembrance of expropriations, soldiers, and bombing – relevant in activating structures of mobilization? How is this discussion of remembrance relevant to our understanding of the link between issues with the past and social movements? Fredrick Harris (2006) has argued that movement organizers engage certain events from social memory through "social appropriation" to generate collective action (p 22). This process suggests that, given the structural opportunities, movement organizers have the capacity to utilize past events in such a way that they are "framed" into claims for mobilization. While this model resonates with the idea of redefining events of the past for the purposes of mobilization, it tends to underplay the role of meaning systems in collective memory. Remembrance involves a process of allocating meaning to the past, one which is key for cognitive liberation, I will add. It is in situating new events in relation to past events through remembrance that meanings are elicited and actions triggered (Armstrong and Crage, 2006). Hence, movement organizers and activists are simultaneously political actors and mnemonic agents.

For a long time the military presence experience in Vieques was assumed as a taken for granted aspect of the island with no bearings on the mobilization process beyond the obvious illustration of an oppositional force or physical source of grievance. Hence, most attributed the triggering effect we saw between 1999 and 2004 to the event of David Sanes's death and the outcry of ending the bombing that followed. However, our examination of the role of remembrance in the wake of the 1999 incident and the call for mobilization that followed shows a more dynamic process around how this experience was rendered and interpreted. The remembering process in Vieques involved the articulation of the expropriations, the soldiers, and the bombing as signifiers of the military presence. These signifiers were central to the mnemonic process which provided meaning to the death of David Sanes. In other words, the death of David Sanes had to be integrated within the "stock of plots" of the mnemonic community to be understood and interpreted (Polletta, 2002: p 34). As the accident was socially appropriated within the existing social frameworks – familiar stories or narratives – and the current context – via anti-military mobilization – it was defined by the signifiers and their meaning structures through remembering the experiences of military presence. Thus, the narrative *¡Ni una bomba más!,* as articulated and enacted in the shadows of the tragedy, gained traction as the memories of members of the community were revisited along with images and emotions, which were constructed and contained for 60 years. As the community recognized and reflected upon those memories and the meanings that such memories provided, a response was articulated that spurred social movement action.

By looking at mobilization narratives through a lens of mnemonic dynamics, we are best situated to observe, analyze, and critique how mobilization processes are explained. The interpretative lens of mnemonic practices emphasizes the role of meaning construction as a dynamic process that involves negotiation and conflict regarding how the past is rendered and presented. The problematization of the past through mnemonic dynamics – activation of mnemonic signifiers to decode and reconstruct a remembrance of the military presence experience – produced the cognitive liberation that supported the mobilization to stop the bombing and, eventually, close the military base.

Considering this analysis, we can argue that mobilization narratives, however effective in articulating the discourse and contextualizing a tragic event, often achieve their triggering effect because of embedded meanings established by mnemonic signifiers. It was because the military presence was condensed into representations of the past – expropriations, soldiers, and bombing signifiers – and reenacted in the remembrance process, that those meanings were elicited, and individuals were compelled to act (Jansen, 2007). The interaction of activists with their memories in the interpretative process – retelling stories, revisiting images and memories, and reconnecting with attributes– produced the meaning allocation necessary to legitimize them as narratives of mobilization. How they remembered the military presence mattered for how they would envision a future without it; a Vieques without the Navy.

Notes

[1] Committee for the Rescue and Development of Vieques, in English.
[2] It is important to clarify that such a distinction is only nominal, and they do not imply the existence of a real expectation among the residents of the island on the events and experiences with the military. The rationale behind this order difference is in their position vis-à-vis the storyline rather than *importance* for individuals' lives. It is important not to assume order as level of importance because this would undermine individual experiences and their heterogeneous impact.
[3] An estimate of over a thousand families were relocated between 1941 and 1943. The first wave removed families from the eastern part of the island, now occupied by the former Camp Garcia training lands, to the center of the island. Further expropriations in the western part would reduce the civilian space to a north-south corridor contained between two military installations. For more on this see Ayala and Bolivar (2006) and McCaffrey (2006).
[4] Luquillo is a municipality in the northeastern part of Puerto Rico, 25 miles from Vieques.
[5] Common term for pier or jetty, usually characterized by boardwalks along the shore.
[6] This view has been strongly criticized and challenged by others in memory studies. For a good description of this debate see Kansteiner and Weilnböck (2008).

Acknowledgments

Data used and presented in this chapter was collected using ethnography and qualitative in-depth interviews between 2001 and 2006 as part of a dissertation project titled *"Because History Does Not Allow Us ..." Collective*

Memory and the Articulation of Mobilization Narratives in the Antimilitary Movement of Vieques (1999–2003).

References

Armstrong, E.A. and Crage, S.M. (2006) "Movements and Memory: The Making of the Stonewall Myth," *American Sociological Review* 71(5): 724–751.

Ayala, C. and Bolivar, J. (2006) "The Cold War and the Second Expropriations of the Navy in Vieques," *Centro Journal* 18(1): 10–35.

Ayala, C. and Carro-Figueroa, V. (2005) "Expropriation and Displacement of Civilians in Vieques, 1940–1950," in R. Bosque-Pérez and J.J. Colón Morera (eds) *Puerto Rico Under Colonial Rule: Political Persecution and the Quest for Human Rights*, Albany, NY: SUNY Press, pp 173–207.

Barreto, A.A. (2001) *Vieques, the Navy and Puerto Rican Politics*, Gainesville, FL: University Press of Florida.

Benford, R. (2002) "Controlling Narrative and Narratives as Control within Social Movements," in J. Davis (ed) *Stories of Change: Narratives and Social Movements*, Albany, NY: SUNY Press, pp 53–75.

Colombani, J. (1999) "Bomb Takes a Life in Vieques," *El Nuevo Día*, April 20.

Davis, J.E. (2002) "Narratives and Social Movements: The Power of Stories," in J.E. Davis (ed) *Stories of Change: Narrative and Social Movements*, Albany, NY: SUNY Press, pp 3–29.

Eyerman, R. (2001) *Cultural Trauma*, Cambridge: Cambridge University Press.

Eyerman, R. (2003) "Performing Opposition, or How Do Social Movements Move," in *Working Papers*, New Haven, CT: Yale University Press.

Falasca-Zamponi, S. (2003) "Of Storytellers and Master Narratives: Modernity, Memory, and History in Fascist Italy," in J. Olick (ed) *States of Memory: Continuities, Conflicts and Transformations in National Retrospection*, Durham, NC: Duke University Press, pp 43–71.

Feindt, G., Krawatzek, F., Mehler, D., Pestel, F., and Trimçev, R. (2014) "Entangled Memory: Toward a Third Wave in Memory Studies," *History and Theory* 53(1): 24–44.

Fine, G.A. (1995) "Public Narration and Group Culture: Discerning Discourse in Social Movements," in H. Johnston and B. Klandermans (eds) *Social Movements and Culture*, Minneapolis, MN: University of Minnesota Press, pp 127–143.

Fine, G.A. (2002) "The Storied Group: Social Movements as 'Bundle of Narratives,'" in J.E. Davis (ed) *Stories of Change: Narrative and Social Movements*, Albany, NY: SUNY Press, pp 229–245.

García Muñiz, H. (1987) *Boots, Boots, Boots: Intervention, Regional Security, and Militarization in the Caribbean, 1979–1986*, Militarism Series 2, San Juan: Projecto Caribeño de Justicia y Paz.

Halbwachs, M. (1992) *On Collective Memory*, Chicago, IL: University of Chicago Press.

Harris, F.C. (2006) "It Takes a Tragedy to Arouse Them: Collective Memory and Collective Action during the Civil Rights Movement," *Social Movement Studies* 5(1): 19–43.

Jansen, R.S. (2007) "Resurrection and Appropriation: Reputational Trajectories, Memory Work and the Political Use of Historical Figures," *American Journal of Sociology* 112(4): 953–1007.

Jasper, J.M. (1997) *The Art of Moral Protest: Culture, Biography, and Creativity in Social Movements*, Chicago, IL: University of Chicago Press.

Johnston, H. and Klandermans, B. (1995) *Social Movements and Culture*. Minneapolis, MN: University of Minnesota Press.

Kane, A. (1997) "Theorizing Meaning Construction in Social Movements: Symbolic Structures and Interpretation during the Irish Land War, 1879–1882," *Sociological Theory* 15(3): 249–276.

Kansteiner, W. and Weilnböck, H. (2008) "Against the Concept of Cultural Trauma," in A. Erll and A. Nünning (eds) *Cultural Memory Studies: An International and Interdisciplinary Handbook,* Berlin: Walter de Gruyter, pp 229–243.

Kidron, C.A. (2003) "Surviving a Distant Past: A Case Study of the Cultural Construction of Trauma Descendant Identity," *Ethos* 31(4): 513–544.

Langenohl, A. (2008) "Memory in Post-Authoritarian Societies," in A. Erll and A. Nünning (eds) *Cultural Memory Studies: An International and Interdisciplinary Handbook,* Berlin: Walter de Gruyter, pp 163–172.

McCaffrey, K.T. (2002) *Military Power and Popular Protest: The US Navy in Vieques, Puerto Rico*, New Brunswick, NJ: Rutgers University Press.

McCaffrey, K.T. (2006) "Social Struggle against the US Navy in Vieques, Puerto Rico: Two Movements in History," *Latin American Perspectives* 146(33): 83–101.

McCaffrey, K.T. (2008) "Because Vieques Is Our Home: Defend It! Women Resisting Militarization in Vieques, Puerto Rico," in B. Sutton, S. Morgen, and J. Novkov (eds) *Critical Perspectives on Gender, Race and Militarization,* New Brunswick, NJ: Rutgers University Press, pp 157–176.

Meléndez, M. (1989) *La Batalla de Vieques*, Santurce: Editorial Edil, Inc.

Mullenneaux, L. (2000) *¡Ni una bomba más! Vieques vs. US Navy*, El Dorado Hills, CA: Pennington Press.

Olick, J. (2003) "What Does It Mean to Normalize the Past? Official Memory in German Politics since 1989," in J. Olick (ed) *States of Memory: Continuities, Conflicts and Transformations in National Retrospection,* Durham, NC: Duke University Press, pp 259–288.

Olick, J. and Levy, D. (1997) "Collective Memory and Cultural Constraint: Holocaust Myth and Rationality in German Politics," *American Sociological Review* 62(6): 921–936.

Olick, J. and Robbins, J. (1998) "Social Memory Studies: From 'Collective Memory' to the Historical Sociology of Mnemonic Practices," *Annual Review of Sociology* 24(1): 105–140.

Olick, J., Vinitzky-Seroussi, V., and Levy D. (eds) (2011) *The Collective Memory Reader*, New York: Oxford University Press.

Paralitici, J. (2005) "Desmilitarización y educación," in *Universidad y (Anti) Militarismo: Historia, luchas y debates*. San Juan: Universitarios por la Desmilitarización, pp 77–90.

Polletta, F. (2002) "Plotting Protest: Mobilizing Stories in the 1960 Student Sit-Ins," in J. E. Davis (ed) *Stories of Change: Narrative and Social Movements*, Albany, NY: SUNY Press, pp 31–51.

Polletta, F. (2003) "Legacies and Liabilities of an Insurgent Past: Remembering Martin Luther King Jr. on the House and Senate Floor," in J. Olick (ed) *States of Memory: Continuities, Conflicts and Transformations in National Retrospection*, Durham, NC: Duke University Press, pp 193–226.

Polletta, F. (2005) *It Was Like a Fever: Storytelling in Protest and Politics*, Chicago, IL: University of Chicago Press.

Rodríguez Beruf, J. (1999) "Guerra contra las drogas, militarización y democracia: Políticas y fuerzas de seguridad en Puerto Rico," in H. García Muñiz and J. Rodríguez Beruff (eds) *Fronteras en conflicto: Guerra contra las drogas, militarización y democracia en el Caribe*, San Juan: Red Caribeña de Geopolítica, pp 51–115.

Sztompka, P. (2000) "Cultural Trauma: The Other Face of Social Change," *European Journal of Social Theory* 3(4): 449–466.

Vélez-Vélez, R. (2010) "Reflexivity in Mobilization: Gender and Memory as Cultural Features in the Mobilization of Women in Vieques (1999–2003)," *Mobilization* 15(1): 405–422.

Vélez-Vélez, R. (2013) "Moving Memories in Vieques: Towards a Memory Approach in Mobilization Research," *International Journal of Liberal Arts and Social Science* 1(2): 53–66.

Yates, J.J. and Hunter, J.D. (2002) "Fundamentalism: When History Goes Awry," in J. Davis (ed) *Stories of Change: Narratives and Social Movements*, Albany, NY: SUNY Press, pp 123–148.

Wagner-Pacifici, R. (1996) "Memories in the Making: The Shapes of Things that Went," *Qualitative Sociology* 19(3): 301–321.

Zamponi, L. (2013) "Collective Memory and Social Movements," in D. Snow, D. della Porta, B. Klandermans, and D. McAdam (eds) *Wiley-Blackwell Encyclopedia of Social and Political Movements*, Hoboken, NJ: Blackwell Publishing, pp 1–4.

Zerubavel, E. (1996) "Social Memories: Steps to a Sociology of the Past," *Qualitative Sociology* 19(3): 283–299.

Zerubavel, Y. (1995) *Recovered Roots*, Chicago, IL: University of Chicago Press.

5

The Ballot of Donald and Hillary: Hateful Memories of Celebrity Leaders

Gary Alan Fine, Christopher Robertson, and Cal Abbo

Shortly after the presidential election of 1968, the honored liberal cartoonist Herblock, a longtime and bitter critic of Richard Nixon, published a cartoon in the *Washington Post*. Herblock had previously depicted Nixon with a nasty-looking five o'clock shadow. Now, there is a sign in the cartoonist's barbershop: "This shop gives to every new president of the United States a free shave." Herblock suggested that each elected leader deserves a fresh start, even the ones we dislike.

Some presidents do not receive their free shave. For some elected leaders, a significant portion of the population *despises* them during the campaign, and these emotions only grow stronger after the election. This is often true for the victors and the vanquished alike, who can each generate feelings of disgust.

In a political system committed to electoral democracy, this is puzzling. Given the likelihood of skeletons in the closets of some (if not most) prominent public servants, why should the public reputation of political figures adored by many come to be reviled by others? How is partisan success meaningfully linked with public representations of moral failure or despicable character? How might collective memory of polarizing presidencies in polarized times be shaped through the uses (and abuses) of the reputations of controversial political figures? Why, given our case, were Donald Trump and Hillary Clinton, two accomplished Americans in their own ways, so intensely disliked by large segments of the electorate? Why, once elected, did Donald Trump not receive his free shave?

To explore the creation of contentious reputations, our chapter builds on an earlier analysis (Fine and Eisenberg, 2002) that described the barbed animosity aimed at Richard Milhous Nixon and William Jefferson Clinton. These two United States presidents were elected for two terms each despite numerous detractors who not only rejected their policies – a legitimate practice in competitive democracies – but loathed their personas and their pasts, suggesting that as persons they lacked integrity and as presidents they lacked legitimacy. In the eyes of detractors, a president with a loathsome reputation threatens the authority of the office. That essay argued that the hatred was tied to generational politics: Nixon was linked to his role in the McCarthy, communist-hunting era of the late 1940s and early 1950s, and Clinton to the radical youth politics of the 1960s that he and his wife symbolized. Although not an example addressed in that paper, President Franklin Delano Roosevelt, seen as a class traitor to the wealthy community in which he had been born and raised, also generated considerable and comparable animus from a significant segment of the population.

To understand the dynamics of contentious collective memories in American politics, we refine this argument in light of responses to the 2016 presidential race between Donald J. Trump and Hillary Rodham Clinton. For the victor – Donald Trump – the public hatred continued and even expanded, but it didn't vanish for Hillary Clinton either. For this chapter, we do not take sides in the conflict; we are bystanders at the edge of a national crackup.

Our analysis is based on data collected from op-eds, articles, and essays written for non-specialist audiences in popular print and online news outlets. When possible, we also took advantage of the comments sections of web articles that afford partisans the opportunity to express their strong feelings. Sources included the most popular and influential outlets of political opinion across the ideological spectrum: from well-known left-of-center newspapers like the *New York Times*, to more niche journals like the right-wing *Claremont Review of Books*. (We focused on polarized positions within the ideological mainstream, broadly construed. Thus, we did not sample from the fringes of either the unapologetically reactionary right or the revolutionary left.) We used keyword searches to identify articles with titles suggesting the author's negative evaluation of either candidate Trump or Clinton, starting in the 2015 primaries up through the first years of the Trump presidency. Articles were searched for expressions of antipathy, the results collected in spreadsheets, and then sorted for close reading. While our collection procedures were neither random (not statistically representative) nor automated, we are nonetheless confident, given the abundance of material, that our data are indicative of the kinds of articles that politically astute conservatives and liberals are likely to have encountered.

Through some combination of chance and deepening divisions in American society, the 2016 election constituted a case study in how political tensions are linked to intense emotional energy. While many progressive, liberal, moderate, and even some conservative voters hated Donald Trump, and were willing to express this animus, his opponent had her devoted haters as well. We do not judge whether such animus was justified. Instead, we focus on showing how reputations are potentially at risk. Partisan ties bound by reputation have the power to transform reparable breaches among allies into irreparable ruptures between rivals (Fine and Robertson 2020), and controversial figures with irredeemable reputations (for some) can deepen and widen existing fissures among a citizenry. Loathsome public images are foregrounded by their backstories and the ways in which their "celebrity" – that is, their knownness – develops and spreads. As such, for our case, the fact that Trump's and Clinton's reputations preceded them was consequential for structuring the possibilities of partisan hatred that followed.

As noted, political loathing is not simply a disagreement on policy; disagreeing, belittling, or satirizing is not the same as despising. One might argue that Richard Nixon and Bill Clinton were more ideologically centrist than many in their parties and, during their time in office, made widely popular decisions. Donald Trump was, at one time, a liberal democrat and his achievements as a developer-cum-reality TV celebrity were real. Hillary Clinton pursued a realist, centrist set of policies as President Obama's Secretary of State for which she received high marks in national surveys and for being a hard-working United States Senator. She was one of the most accomplished and qualified persons to run for the presidency in many decades.

However, accomplishments are not all that matter. Political hatred has an emotional root and can be attached to presidents or candidates of either party, although their detractors are non-overlapping groups. Still, it is important to recognize that not all political leaders are detested by their opponents. For example, consider Dwight Eisenhower, Jimmy Carter or George H.W. Bush, and, as of this writing, Joe Biden. Simply because one is a political leader in a competitive democracy does not mean that hatred is inevitable, although partisan opposition surely is – disagreeing or disliking is not the same as detesting.

The reality that animus can be aimed at an individual whom one does not know personally is startling. How can a stranger be such a villain? These reactions operate through the power of mediated representations. This constitutes a form of *parasocial interaction* (Horton and Wohl, 1956; Caughey, 1984). These imagined relationships can be so intensely motivating that one may throw objects at a television screen or may refuse to speak the name of the target. In contemporary politics, many chose not to refer to President Trump by name, calling him "45" – or much worse. The attacks can be brutal. Bill Clinton was said to have the "sexual glands of an orangutan" (Tyrrell Jr, 1998). Said one critic of Nixon, "everything anyone has suspected about Richard Nixon has been true, with or without evidence" (Fine and Eisenberg, 2002). Even in 2021, some claim that they still despise Richard Nixon (Jason Shapiro in Obermann, 2021). Added to this is the sexualization of the opponent, either suggesting an insatiable sexual appetite or addiction (as in the case of Bill Clinton) or abnormally small genitals (as in the "small hands" syndrome attached to Donald Trump).

From where does this loathing derive? We argue that the evaluation of persona precedes – and often overwhelms – the judgements of political adequacy, and further that the understanding of persona stems from the politician's place in a contentious past, even if that history is first recognized at the point that the person emerges as a public figure. In other words, the politician enters the presidential arena with a personal history that is then judged and found wanting by opponents who are primed to pounce.

The argument we present is that despised politicians are not loathed primarily because of the policies that they endorse, but as part of their pre-established identities. Their quality of being known – their reputational persona – provides the emotional substrate for being reviled. As a consequence, their character is set for a sizeable segment of the electorate at the time of their emergence and then is cemented through the events of the campaign. Paradoxically, then, the candidate's success all but guarantees that public detractors will view them as irredeemable personally – regardless of any post-election policy accomplishments. The specific grounds for scorn are interpreted through and integrated into their pre established reputation. This distaste is less evident among the members of the political class in which they interact as colleagues (although some animosity remains), but among those members of the public who follow politics and for whom reputation is better known than the kind of person the candidate is in private.

Political enemies are primed to search for reasons to attack and in a contentious political environment – one with an abundance of "evidence" – often they discover them. Errors that might be perceived as innocent mistakes or the unintended consequences of best intentions are treated as deliberate sins. While politicians on the receiving end of this emotional attack are typically prominent figures, they need not be presidential candidates, although being a president-in-waiting contributes to the desire to diminish. Some Senators and Congressional Representatives receive these attacks (Ted Cruz, Nancy Pelosi), although relatively few do. These detested public figures have celebrity status, and, being known by many, receive considerable attention from the partisan media.

Partisan attention leaves a temporal record, creating the possibility that what is forgotten today might be remembered tomorrow. Time, Maurice Halbwachs (1992: p 8) reminds us, is real "insofar as it offers events as material for thought." These materials afford reputational entrepreneurs opportunities to recollect and reconstruct biographical memories of political figures' failings and foibles as mnemonic means for pugilistic ends. By reminding publics of disreputable biographies, partisan agents of memory cast harsh light on forgotten, repressed, or hitherto unknown times of yesteryear that resonate with the contemporary political moment.

Herein lies the centrifugal power of memory-making and reputation work. On the one hand, because reputations are "sticky" objects (Fine, 2012), attempts at tarring the public personas of partisan figures today bind the identities of their supporters to an unsavory past. In contrast, the reputational implications of being judged morally complicit in the shameful histories of divisive public figures can lead supporters to reject the truthfulness of otherwise uncontested facts or the premise that such actions were ever shame-worthy to begin with. In other words, highlighting vices in the biographies of polarizing political leaders may set in motion a dialectical process of partisan collective memory-making, such that public gaffes can be negated by the upside-down-reality of "fake news," and private vices can be reformed as politically-incorrect virtues.

Where the process leads next – that is, how partisans recognize and respond to the risks and rewards of mnemonic disputes – depends on collectively held definitions of the situation and shared interpretation of who bears responsibility for how they ended up there. Lewis Coser (quoted in Halbwachs, 1992: p 22), describing a comparable case of contentious memory at the fall of the Soviet Union, analogized: "It is perhaps a similar experience to that when two married persons suddenly discover that both of them have a hitherto unknown disreputable past. How they manage to deal with this sudden revelation will largely determine the future of their relationship." Like interpersonal relations, the use and abuse of biographical memory can have significant effects on the tenuous balance between trust and truth in a polarized civil sphere (Alexander, 2006). Partisans of American politics increasingly find themselves in equally uncomfortable situations.

In the case of despised presidents, surveys suggest that committed antagonists constitute about 20 percent of the electorate, as in the case of Nixon and Clinton, the two most hated presidents of the 20th century (Fine and Eisenberg, 2002). (We must wait a few years to determine whether the level of distaste for Donald Trump declines, although his continued engagement in the political arena suggests that this is unlikely.) Hillary Clinton spoke of the existence of "a vast right-wing conspiracy" that targeted her husband, and that was later attached to her own persona as a secret Socialist and/or Lady Macbeth. This involves what has been termed Clintipathy (Troy, 2016). But there are vast left-wing conspiracies as well, especially given the liberal media environment. Enraged partisans on both left and right find evidence that gives them comfort.

This dynamic is similar to what social psychologists call attribution error, the idea that people interpret the actions of others (if they dislike them) as emanating from internal motives – who a person *is*, that is, their character – whereas individuals have greater sensitivity to external causes when it comes to their own actions (especially if they did something wrong or failed in some endeavor) (see Kelley, 1973; Hunt, 1993). Every mistake – actual or imagined – becomes grist for the mill that pulverizes a reputation.

In this regard, it is significant that the first impeachment resolution aimed at Richard Nixon occurred prior to the Watergate break-in. Talk of impeachment surrounded Bill Clinton before citizens knew of Monica Lewinsky. Likewise, impassioned partisans called for the impeachment of Donald Trump prior to his taking office. No doubt something similar would have been attached to Secretary Clinton had she been elected ("Lock her up!"). The materials that constitute a scandal are assumed to be waiting to be uncovered. Such assumptions prime partisans to accept the truthfulness of a rumor if it aligns with their moral evaluation of the rumored.

Recalling Herblock's cartoon, for leaders whom enemies can construct an evil persona from personal history, sharp razors are to be used for backstabbing, not for barbering. Why does this matter for scholars of collective memory and contentious reputations? Certainly this dynamic shapes campaigns and how a targeted candidate must respond, perhaps presenting the attackers as evil in themselves, hoping that other citizens will sympathize with their plight, finding the diatribes too constant, too extreme, and too unjust. Further, when the hated politician is elected and is inaugurated, these reputational entrepreneurs (Fine, 2001) do not disappear. Perhaps they even experience a certain frisson in embracing their public disdain as some considered the repeated attacks by Rush Limbaugh on Bill Clinton crucial to helping "El Rushbo" become a national brand.

There are also consequences for governance. Knowing that there are those who attempt to cast each decision in a negative light might constrain policy choices. These enemies are citizens who take pleasure in watching failure, as when Rush Limbaugh admitted that he hoped that Barack Obama would fail. Such a claim surely had a double meaning: that Obama would fail in being unable to enact his desired policies (a legitimate concern of partisan rivals), but also that Obama's tenure would be seen as a failed presidency. In the latter, we perceive a not-so-hidden hope for personal destruction. Every error can become a scandal and every ambiguity a conspiracy.

Often the political target gives their enemies fodder for condemnation. But these scandals are treated not just as wrong actions, but as reflecting malformed character. Some of this expressed hatred, now so evident on social media, might be something of a game, bringing satisfaction to the hater for their creativity in a community that shares their perspective. Partisans come to believe that they "own" their opponents, producing a *jouissance* in distaste. One can recognize this enjoyment in the communal hatred of Donald Trump, reflected in memes, slogans, and images. An anti-Trump rally reflected a space of partisan creativity. One need not assume that hatred necessarily reveals trauma, only a sense of belonging.

For Richard Nixon, the hatred developed from his role in the Alger Hiss hearings. For Bill Clinton, it was his role as a draft-dodging child of the 1960s. And for Donald Trump, the origins of the hatred came, in part, from his exemplification of the Decade of Greed and Self-Indulgence of the 1980s. The presence of these committed antagonists did not prevent the president from gaining national popularity. Unintentionally, they might have helped increase it. Hated political figures can come to serve as a binding agent for many people who otherwise feel looked down upon or ignored. Richard Nixon and Bill Clinton were re-elected and Donald Trump received nearly 75 million votes in his own re-election bid (and Hillary Clinton received the plurality of cast votes in 2016).

The great Trumpian hatred

Having described some of the general processes of political hatred, we turn to the profound contentious reputational work that surrounded Donald Trump and his 2016 opponent Hillary Clinton. Although it is difficult to measure accurately the amount of distaste towards political candidates, it is hard to think of a recent election in which there was more animus directed towards both major presidential candidates.

Although Richard Nixon and Bill Clinton certainly gathered a devoted coterie of haters, these did not compare with those who were willing to announce their hatred of Donald Trump and Hillary Clinton – a difference that was no doubt fueled by the explosive growth of social media and new technologies in the intervening years. Hating Trump became for many a mark of intellectual sophistication and moral virtue. While hating Hillary was not as evident among cultural elites, it was fully present in many corners of the white American middle class.

The hatred of Donald Trump was so evident that the prominent broadcaster Keith Obermann (2021; the comments presented are from responses to Obermann's op-ed) felt comfortable in announcing – proudly – in the pages of the *New York Times*, "I hated Donald Trump when hating Donald Trump wasn't cool." Obermann felt that he would gain status by the fact that he recognized Donald Trump's faults long before most other Americans. By the time of Donald Trump's second impeachment, Obermann spoke of these emotions as constituting "the Great Hate." His anger was such that he could write, "I, for one, have gotten loud and blasphemous enough to peel the paint off my walls." In response to the op-ed, readers competed in the drama of their online comments: Eliot claimed that Trump was a "despicably vapid human." Sheila suggested that "His evil is obvious when you view any segment of his career." John responds: "I consider Trump to be an enemy …

I wish him the worst. ... I'm opposed to the death penalty but he makes me question my position." Peyton remarks, "I hate him and plan to do so until I hear he's breathed his last and then I'll despise his memory. ... Loathing him has been a passion, an addiction, a compulsion." Cathy claimed: "I've been on medication for 4 years because of that monster and am only now beginning to feel calm." These comments could easily be multiplied. There were over 1800 responses to the op-ed when the *New York Times* closed the page. While by no means a random sample, most respondents agreed that President Trump was hate-worthy – he made America hate again. Few insults were off-limits, evident in the remarks by Larry:

> "I will never stop hating Donald J Trump. I have never hated a person with more intensity than I do this man who has gone to great lengths to destroy this great Nation of ours for the sole purpose of his own personal gain. ... Get over it, you say? Has the world gotten over the evil that overtook it eight decades ago?"

At a moment in which many condemn hateful speech and vitriol in many different forums, *Times* readers embraced hatred in describing their feelings toward Donald Trump.

Beyond the loathing texts, other forms of humiliation were prepared. Trumpian opponents created statues (even actors pretending to be living statues) or insulting balloons. Artists utilized their skills to create what might be described as anti-shrines, idols of derision. For instance, in Washington, DC, outside the Lincoln Memorial – the pointed implication being that Donald Trump is no Abraham Lincoln – "a street artist covered in metallic gold paint stood on a pedestal ... hands in front of his crotch, he appeared to be peeing into a chair beside him" (Lefrak, 2020). One statue of Donald Trump on display in London made farting noises (Perrone, 2019). An artist placed busts of Donald Trump on various Brooklyn sidewalks, with the sign "Pee on Me," allowing dogs to express their canine irritation (or that of their owners) by urinating on the President. As the artist, Phil Gable, remarked, "It was largely just a personal expression of my own disdain for Donald Trump, both as a President and as a human being" (Schwartz, 2018). Another statue on display in New York and four other cities depicts President Trump in the nude with tiny genitals – a photographic magnet for anti-Trump Americans to take selfies with the humiliated president's likeness (Tiffany and Bareham, 2016). As the *Washington Post* headlined their article, "These protestors wanted to humiliate 'Emperor' Trump. So they took off his clothes" (Holley, 2016). Significantly, the first of these statues appeared prior to President Trump's election. As will be clear, Hillary Clinton received similarly sexualized gestures of ridicule, suggesting that she was either lesbian or frigid, and similar statues were created to humiliate her.

Both supporters and critics of Donald Trump recognize that he thrives on publicity, and, as a result, there is much material from which critics can express their evaluation of his moral selfhood. In such a circumstance, both admirers and haters believe that they know him. Parasocial interaction with Donald Trump is bipartisan.

Donald Trump exemplifies the symbolism of contentious memory based on his history as a known figure and as a provocateur. In the next section, we begin by considering how Donald Trump's pre-political actions as a celebrity developer and as a representative of the 1980s "Decade of Greed" served as a basis for the hatred that evolved as he became president. We then turn to his role in publicizing the conspiratorial claim that Barack Obama was possibly born in Kenya and was not a legitimate American president. We argue that these acts – in addition to myriad lesser-known ones – established biographical predicates for hatred that led to a context in which some of Trump's actions that might otherwise have been excused or overlooked were instead highlighted.

The predicate: Donald Trump as master of greed

As noted, Donald Trump was a known celebrity for over three decades when he rode his Gold Escalator into the political fray. At first, most Americans felt that his entrance into Republican politics was a publicity stunt that would lead nowhere. How could this recent convert – as new to conservatism as he was to evangelicalism – a man with no political experience and few durable ideological commitments, be taken seriously as a legitimate candidate? Much of the early animus responded to his showy display of wealth (as well as his targeting President Obama). Donald Trump was the Thorstein Veblen candidate, an avatar of conspicuous consumption. This theme emerged early in Donald Trump's career. In the *New York Times*, he had been described as a "slumlord" and a "humbug" (Schanberg, 1984). In the words of one critic, Donald Trump was "a gross entitled jerk." His battles with his tenants as a real estate developer were reported as exemplifying his lack of character (Cohen, 2017).

The iconic escalator on which Donald Trump travelled to announce his presidential ambitions was, notably, located in Trump Tower. The fact that so many Trump buildings are self-named justified the distaste of many, even though for his supporters it indicated that his talents could be applied to governance. Trump had become as much a corporate brand as a human person. His great wealth as displayed and as reported on (however much was present in reality) was matched by what detractors considered garish vulgarity. While the hatred for Donald Trump cannot entirely be attributed to how his celebrity developed in the 1980s so-called Decade of Greed, when, after all, he was a liberal democrat, those images provided the frame for later interpretations. His affiliation with a centrist liberalism was such that in 1987 the Democratic Congressional Campaign Committee asked Donald Trump to serve as the host for the committee's dinner the following year, a choice that some progressives found unappetizing. Ross Baker (1987: p 23), a political science professor at Rutgers University, remarked in the *New York Times*, focusing on Trump's wealth, "Mr. Trump as the master of ceremonies at a function to boost the Democrats' fortunes is like the Sheriff of Nottingham presiding over a fund-raiser for Robin Hood," but then adding significantly, "There is nothing wicked or sinister about Mr. Trump." A *Time* magazine essay from 2015, recognizing that he had been depicted on the cover of the magazine in 1989, commented in light of his outrageous self-inflating comments, that "Trump rose to fame in the go-go 1980s, and he was a perfect symbol of that ego-driven era" (Mitchell, 2015). He was a man who was quoted as remarking in 1989, "Who has done as much as I have? No one has done more in New York than me" (Mitchell, 2015). However doubtful this claim might be, at first it seemed more eccentric than perverse.

By 1990, Donald Trump was sufficiently well-known in New York and elsewhere that Alexander Cockburn (1990: p 334) could write about the estrangement of Donald and Ivana Trump as an "elegy to the eighties ... theirs was but two notes in a blare of vulgarity and remorseless self-aggrandizement." Donald Trump became known by the enduring description of journalist Kurt Anderson as a "short-fingered vulgarian." The word vulgar stuck as a compelling description of Donald Trump by those who considered good taste defining of a proper self and served as a framework for how he was judged.

Consider the remarks of Jay in response to Keith Obermann's op-ed, recalling the 1980s:

> "My own awareness of Donald Trump began ... in 1986. I was reading an article ... about this crazy real estate developer who wanted to build all these completely inappropriate and tasteless buildings in New York like Trump Castle and other similarly awful things. My hope at the time was that he flamed out quickly so that he didn't have a chance to destroy New York's skyline. ... He may not have succeeded in destroying Manhattan's skyline but he did a pretty good job of demolishing America as we thought we know it."

Likewise, Bob responds,

> "I have hated Donald Trump since I first laid eyes on the ostentatious Trump Tower nearly 40 years ago. My hatred grew in the years that followed. ... As one of the most vile, disgusting, evil individuals to

ever walk the Earth I will continue to feel towards him an emotion so dark that no words can capture."

That architecture can produce such lasting emotion is a tribute to how the discourse of hatred can be expanded, as well as the fact that Donald Trump represented an aesthetic violation.

These strong reactions, ignoring the achievements of his presidency for supporters, while emphasizing the failures as resulting from character deficits, leads to reputational stigma. The linkage of Donald Trump as preparing the ground for a coup d'état, fearing that the President could declare martial law (Abramsky, 2020: p 15), may seem implausible to some, even with hindsight of the violent incursion of the Capitol on January 6 by Trump supporters attempting to overturn the outcome of the election. Some liberals admitted similar anxieties about the final days of the Nixon administration.

Liberals and even some Republicans drew parallels between Trump's attempts to motivate his supporters and events in Germany in the 1930s. The claim that Donald Trump was a fascist was common. Charles Fried, Ronald Reagan's solicitor general, opined that Trump and his administration were

> certainly racist, contemptuous of ordinary democratic and constitutional norms, and they believe their cause, their interests, are really the interests of the nation and therefore anything that keeps them in power is in the national interest. Does that make you a fascist? It kind of looks that way, doesn't it? (Abramsky, 2020: p 13)

Laila Lalami (2016: p 10), writing in *The Nation*, claimed that Trump has "brought fascism back into the mainstream." This was one F-word often spoken on the left, just as socialism or communism have long been spoken on the right. No matter the differences in actual policy, governing philosophy, or historical context, the term seemed to fit. A connection between Trump and Hitler was often raised in progressive circles (Cillizza, 2018).

These extreme pronouncements, in time, came to be labelled by Trump-admiring conservatives as constituting "Trump Derangement Syndrome," referencing similar attacks on President George W. Bush and, later, Vice-Presidential candidate Sarah Palin. The condition was defined in the online *Urban Dictionary*: "Trump Derangement Syndrome (TDS) is a mental condition in which a person has been driven effectively insane due to their dislike of Donald Trump, to the point they will abandon all logic and reason." Although partisan animosity is characteristic of American democracy, this pseudo-psychiatric "syndrome," at least as it is imagined, prevents liberals and conservatives from engaging in cordial conversation, much less in developing lasting friendships. In the aftermath of COVID-19, essayist Joseph Epstein

(2020) even suggested that Trump Derangement Syndrome constitutes "the next pandemic."

The Donald and Kenya: a boomerang effect

Donald Trump surely contributed to the appeal of Trump Derangement Syndrome, being deliberately provocative as his brand. One reaps what one sows. Attacks can boomerang on their maker, as supporters of those attacked embrace a similar level of animus. This was surely the case with Richard Nixon, whose attacks on allegedly pro-communist leftists inspired a generation of opponents who would never forget his politically effective diatribes when serving on the House Un-American Activities Committee in the late 1940s.

The actions of Donald Trump, while not identical, similarly inspired a boomerang of hatred. During the presidency of Barack Obama, a man admired, even loved, by many liberals, a controversy was fueled by right-wing talk radio and television as to whether his birthplace was in Hawaii or in Kenya, and whether, consequently, he could legitimately serve as President of the United States, the first African American so elected. Today it is clear that President Obama was born in Hawaii, but his long form birth certificate was not available at first, a documentary ambiguity constructed as an obstetric conspiracy. Donald Trump was a leader in questioning Barack Obama's legitimacy and in pushing the unsupported claim into the national conversation. While he never definitively asserted that President Obama was born in Kenya, Trump remarked on many occasions that the claim needed to be investigated and suggested that he was sponsoring the investigation. This rhetorical move – using ambiguity to avoid accountability – would be deployed later in Trump's presidency. To attack the legitimacy of a man who was for many a path-breaking hero generated anger and the implication that the claim was based on racial insensitivity at best and racist malice at worst, although Trump's willingness to attack numerous others leaves open whether racism, resentment, or some combination of the two was at the root of his involvement.

There is a racial backstory that some opponents recalled. In 1989, a young (white female) jogger was allegedly physically and sexually assaulted by a group of Black men, who became known collectively as the Central Park Five. These young men were arrested, confessed under police pressure, and were sentenced to years in prison. Trump, donning the rhetorical garb of civic protector, led a campaign against these young men, appeared on television, and even placed full-page advertisements in the *New York Times* urging the death penalty. Years later, their convictions were overturned, and the men became public symbols of injustice in America's legal system. For many, the story served to exemplify racism, irrational fear of crime, and

Donald Trump's role as a divisive and dangerous political figure (Wicker, 1989). For liberals, Donald Trump's role in the tragedy of justice marked him as a leader of what was considered a media-led lynch mob.

Together these aspects of Donald Trump's past set the predicate for the hatred just described. Our argument is not that these actions were sufficient for the establishment of political hatred or to deny that Trump's behaviors warranted this emotional response, but that the known celebrity of "The Donald" – much like the known celebrity of "Hillary" – provided the material from which a target of derision was built.

It takes a village to hate Hillary

Despite the differences among those who despised Donald Trump and those who reviled Hillary Clinton, certain themes were similar. The hatred occurring within a shared moral community seems so self-evident that it requires no justification. The legitimacy of public hatred is available in contemporary American politics, in which opposing silos are carefully situated and well-armed. Hatred may bolster support for one's own candidate. Indeed, it has been suggested that hatred for an opponent may justify increasing support for a chosen candidate when one's support is uncertain or ambivalent. If one can believe that electing Hillary would lead to the American equivalent of the fall of Rome, voting for the flawed Donald Trump – "the lesser of two evils" – might seem to be necessary. As Conor Friedersdorf (2016) suggested in *The Atlantic*:

> Many partisans will always find a way to persuade themselves that the other party's candidate is bad enough to clearly justify their support for their party's candidate. ... Insofar as he or she is unusually hard to support, the opposing candidate will come to be regarded as even more unusually evil or dangerous.

Certainly, the attacks directed towards Hillary Clinton in 2016 were venomous, although found in different social quarters from those aimed at Donald Trump. The communities were not mirror images, but related themes of morality and sexuality were evident. It might be claimed that whichever candidate was defeated, it would be because they were not sufficiently likeable. How many would willingly share a beer with either Hillary or Donald? While the absence of likeability is not the cause of hatred per se, it suggests something significant, perhaps touching on a perceived lack of authenticity or sincerity. As William Voegeli (2016) phrased it, "Hillary Clinton suffers from profound authenticity deficiencies ... She comes across as an office-seeker who doesn't really believe in anything ... half as fiercely as she believes in her right and destiny to be president." This permitted her opponents to claim that in order to gain power, she deliberately hid what she truly and secretly believes (that is, "socialism"). Adding to this is the fact that opponents see her as "sour, dour, and without a humorous molecule in her body. Her laughter is always feigned" (Smith, 2020). The absence of a sense of humor, central to being likeable, was a charge also levelled at Richard Nixon and Donald Trump, although not, it must be admitted, at Bill Clinton. Michelle Goldberg (2016), reporting on those who label Hillary a "sociopath," quotes Henry Louis Gates as writing in 1996, "Like horse-racing, Hillary-hating has become one of those national pastimes which unite the elite and the lumpen. … There's just something about her that pisses people off," the renowned Washington hostess Sally Quinn told Gates.

One blogger made this generic dislike central in a letter to "Madam Not-President," noting in passing hatred towards Trump by his opponents,

> Here's the real truth … you lost the presidential election because America hates you. "Hate" is not a word I use as flippantly as your side of the ideological aisle. "Dislike" isn't a strong enough term for someone who tests the upchuck reflexes of even those with the most resilient of stomachs. (Kirchoff, 2017)

Recall the various creative, if unattractive, statuary insults aimed at Donald Trump. In the heart of New York, Donald Trump would find few who wished to tear down or cover over these offensive effigies. But when a nude statue of Hillary Clinton was unveiled in Manhattan, the response was swift.

> In August, a gross statue of a nude Donald Trump was "art," and crowds gathered to celebrate it. But when a similarly dysmorphic nude statue of Hillary Clinton … was unveiled on Tuesday, it was declared "obscene" … and taken down by women at the scene. Both statues seemed designed to humiliate their subject. But from city officials on down to passersby, New Yorkers seemed OK with a grotesque nude vision of the GOP candidate for president. (Ventura, Culliton, and Ness, 2016)

The artistic representation of public disdain is linked to what is permitted on one's home turf.

A nude statue was just one means of disdaining the former First Lady, an abhorrence that was as deep as that for Donald Trump. Professor Herbert London (2016) was explicit, "she is, in my judgment, an evil force, an embodiment of evil." Given that this quotation is found on the conservative Breitbart website, the comments in response are as colorful as those on the *New York Times* website: "Hillary is a lying, corrupt sociopath" and "I like to think of her as an evil, malignant succubus." "Her real father is the Prince of Darkness, the Father of Lies, the Champion of Chaos, Satan," said another.

As a writer in *The Nation*, the progressive journal, assessed the attacks, "she has been reduced at every turn to a physically unhealthy yet nut-crackingly strong, pantsuit-wearing, man-hating closet lesbian, a castrating and shrewish fish without a bicycle" (Williams, 2016: p 11). This overview is evident in a lurid imaginary by DJR to Herbert London's essay, sexualizing her:

> She is disgusting – her looks, bad breath and the noises she makes when pulling her finger not to mention the robust aroma that follows ... Imagine her in scanty swimwear or nothing at all ... I see her doing a sophisticated dance in a short dress, on dancing with the stars, wearing no underwear. When she twirls around she unapologetically exposes her mangy pelt.

This vulgar mental image is mirrored in the body-shaming calumny that she is excessively fat, claiming that for a jumpsuit, she would need canvas from the circus. Again, we find a parallel in our collective emotional code as similar claims about weight were also made about Donald Trump, a striking choice by liberals who have rejected such forms of attacks on physiognomy.

Similar to Trump haters, there is a certain *jouissance* through which the insults flow. Calling out "Lock Her Up" seems to be a form of crowd joy. One critic describes Hillary as "a lying, manipulative, narcissistic woman who deserves nothing except to be put in jail for life," describing disgust in listening to "that painful scratching noise that you like to call intelligence spew from your mouth like typical Clinton diarrhea." In the same article, Alex Jones, the conspiracy-promoting radio talk-show host, piled on, suggesting, "She's a creep, she's a witch ... Look at her face ... All she needs is green skin" (Taylor-Coleman, 2016).

Hatred for Hillary Clinton becomes linked to the sexuality of her husband. This is a key indicator that political disagreement is readily transformed into an imaginative repulsion. Recall an infamous retweet by Donald Trump, soon deleted (there were some things even The Donald recognized were beyond the pale), "If Clinton can't satisfy her husband, what makes her think she can satisfy America?" Hillary could not be the Father of the Country, nor even its paramour. The politics of gender is undeniably implicated in the sexualized hatred for Hillary (as it is for The Donald). As sociologist Todd Gitlin (2016) suggests, misogyny is a "big hunk" of the "Hang the Bitch mentality." This is well-represented in an attack in the Trumpist publication, *American Greatness*:

> What do you call – rather, whom should you call when a 70-year-old woman in a house dress and slippers storms the stage at a conference

in Central Park, a Woodstock for the wealthy, in which this gate-crasher, with her bedraggled hair and belligerent attitude, seizes a wireless microphone and proceeds to rant against Russia; while security guards stand backstage and whisper into their mouthpieces about a "Code Bravo," as an ambulance speeds toward 5th Avenue and 69th Street; while paramedics answer this call and the doctor, sitting atop a wheel well and next to a gurney in the back of the ambulance, fills a syringe with Thorazine? The question answers itself, except when the woman is Hillary Clinton. How else to explain the appeal of someone so appalling? (Hamilton, 2018)

This attack, which perhaps refers to a short-lived kerfuffle about Clinton's supposed deteriorating health, is not sexual per se but relies on images of proper gender presentation. Defenders are ready to suggest that these attacks are illegitimate and, more than this, reflect male privilege, contrasting the rejection of Hillary with the authors' own clearly expressed dislike for Donald Trump. It is in these remarks that we find the comparative hatreds playing off each other, unable to be separated:

People so hate Hillary Clinton that almost half of all Americans are voting for a man who is widely considered the most unqualified and even dangerous person ever to run for the Presidency ... If we threaten people in the areas of sexual identity, then swamp them with feelings of envy and paranoia we can do a pretty good job of disabling their mental apparatus ... This is what has been done to the American political right ... The primary reason Hillary Clinton is so hated is because she is a woman who is exceptionally competent in a world of human minds that have become increasingly sexually perplexed, envious, and paranoid. (Welch, 2016)

This author's account of why Clinton is targeted with vitriol highlights an asymmetry in who can rightly lay claim to political anger based on the substance of policies that are embraced. At issue is whether the attack is on a person or on a demographic category.

It's time to stop pretending that this is about substance. This is about an eagerness to believe that a woman who seeks power will say or do anything to get it. This is about a Lady Macbeth stereotype that, frankly, should never have existed in the first place. This is about the one thing no one wants to admit it's about. Consider, for a moment, two people. One, as a young woman at the beginning of a promising legal career, went door to door searching for ways to guarantee an education to the countless disabled and disadvantaged children who had fallen through the cracks. The other, as a young millionaire, exacted revenge on his recently deceased brother's family by cutting off the medical insurance desperately needed by his nephew's newborn son, who at eighteen months of age was suffering from violent seizures brought on by a rare neurological disorder. What kind of a society treats these two people as equal in any way? ... Generations from now, people will shake their heads at this moment in time, when the first female major party presidential nominee – competent, qualified and more thoroughly vetted than any non-incumbent candidate in history – endured the humiliation of being likened to such an obvious grifter, ignoramus and hate monger. (Womack, 2016)

Finally, there is the account of prominent gender theorist Laura Kipnis (2014), who connects Hillary Hatred with male desire allegedly felt by Trump supporters:

Despise her they do, yet they're also strangely drawn to her, in some inexplicably intimate way. She occupies their attention. They spend a lot of time thinking about her – enumerating her character flaws, dissecting her motives, analyzing her physical shortcomings with a penetrating, clinical eye: those thick ankles and dumpy hips, the ever-changing hairdos. You'd think they were talking about their first wives. There's the same over-invested quality, an edge of spite, some ancient wound not yet repaired. And how they love conjecturing upon her sexuality! Or lack of, heh. Is she frigid, is she gay? Heh ... My point is that you can tell a lot about a man by what he thinks about Hillary, maybe even everything. She's not just another presidential candidate, she's a sophisticated diagnostic instrument for calibrating male anxiety, which is running high. Understandably, given that the whole male-female, who-runs-the-world question is pretty much up for grabs. Hillary seems to attract a certain type: guys with a lot of psychological baggage, emotional intensity, and messy inner lives.

As with those who speak of Trump Derangement Syndrome, this is an attempt to turn the hatred back on the hater, connecting two pools of disgust as a cesspool of similar odor, both filled with reputationally toxic refuse from the candidates' pasts.

Coda

The existence of widespread public disdain poses a challenge for a democratic nation. At its core, democracy assumes the presentation of legitimate alternatives. Either side could plausibly win and, should that happen, the result should be accepted. Does this require the demeaning of the opposition? Does democracy depend on respect for rivals? At various junctions of American history, political divides have been more or less salient and violent. Today the chasm is deep, wide, and perhaps unbridgeable.

How does this demeaning emerge? We claim that it develops in response to a political figure who is a known person, celebrated by a community, but linked to a contentious moral order. Within the context of the hatred, while policy differences are never absent, often the character of the rejected figures is expressed through claims of a thoroughgoing immorality or a perverse sexuality. In other words, a troubling backstory becomes embedded in a deviant self that requires the rejection of the political figure by communities committed to a contentious moral order. Reputation affords partisans a way of positioning themselves vis-a-vis allies and enemies within a shifting moral topography.

We entered 2021 with a new president. One with a long past but, given his Amtrak commute, without much baggage. As we noted, not every president is hated. However, every profoundly hated president has a backstory that supplies material, motive, and justification for hatred. This was the case with Richard Nixon and with Bill Clinton and is true of Donald Trump and Hillary Clinton. George W. Bush (Bush 43) had a less contentious backstory, and while there was visceral dislike as a result of what some considered a privileged upbringing and career successes owing to family connections, the hatred did not reach the level of that directed to Nixon, Clinton, and Trump, and diminished quickly in his kindly and mild post-presidency. What hatred there was developed from the very close election of 2000, in which some Democrats felt that Bush was illegitimately anointed by the Supreme Court. This was coupled with Bush 43's belligerent responses to the attacks on 9/11 and his administration's perceived mishandling of the aftermath of Hurricane Katrina. However, while there was anger directed at Bush 43, it never created the extended hostile community that afflicted other hated presidents and, as noted, diminished rapidly after his presidency. More important, the animosity was primarily linked to issues of contemporary politics and policy.

The animosity shown to Barack Obama was related to that shown to Bush 43, but different as well. By the dawning of the 21st century, the gap between Democrats and Republicans – liberals and conservatives – had widened, solidified by the epistemic (or informational) silos that were established by talk radio, cable news networks, and social media. The politics of racial politesse made it rare for many Americans to announce publicly that they "hated" the first African American president for his racial background, whatever their underlying prejudices might be. His politics – or at least the imagining of that politics – served as the grounds of criticism. Unapologetically racist hate speech was rare in most public settings. More often Obama's opponents would emphasize that they thought that he was a good person, a devoted husband and father, but a duplicitous Muslim conspirator ("Barack Hussein Osama") and/or a radical Marxist ideologue. The attacks on his identity were linked to beliefs that were felt to be radical, socialist, or Islamicist. In this regard, Obama was transformed into a dangerous Other to be feared more so than hated. His personal biography provided the cultural material for constructing reputational attacks against him. Barack Obama did not reflect a past historical moment as was true for Nixon, Clinton, and Trump, but rather a cultural disturbance in a swirling present. Despite its intensity, Obamanation was as much about the moment as the man.

Will Joe Biden be a despised President? So far, derision but not hatred has emerged ("Let's go, Brandon!"), even though some strongly oppose his policies and worry about their effects. His approval rating is not high among voters, similar to that of Donald Trump, but the emotional context is vastly different. We suspect that Joe Biden will be protected in that he lacks an evil backstory, coupled with a set of family tragedies that protect and inoculate his reputation and provide a penumbra of sympathy. The possible corruption of members of the Biden clan has not yet spilled over to tar the President among most voters. The contrast with his predecessor will likely help, along with more sympathetic mainstream media accounts. Perhaps we will choose to take an intermission from the daily drama and emotional investment that hatred demands. President Biden will be attacked, he will be scorned, and he will be mocked. But will he be hated? While it is doubtful, four years is forever in politics.

References

Abramsky, S. (2020) "Is Trump Planning a Coup D'état?," *The Nation* September (21/28): 12–15.
Alexander, J. (2006) *The Civil Sphere*, New York: Oxford University Press.
Baker, R. (1987) "Dump Trump," *New York Times*, November 24: A23.
Caughey, J. (1984) *Imaginary Social Worlds: A Cultural Approach*, Lincoln, NE: University of Nebraska Press.
Cillizza, C. (2018) "What Is 'Trump Derangement Syndrome' – and Do You Have It?," *CNN*, [online] July 20, Available from: www.cnn.com/2018/07/19/politics/trump-derangement-syndrome/index.html [Accessed April 23, 2021].
Cockburn, A. (1990) "Trumpery City," *The Nation*, March 12: 334–335.
Cohen, R. (2017) "Wondering, if This Is America," *New York Times*, December 23: A23.
Epstein, J. (2020) "The Next Pandemic: Trump Derangement Syndrome," *Wall Street Journal*, [online] July 9, Available from: www.wsj.com/articles/the-next-pandemic-trump-derangement-syndrome-11594336574 [Accessed April 23, 2021].

Fine, G.A. (2001) *Difficult Reputations: Collective Memories of the Evil, Inept, and Controversial,* Chicago, IL: University of Chicago Press.

Fine, G.A. (2012) *Sticky Reputations: The Politics of Collective Memory in Midcentury America,* New York: Routledge.

Fine, G.A. and Eisenberg, E. (2002) "Tricky Dick and Slick Willie: Despised Presidents and Generational Imprinting," *American Behavioral Scientist* 46: 553–565.

Fine, G.A. and Robertson, C. (2020) "Reputation in Rupture: Broken Alliances and Relational Politics in the Roosevelt-Taft Split," *Sociological Forum* 35(1): 73–94.

Friedersdorf, C. (2016) "Is Clinton Hatred Fueled by Dislike for Trump?," *The Atlantic,* [online] October 6, Available from: www.theatlantic.com/politics/archive/2016/10/the-relatively-worse-theory-of-strong-partisanship/502613/ [Accessed June 6, 2021].

Gitlin, T. (2016) "What's Behind the Hillary Hatred Syndrome?," *Bill Moyers,* [online] October 29, Available from: https://billmoyers.com/story/hillary-hatred-revisited/ [Accessed June 6, 2016].

Goldberg, M. (2016) "The Hillary Haters," *Slate,* [online] July 24, Available from: www.slate.com/articles/news_and_politics/cover_story/2016/07/the_people_who_hate_hillary_clinton_the_most.html [Accessed June 16, 2021].

Halbwachs, M. (1992) *On Collective Memory,* Chicago, IL: University of Chicago Press.

Hamilton, A. (2018) "House Dress Hillary," *American Greatness,* [online] July 23, Available from: https://amgreatness.com/2018/07/23/house-dress-hillary/ [Accessed June 16, 2021].

Holley, P. (2016) "These Protesters Wanted to Humiliate 'Emperor' Trump. So They Took Off His Clothes," *Washington Post,* [online] August 19, Available from: www.washingtonpost.com/news/morning-mix/wp/2016/08/18/anarchists-unveil-naked-donald-trump-statues-in-several-u-s-cities/ [Accessed April 6, 2021].

Horton, D. and Wohl, R.R. (1956) "Mass Communication and Para-Social Interaction: Observations on Intimacy at a Distance," *Psychiatry* 19(3): 215–239.

Hunt, M. (1993) *The Story of Psychology,* New York: Doubleday.

Kelley, H.H. (1973) "The Processes of Causal Attribution," *American Psychologist* 28(2): 107–128.

Kipnis, L. (2014) "A Deformed Woman: Hillary Clinton and the Men Who Hate Her," *Talking Points Memo,* [online] December 5, Available from: https://talkingpointsmemo.com/theslice/men-who-hate-hillary-clinton [Accessed June 16, 2021].

Kirchoff, C. (2017) "Dear Hillary Clinton: You Lost Because America Hates You …," *Louder with Crowder,* [online] September 8, Available from: www.louderwithcrowder.com/dear-hillary-clinton-you-lost-because-america-hates-you [Accessed June 16, 2021].

Lalami, L. (2016) "Donald Trump's Hate-In," *The Nation*, March 7: 10–11.

Lefrak, M. (2020) "'Living Statues' Mock the President in Front of Lincoln Memorial and Trump Hotel," *National Public Radio*, [online] October 28, Available from: www.npr.org/local/305/2020/10/28/928627665/living-statues-mock-the-president-in-front-of-lincoln-memorial-and-trump-hotel [Accessed April 6, 2021].

London, H. (2016) "Hillary Clinton is 'Embodiment of Evil,'" *Breitbart*, [online] May 24, Available from: www.breitbart.com/radio/2016/05/24/dr-herbert-london-hillary-clinton-embodiment-evil/ [Accessed June 16, 2021].

Mitchell, D. (2015) "How Donald Trump Became Donald Trump," *Time*, [online] July 23, Available from: https://time.com/3969794/donald-trump-history. [Accessed April 23, 2021].

Obermann, K. (2021) "Is This the End of Obsessively Hating Donald Trump?," *New York Times*, [online] February 12, Available from: www.nytimes.com/2021/02/12/opinion/trump-impeachment-media.html [Accessed February 16, 2021].

Perrone, A. (2019) "Trump Protests: Giant Model of President Sitting on Golden Toilet While Tweeting Appears in Central London," *Independent*, [online] June 4, Available from: www.independent.co.uk/news/uk/home-news/trump-protests-toilet-robot-tweeting-trafalgar-square-london-state-visit-a8943061.html [Accessed April 6, 2021].

Schanberg, S. (1984) "Donald Humbug," *New York Times*, February 7: A25.

Schwartz, D. (2018) "You or Your Dog Can Now Pee All over Trump Thanks to These Statues," *Vice*, [online] October 10, Available from: www.vice.com/en/article/kzjkkx/trump-pee-on-me-statues-new-york-dogs-vgtrn [Accessed June 6, 2021].

Smith, K. (2020) "Inside the Hillary Bubble," *National Review*, [online] January 28, Available from: www.nationalreview.com/2020/01/television-review-hillary-documentary-clinton-still-blaming-america-for-her-failures/ [Accessed June 16, 2021].

Taylor-Coleman, J. (2016) "The Dark Depths of Hatred for Hillary Clinton," *BBC*, [online] October 12, Available from: www.bbc.com/news/magazine/36992955 [Accessed June 6, 2021].

Tiffany, K. and Bareham, J. (2016) "11 Photos of NYC's Naked Trump Statue," *The Verge*, [online] August 18, Available from: www.theverge.com/2016/8/18/12538672/nude-donald-trump-statues-union-square-los-angeles-indecline [Accessed April 6, 2021].

Troy, G. (2016) "Understanding 'Clintipathy': A Pathological Hatred of the Clintons," *Time*, [online] October 30, Available from: http://time.com/4550665/why-people-hate-the-clintons/ [Accessed June 6, 2021].

Tyrell Jr, R., (1998) "The Continuing Crisis," *The American Spectator* 31(3): 8–9.

Ventura, M., Culliton, K., and Ness, J. (2016) "A Nude Trump Statue? That's 'Art,' Similar Clinton Statue? 'Obscene,'" *DNAinfo*, [online] October 18, Available from: www.dnainfo.com/new-york/20161018/battery-park-city/naked-donald-trump-hillary-clinton-statues-bowling-green-union-square-nyc/ [Accessed April 6, 2021].

Voegeli, W. (2016) "Hillary's Female Problems," *Claremont Review of Books*, [online] February 8, Available from: https://claremontreviewofbooks.com/digital/hillarys-female-problems/ [Accessed June 16, 2021].

Welch, B. (2016) "Why Do They Hate Hillary So Much? A Psychologist's View," *Huffington Post*, [online] November 3, Available from: www.huffpost.com/entry/why-do-they-hate-hillary-_b_12720840 [Accessed June 16, 2021].

Wicker, T. (1989) "In the Nation; Making Things Worse," *New York Times*, [online] May 2, Available from: www.nytimes.com/1989/05/02/opinion/in-the-nation-making-things-worse.html [Accessed June 25, 2021].

Williams, P.J. (2016) "Trump L'Oeil," *The Nation*, September 26–October 3: 10–11.

Womack, L. (2016) "Stop Pretending You Don't Know Why People Hate Hillary Clinton," *Huffington Post*, [online] September 26, Available from: www.huffpost.com/entry/stop-pretending-you-dont-_b_12191766 [Accessed June 16, 2021].

PART II

Racism, Exclusion, and Mnemonic Conflict

6

Building a Case for Citizenship: Countermemory Work among Deported Veterans

Sofya Aptekar

Tijuana, 2016. A middle-aged man with a buzz cut sits on a futon draped with crocheted blankets. Wearing a zipped up beige windbreaker, his bare knees hold up the stained card table. The man is bent over a paper intake form, his ballpoint pen tentatively poised mid-air, the fingers of the left hand carefully pressing the paper down. The form says "DEPORTED VETERANS" on top in large font. The window into this scene is the public Facebook page of the Deported Veterans Support House. Dominating the photograph is a large US flag hanging on the wall. In fact, there are at least five other US flags visible: a small flag attached to the card table, a flag in the background of a memorial flyer for a deceased deported veteran, a flag carried by a deported but still living veteran on a flyer for a Memorial Day action, a 13-fold flag on a metal bookshelf[1] – and one of the crocheted blankets is a US flag. Also visible are other flyers with helmet imagery and words like "banished veterans."

As he fills out the intake form with information about his military service and demographics, the man is enveloped in patriotic symbols of the United States that fill the modest space. If he becomes part of the deported veteran community, he will work with other deported veterans and their allies to re-create himself as a banished veteran, "honorably discharged, dishonorably deported." He will reconstruct his own biography to foreground his military service, reconfiguring his past to open up a future of return. And he will contribute to the shared countermemory project with which deported veterans establish their claims of belonging in the United States.

In this chapter, I discuss how US military veterans deported to Mexico work together to co-construct autobiographical memories to build a shared case for US citizenship and national belonging through military service. The countermemory they work on surfaces the existence of immigrants in the US military and establishes the connection between the US military, prison, and immigration systems amidst a dominant collective memory of war and the US military that excludes the deportee. I show the tensions and struggles between this shared and social autobiographical memory work and the dominant cultural schema through which veterans, immigrants, and deviance are commonly understood, as well as the challenges that deported veterans experience to their mnemonic authority. I draw on materials produced by deported veterans affiliated with the Deported Veterans Support Houses, as well as interviews and fieldwork.

How veterans get deported

To understand the deportation of US military veterans, we have to start with two basic facts. The first fact is that it is possible to enlist in the US military without having US citizenship and to serve without ever acquiring it. In 2008, the Department of Defense estimated that a third of immigrants serving in the US armed forces were not US citizens (Batalova, 2008). Eighteen percent of foreign-born US military veterans are estimated to lack US citizenship (Zong and Batalova, 2019). While there are special provisions for naturalization among military personnel, naturalization has not been easily accessible to many immigrant service members (Aptekar, 2023). The second fact is that until recently, there have not been any special provisions for veterans within the mass deportation apparatus in the United States, and even those checks or protections that have been instituted are exceedingly weak.[2]

The US government deports veterans of its own military the same way it deports immigrants who are not veterans. Particularly since legislative changes in the mid-1990s under the Clinton administration, non-citizens convicted of aggravated felonies are deported even if they are legal permanent residents.[3] Aggravated felony is a category of crime that exists for the purposes of adjudicating immigration cases and includes any crime punishable by a year or more, even if the immigrant was not actually sentenced to that (Golash-Boza, 2017). In a 2014 report, the Immigrant Legal Resource Center listed examples of offenses that have been found to be aggravated felonies:

- Misdemeanor theft of items of minimal value such as a $10 video game, $15 worth of baby clothes, or tire rims from an automobile.
- Writing a bad check for $1500 worth of construction supplies.
- The sale of $10 worth of marijuana or pointing out a suspected drug seller to a potential buyer.
- Allowing friends to use a car to commit a burglary.
- Pulling the hair of another during a fight over a boyfriend.[4]

Unlike in earlier eras of US history, judges no longer have discretion, making detention and deportation mandatory for non-citizens convicted of an aggravated felony (Golash-Boza, 2015). The number of immigrants deported grew after 2003, peaking under the Obama administration at over 400,000 people each year.[5] The Department of Homeland Security does not keep track of the number of deported veterans and estimates vary, ranging from 3000 to 30,000.[6] Moreover, although deported veterans qualify for naturalization based on their military service, an aggravated felony forecloses that possibility, as they are deemed to lack good moral character (Martinez, 2017). Caldwell (2019) reports that some veterans are deported based on convictions prior to their military service. In other words, these convictions did not disqualify them from serving in the military but were enough to get them deported.

The deportation of immigrant veterans takes place in the context of a racist system of criminalization and incarceration in the United States. Racial inequity pervades the criminal justice system, disproportionately targeting African Americans and Latinx people. It's important to keep in mind that fewer than three percent of defendants go to trial in the United States.[7] Whether or not they are guilty, people are pressured to plead guilty to avoid the risk of longer sentences were they to be found guilty in court. Having served in the US military – and sometimes even told that they were US citizens automatically – many immigrant veterans do not realize that pleading guilty will result in eventual deportation. The imbrication of the deportation regime with the criminal justice system results in gendered racial removal, with deportees being almost entirely men sent to Latin American and Caribbean countries (Golash-Boza and Hondagneu-Sotelo, 2013; Golash-Boza, 2015). Black and Latinx men are also heavily recruited by the US military, including through targeted Spanish-language marketing ploys, military charter schools concentrated in predominantly minority urban neighborhoods, and recruiters deployed to sell military service to youth facing few options due to poverty and racist criminalization (Mariscal, 2007).

Deported veterans in Mexico who are the focus of this chapter have been through the gears of the military, criminal justice, and immigration systems in the United States. They were recruited into the military as impoverished teens, struggled with substance abuse and poverty when they left the military, were convicted of crimes, imprisoned, transferred to immigration detention, and deported to Mexico. Their struggles in Mexico varied based on the presence of social networks and extended family they could count on for support, although all shared difficulty fitting in as US-raised Mexicans with accented or even rudimentary Spanish abilities amidst the stigma attached to deportees (Golash-Boza, 2015; Caldwell, 2019; Slack, 2019). Some were unhoused, ill, and dying. Others had rebuilt their lives and started new families. Their very existence challenges the hegemonic memory construction around military service and veterans, which tends to spotlight the US military in isolation from its thick connections to other institutions of US imperialism and oppression, such as prisons and borders.

The Deported Veteran Support Houses provide a much-needed social connection and hope for remedy, but also survival provisions such as food and temporary shelter for this extremely vulnerable population of deportees. The Support Houses originated in large part from the organizing and advocacy work of Hector Barajas, himself a deported veteran, and his supporters, in the mid-2010s.[8] There is also a chapter of Veterans for Peace in Tijuana, which engages in advocacy work with deported veterans, and there are complicated and overlapping spheres of relationships between the two groups. For analytical clarity and conciseness, I focus primarily on the Deported Veterans Support House network, since it has had more visibility in the media and political sphere, and whose specific framing of deported veterans' plight has been key in raising awareness and improving access to veteran benefits and even, in some cases, US citizenship. As I show, this framing does not engage with critiques of the military or war or challenge official definitions of military past.

Methods

I learned of deported veterans from a colleague who mentioned that when giving an academic talk in Tijuana on his deportation research, he was surprised to see a group of men at the back of the room who rose at the end of his presentation to unfurl a banner identifying themselves as deported US veterans. Although I had written a book about citizenship and naturalization and was familiar with the special provisions for naturalization for members of the military, I had been unaware that deported veterans existed. In this chapter, I draw on data collected as part of a larger project on immigrants serving in the US military (Aptekar, 2023). Although I focus on the ways that specifically deported veterans co-construct and use autobiographical memories to challenge official collective meanings of military service and the nation, my research on immigrants who served in the military and were *not* deported informs my analysis.

Since 2014 or so, I have been following deported veterans on social media, and collecting news stories, videos, and other media materials that had to do with deported veterans. Deported veterans in Mexico have produced a profusion of content, particularly on several group Facebook pages, which they have used as public-facing arena for making claims of deservingness through textual posts, photographs, artwork, and videos. This was not an entirely one-sided research process of collection and archiving. Through online interactions, I got to know Hector Barajas, a prominent organizer of deported veterans in Mexico and beyond. Hector stayed in my home in

New York when he came to the area to organize local families of military deportees, following his pardon and naturalization. I conducted in-depth semi-structured interviews with five Mexican American deported veterans between 2017 and 2020. Finally, I was able to visit the Deported Veterans Support House in Ciudad Juarez in the fall of 2019, meeting some of the veterans in person, spending time in the space they created, and sharing a meal and a tour of the city.

Constructing the banished veteran

Deported veterans collectively develop identities as veterans in exile. Veteran identity among those who have served in the US military is not a given. Some deported veterans had not strongly identified as veterans after their service. After all, dominant frames of veterans encompass both damage/danger and honor/deservingness, and some may shy away from being associated with veteran identity (Kleykamp and Hipes, 2015). Other deported veterans hid their veteran status after deportation because veterans are targeted for recruitment by cartels and otherwise stigmatized on the Mexican side of the US-Mexico borderlands (Slack, 2019). For example, one deported veteran I call Tadeo did not start building his veteran identity until he connected with other deported veterans a decade after being deported. When Tadeo left the military, he did not feel a strong veteran identity. Tadeo said that as a deportee, being a veteran was not something he thought about much. But years later, alongside other deported veterans, Tadeo began to construct his past as a veteran, feeling pride in his veteran identity:

> "I forgot all about the Marines for a while, all about the United States, I was, figured Mexico was my life. If I wanted to go anywhere, I was going Canada. Not the United States, I'd just erase it off the map. But I can't. Anyways, the Deported Veterans helped me along with this. I'm there. I'm back with my military friends. I'm back with them. Yes, I started wearing my dog tags again. And I proudly sport my t-shirts that say 'Deported Veterans.'"

Tadeo got a membership in an American Legion chapter in California, listing his parents' address. During our video call, he held up his dog tags and an issue of a veterans' magazine and talked about ordering military paraphernalia and dreaming of getting a set of his dress blues, the formal uniform of the Marine. Reconfiguring his past as a veteran opened up a different future for Tadeo, a future where return to the United States was a possibility.

Collecting and displaying materials, such as Tadeo's dog tags, T-shirts, magazines, patches, and uniforms, are key to rebuilding the veteran identity in exile. This is material evidence that deported veterans use to establish their claim on the US military as members of the warrior brotherhood, and through it, on belonging to the United States. As criminalized Latinx immigrant men, they need all the evidence they can gather to buttress their identities as veterans, while also distancing themselves from negative stereotypes of violent, damaged veterans. It is a delicate balancing act. Deported veterans use a range of materials as biographical signifiers to build community with each other and to project their identities north across the border. Their matching black T-shirts with a white silhouette of a Revolutionary-era soldier in a tricorner hat leaning on a barbed wire fence are the uniform that identifies them as banished veterans. Donning these T-shirts in formation, they are a battalion of banished veterans recreating the brotherhood they were supposed to have experienced in the military. The T-shirts, hats, patches, and uniforms are all tools in framing their deportation as an aberration. Thus, when Hector Barajas draped a large flag of the Army's airborne division over his tent when he lived in an encampment of unhoused deportees in Tijuana, it set him apart from other deportees, ostensibly more deserving of banishment than a US military veteran. Hector's use of the flag is suggestive of defensive othering, a type of identity work seen among members of disadvantaged and oppressed groups who try to differentiate themselves from other stigmatized people and attempt to claim membership in a more valued social group (Schwalbe et al, 2000). The display of veteran identity through material objects can be situational and is strategically collective. Some deportees project their veteran identity on US-facing social media and when spending time with other deported veterans. In other spheres of their lives, they de-emphasize veteran identity. Ricardo hid his past in the US military when he was first deported, both for safety and to avoid discrimination in employment. Once he started to organize with other deported veterans, Ricardo began to emphasize it on social media:

> "And in my sense, a lot of people on Facebook didn't know I was a veteran, and now I ... post things, Happy Veterans Day to me and to all my veterans and especially my deported veterans. And I'm not afraid because I'm kind of like at peace with it. I try to be careful with it as much as I can, but if you go to my profile, you'll see a bunch of deported veterans articles and stuff."

When Ricardo's high school teacher thanked him for his service on Facebook, the validation pleased Ricardo. A person Ricardo described as "a white guy" publicly recognizing Ricardo's veteran status is valuable because white US masculinity is inextricable from Americanness. Ricardo's claim on the United States as a Mexican American is much weaker in the context of white supremacy and conflation of Mexican Americans with foreign invasion, sexual deviance, and criminality (Chavez, 2013). The display of veteran identity is more effective when it is collective because it helps establish the reality of deported veterans – which continues to baffle US observers – and that is less likely to be doubted when faced with groups of deportees performing it. It is also done in cooperation with US-based veterans and allies, who supply deported veterans with material needed for their identity work, such as uniforms and military paraphernalia. Deported veterans work to build connections with other veterans and veteran organizations in the United States, but the latter sometimes dismiss their bids for shared identity because of the stain of criminality that marks deported veterans.

Deported veterans develop and share stories of their recruitment and military service, all to make a case that they deserve to return, belong, and be claimed by the United States. Two types of materials are especially important in connecting past military service to deportee present: certificates of honorable discharge from the military and photographs of deportees as service members. Proof of honorable discharge supports the narratives of respectability and lawfulness that deported veterans use to offset being marked as criminalized. In fact, deported veterans police each other for stolen valor, meaning that they attempt to draw boundaries about who gets to claim the status of deported veteran, excluding not only those who completely make up military service but also those who have been dishonorably discharged or did not finish basic training. The slogan "honorably discharged, dishonorably deported" performs the boundary work of defensive othering by reinforcing the racist structures of the US military, since service members of color are more likely to be charged in military justice proceedings and thus more likely to be dishonorably discharged (Schwalbe et al, 2000; Burk and Espinoza, 2012).

Deported veterans extensively use photographs of themselves as service members. Mostly formal portraits in uniforms, usually made at the completion of basic training, or sometimes informal snapshots taken during military service, the photographs are dramatic claims on US citizenship. Veterans pose holding these photographs of their adolescent incarnations with ageing hands, pressing them against bodies injured by military and prison labor and deportee life. They collate them into wall posters and large banners that they hold up during ceremonies or attach to the border wall. They post them on social media. Significantly, the pictures of those who served in a theatre of war are marked "combat veteran" rather than just "veteran," marking internal hierarchies of deservingness within the group.

Attached to one such photograph on the Deported Veteran Support House Facebook page is a note from Steven Pierre St. Louise, deported to Haiti:

"This picture was taken at NTC [National Training Center] at boot-camp post-graduation!!! This is proof that I am like many others more

American than 'APPLE PIE' proof enough to make America great again cause we were taught to leave no men behind 'today we are forgotten and forsake not just left behind' [sic]."

In the photograph, St. Louise is a young sailor in a dress uniform posed in front of the US flag, white Dixie cup hat contrasting with his brown skin. St. Louise uses the photograph to prove the strength of his claim on belonging and to critique the hypocrisy of the military ethos of "no man left behind."

Memory work is not simply the collection and display of photographs, certificates, patches, ribbons, uniforms, and flags, it is also an embodied construction of the past, conducted in the everyday and in special ceremonies. When deported veterans stand in formation, march, and salute, mnemonics of the body link the present to the past. They document these shared and learned practices of military discipline of the body to communicate with the media, US politicians, and the public (Connerton, 1989). Many decades after their separation from the military, deported veterans squeeze their ageing bodies into military uniforms when they have them, or wear hats, deported veteran T-shirts, and camouflage gear. Hector Barajas dons the maroon beret of the airborne division and shines his army boots, even though wearing them cuts off the circulation to his feet.

US holidays like Memorial Day and Veteran's Day, along with the tragically too frequent deaths of deported veterans, are ceremonial occasions during which embodied and collective memory work takes place. Deaths of deported veterans mark their homecoming, as their bodies – banned from the United States during life – can be buried in US military cemeteries. When 64-year-old Vietnam veteran Gonzalo Chaidez died of tuberculosis in 2015,[9] the deported veteran community gathered in a somber ceremony to perform such a homecoming and send him off. Dressed in their best clothes – polos and jeans, ill-fitting suit jackets, and not a few military uniforms – they carefully performed the 13-step flag folding ceremony, passing the flag to each other and saluting. They drove the small wooden box bearing Chaidez's cremated remains in a makeshift altar inside a truck, then constructed an altar against the border wall at Friendship Park in Tijuana. Flanked by flowers and small flags, the altar featured a photograph of Chaidez holding the folded flag at the border wall in another memorial ceremony. On the other side of the border wall, an Army honor guard composed of middle-aged men in camouflage slowly folded another flag, accompanied by taps, and presented it to Chaidez's elderly mother. The message of the numerous photographs and montages from Chaidez's funeral shared on social media was underscored by the captions: "Gonzalo Chaidez US Army Presente! ... Bring all deported US veterans home! Alive[,] not under these circumstances[.] If we are allowed to be buried as American, we should be allowed to live with our families as Americans."

While some deported veterans had not participated in Veterans Day events when they lived in the United States, now Veterans Day offered them a venue for collectively constructing their shared history as veterans. When performed on the Mexican side of the US-Mexico border, presentations of colors, moments of silence, marching, and salutes cement the connection between their years in the US military and their present identities as veterans. Between these lie decades of life where the biographical thread of military service may have been hardly prominent or was lost entirely. The emphasis on the US flag is not only a tool in the presentation of patriotism needed to bolster their claims as veterans, but a crucial symbol for them as immigrants and deportees. The abundance of US flags in deported veteran space and on their bodies acts an armor for them as immigrants who have been expelled from the United States. Although they often distinguish themselves from the mainstream immigrant rights movement, the way deported veterans use flags is in some ways similar to the use of US flags in the mass immigrant demonstrations that took over US cities in 2006: immigrants literally wrapped themselves in US flags as a claim to belonging and attempt at self-protection from the state (Bauder, 2006). The personal narratives of the past contribute to a collective narrative of honor, belonging, and unjust exile that also helps deported veterans cope and adjust to their deportation.

So far, I have focused mostly on the public-facing work of deported veterans to construct themselves as veterans deserving of returning home. From interviews with deported veterans and spending time in one of the support houses, I was able to learn about memory work that is more internally oriented. I observed deported veterans share their memories of military service over a restaurant meal in Ciudad Juarez. The men traded stories of bodily injury. Each contributed examples that added to a narrative of warrior masculinity both at odds with their poor physical state at the time of the conversation, and completely in line with it, since the poor physical state stemmed from the injuries they sustained in the military. Laughing at memories of their youth, they talked about dramatic falls, walking on broken ankles, ignoring fractured ribs, long periods of lost consciousness. All agreed that injuries in the military were routine and service members were expected not to ask for medical care. On other occasions, deported veterans revealed drug use promoted by the military to enhance performance, exposure to poisonous chemicals, and other ways in which the military has routinely subjected the bodies of service members to harm (Hamilton, 2016; Kieran, 2019; Lutz and Mazzarino, 2019). The memories of this harm and injury resided in deported veterans' bodies and connected their pasts as young recruits to their middle-aged and elderly present, in which they fought to access medical care and disability pay.

There was at most a muted note of critique in these shared memories of injuries: not only does victimhood undermine warrior masculinity, but deported veterans are constrained in their capacity to critique the institution central to their claims to recognition and belonging. They strategically background their experiences of violence, abuse, and racism in the military to organize their memories towards a strategic end. That they dial down critiques of the military in their public presentation does not mean that they do not have a sharp analysis of what happened to them. These veterans' adversary is the government that they served. As Jack put it: "The same system that I vowed to protect and die for, is the same system that I got screwed in." Or Ricardo: "I'm angry at the government for not protecting us." One of my interviewees confided that some deported veterans want to sue the US government. The tensions of co-constructing and sharing deported veteran memories are challenging. The anger at the US government for discarding them is at odds with the carefully constructed image of the past where upstanding and patriotic military service members risk their lives for love of country. The experience of having been a disposable military worker and now a disposed-of veteran is also collective, and it is a countermemory that resides below the patriotic surface of deported veterans' memory work. The youthful military portraits that deported veterans use so heavily paper over the contentious memories that threaten to burst forth, starting with recollections of exploitative military labor, civilian lives of racialized and criminalized precarity in the United States, and finally the violent rupture of incarceration and deportation.

Yet another contradictory aspect of autobiographical memory that deported veterans collectively suppress involves the memories of the lives they have built after deportation. Without a doubt difficult, these lives are not unremittingly painful, as some deported veterans have found forms of family, community, and belonging. Some do not actually want to return to live in the US, they just want to be able to go back and forth and to be recognized. To admit this in the ceremonial production of veteran identity, however, would dramatically disrupt the story of good soldiers unfairly banished from the American Dream.

Mnemonic tensions

Deported veterans draw on autobiographical memories to remember a past that foregrounds their honorable military service, establishing them as a group with a legitimate grievance deserving of redress. The work of foregrounding and backgrounding memories is necessary for deported veterans' construction of countermemory that resists their forgetting and exclusion from dominant narratives of military service in the United States. As DeGloma (2015) shows, personal narratives are a tool in the coordination of autobiographical and collective memory in contested cultural spheres. The mnemonic authority of deported veterans – their very ability to be recognized as authorities in telling their stories – is challenged amidst a complex intersection of schema around veterans, immigrants, and criminality. First, the very existence of deported veterans provokes disbelief, which can quickly turn into challenges to the reality of their veteran status. Second, deported veterans face contestation over the nature of their past, including their military service, their failure to get US citizenship, and their criminality. Third, even given acceptance of deported veterans' military service, there are challenges to the primacy of veteran histories over histories of racialized immigrant criminality.[10]

As I mentioned, many people are surprised to learn of the existence of deported US veterans. Veterans symbolize Americanness. Veterans are honored and respected. The US *owes* veterans. How can they be deported? Deportation is for aliens, illegals, and criminals. It is for immigrants who are perpetually in relationship of debt to the United States (Park, 2011). Yet, here are social media and news stories that present deported veterans as a real phenomenon. They are surrounded by military paraphernalia and US flags. They hold up certificates that prove their military service. At the very basic level, deported veterans' mnemonic authority is challenged by doubts about their existence. It is easy to accept images of Latinx men deported – even easier when they are covered with tattoos and exhibit a working-class habitus. Thus, the doubts are not that they are deported, but that they are real veterans. Deported veterans know this, and that's why they are continuously proving that they are veterans while policing within their group for anyone with weak claims to being a veteran.

Yet the mnemonic tension reaches beyond questions about the very existence of the past because there is a dark underside to the honored veteran narrative. Particularly in the era of the all-volunteer military, Americans owe those who join the military. They owe them for ostensibly protecting the American way of life, but also for bearing the costs of imperial labor in their minds and bodies. Even as they are celebrated at football games, parades, and school assemblies, the veteran is also a feared figure, unsafely containing the imperial damage, which at any point may erupt in violence, dysfunction, and profound maladjustment (Wool, 2015).[11] Thus the emphasis on veteran identity triggers this complex coexistence of honor and stigma, and makes for a narrative minefield when it comes to reporting damage and disability in trying to get veterans' benefits. Such reports, particularly of trauma and substance abuse, evoke the feared, damaged veteran, even as they may evoke pity and get them closer to the benefits to which they are entitled.

Moreover, deported veterans remember their military service in the borderlands of the United States and Mexico, where the meanings and memories connected to the military are even more complex. Itself a highly militarized zone, the US-Mexico border hosts personnel and equipment handed down from US imperial projects overseas, as well as personnel from multiple divisions of the US military. As Correa and Thomas (2019) argue, the militarization of the border is part of a military-police assemblage spurred on by the War on Drugs and evident in the urban neighborhoods of color across the United States where youth are pushed into military service. In the borderlands, narratives of the US military are imbricated more explicitly with the violent construction and enforcement of the settler colonial borders of the United States. Perhaps more so than in other US locations, the borderlands disrupt US colonial aphasia, illuminating the role of the US military as an imperial force (Stoler, 2016). At the same time, US service members participate in human and drug trafficking across the border[12] and Mexican drug cartels view veteran deportees as desirable low-level workers (Caldwell, 2019; Slack, 2019). It is for these multiple reasons that some deported veterans deemphasize their military service in that context. The Mexican military's own troubled relationship with the drug cartels casts another layer of stigma, violence, and power over the image of the soldier (Correa-Cabrera, 2017). Deported veterans in Mexico's borderlands with the United States are navigating a minefield of transnational meanings, highlighting the need to pay attention to where memories are constructed, by whom, for whom, and against what.

The second area of mnemonic tensions is over the nature of deported veterans' past. What kind of service members were these people who enlisted without US citizenship? Why didn't they get US citizenship? These very questions are regularly broached in the comments on deported veteran news stories and social media, casting doubt on the character of deported veterans as veterans and patriots. To combat these aspersions, deported veterans highlight the experience of combat when they are able to prove it, even as that risks invoking the specter of damage and violence. But many service members never see combat, and this is true of deported veterans as well. Another mnemonic strategy, then, is to tell the story of enlistment and service in a way that emphasizes commitment and patriotism. So deported veterans insist that if given a do over, they would enlist again. Even when they tell stories of damage they sustained in the military, the stories end with this insistence that they would repeat their military service if they could.

The mnemonic tensions over citizenship and naturalization point to the steep costs of citizenship and the few narrow options apportioned to deserving immigrants in the United States. As critical refugee scholars such as Espiritu (2014) and Tang (2015) show, to be a refugee is to be the ultimate victim onto whom the imperial power grafts a set of memories and meanings legitimating empire and redeeming military defeat. With deported veterans, we encounter in many ways the opposite but equally narrow imperial pathways: to be deserving of reinstatement into the US nation means participation in violence, placing oneself near death in pursuit of murder in the service of empire. In both cases, it is a militarized field that frames the question of citizenship in terms of what one must do for the US empire in order to be admitted. Deported veterans face the high bar of proving their worth as the ultimate soldiers of empire. Like all immigrants, they have to demonstrate their utmost loyalty and deference to the state and its rules, even when the rules are set up to exclude them.

Avowing their commitment to the US military and the United States itself is necessary to counteract suspicions of deported veterans as non-citizen immigrants, who are always already suspect in their motivations to enlist. Not getting US citizenship then works at cross purposes. On the one hand, deported veterans clearly did not enlist in the US military for the shortcut to US citizenship that it theoretically provides. Yet if they were truly patriotic, why did they not get it during or after their service? Some deported veterans address this area of biographical tension by recounting the false promises made to them about automatic US citizenship upon enlistment.[13] Or, they attempt to describe the very real obstacles to naturalization faced by immigrants in the US and exacerbated by the strictures of military service (Aptekar, 2023). The latter set of memories is less likely to resonate with those outside the immigrant advocacy world: "why didn't they just become a citizen?" is a common trope in the anti-immigrant rhetoric. Not becoming a US citizen casts deported veterans – specifically Latinx men already assumed to be criminal (Cacho, 2012) – with the mass of criminalized and deportable immigrants. That some have histories of substance use disorder make this even more so, even when veterans trace their substance issues to their military service. In fact, memories of the military's neglect and abuse of service members undermine claims to belonging through veteran status, which are predicated on the integrity of the institution of the military itself. Deported veterans tread a narrow path in remembering their failure to naturalize while upholding the military and immigration systems that oppress them.

Finally, even when critics accept that deported veterans really did serve in the military honorably and patriotically, and do not fault them for not getting US citizenship, they may still question the relevance of their past. Does it really matter that these deportees served in the military? After all, they are criminals. For instance, when reporters asked him to comment on the plight of deported veterans, House of Representatives minority leader Kevin McCarthy of California District 23 said the following:

> "I have long fought for quality benefits for veterans who have bravely served our country, and believe that these benefits are just one way for our nation to pay its respects to our heroes. However, as is to be expected of all living in the U.S., respect must also be paid to the rule of law, by veterans and non-veterans alike."[14]

For McCarthy and many others, deported veterans' criminality trumps being a veteran. The nation pays its respects to heroes, not criminals. Deported veterans are keenly aware of the pall cast by criminality on their chances of reversing their deportations. Aside from connecting criminality to military service via damage sustained or addictions developed, deported veterans claim deservingness based on the relative seriousness of their criminal convictions. As is common in the criminal justice system reform movements, which make distinctions between those deserving of reforms (drug possession) and those who are not (rapists),[15] deported veterans like Ricardo draw distinctions between types of crimes: "If you see, most of us are not violent. Most of us are first time offenders. Most of us are not career criminals." Ricardo's response to critics like McCarthy is to double down on the primacy of veteran status: "Any other soldier, he would have done his time, gone home. VA clinic, a rehabilitation program if he was like an addict or something. A second chance, you know. So why not us." But deported veterans are not like "any other soldiers." They are non-citizens who are deportable.

Foregrounding veteran identity is a complex process for deported veterans as a group confronting the dominant construction of the veteran. It is also the case that individuals struggle over which aspects of their autobiographical pasts to highlight and which to downplay or ignore, especially when different aspects of their pasts have conflicting impact on present identity. Remembering the veteran above all else subjugates other memory strands. This was poignantly explained by Hector:

> "The one [identity] that I focus because of the work that I do is just veteran, veteran, veteran. <laughs> You know, you have to use certain things to your advantage and you know how to reach people. I think I kind of, it's kind of been my role, not my character, no. But I have yet to find an identity. Especially this endeavor that I am going on [as a US citizen]. A new man … Before, it was like this big Mexican and I got tattoos on my arms that say Mexico. And I guess I have these different identities over the years, from being a smart kid to being a lost kid <laughs>, deported, soldier, addict, homeless, lots of different things. American. That's one of the identities that are there, that I can relate to, that I think about."

Pardoned by the California governor, Hector is one of the few deported veterans who was able to acquire US citizenship. His new standpoint allows him to step back from "just veteran, veteran, veteran" and reflect on all the other memories that constitute his life and that might distract or detract from the push to claim deservingness and recognition.

The interpretative process

Hector's admission of personal mnemonic tensions is indicative of the insight provided by triangulating multiple sources of data and methodology.

Particularly revealing are the points of disjuncture between the public-facing narratives of the deported veterans, which I gathered through analysis of their social media and news stories, and what they revealed in interviews. It is not simply that deported veterans told me their *true* memories in interviews, ones they suppressed in public. All memory is constructed memory and deported veterans engage in the social process of remembering while responding to their current needs (Halbwachs, 1992). Talking to me was part of the work of spreading awareness of deported veterans' plight and an opportunity for public-facing memory construction. Yet, these interviews, leisurely paced, confidential, and largely open-ended, occasioned the surfacing of mnemonic tensions.

I do not take credit for creating a space in which deported veterans could go beyond practiced stories. Rather, the fact that they shared the messy complexity of their memories is a data point in itself. I think it reveals that the pressure of constructing the patriotic veteran memory is significant, and one welcomes an opportunity for relief from the pressure. Perhaps talking to me – a white woman professor from a lesser-known university who has no military history or affiliation but who introduced herself as an immigrant – lowered the stakes of the conversation just enough. Were I a reporter, a political staffer, an Ivy League professor, or an immigration attorney, I suspect I would have heard less mnemonic tension. It did also help that I had interviewed dozens of immigrant veterans who were not deported. The questions I asked drew on what I learned from those other interviews, including the unglamorous role of the poverty draft among criminalized youth of color and the logistical difficulties of getting citizenship through the military. The interviews progressed in chronological order through the participants' life stories. For the most part, I asked participants to tell me their stories "starting from the beginning," and I used short prompts to keep the stories going, reacting empathetically. I referred to markers dropped by participants (for example, "there were things here and there"), encouraging them to expand (Weiss, 1995). I asked participants about identifying as a veteran, what it felt like to live in Mexico, and the meaning of US citizenship to them, although some brought these topics up without my prompting.

By merely existing, deported veterans explode many US cultural schemes around veterans and the military. Their memories are countermemories to the autobiographical frameworks which are rooted in the dominant histories of the US military and the nation. These autobiographical threats and collective tensions are resolved by expelling them from the veteran brotherhood into the category of racialized immigrant criminality. But deported veterans also wreck the narratives of many migration scholars and military sociologists who conceptualize military service as a mechanism of upward social mobility for immigrants (Barry, 2013; Chen, 2020; Strader, Lundquist, and Dominguez-Villegas, 2021). For these immigrants certainly did not experience upward mobility because of their military service. Their lives can hardly support assimilationist theories and challenge narrow analyses that quantify immigrant contributions and immigrant integration into systems of oppression. My recognition of the social location of deported veterans at the intersection of US imperialism, the US immigration system, and the prison-industrial complex shaped my interpretations of the mnemonic tensions that surround them.

Despite my analytical framework and being a critic of the US military, I did and do experience the pull of the deservingness narratives produced by the deported veterans. Aware of my own positionality as a far more privileged type of immigrant, I have wanted to affirm and amplify deported veterans' mnemonic claims. Bracketing my concerns about the limitations of the tactics and the moral claims that underlie them, I have done my small share of disseminating that particular version of their memories as veterans through campus events, talks, and my own social media. Like other allies, I have amplified the claims of these immigrants to deservingness as veterans, even when it was done at the expense of other immigrants, other criminalized people, and the victims of US imperial aggressions. Even as I reject the deportation of people regardless of immigration or veteran status, their criminal convictions – and, most importantly, the harm they caused other people – I have found myself echoing deported veterans' arguments about the relative harmlessness of their crimes and their merit as veterans. I have even done that in this chapter when listing the shockingly not aggravated examples of what might constitute an aggravated felony. In doing so, I, too, risk advocating solutions that absolve systems of oppression in favor of neoliberal remedies.

Who am I to feel frustrated at the organizing choices of a multiply-marginalized group like the deported veterans? I largely do what they ask of their allies: donate and spread the word. And yet I want to raise these questions: *What would happen were the deported veterans to weave together and release their countermemories publicly? Would they find common cause with non-veterans that the US deports, including those who have also spent time in US prisons? Would their struggle resonate with the freedom fighters and abolitionists inside and outside US prisons and detention centers? Would they call for open borders, for decolonization of indigenous lands? Would they participate or even lead the movement against military recruitment in communities of color and against US militarism and empire across the globe?* While offering these questions, I continue to support the claims made by deported veterans and sit with the strategic contradictions and inconsistencies of their organizing, even as I support the claims of those pushed to the edge of deservingness by these claims to belonging and citizenship. To do otherwise would be playing a different kind of deservingness game. I also recognize my own complicity as a US citizen in the violence and destruction perpetrated by the US military, as well as the way my own immigrant story contributes to the harmful ideology of the nation of immigrants (Dunbar-Ortiz, 2021). Deported veterans struggle with how to present themselves to those with power to bring them home, and it is a struggle to describe and analyze their memory work.

Conclusion

The possibilities that my questions raise are contained in the memories of deported veterans and the harm they continue to experience at the crux of multiple systems of violence and oppression. The mnemonic tensions that arise when deported veterans remember US military service in the sociohistorical location of the US-Mexico borderlands complicate their strategic attempts to conform to the hegemonic neoliberal script for the marginalized and prove their deservingness to belong in ways that preserve the systems that oppress them. They channel their shared autobiographical memory work into narratives that resonate with the public and policy makers in the context of immigrant dehumanization, white supremacy, and entrenched militarism. These narratives struggle with the dual frames of veterans as violent/damaged and heroic/victims as they construct exceptionality: deported veterans as better than other immigrants and more deserving of sympathy than non-veteran felons – and even more victimized than US born veterans.

The inclusion of a countermemory project of deported veterans in this volume contributes to collective memory scholarship not only through its somewhat unusual research site, but through its analysis of the ways in which the transborder context influences and complicates remembering. It highlights the struggle of banished veterans to survive deportation and remember their way back to the United States while navigating a minefield of what Lisa Yoneyama (2016) calls "complicit amnesia" endemic to imperial violence and war. In this analysis, it is imperative to center the US military as a transborder force connected to multiple other institutions of violence and oppression, which in itself requires a commitment to surfacing and engaging the countermemories of the US military and US empire against the strong pull of amnesia.

The case of the deported veterans demonstrates the rich possibilities of incorporating investigations of memories and countermemories into migration research. We can see this focus on mnemonic tensions in the research of critical scholars such as Espiritu (2014), who has written on memories and countermemories of the Vietnam War and Vietnamese refugees to the United States. Attention to memory in refugee research is likely more obvious because of the explicit mnemonic labors of asylees and refugees in constructing memories for their legal cases. But it is no less relevant to broader immigration topics, including surfacing the memories and countermemories of why people migrate and analyzing the tensions that are too often overwritten by simplified migration narratives of the American Dream. How are immigrant memories weaponized in the United States in the service of the settler colonial project, white supremacy, and capitalist exploitation? What kind of memory work happens within the different strands of the migrant justice movement? Addressing the issue of memory deepens our explorations of the political, social, and moral significance of migration and borders. With its focus on war, violence, and genocide, collective memory scholarship provides some intriguing frameworks and avenues of questioning for migration scholars who study cultures of migration, migrant collective organizing, and immigrant narratives, particularly when it engages transnational processes.

More broadly, for scholars of memory, my approach underscores the analytical rewards of studying how people use their personal memories to engage with and challenge official definitions and categories. Moving between levels of analysis from the autobiographical to social and organizational to the level of national narratives of patriotism and citizenship reveals the ways in which individual memory work done in social contexts reinforces dominant mnemonic constructs, even as it provides glimpses into tensions and opens possibilities of change. This necessitates drawing on multiple forms of data and being attuned to the sometimes-subtle differences in what they reveal, including silences. Too often reserved for the study of youth and social movements, social media in the third decade of the 21st century is a rich research site for studying contentious memory, providing audiovisual material and opportunities to observe digitally mediated social interaction. Finally, in the words of Kristin Luker (2008), we are fish studying water, which means that it is difficult to overstate the significance of self-reflexivity for researchers attempting to understand memory work of others even as we continuously engage in constructing ourselves with integrity and authenticity.

Notes

[1] A 13-fold flag is a ceremonious flag given to survivors of a deceased veteran (www.legion.org/flag/folding).

[2] However, since 2004, ICE agents (both in Enforcement and Removal Operations and in Homeland Security Investigation units) operate under policies that require them to conduct additional evaluations and consult managers in cases involving deportable veterans when issuing Notices to Appear (charging documents). A 2019 GAO report found serious gaps in ICE's implementation of its own policies. However, Garcia (2017) reported several examples of ICE agents referring to their own veteran status when letting immigrant veterans go instead of arresting them. In all these examples, other ICE agents eventually came to arrest the veterans. (US Government Accountability Office (2019) *Immigration Enforcement: Actions Needed to Better Handle, Identify, and Track Cases Involving Veterans*, June 2019, www.gao.gov/assets/gao-19-416.pdf.)

[3] Golash-Boza, 2015; Texas Civil Rights Project. 2018. Land of The Free, No Home to the Brave: A Report on the Social, Economic, and Moral Cost of Deporting Veterans.

4. Immigrant Legal Resource Center. Aggravated Felony Factsheet. www.ilrc.org/sites/default/files/resources/ijn-aggravated-felony-factsheet.pdf
5. Gramlich, 2020. www.pewresearch.org/fact-tank/2020/03/02/how-border-apprehensions-ice-arrests-and-deportations-have-changed-under-trump/
6. Rivas, 2013. https://splinternews.com/it-s-veterans-day-and-u-s-veterans-are-getting-deporte-1793840071
7. National Association of Criminal Defense Lawyers. 2018. www.nacdl.org/Document/TrialPenaltySixthAmendmentRighttoTrialNearExtinct
8. Kao, Joanna. 2014. "Deported Vets: Life in 'The Bunker.'" *Al Jazeera America*. http://projects.aljazeera.com/2014/deported-veterans/
9. www.youtube.com/watch?v=dW4CiPzBgXw
10. These mnemonic conflicts are congruent to the typology outlined by DeGloma (2015).
11. Zoë Wool describes this as "the pathologizing monster-out-of-place soldier figure of many PTSD-tinged news stories about soldiers' rocky homecomings" (2015: p 151).
12. Watson, Julie. 2019. "Smugglers Offer Cash to Troops, Others to Drive Migrants." *AP*. https://apnews.com/article/47c9799c15e64e64848cff1a7dca92be
13. Texas Civil Rights Project. 2018.
14. www.bakersfield.com/columnists/jose-gaspar/jose-gaspar-deported-veterans-still-fighting-to-come-back-to-the-place-they-call-home/article_8fb1cd8a-02cb-11ec-b2b0-6f354e8b8b95.html
15. Jones, Alexi. 2020. "Reports without Results: Why States Should Stop Excluding Violent Offenses from Criminal Justice Reforms." Prison Policy Initiative. www.prisonpolicy.org/reports/violence.html

References

Aptekar, S. (2023) *Green Card Soldier: Between Model Immigrant and Security Threat*, Cambridge, MA: Massachusetts Institute of Technology Press.

Barry, C. (2013) *New Americans in Our Nation's Military: A Proud Tradition and Hopeful Future*, Washington, DC: Center for American Progress.

Batalova, J. (2008) *Immigrants in the US Armed Forces*, Washington, DC: Migration Policy Institute.

Bauder, H. (2006) "And the Flag Waved on: Immigrants Protest, Geographers Meet in Chicago," *Environment and Planning A: Economy and Space* 38(6): 1001–1004.

Burk, J. and Espinoza, E. (2012) "Race Relations within the US Military," *Annual Review of Sociology* 38(1): 401–422.

Cacho, L.M. (2012) *Social Death: Racialized Rightlessness and the Criminalization of the Unprotected*, New York: NYU Press.

Caldwell, B.C. (2019) *Deported Americans: Life after Deportation to Mexico*, Durham, NC: Duke University Press.

Chavez, L. (2013) *The Latino Threat: Constructing Immigrants, Citizens, and the Nation*, Stanford, CA: Stanford University Press.

Chen, M.H. (2020) *Pursuing Citizenship in the Enforcement Era*, Stanford, CA: Stanford University Press.

Connerton, P. (1989) *How Societies Remember*, Cambridge: Cambridge University Press.
Correa, J. and Thomas, J.M. (2019) "From the Border to the Core: A Thickening Military-Police Assemblage," *Critical Sociology* 45(7–8): 1133–1147.
Correa-Cabrera, G. (2017) *Los Zetas Inc.: Criminal Corporations, Energy, and Civil War in Mexico*, Austin, TX: University of Texas Press.
DeGloma, T. (2015) "The Strategies of Mnemonic Battle: On the Alignment of Autobiographical and Collective Memories in Conflicts over the Past," *American Journal of Cultural Sociology* 3: 156–190.
Dunbar-Ortiz, R. (2021) *Not a Nation of Immigrants: Settler Colonialism, White Supremacy, and a History of Erasure and Exclusion*, Boston, MA: Beacon Press.
Espiritu, Y.L. (2014) *Body Counts: The Vietnam War and Militarized Refugees*, Berkeley, CA: University of California Press.
Garcia, J.M. (2017) *Without a Country: The Untold Story of America's Deported Veterans*. New York: Hot Books.
Golash-Boza, T.M. (2015) *Deported: Immigrant Policing, Disposable Labor and Global Capitalism,* New York: NYU Press.
Golash-Boza, T.M. (2017) "Structural Racism, Criminalization, and Pathways to Deportation for Dominican and Jamaican Men in the United States," *Social Justice* 44(2–3): 137–162.
Golash-Boza, T.M. and Hondagneu-Sotelo, P. (2013) "Latino Immigrant Men and the Deportation Crisis: A Gendered Racial Removal Program," *Latino Studies* 11(3): 271–292.
Gramlich, J. (2020) "How Border Apprehensions, ICE Arrests and Deportations Have Changed under Trump," Pew Research Center, [online] March 2, Available from: www.pewresearch.org/fact-tank/2020/03/02/how-border-apprehensions-ice-arrests-and-deportations-have-changed-under-trump/ [Accessed August 7, 2022].
Halbwachs, M. (1992) *On Collective Memory*, Chicago, IL: University of Chicago Press.
Hamilton, J.W. (2016) "Contamination at US Military Bases: Profiles and Responses," *Stanford Environmental Law Journal* 35(2): 223–249.
Jones, A. (2020) "Reports without Results: Why States Should Stop Excluding Violent Offenses from Criminal Justice Reforms," Prison Policy Initiative, [online] April 7, Available from: www.prisonpolicy.org/blog/2020/04/07/violence-report/ [Accessed August 7, 2022].
Kao, J.S. (2014) "Deported Vets: Life in the 'Bunker,'" Al Jazeera, [online] September 26, Available from: http://projects.aljazeera.com/2014/deported-veterans/ [Accessed August 7, 2022].
Kieran, D. (2019) *Signature Wounds: The Untold Story of the Military's Mental Health Crisis*, New York: NYU Press.
Kleykamp, M. and Hipes, C. (2015) "Coverage of Veterans of the Wars in Iraq and Afghanistan in the US Media," *Sociological Forum* 30(2): 348–368.

Luker, K. (2008) *Salsa Dancing into the Social Sciences: Research in an Age of Info-glut*, Cambridge, MA: Harvard University Press.

Lutz, C. and Mazzarino, A. (2019) *War and Health: The Medical Consequences of the Wars in Iraq and Afghanistan*, New York: NYU Press.

Mariscal, J. (2007) "Immigration and Military Enlistment: The Pentagon's Push for the Dream Act Heats Up," *Latino Studies* 5: 358–363.

Martinez, A. (2017) "Veterans Banished: The Fight to Bring Them Home," *The Scholar: St. Mary's Law Review on Race and Social Justice* 19(3): 321–360.

Park, L.S.-H. (2011) *Entitled to Nothing: The Struggle for Immigrant Health Care in the Age of Welfare Reform*, New York: NYU Press.

Rivas, J. (2013) "It's Veterans Day and US Veterans Are Getting Deported," *Splinter*, [online] November 11, Available from https://splinternews.com/it-s-veterans-day-and-u-s-veterans-are-getting-deporte-1793840071 [Accessed August 7, 2022].

Schwalbe, M., Godwin, S., Holden, D., Schrock, D., Thompson, S., and Wolkomir, M. (2000) "Generic Processes in the Reproduction of Inequality: An Interactionist Analysis," *Social Forces* 79(2): 419–452.

Slack, J. (2019) *Deported to Death: How Drug Violence Is Changing Migration on the US–Mexico Border*, Berkeley, CA: University of California Press.

Stoler, A.L. (2016) *Duress: Imperial Durabilities in Our Times*, Durham, NC: Duke University Press.

Strader, E., Lundquist, J., and Dominguez-Villegas, R. (2021) "Warriors Wanted: The Performance of Immigrants in the US Army," *International Migration Review* 55(2): 382–401.

Tang, E. (2015) *Unsettled: Cambodian Refugees in the New York City Hyperghetto*, Philadelphia, PA: Temple University Press.

Watson, J. (2019) "Smugglers Offer Cash to Troops, Others to Drive Immigrants," Associated Press, [online] July 26, Available from: https://apnews.com/article/47c9799c15e64e64848cff1a7dca92be [Accessed August 7, 2022].

Weiss, R.S. (1995) *Learning from Strangers: The Art and Method of Qualitative Interview Studies*, Riverside, CA: Free Press.

Wool, Z.H. (2015) *After War: The Weight of Life at Walter Reed*, Durham, NC: Duke University Press.

Yoneyama, L. (2016) *Cold War Ruins: Transpacific Critique of American Justice and Japanese War Crimes*, Durham, NC: Duke University Press.

Zong, J. and Batalova, J. (2019) "Immigrants from New Origin Countries in the United States," Migration Policy Institute, [online] January 17, Available from: www.migrationpolicy.org/article/immigrants-new-origin-countries-united-states-2017#NaturalizationPathways [Accessed November 16, 2021].

7

Commemorations as Transformative Events: Collective Memory, Temporality, and Social Change

Claire Whitlinger

In the late 2000s, contemporary observers were quick to identify Philadelphia, Mississippi, as ground zero of a nascent memory movement, a notable development given the city's dubious racial history. The community, situated in the state's east-central region, was notorious as the site of the 1964 "Mississippi Burning" murders of three civil rights workers – James Chaney, Andrew Goodman, and Michael Schwerner – and had long maintained a reputation as a "strange, tight, little town" for its citizens' silence, denial, and obstruction of justice in the case (Nevin, 1964). For decades, travelers avoided the city and its surrounding county, Neshoba, out of fear of harassment or worse (Mars, 1977).

That began to change in 2004. Historians and racial justice practitioners were beginning to describe Philadelphia as a "beacon of racial reconciliation," accolades that I heard repeatedly as I travelled throughout the state in 2009 to investigate efforts to establish a statewide truth commission. I would soon learn that an interracial coalition of citizens from Philadelphia and the surrounding county had coalesced in 2004 around the fortieth anniversary of the 1964 killings, ultimately calling for justice in the case. Such a group, let alone such a demand, would have been unthinkable just decades before when the mere suggestion would have likely provoked the retaliation of nightriders. Throughout the 1960s, the White Knights of the Ku Klux Klan exerted significant social control in Neshoba County, reinforcing white supremacy through intimidation and violence (Huie, [1965] 2000). Thus, given the history of racial violence in the county, the Philadelphia Coalition was an extraordinary development. Whether the fortieth anniversary commemoration spearheaded by the coalition would mark a turning point in the long-standing trajectory of public silence as many observers projected, however, remained to be seen.

Just 15 years before, in 1989, a similar interracial coalition of Neshoba Countians hosted a large-scale community-wide commemoration ceremony marking the twenty-fifth anniversary of the murders. They, too, identified the event as a critical juncture in its immediate aftermath, a turning point between past denial and present atonement. But these projections were short-lived. The 1989 commemoration, while not without reverberations, failed to transform local memory policies and practices. In contrast, the 2004 commemoration appeared to provoke subsequent transformations in Neshoba County and across Mississippi's legal, educational, and civil spheres (Whitlinger, 2020). In 2005, the state prosecuted and convicted Edgar Ray Killen for his role as the mastermind of the 1964 murders; in 2006, the Mississippi legislature passed groundbreaking education legislation mandating civil and human rights curriculum at every grade level; and in 2009, Mississippi citizens launched the Mississippi Truth Project, initially modelled after the South African Truth Commission and later transformed into a statewide oral history project. That these developments occurred after the 2004 commemoration does not, of course, mean that the 2004 commemoration caused these developments.

Nonetheless, this historical sequence prompted me to ask several questions on the relationship between commemoration and social change. Given Philadelphia's long public silence on the 1964 killings, how did large-scale community-wide commemorations come to punctuate the mnemonic landscape in 1989 and then again in 2004? Could the Killen trial, the civil rights education bill, and the Mississippi Truth Project be reasonably attributed to the fortieth anniversary commemoration in Neshoba County, and if so, how? And finally, if these three transformations can be traced back to the fortieth anniversary commemoration, what factors were present in 2004 and *not* in 1989 that enabled the 2004 commemoration to be transformative?

Answering these questions required deep sociohistorical research – trips to half a dozen archives, 61 in-depth interviews, and over a year of participant observation – for no scholar had yet written a comprehensive history of these more recent events. Despite prior historical works on the Civil Rights Movement, Mississippi, and Neshoba County – some authored by fellow sociologists equally inspired by the state's rich legacy (Morris, 1984; McAdam, 1990; McCord, 2016) – a sociologist's ultimate task is to identify patterns and more general social processes. Thus, as I sought to better understand Philadelphia's mnemonic practices in the 50 years following the murders, I looked for broader insights on the causes and consequences of commemorating racial violence.

Over the past 30 years, commemorations of difficult pasts have become a staple of collective memory research, and out of this scholarship has emerged a rich body of knowledge about the causes and composition of commemorative projects (Wagner-Pacifici, 1996; Vinitsky-Seroussi, 2002; Armstrong and Crage, 2006; Steidl, 2013). However, research on commemorative consequences has remained less developed, perhaps because of its complexity. A commemoration's possible reverberations are infinite, ranging from the political to the cultural, the macro to the micro, the intended to the unintended. For this reason, I found it advantageous to begin with hypothesized outcomes and to work my way back to their origins, a process that entailed counterfactual logic and systematic comparison. Yet before I could explore the consequences of Philadelphia, Mississippi's, commemorations, I had to investigate how these commemorations came to be, for as I would come to find, the context of a commemoration's emergence matters for its outcomes.

This research design was shaped by a distinct analytical perspective, one inspired by William Sewell's (1996) notion of "eventful temporality," that conceptualizes commemorations as "events" with the potential to transform social structures. In what follows, I will review the literature on eventful temporality, demonstrating how this perspective shaped my methods and findings, as well as its broader implications for the study of contested memories. After all, we know little about what commemorations of difficult pasts do and whether they can transform the often-tragic conditions out of which they emerge.

Conceptualizing commemorations as events

When considering the causal power of commemoration, the sociological literature on the role of events in transforming social life is particularly instructive (Abbott, 1992; Sewell, 1996; Mahoney, 2000; Hess and Martin, 2006; Haydu, 2010; Wagner-Pacifici, 2010; Moore, 2011; Berezin, 2012; Meyer and Kimeldorf, 2015). Building on William Sewell's (1996) seminal work of historical sociology, "Three Temporalities: Towards an Eventful Sociology," this research embraces a form of temporality that recognizes the power of events. In contrast to teleological temporality, which emphasizes linear development through necessary stages (industrialization, urbanization, secularization, and so on), and experimental temporality, which compares different historical pathways (revolution versus non-revolution), eventful temporality understands history as "lumpy, uneven, unpredictable, and discontinuous" (Sewell, 2005: p 9). This perspective therefore requires analysts to engage complex, conjunctural, and often, contingent temporal sequences that shape social relations and structures in unexpected ways.

Such temporal sequences are conceptualized as "events" – a "relatively rare subclass of happenings that transform structures," according to Sewell's (1996: p 262) now classic formulation based on his study of the French Revolution. By affecting "actors' ability to understand and act in the world," events, Sewell (2005: p 225) explains, "lead to changes in durable patterns of relations." Recent research, however, challenges the rarity of structure-transforming events, identifying more frequent, smaller-scale common occurrences as "eventful" (della Porta, 2008; Meyer and Kimeldorf, 2015). Yet all events – big or small – represent ruptures or turning points between more stable and durable trajectories or what Andrew Abbott (2001: p 247) has described as the "smooth befores and afters." This dislocation from the ordinary routines of social life is what shapes an event's transformative potential. By disrupting the quotidian, events become "templates of possibility," offering "visions of possible paths – even if those paths are not pursued" (Berezin, 2012: p 15). After all, it is not the event itself that is significant, but the meaning assigned to it that determines an event's transformative potential (McAdam and Sewell, 2001; Wagner-Pacifici 2010).

Social movement scholars have begun to embrace an eventful approach to the study of collective action by analyzing protests as events, in which a protest significantly alters the relationship between activists or the trajectory of the campaign (McAdam and Sewell, 2001; della Porta, 2008; Meyer and Kimeldorf, 2015; Wood et al, 2017; Gillan, 2020). Donatella della Porta (2008), for example, finds that protest events transform identities, networks, and movement practices through a combination of affective, relational, and cognitive mechanisms. Likewise, Meyer and Kimeldorf (2015: p 430) develop the idea of "eventful subjectivity" in their study of the Chicago Living Wage Campaign, finding that the non-routine nature of mobilization for movement novices generated novel ideas and practices that unified a diverse community of low-wage workers through a more expansive understanding of solidarity. This work demonstrates that an eventful approach need not only be applied to large-scale happenings such as revolutions, royal successions, and religious revivals. Smaller-scale protests can also transform the lives of activists, and in some cases, the fate of their movement.

Memory movements are shaped by similar processes of transformation and unification (Zamponi, 2013; Kubal and Becerra, 2014; Eyerman, 2016). Defined as sustained collective efforts to change representations of the past, memory movements resemble "new social movements" whose goals can be understood as more cultural than political, and whose very existence is a victory (Melucci, 1980). Like new social movements, memory movements raise awareness of marginalized pasts, or marginalized interpretations of the past, by their very existence (Ghoshal, 2013). So, when long-suppressed countermemory enters the public sphere, commemoration functions *as* protest. And like protest, commemorative projects are often the result of social movement-like activities. Memory activists, sometimes referred to as "agents of memory," "mnemonic entrepreneurs," or "memory choreographers," operate much like Howard Becker's "moral entrepreneurs," encouraging collectivities to adopt or maintain a social norm related to their moral viewpoints (Becker, 1963; Jelin, 2003). Such activists engage in "mnemonic battles," negotiating the meaning of the past in the context of present institutional constraints in competition with other agents of memory (Zerubavel, 1997; DeGloma, 2015). Consequently, those who can frame the commemoration in a way that appeals to powerful constituencies, mobilize sufficient financial and human resources, and take advantage of political opportunities, are more likely to transform representations of the past successfully (Kubal, 2008).

It is important, however, to distinguish memory movements from the commemorative work they pursue. Extant research overwhelmingly conceptualizes commemorative projects – such as those in Philadelphia, Mississippi – as mere consequences of memory movements. But, as I have come to find, commemorative projects may also *provoke* subsequent – and distinct – memory movements. Embracing eventful temporality therefore challenges researchers to consider how commemorative initiatives transform structures and relations, including cultivating memory movements that are analytically distinct from the conditions out of which they emerged.

While commemorations are, in one sense, "events," as social phenomena that distinguish the "sacred" from the "profane," rupturing the ordinary routines of social life (Durkheim, [1912]1995), not all commemorations are *eventful* (Sewell, 1996). Most commemorative projects, including those commemorating racial violence, are often banal in a broader social sense despite being meaningful to those involved. Many commemorative activities happen with modest fanfare and leave little in their wake other than the satisfaction or frustration of those who participated, and major social structures remain unchanged. But the fortieth anniversary commemoration in Philadelphia appeared to have significant reverberations across various spheres of social life, contradicting general patterns and allowing a more nuanced analysis of commemoration's consequences. The question is, how?

Studying commemorations as events: a methodological approach

To assess whether and how the fortieth anniversary commemoration in Philadelphia, Mississippi, was, in fact, a turning point toward more stable and durable trajectories, I had to begin at the end, starting not with the commemoration and moving forward but with the outcomes that might reasonably be linked to it and working my way backward in time. Given the range of possible outcomes, I approached this process inductively, first probing archival materials for insight into the commemoration's aftermath and later conducting interviews. Interviews with key informants became an essential part of my research; the people closest to the commemoration planning process were deeply invested in the event's potential reverberations and provided rich insights into the sequence of events and the motivations underlying key decisions. Their understanding of their work provided focus as I investigated whether these reported outcomes could be verified empirically and systematically. The archival and interview data revealed numerous outcomes. New friendships were formed, new organizations were founded, new policies were written, and new fissures were opened.

Given this panoply of outcomes, I focused the second stage of my research on three potential (or hypothesized) institutional outcomes: the 2005 prosecution of Edgar Ray Killen; the passage in 2006 of the civil and human rights education bill; and the 2009 public launch of Mississippi's Truth Project. To assess whether and how these three key events were causally connected to the fortieth anniversary commemoration in 2004, I utilized a multi-stage approach drawing on two distinct, but complementary, comparative historical methodologies: counterfactual analysis and systematic comparison.

Counterfactual analysis

Counterfactual analysis has a long history in sociology going back to Max Weber (Reiss, 2009; Pavone, 2015). In one of his widely read essays, "Objective Possibility and Adequate Causation in Historical Explanation," Weber ([1905] 1949) seeks to reconcile structural determinism with contingency, foreshadowing research on "eventful temporality" and "critical junctures" with his focus on contingency (Sewell, 2005; Capoccia and Kelemen, 2007; Soifer, 2012). "If history is to rise above the level of chronicle," Weber wrote in 1905, "then the historian must be explicit about possible developments that did not occur" (quoted in Ringer, 2002: p 166).

Despite its long history in the discipline, counterfactual analysis has been derided as "virtual history" (Ferguson, 1999) or mere "cocktail conversation" (Bulhof, 1999). After all, how can we know with any certainty what would have happened? Historical outcomes are contingent on long chains of happenings often shaped by chance occurrences. "Replaying the tape," according to the late paleontologist, Stephen Jay Gould (1989), in his book, *Wonderful Life: The Burgess Shale and the Nature of History*, would inevitably result in different evolutionary outcomes. If the natural world is shaped by random mutations and chance historical events, surely the social world is equally unpredictable.

History's unpredictability, however, does not preclude social theorizing. Theories of social change can illuminate what happened and why even if unable to predict the future. Theorizing causes of social change is central to historical analysis, albeit often implicit (Bulhof, 1999). Any attempt to make causal claims about historical phenomena involves counterfactual reasoning. To claim that X caused Y is also to suggest that if X had *not* occurred, neither would have Y. In other words, "[c]ounterfactuals, causes, and explanations are three sides of the same strange three-sided coin; you cannot have one without the other two" (Bulhof, 1999: p 147).

But not all counterfactuals are created equal. In recent years, social scientists have differentiated between counterfactuals as thought-provoking but insufficiently rigorous imaginative exercises and counterfactuals that meet the criteria of rigorous social science. The latter, which are based on indirect evidence and are what I hoped to accomplish, must fulfil several criteria. In particular, counterfactuals must specify antecedents (hypothesized independent variables) and consequents (dependent variables); generate plausible hypotheses that require minimal rewriting of history; and articulate mechanisms or connecting principles that are consistent with well-established theory and statistics.

To systematize my counterfactual analysis, I employed Event Structure Analysis (Griffin, 1993), a formal qualitative method that allowed me to trace the causal connections *between* acts of remembrance and subsequent episodes of social repair. Originally developed by David Heise (1989) and extended by Larry Griffin for historical analysis, Event Structure Analysis (ESA) is an iterative, interactive qualitative methodology that is structured by a computer software program, ETHNO, which guides researchers through a series of counterfactual questions based on a chronology of actions. In effect, this methodology structures the qualitative historical analysis by challenging analysts to consider alternative hypotheses at each stage of the chronology, making visible the causal assumptions that often remain implicit within historical analysis (Isaac, Street, and Knapp, 1994). Thus, ESA does not *reveal* causality but *elicits* the researcher's understanding of complex causal relationships by scrutinizing whether and how the relationship between two temporally ordered events are, in fact, causal.

This iterative process served as a constant check, helping me to identify empirical gaps in the sequence of actions that I otherwise may have missed, challenging me to revisit my data when I was uncertain about the connections between two actions, and enabling me to ask more refined targeted questions. ESA was thus a vital tool in my research process, illuminating the causal connections between the fortieth anniversary commemoration and the Killen trial, education bill, and truth project. In particular, this analysis highlighted how the fortieth anniversary commemoration mobilized local mnemonic activists; concentrated local, state, and global resources; shifted the state's political culture regarding rituals of remembrance; and broadened political opportunities for subsequent commemorative work. Taken together, these developments enabled the Killen trial, education bill, and truth project to emerge (see Whitlinger, 2020).

Systematic comparison

After using ESA to establish that the Killen trial, the education bill, and the Mississippi Truth Project were causally connected to the fortieth anniversary commemoration, I set out to explain why, drawing analytical leverage from a different methodology: structured comparison. Fifteen years before the 2004 anniversary commemoration an interracial coalition of local citizens had organized a remarkably similar event to mark the twenty-fifth anniversary of the murders that failed to yield such transformative outcomes. This assumes that the 1989 commemoration could have been transformative, and thus can be conceptualized as a negative case or "near miss" (Capoccia and Kelemen, 2007: p 352; see also, Lewis-Beck, Bryman, and Liao, 2004). Thus, by comparing the twenty-fifth and fortieth anniversary commemorations, I hoped to isolate what factors were present in 2004 – and missing in 1989 – that enabled the fortieth anniversary commemoration to be transformative.

Here, I drew inspiration from – but did not seek to replicate – Theda Skocpol's two-stage comparative design in *States and Social Revolutions* (1976), which sought to explain how France in the late 18th century, China after 1911, and Russia after 1917 all experienced social revolutions for similar analytic reasons. Drawing on John Stewart Mill's ([1888] 1970) comparative method, Skocpol looks for common causal factors among cases that vary in all other ways that seem causally relevant (Mill's "Method of Similarity") *and* examines intra-country comparisons such as the "abortive" Russian Revolution of 1905 to the Russian Revolution of 1917 (Mill's "Method of Difference"). Likewise, I first engaged the "Method of Similarity," establishing that the 1989 and 2004 commemorations were both silence-breaking commemorations precipitated by similar social forces. I then shifted my analytic focus by examining the cases through the "Method of Difference" to explain the variation in outcomes.

Few works of comparative history have been more scrutinized than Skocpol's (cf. Mahoney, 1999) with critics suggesting that Skocpol's method departs from or fails to uphold a Millian logic (Sewell, 1996; Goldstone, 1980). For William Sewell, the major proponent of eventful temporality, Skocpol's argument is convincing not because of her Millian comparison, but because of her historical narrative. "The true payoff of Skocpol's comparative history," according to Sewell (1996: p 262), "is not rigorous testing of abstract generalizations but the discovery of analogies on which new and convincing narratives of eventful sequences can be constructed."

Taking note of these critiques, I engaged these historical comparisons with sensitivity to timing and sequence. After all, a particular challenge to a

Millian methodology comes from the fact that a comparative logic assumes that the units being compared are independent of one another (Kiser and Hechter, 1991: p 13; Steinmetz, 2008: p 382). And while "[i]ndependence is defined analytically according to what it is that is being problematized and thus along substantive, not logical dimensions" (Somers, 1998: p 758; see also Ragin, 1992; Hall, 2003), the 1989 and 2004 commemorations have deep substantive connections that could not be ignored. Phenomena such as commemorations occur within particular spatio-temporal mnemonic contexts and are, at least partially, determined by previous commemorations, what collective memory scholars refer to as "genre memory" or more simply, the "memory of commemoration" (Olick, 1999b). Thus, I incorporated into my analysis the impact of previous commemorations as well as changing local and national norms regarding commemorative practices. This echoes more recent "process-oriented" approaches in the field of comparative history including the "comparative sequential method" (Falleti and Mahoney, 2015). As Tulia Falleti and James Mahoney (2015) remind us, Mill's method, in practice, compares *sequences* rather than *cases*.

The sequences of actions certainly mattered, although not in the way (or as much) as one might expect. Indeed, several of the actors involved in the 2004 project had also been involved in 1989, enhancing the 2004 group's mnemonic capacity by providing access to "lessons learned" in a general sense. But these actors were not central actors or primary decision-makers in 2004. It is also true that, by 2004, the state's institutional capacity to support commemorative work had developed. A civil society organization, the William Winter Institute for Racial Reconciliation, had been established following President Clinton's "One America" initiative on race in 1998, which had hosted its only public forum in the deep south at the University of Mississippi (Lawson, 2009). The Winter Institute's entire mission was to support local communities' efforts to confront their difficult racial pasts, and as a result, the professional staff proved to be a remarkable resource for the local group in Neshoba County, providing access to specialized knowledge and resources and taking on many of the organizational tasks that would be difficult for private individuals with full-time jobs to perform.

Yet looking more closely at the 1989 case reveals that the local mnemonic capacity was similarly buttressed by external resources, albeit from outside the state. The mayor's office in Philadelphia, Pennsylvania, had taken an interest in supporting their sister city's reconciliatory efforts following the 1988 release of the film, *Mississippi Burning*, which reignited national interest in the case and coincided with reputational management issues for the mayor in Philadelphia, Pennsylvania. Several members of the 1989 commemoration committee later speculated that the Pennsylvania mayor desired positive press in the wake of a racially charged incident where city police dropped a bomb on occupied rowhouses attempting to end an armed impasse with MOVE, a

Black liberation organization, killing 11 and leaving 250 homeless (Sanders and Jeffrey, 2013). Regardless of the motivation, the Pennsylvania contingent provided substantial financial and human resources through the "Philadelphia to Philadelphia" project that supported commemorative work in Mississippi. These structural factors thus only partially shaped the 2004 commemoration's outcomes. To fully understand what happened in 2004, I had to look more deeply at the planning process itself, a process revealed by the Event Structure Analysis, and which highlighted the significance of interactional dynamics for shaping a commemoration's transformative potential.

Interactional dynamics and commemorative outcomes

After returning to my data, I realized that comparing the commemoration ceremonies had been misleading. While the content, structure, and sponsoring organizations had been remarkably similar, the *process* of planning the ceremonies differed considerably. By refocusing my attention on the planning processes – a process unpacked by the preceding Event Structure Analysis – I discovered the missing piece to my analytical puzzle. In short, this process-oriented comparative analysis revealed that interracial efforts to commemorate racial violence (which are increasingly common) need to be conceptualized as instances of intergroup contact where members from one or more social groups engage with each other for a sustained period (Wagner and Hewstone, 2012). Doing so highlights critical – and often-overlooked – meso-level dynamics of commemorative work, including intergroup interactions. Commemorating racial violence, I came to learn, involves at least two major tasks: constructing the commemorative vehicle *and* maintaining intergroup relations. Without sustaining interpersonal relationships across social divides, organizing the commemoration would be impossible. By expanding my object of analysis (the commemoration) to include not only the ceremony but the process of planning the ceremony, I better understood why the 2004 commemoration had been "eventful" when previous attempts had failed to transform local mnemonic practices.

Looking more deeply into the research on intergroup contact, I learned that social psychologists have examined the consequences of intergroup contact as well as its ideal conditions for over 50 years, drawing Gordon Allport's (1954) seminal work, *The Nature of Prejudice*. While Allport himself noted that "superficial" intergroup contact could do more harm than good by reinforcing adverse associations and implicit bias, a substantial body of research confirms that intergroup contact reduces intergroup prejudices provided that certain conditions are met (Pettigrew and Tropp, 2006). These conditions include (i) equal status within the situation so that each group can fully participate in the relationship; (ii) cooperation towards a common "superordinate" goal or task that requires groups to work together;

(iii) support of relevant authorities, laws, or customs, which help to normalize the interaction between groups; and, more recently, (iv) possibilities for intimate, informal contact, or what Thomas Pettigrew (1998: p 76) calls "friendship potential."

The research supporting Allport's initial findings has been resounding. A recent meta-analysis synthesizing over five hundred studies finds that "[t]here is a fundamental, robust, and positive impact of contact on intergroup attitudes regardless of target group, age group, geographical area, or contact setting" (Crisp et al, 2009: p 2; see also, Pettigrew and Tropp, 2006). And while this social-psychological research focuses on individual-level outcomes (prejudice reduction), these interactional dynamics can have macro-level consequences by reconstituting the boundaries of in-groups and out-groups, a necessary step in the formation of collective identity formation.

Social movement scholarship suggests that strong identification with a collectivity makes participation on behalf of that collectivity more likely, as well as a deep and enduring commitment to continued activism (Hunt and Benford, 2004; Nepstad, 2013). Despite these findings, collective identity, according to James Jasper (2018: p 105), remains "a necessary fiction." "All groups," he writes, "face the same challenge: the individuals who compose them may share some tastes, feelings, and goals, but never all." Maintaining constructive intergroup relations even with these potential cleavages is, therefore, key to cultivating and sustaining the capacity to commemorate across significant social divides such as race in the United States. After all, few participants of commemoration planning task forces (including those in Philadelphia, Mississippi) have had the opportunity to discuss racial issues in interracial settings. In the United States and other societies with high levels of social inequality, socio-spatial segregation provides few opportunities for interracial interactions, as individuals live, work, worship, and play in overwhelmingly racially homogeneous settings (Massey and Denton, 1993). In turn, these social experiences influence cognitive understandings and worldviews, including the events one remembers as significant (May, 2000; Griffin and Bollen, 2009). Consequently, these cognitive differences pose challenges to collective action, including memory projects, as past events must be understood in a generally consensual way for a group to connect past experiences and present problems (Schuman and Rieger, 1992).

Returning to my empirical data with new insight on the significance of interactional dynamics in the planning process, I began to see that the 2004 commemoration planners had, albeit unintentionally, fulfilled all the conditions of positive intergroup contact while the 1989 participants had failed to do so. This is most evident when examining how each task force formed. While the twenty-fifth-anniversary commemoration in 1989 was initiated and almost entirely planned by local white men in prominent leadership positions with largely tokenistic participation from local Black leaders, the 2004 task force prioritized racial inclusivity from the start. This included the selection of the task force co-chairs who represented the community's two largest racial groups, Black and white. (Neshoba County was also home to the Mississippi Band of Choctaw Indians.) From the beginning of the planning process, the 2004 task force co-chairs (Leroy Clemons, the head of the local branch of the NAACP, and Jim Prince, the editor of the local newspaper) conceptualized the commemoration as an interracial project that depended on diverse representation. This is evident in their first conversations about the project, when they agreed, in Clemons's words, to "do a memorial service ... [but] make it a communitywide memorial service." Consequently, the co-chairs were intentional about the composition of the task force, reaching beyond their immediate social networks to ensure that various stakeholder groups were represented, including government representatives from the city, county, and nearby Choctaw tribe. In sum, the leadership and composition of the 2004 planning committee provided equal status to those from the community's major racial demographic groups and represented (at least tacit) approval from local political authorities.

Once the commemoration planning started in earnest, the differences between 1989 and 2004 become even more clear. In 1989, the commemoration planning committee's mandate had been fairly circumscribed: to plan the twenty-fifth-anniversary commemoration. Its process flowed from the top down, and its agenda – implicit and explicit – did not embrace developing a shared common goal from the bottom up. A Philadelphia resident who participated in both commemoration services described the 1989 mandate as confined only to the commemoration's planning: "We were planning an event ... It could have been a festival." Although the 1989 commemoration did have a shared goal (event planning), it was not a goal that required interracial cooperation and collaboration in a meaningful sense. In contrast, the 2004 commemoration developed cooperation towards common goals from the ground up, beginning with the first meeting. Jim Prince, a 2004 task force co-chair, jokingly described the first task force meeting in 2004 as "kind of like an AA [Alcoholics Anonymous] meeting," with participants introducing themselves following the classic self-help formula: "Hi, my name is so-and-so, and I'm here because ..." As each participant shared their experiences of race and racism in Neshoba County, one thing became clear: regardless of race, all shared affection for their community. For them, Neshoba County was not the cold, unfeeling place depicted in the film *Mississippi Burning*. And it certainly was not a place to be feared or avoided – feelings that were still held by many outside the county. Underlying this impulse for impression management was also a desire to seek justice for the three civil rights workers. This was the shared goal that united members of the 2004 task force and one that had emerged organically.

In other words, while the 1989 task force had begun with the fundamental tasks of event planning, focusing on funding and other organizational concerns, the 2004 task force began with stories, revealing their personal connections to race and violence in Neshoba County. Most significantly, this storytelling served as a form of consciousness-raising, linking personal experiences to structural forces while also deepening and complicating participants' understandings of their own pasts and the racial experiences of others. Furthermore, this growing emotional affinity began to transform the boundaries between in-groups and out-groups, generating a new sense of collective identity when participants of the task force began to identify themselves by a new name: Philadelphia Coalition. Thus, by addressing issues of power within the task force, the equal status among participants and co-chairs in 2004 enabled storytelling as a form of intimate contact – which, in turn, clarified the group's collective goals and cultivated their shared identity as the Philadelphia Coalition, an identity that helped establish their legitimacy for local and state political actors, which led to the legal, educational, and civil transformations mentioned earlier. These findings not only suggest that commemorations can be understood as structure-transforming; they also indicate – perhaps ironically – that commemorations are most *eventful* when they are not treated as mere *events*.

Conclusion

Anyone engaged in commemorative work knows that planning a large-scale commemorative ceremony is a complicated undertaking. Those engaged in the planning process must constantly shift between the sacred and the profane, attending to the potent cultural representations of the past – its symbols, songs, and artistic renderings – while also managing mundane organizational details such as securing sound equipment and setting up chairs. This may help explain why local memory activists so often tend to overlook the social-psychological dimensions of the planning process itself, an omission that is especially consequential when commemorating racial violence.

When members of the 2004 commemoration task force first gathered in Philadelphia, few had engaged in public discussions of the 1964 murders, and those who had rarely did so within an interracial group setting. For Neshoba Countians, like many others in the United States, race was a topic to be avoided, a potential minefield of divisive issues and reactions (Sue, 2015). Moreover, opportunities for discussing the city's racial past remained few and far between as de jure, and later de facto, segregation of Neshoba County's schools, neighborhoods, churches, and other civil society organizations constrained possibilities for interracial interactions, a dynamic that undoubtedly shaped understandings of the past as well as possibilities for race relations in the future (May, 2000). Given these dynamics, when the interracial commemoration task forces began their work in Neshoba County in 1989 and again in 2004, their interactions represented instances of intergroup contact (Wagner and Hewstone, 2012).

Herein lies the key to understanding why the 2004 commemoration had been transformative when previous attempts failed to change local memory practices. Comparing the 1989 and 2004 commemoration reveals that commemorating racial violence is not sufficient to cultivate broader social change. Rather, the process of planning the commemoration – which includes maintaining intergroup relations – powerfully shapes possibilities for subsequent outcomes. Notably, the fortieth anniversary fulfilled the four major facilitating conditions for positive intergroup contact. Interracial co-chairs recruited a representative and roughly racially balanced group of participants, thus maintaining *equal status* for the county's two largest racial groups (white and Black); storytelling enabled participants to identify common experiences and concerns that cultivated intergroup collaboration on a common goal (justice); this seemingly united interracial group of local citizens received support from relevant political authorities including the city, the county, and the tribe; and finally, the initial focus on storytelling represented the sort of self-disclosure that provides possibilities for friendship, even across notable social divides. Taken together, these factors enabled the 2004 commemoration to cultivate a collective identity and local organizational infrastructure – the Philadelphia Coalition – that helped sustain their memory work even after the commemoration itself had concluded.

These insights emerged only after considering commemorations as potentially structure-transforming events, inspired by William Sewell's foundational work on "eventful temporality" (Sewell, 1996), an analytical approach that shaped my research methods and findings. This approach emphasizes causation and counterfactual analysis, concerns that ESA is particularly well-suited to address. This formal (computer-assisted) qualitative analysis enabled me to deconstruct the commemorative events into their component parts using counterfactual reasoning and revealed differences between the 1989 and 2004 commemorations that would have been otherwise obscured. To my surprise, these differences appeared not in the form and content of the commemorative ceremony, but the interactions leading up to the commemorations, suggesting that the transformative potential of commemoration lies in its planning process.

Aside from these theoretical findings, an eventful approach to the study of commemoration reveals broader insights for the study of contested memories. First, researchers exploring the memory-movement nexus overwhelmingly conceptualize commemorations (memorials, marches, and the like) as *products* of memory movement, the outcomes of collective memory mobilization. Undoubtedly, this is an important insight. Commemorative vehicles, like the twenty-fifth- and fortieth-anniversary commemoration services examined here, require many of the components that are characteristic of a successful social movement mobilization. They must cultivate sufficient resources, seize advantageous political opportunities, and frame their projects in ways that compel their target audiences. Yet as I have come to find, commemorations may also *promote* memory movements, helping to solidify commitment to memory work and building the commemorative capacity of those communities undertaking such projects. Rather than conceptualizing the relationship between memory movements and commemorations as unidirectional, it is more advantageous to understand this interaction as iterative, a feedback loop where movements produce commemorations and commemorations produce movements.

Second, despite the significance of race in the United States, and its apparent influence on commemorative possibilities, those orchestrating commemorations of racial violence (and those studying these occurrences) often underestimate the role of social identities in the planning process. When local agents of memory enact commemorations in racially homogenous social spaces, those events, while meaningful, may lack the capacity to transform surrounding social structures, given their social isolation. On the other hand, engaging in commemorative work with individuals from multiple social groups that have historically been in conflict introduces intergroup dynamics that can be difficult to manage, and in some cases, threaten the viability of the commemoration. We must therefore understand commemorations of racial violence as having two primary tasks: orchestrating a commemorative vehicle *and* maintaining intergroup relations.

This emphasis on intergroup processes suggests a final, critical point. Meso-level analysis in the study of contested memories has been outshadowed by macro and micro approaches, exemplified by Jeffrey K. Olick's (1999a) distinction between "collective" and "collected" memory. While the former refers to collective representations of the past enshrined in objects and rituals, the latter highlights how social group membership shapes individual perceptions of the past as demonstrated by survey research (see Schuman and Reiger, 1992; Griffin and Bollen, 2009; Corning and Schuman, 2015). Neither "collective" nor "collected" memory accounts for the interactional dynamics that shape commemorative outcomes. So, as researchers continue to explore what commemorations do and how they transform social relations and social structures, meso-level approaches may be especially advantageous.

References

Abbott, A. (1992) "From Causes to Events: Notes on Narrative Positivism," *Sociological Methods and Research* 20(4): 428–455.

Abbott, A. (2001) *Time Matters: On Theory and Method*, Chicago, IL: University of Chicago Press.

Allport, G.W. (1954) *The Nature of Prejudice*, Boston, MA: Addison-Wesley Publishing Company.

Armstrong, E. and Crage, S. (2006) "Movements and Memory: The Making of the Stonewall Myth," *American Sociological Review* 71(5): 724–751.

Becker, H. (1963) *Outsiders: Studies in the Sociology of Deviance*, New York: Free Press.

Berezin, M. (2012) "Events as Templates of Possibility: An Analytic Typology of Political Facts," in J. Alexander, R. Jacobs, and P. Smith, (eds) *The Oxford Handbook of Cultural Sociology*, New York: Oxford University Press, pp 613–635.

Bulhof, J. (1999) "What If? Modality and History," *History and Theory* 38(2): 145–168.

Capoccia, G. and Keleman, D. (2007) "The Study of Critical Junctures: Theory, Narrative, and Counterfactuals in Historical Institutionalism," *World Politics* 59(3): 341–369.

Corning, A. and Schuman, H. (2015) *Generations and Collective Memory*, Chicago, IL: University of Chicago Press.

Crisp, R.J., Stathi, S., Turner, R. and Husnu, S. (2009) "Imagined Intergroup Contact: Theory, Paradigm and Practice," *Social and Personality Psychology Compass* 3(1): 1–18.

DeGloma, T. (2015) "The Strategies of Mnemonic Battle: On the Alignment of Autobiographical and Collective Memories in Conflicts over the Past," *American Journal of Cultural Sociology* 3(1): 156–190.

della Porta, Donatella. (2008) "Eventful Protest, Global Conflicts," *Distinktion: Scandinavian Journal of Social Theory* 9(2): 27–56.

Durkheim, E. ([1912] 1995). *The Elementary Forms of Religious Life*, New York: Simon & Shuster.

Earl, J. (2004) "The Cultural Consequences of Social Movements," in D.A. Snow, S. Soule, and H. Kriesi (ed) *The Blackwell Companion to Social Movements*, Oxford: Blackwell, pp 508–530.

Eyerman, R. (2016) "Social Movements and Memory," in A.L. Tota and T. Hagen (eds) *Routledge International Handbook of Memory Studies*, New York: Routledge, pp 101–105.

Falleti, T.G. and Mahoney, J. (2015) "The Comparative Sequential Method," in J. Mahoney and K. Thelen (eds) *Advances in Comparative-Historical Analysis*, Cambridge: Cambridge University Press, pp 211–239.

Ferguson, N. (1999) *Virtual History: Alternatives and Counterfactuals*. New York: Basic Books.

Ghoshal, R.A. (2013) "Transforming Collective Memory: Mnemonic Opportunity Structures and the Outcomes of Racial Violence Memory Movements," *Theory and Society* 42(4): 329–350.

Gillan, K. (2020) "Temporality in Social Movement Theory: Vectors and Events in the Neoliberal Timescape," *Social Movement Studies* 19(5–6): 516–536.

Goldstone, J.A. (1980) "The Weakness of Organization: A New Look at Gamson's The Strategy of Social Protest," *American Journal of Sociology* 85(5): 1017–1042.

Gould, S.J. (1989) *A Wonderful Life: The Burgess Shale and the Nature of History*, New York: W.W. Norton.

Griffin, L.J. (1993) "Narrative, Event-structure Analysis, and Causal Interpretation in Historical Sociology," *American Journal of Sociology* 98(5): 1094–1133.

Griffin, L.J. and Bollen, K.A. (2009) "What Do These Memories Do? Civil Rights Remembrance and Racial Attitudes," *American Sociological Review* 74(4): 594–614.

Hall, P.A. (2003) "Aligning Ontology and Methodology in Comparative Research," in J. Mahoney, and D. Reuschemeyer (eds) *Comparative Historical Analysis in the Social Sciences*, Cambridge: Cambridge University Press, pp 373–404.

Haydu, J. (2010) "Reversals of Fortune: Path Dependency, Problem Solving, and Temporal Cases," *Theory and Society* 39(1): 25–48.

Heise, D. (1989) "Modeling Event Structures," *Journal of Mathematical Sociology* 14: 139–168.

Hess, D. and Martin, B. (2006) "Repression, Backfire, and the Theory of Transformative Events," *Mobilization* 11(2): 249–267.

Huie, W.B. ([1965] 2000) *Three Lives for Mississippi*. Jackson, MS: University of Mississippi Press.

Hunt, S.A. and Benford, R.D. (2004) "Collective Identity, Solidarity, and Commitment," in D.A. Snow, S.A. Soule, and H. Kriesi (eds) *The Blackwell Companion to Social Movements*. Oxford: Blackwell, pp 433–457.

Isaac, L.W., Street, D.A., and Knapp, S.J. (1994) "Analyzing Historical Contingency with Formal Methods," *Sociological Methods and Research* 23: 114–141.

Jasper, J. (2018) *The Emotions of Protest*, Chicago, IL: University of Chicago Press.

Jelin, E. (2003) *State Repression and the Labors of Memory*, Minneapolis, MN: University of Minnesota Press.

Kiser, E. and Hechter, M. (1991) "The Role of General Theory in Comparative-historical Sociology," *American Journal of Sociology* 97(1): 1–30.

Kubal, T. (2008) *Cultural Movements and Collective Memory: Christopher Columbus and the Rewriting of the National Origin Myth*, New York: Palgrave Macmillan.

Kubal, T. and Becerra, R. (2014) "Social Movements and Collective Memory," *Sociology Compass* 8(6): 865–875.

Lawson, S. (ed) (2009) *One America in the Twenty-first Century*, New Haven, CT: Yale University Press.

Lewis-Beck, M.S., Bryman, A., and Futing Liao, T. (2004) "Negative Case," in *The SAGE Encyclopedia of Social Science Research Methods*. Thousand Oaks, CA: Sage Publications, pp 716–717.

Mahoney, J. (1999) "Nominal, Ordinal, and Narrative Appraisal in Macrocausal Analysis," *American Journal of Sociology* 104(4): 1154–1196.

Mahoney, J. (2000) "Path Dependence in Historical Sociology," *Theory and Society* 29(4): 507–548.

Mars, F. (1977) *Witness in Philadelphia*, Baton Rouge, LA: Louisiana State University Press.

Massey, D.S. and Denton, N.A. (1993) *American Apartheid: Segregation and the Making of the Underclass*, Cambridge, MA: Harvard University Press.

May, R.A.B. (2000) "Race Talk and Local Collective Memory Among African American Men in a Neighborhood Tavern," *Qualitative Sociology* 23(2): 201–214.

McAdam, D. (1990) *Freedom Summer*, New York: Oxford University Press.

McAdam, D. and Sewell Jr, W.H. (2001) "It's about Time: Temporality in the Study of Social Movements and Revolutions," in Aminzade, R.R., J.A. Goldstone, D. McAdam, E.J. Perry, W.H. Sewell, S. Tarrow, and C. Tilly (eds) *Silence and Voice in the Study of Contentious Politics*, Cambridge: Cambridge University Press, pp 89–125.

McCord, W. (2016) *Mississippi: The Long, Hot Summer*, Jackson, MS: University Press of Mississippi.

Melucci, A. (1980) "The New Social Movements: A Theoretical Approach," *Social Science Information* 19(2): 199–226.

Meyer, R. and Kimeldorf, H. (2015) "Eventful Subjectivity: The Experiential Sources of Solidarity," *Journal of Historical Sociology* 28(4): 429–457.

Mill, J.S. (1970) "Two Methods of Comparison" (excerpt from A System of Logic), in A. Etzioni and F.L. Du Bow (eds) *Comparative Perspectives: Theories and Methods*, Boston, MA: Little Brown, pp 205–210.

Moore, A. (2011) "The Eventfulness of Social Reproduction," *Sociological Theory* 29(4): 294–314.

Morris, A. (1984) *Origins of the Civil Rights Movement*, New York: Free Press.

Nepstad, S.E. (2013) "Commitment," in Snow, D., D. della Porta, D. McAdam, and B. Klandermans (eds) *The Wiley-Blackwell Encyclopedia of Social and Political Movements*, Oxford: Blackwell, pp 229–230.

Nevin, D. (1964) "A Strange, Tight Little Town, Loath to Admit Complicity," *Life*, December 18, pp 38–39.

Olick, J.K. (1999a) "Collective Memory: The Two Cultures," *Sociological Theory* 17(3): 333–348.

Olick, J.K. (1999b) "Genre Memories and Memory Genres: A Dialogical Analysis of May 8, 1945 Commemorations in the Federal Republic of Germany," *American Sociological Review* 64(3): 381–402.

Pavone, T. (2015) "Causal inquiry in historical social science: Reading Max Weber in light of contemporary approaches," Available from: https://scholar.princeton.edu/sites/default/files/tpavone/files/max_weber_causal_inquiry_in_historical_social_science.pdf [Accessed November 9, 2022].

Pettigrew, T.F. (1998) "Intergroup Contact Theory," *Annual Review of Psychology* 49(1): 65–85.
Pettigrew, T.F. and Tropp, L.R. (2006) "A Meta-analytic Test of Intergroup Contact Theory," *Journal of Personality and Social Psychology* 90(5): 751–783.
Ragin, C.C. and Becker, S.H. (eds) (1992) *What Is a Case? Exploring the Foundations of Social Inquiry*, New York: Cambridge University Press.
Reiss, J. (2009) "Counterfactuals, Thought Experiments, and Singular Causal Analysis in History," *Philosophy of Science* 76(5): 712–723.
Ringer, F. (2002) "Max Weber on Causal Analysis, Interpretation, and Comparison," *History and Theory* 41(2): 163–178.
Sanders, K. and Jeffries, J.L. (2013) "Framing MOVE: A Press' Complicity in the Murder of Women and Children in the City of (Un)Brotherly Love," *Journal of African American Studies* 17: 566–586.
Schuman, H. and Rieger, C. (1992) "Historical Analogies, Generational Effects, and Attitudes Toward War," *American Sociological Review* 57(3): 315–326.
Sewell, W.H. (1996) "Historical Events as Transformations of Structures: Inventing Revolution at the Bastille," *Theory and Society* 25(6): 841–881.
Sewell, W.H. (2005) *Logics of History: Social Theory and Social Transformation*, Chicago, IL: University of Chicago Press.
Skocpol, T. (1976) *States and Social Revolutions*, Cambridge: Cambridge University Press.
Soifer, H.D. (2012) "The Causal Logic of Critical Junctures," *Comparative Political Studies* 45(12): 1572–1597.
Somers, M.R. (1998) "We're No Angels: Realism, Rational Choice, and Relationality in Social Science," *American Journal of Sociology* 104(3): 722–784.
Steidl, C.R. (2013) "Remembering May 4, 1970: Integrating the Commemorative Field at Kent State," *American Sociological Review* 78(5): 749–772.
Steinmetz, G. (2008) "Logics of History as a Framework for an Integrated Social Science," *Social Science History* 32(4): 535–553.
Sue, D.W. (2015) *Race Talk and the Conspiracy of Silence: Understanding and Facilitating Difficult Dialogues on Race*, Hoboken, NJ: Wiley.
Vinitzky-Seroussi, V. (2002) "Commemorating a Difficult Past: Yitzhak Rabin's Memorials," *American Sociological Review* 67(1): 30–51.
Wagner, U. and Hewstone, M. (2012) "Intergroup Contact," in L. Tropp (ed) *The Oxford Handbook of Intergroup Conflict*, Oxford: Oxford University Press, pp 193–209.
Wagner-Pacifici, R. (1996) "Memories in the Making: The Shapes of Things that Went," *Qualitative Sociology* 19(3): 301–21.
Wagner-Pacifici, R. (2010) "Theorizing the Restlessness of Events," *American Journal of Sociology* 115(5): 1351–1386.

Weber, M. ([1905] 1949) "Objective Possibility and Adequate Causation in Historical Explanation," in E. Shils and H. Finch (eds) *The Methodology of the Social Sciences*, Glencoe, IL: Free Press, pp 164–188.

Whitlinger, C. (2020) *Between Remembrance and Repair: Commemorating Racial Violence in Philadelphia*, Mississippi, Chapel Hill, NC: University of North Carolina Press.

Wood, L.J., Staggenborg, S., Stalker, G., and Kutz-Flamenbaum, R. (2017) "Eventful Events: Local Outcomes of G20 Summit Protests in Pittsburgh and Toronto," *Social Movement Studies* 16(5): 595–609.

Zamponi, L. (2013) "Collective Memory and Social Movements," in D.A. Snow, D. della Porta, B. Klandermans, and D. McAdam (eds) *The Wiley-Blackwell Encyclopedia of Social and Political Movements*, Oxford: Blackwell, pp 225–229.

Zerubavel, E. (1997) *Social Mindscapes: An Invitation to Cognitive Sociology*, Cambridge, MA: Harvard University Press.

8

Contentious Pasts, Contentious Futures: Race, Memory, and Politics in Montgomery's Legacy Museum

Amy Sodaro

In Spring 2020 most of us were trapped in our homes in the eerie quiet of the pandemic shutdown when the excruciating video of George Floyd's murder began to circulate in a way that it may not have had people been out living their lives. Coming after the killing of Ahmaud Arbery in February and Breonna Taylor in March, the murder of Floyd captivated the nation and resulted in massive Black Lives Matter protests. The protests appear to be the largest in history with 15–26 million people participating in the US alone, though they also spread around the world (Buchanan, Quoctrung, and Patel, 2020). They garnered more media coverage than any protest in the last 50 years (Heaney, 2020) and spawned a social media torrent: between May 25 and June 5, race- and Black Lives Matter-related (BLM) videos were watched over 1.4 billion times on Twitter alone (Blake, 2020). Floyd's murder was horrific, but it was also the context in which it occurred that gave it such powerful traction. As sociologist Patricia Fernandez-Kelly (2020) wrote: "The pandemic made visible huge inequalities and fueled existential anxieties magnified by the sight of George Floyd's murder. The crime was a cruel reminder of the neglect with which people of color have been treated. It was also a call to action."

As Fernandez-Kelly suggests, the protests in response to George Floyd's killing were not just about the present moment, but the centuries of racism and racial injustice that created the conditions in which it could occur, from slavery, through Jim Crow, to mass incarceration and current forms of racial terror, often at the hands of the state. The connection between this deeply entrenched racism of the past and its present manifestations is beginning to make its way into contemporary mainstream debates and protests about race in the US, and is part of a larger struggle playing out around the world over the contentious past of colonization, slavery, and their lasting legacies of violence, inequality, and injustice. One space in which these struggles play out is the memorial museum, which encompasses both the educative functions of history museums and the affect of social memory. Memorial museums are created to (re)present past violence and atrocity for visitors and in their telling of violent pasts, they help to shape collective historical narratives and understanding. They are also expensive institutions and generally require significant resources to be created and maintained. As such they are excellent windows into the present political priorities of the societies that build them and their study can help us understand how memory, and in particular memory of contentious pasts, is shaped and circulated within societies.

Until recently, memorial museums in the US, such as the US Holocaust Memorial Museum and the 9/11 Museum, were created to address contentious pasts, but in ways that reinforce patriotic, nationalist narratives of America as beacon of democracy and freedom, ignoring America's own past violence and atrocity. But this has begun to change with new memorial museums that attempt to critically confront America's history of racial violence and oppression, exemplified by The Legacy Museum: From Slavery to Mass Incarceration in Montgomery, Alabama. Unlike other American memorial museums, The Legacy Museum does not smooth over controversial aspects of America's past, but confronts them in material and demanding ways, asking collectives and individuals to acknowledge their role in US racism, past and present, pointing toward a shift in how America(ns) understand and relate to this contentious past. However, while The Legacy Museum and its sister institution, the National Memorial to Peace and Justice, were developed during the Obama era, which many believed indicated a new "post-racial" America, they opened in 2018 in what scholar Alison Landsberg has called a "post-postracial" America (2018). Under Trump's administration, the US saw growing racial tension, white nationalism and political division, even as many on the left sought to draw attention to the ongoing consequences of racial injustice, particularly through the Black Lives Matter movement, signaling a "reemergence of race as a socially and politically significant discourse" (Landsberg, 2018: p 199). In this chapter, I examine The Legacy Museum's confrontation of America's racist past in the context of the current social-political moment in the US and within the larger global commemorative trend of memorial museums as a form of reckoning with contentious pasts and futures.[1]

Contentious memory and memorial museums

In recent decades, something of a memory boom has swept the globe. Evident in everything from academia, with its quickly expanding field of memory studies, to popular culture, where autobiographies and memoirs are surging in popularity, together with museums, memorials and historic sites, this memory boom is particularly evident throughout civil society and political life. However, whereas memory of conflict and violence used to take form as triumphant celebrations of the victors, today there has been a shift to focus on coming to terms with the problems of the past. This change in societies' orientation toward the past has been termed a "politics of regret" (Olick, 2007) or "reparations politics" (Torpey, 2006), and points towards what is often a more introspective and critical – sometimes self-indicting – attempt to reckon with past oppression and injustice. Thus, a big part of the memory boom has taken the shape of memorials, museums, apologies, reparations, truth commissions, and other mechanisms aimed at righting past wrongs.

Memorial museums are one such manifestation of this memory boom; emerging from early efforts to commemorate the Holocaust (Young, 1993; Sodaro, 2018), they have since spread around the globe and nearly any society with conflict in its recent (or not-so-recent) past has created a memorial museum. Where they are built, memorial museums are often extremely popular tourist destinations, demonstrating that it is not just academics, but the general public that is interested in memory of past violence.[2] As a sociologist of memory, I understand memorial museums to be significant public institutions in which the past is represented by and for the present. Sociological analysis of collective memory emphasizes that the past is always reconstructed by the present (for example, Halbwachs, 1992) and that the forms it takes – the social frameworks that enable memory's articulation in the present – help to make meaning of past events and shape present understandings of history (Wagner-Pacifici, 1996). Museums as cultural forms serve various important purposes in contemporary society: from encouraging visitors to engage in a "ritual of citizenship" (Duncan, 1991), to teaching self-regulation and discipline (Bennett, 1988), to embodying and displaying "official nationalism" (Anderson, 1991). They are also believed to be highly trustworthy institutions.[3] Memorial museums thus harness this cultural authority and perceived objectivity to the power and affect of memory to represent and teach about contentious and violent pasts.

My research on memorial museums has found that their ultimate goal in combining museological history-telling and education with affective memory is to change visitors' attitudes and beliefs in a way that will purportedly promote democratic culture and the prevention of future violence – moral transformation vis-à-vis an *ethic of never again* (Sodaro, 2018). However, memorial museums are inevitably and always political institutions and so the transformation they attempt depends very much on the context in which they are created. Memorial museums ultimately tell us more about the present society in which they are created than they do about the past that they recall and in this way are useful institutions for understanding how contestations and conflicts over the past reveal present political and social concerns. They help us to see how entrepreneurs of the present make meaning of the past via exhibits and narratives, revealing important aspects of the broader political and economic context in which they work.

The "global rush to commemorate" using memorial museums (Williams, 2007) has been very selective in the US to date, with a couple of very prominent memorial museums and some striking silences, reflecting US politics and priorities. The US Holocaust Memorial Museum, which opened in 1993, was one of the first memorial museums and has become a global model for others, including dozens of other Holocaust museums in the US. Over 20 years later, the National September 11 Memorial Museum opened as another prominent American memorial museum, using cutting-edge museological design and technology to create a deeply moving and affective experience of 9/11. However, these museums adhere to hegemonic American narratives of US innocence (Sturken, 2016) and the American ideals of democracy and freedom (Sodaro, 2018), providing visitors with what Edward Linenthal (1995) calls a "comfortable horrible memory" of atrocities for which the US was not responsible. What has been missing from the memorial landscape in the US are museums and memory sites focused on past atrocities that implicate the US, such as the genocide of Native Americans and slavery. However, in the last few years there appears to be space opening up in American historical memory to address and incorporate more contentious and difficult pasts, including in new memorial museums like The Legacy Museum.

Race and memory in US museums

While African American history, and that of other minoritized groups, is woefully underrepresented in US historic and heritage sites (Linn-Tynen, 2020) – for example, less than 8 per cent of the almost 100,000 sites listed on the National Register of Historic Places are focused on women, Latinos, African Americans and other minoritized groups (Bronin, 2020) – museums of African American history and culture are not new in the US. Since the founding of the first African American-focused museum, at Hampton University in 1868 (Burns, 2013: p 8), African American museums have proliferated; in 1978 there was enough momentum for the formation of the Association of African American Museums, which currently has over 200 members (Burns 2013: p 10). Scholars (Autry, 2013; Burns, 2013) argue that African American museums have been created in phases. The first consisted of the establishment of neighborhood museums, primarily in northern or midwestern cities, during the 1960s and 1970s civil rights era. This was followed by a second, post-civil rights phase in which museums were created to focus on recent African American history, primarily the Civil Rights Movement, as a part of urban renewal projects (Autry, 2013). In analyzing the political economy of memory in which these phases unfolded, Robyn Autry argues that while the context behind their creations differs, the museums are united in the kinds of "uplifting" stories that they tell: they tend to sanitize past racial violence and avoid narratives of Black victimization in order to fit the "narrative of progress that resonates with more conventional representations of American social values and mores" (2013: p 77). Either with the goal of conveying inspirational messages to highlight resistance and resilience (Autry, 2013), working to "vindicate the race" vis-à-vis white America (Burns, 2013), or accommodating white visitors in order to bring in tourist dollars and burnish a city's image (Dwyer and Alderman, 2008), African American museums have traditionally avoided confrontation with the violence and injustice of slavery and its legacies.

At the same time that these museums were providing African American communities with empowering "free spaces" (Burns, 2013) promoting unity and community pride, the global memory boom was pushing societies and collectives to confront their contentious pasts via a politics of regret. Over the course of the 20th century, the growing emphasis on human rights and burgeoning political power of minoritized and marginalized groups mean that there was a new public validation for victims of historical injustice and new demands for perpetrators of those injustices to confront their implication. Though the US has been very slow to confront its own contentious and implicated past vis-à-vis this politics of regret, some museums across the country have taken tentative steps toward confrontation with the history of slavery. Amidst a backdrop of post-civil rights-era social changes and growing academic and public interest in the history of slavery, museums and exhibits have slowly begun to incorporate stories of slavery. Washington, DC's Anacostia Museum had a 1979 exhibit focused on slavery called "Out of Africa" and the Smithsonian National Museum of American History's 1985 exhibit "After the Revolution: Everyday Life in America, 1780–1800" included stories about slavery (Brooms, 2012: p 509). In the early 1990s, the African Burial Ground was re-discovered in lower Manhattan and a memorial and small museum opened on the site in 2007 and 2010 respectively, paving the way for and complementing the New York Historical Society's 2005 groundbreaking exhibit "Slavery in New York." While many considered the African Burial Ground to be a site of national importance, and continue to today,[4] plans were already underway for a national museum that would firmly usher in the third phase of African American museums in the US: the Smithsonian National Museum for African American History and Culture (NMAAHC).

The NMAAHC was chartered by George W. Bush in 2003 and opened in September 2016. It had been 100 years in the making; initiated in 1915 by the Committee of Colored Citizens, who wished to honor the contributions to the Civil War effort by African American soldiers on the National Mall, the museum's creation went through fits and starts, mirroring the national political, cultural, and economic situation. In the 1990s, momentum grew with the establishment of the African American Museum Project at the Smithsonian, and in 2001 the legislation was passed to make the museum a reality. Its opening, in the waning days of Barack Obama's second term and just over a month before Trump's improbable 2016 victory, was an opportunity to celebrate the museum as a symbol of national unity – if not by putting past racial violence and injustice behind us entirely, then by understanding it as part of the teleological tale of progress that is America. Obama's lofty speech argued: "That's the American story that this museum tells – one of suffering and delight; one of fear but also of hope; of wandering in the wilderness and then seeing out on the horizon a glimmer of the Promised Land."

The American-ness of the museum had to be stressed in order for it to make it through a Congress with many members resistant to a museum focused specifically on African Americans. And as Obama's speech suggested, the museum's story is one that is both "upsetting" and "uplifting" (Cotter, 2016), taking visitors from the suffering and violence of slavery, where artifacts like a slave cabin and shackles are displayed, through the injustice of segregation, where Emmett Till's coffin reminds of the violent enforcement of "separate by equal." But the final historical section, "A Changing America," which focuses on the period from MLK's assassination to Obama's election, the endpoint of the historical exhibit, ensures that the story of race in America ends with uplift and seems to reflect the heady – and misguided – belief that the US had moved on from racism with the election of Obama. The museum thus tells a tale of progress, constructing "consensus" out of a difficult history (Teeger and Vinitzky-Seroussi, 2007). However, despite its framing around unity and racial harmony, the NMAAHC does something new: it centers race and the African American story within American history. Through its in-depth narration of American history centered on racial oppression, "The museum creates the occasion for white people to confront the violence that whites, and white supremacy, have inflicted on Blacks" and to "*own* uncomfortable memories of American whiteness" (Landsberg, 2018: p 209). Thus, the museum's narrative of progress is tempered by caution as the museum works to navigate its complex role as a national institution.

Just 18 months after the NMAAHC opened, The Legacy Museum opened in Montgomery to a very different political and social context. While many celebrated Obama's election and re-election as evidence of a move toward a "post-racial" America, that myth was shattered with Donald Trump's election in 2016. He had campaigned using openly racist rhetoric and promises – his political career was launched by his virulent birther lies about Obama – and his election enabled a rise in racist rhetoric and white nationalism. White supremacist groups were emboldened during Trump's presidency, exemplified by the 2017 Charlottesville Unite the Right rally where white nationalists hoisted tiki torches and shouted racist chants to protest the removal of a statue of Robert E. Lee. Met by anti-racist counterprotests, the rally turned deadly with three people killed and dozens injured. Encouraged in part by Trump's refusal to condemn the racist rally and violence, white nationalist hate groups grew by 55 per cent during Trump's presidency (SPLC, 2019), culminating in the January 6 attack on the US Capitol by an angry mob of Trump supporters, many displaying racist symbols like Confederate flags and nooses. The Legacy Museum opened within this tumultuous, "post-postracial" period (Landsberg, 2018), when it had become painfully clear that the US had not moved beyond race with the election of Obama.

The Legacy Museum

The Legacy Museum: From Enslavement to Mass Incarceration and its sister institution, the National Memorial to Peace and Justice, colloquially known as the Lynching Memorial, were built by the non-profit organization Equal Justice Initiative (EJI). Created and run by civil rights lawyer Bryan Stevenson, EJI primarily provides legal representation for people wrongly convicted, unfairly sentenced or abused in the criminal justice system. But their work within the US's discriminatory criminal justice system demanded a more complete and historical accounting. EJI began investigating this history, producing a 2013 report on slavery, with a focus on Montgomery, which laid the foundation for their groundbreaking investigations on lynching in the South and across the US. Through extensive research, EJI documented over 4400 lynchings in the period between Reconstruction and WWII[5] and, deeming these lynchings racial terror, they decided that this dark side of America's history had to be publicly told.

One part of the telling of this story is the stunning memorial to the 4400 people lynched. Built into a hill just outside of downtown Montgomery, the memorial encircles an open, grassy square with 800 hanging steel monuments. Each column represents a county in which a lynching (or many) occurred and is marked by the dates and names of the victims. As visitors make their way through the memorial, the ground descends and the monuments, which in the beginning were bolted into the ground, rise to hang ominously above the visitors. Wall panels with brief descriptions of some of the lynchings give names and horrifying detail to the staggering scale of violence; a wall of running water, providing a soothing soundtrack, reminds visitors that thousands of victims remain unknown. Outside of the memorial, duplicates of the monuments lie almost like coffins, waiting for counties to acknowledge their past violence and claim their monument (Schult 2020). Though many counties have initiated the process of claiming their duplicate monument, at the time of this writing (summer 2020) not a single monument had yet been claimed, underlining the deeply contentious pasts that these monuments and the memorial evoke.

The rest of the story that EJI's research uncovered is told in The Legacy Museum, which contextualizes the racial terror lynchings within America's long history of racial injustice and which, like the memorial, is intended to "force a reckoning with America's history of racial violence and its continuing legacy" (Woodley, 2022: p 3). Though the museum reopened in October 2021 at four times the size and in a new building, the new museum retains the character and elements of the original. This chapter focuses on the first version of the museum, which was located in a low, whitewashed brick building near Montgomery's waterfront, a former warehouse district that appears to be undergoing revitalization. The museum is located in Montgomery because that is where EJI is based, but the city is symbolically a deeply meaningful place for such a museum (for example, Brand, Inwood, and Alderman, 2022). As the capitol of Alabama, Montgomery is a city of imposing, neoclassical white government buildings; for a deep red state that believes in small government, the government looks anything but small. Among the white government buildings are numerous courts, police stations, sheriff's offices, jails, and parole offices, suggesting an omnipresent criminal justice system – part of the reason that EJI is based here. But this present Montgomery is also steeped in history. All over the city historic markers denote important sites of the Civil War and the Civil Rights Movement, highlighting Montgomery's fame as both the "cradle of the Confederacy" and the "birthplace of the Civil Rights Movement." Just a short walk from the place where Rosa Parks boarded a bus and refused to give up her seat sits the First White House of the Confederacy, where Jefferson Davis resided until 1861. Even the striking Artesian Basin and Court Square Fountain, gracefully poised between the riverfront and the capitol, was the site of slave auctions.

When Stevenson moved to Montgomery in the 1980s there were no references to slavery in Montgomery (The Legacy Museum, 2018), but today a historic marker outside of EJI's offices, around the corner from the museum, tells visitors that these warehouses were used in the slave trade. This point is reiterated on entrance to the museum, where visitors are met with a painted message on a brick wall: You are standing on a site where enslaved people were warehoused. Thus begins a visit to The Legacy Museum in a cramped entry alcove with this stark marker of the building's past. The alcove fills in this grim history with information about the slave trade in Montgomery, which surged after the Transatlantic Slave Trade was banned in 1808, and approximately one million enslaved (and freed) African

Americans were relocated from the upper south to the lower south to work the plantations. While Montgomery thrived on this domestic slave trade, a wall of quotes from testimonies of enslaved people describes the devastating human consequences of slave auctions and family separations, when families were ripped apart in the name of commerce.

Visitors walk down a dark ramp into the main exhibit and on the way encounter the ghosts of this domestic slave trade. In the recreated "slave pens," holograms of enslaved people, awaiting their imminent sale on the auction block, come to life and speak to visitors as they approach the cells; a woman sings mournful hymns, another begs to see her children, two children stand terrified and timidly ask if you can help them find their mother. The figures fade when visitors walk away, but to walk away is to ignore the pleas of people long since lost to history but here given voice (for example, Sturken, 2022); it feels wrong and most visitors stay and listen, many clinging to the bars to get closer.

For visitors familiar with Holocaust and other memorial museums, these figures evoke the video testimony of survivors that has become a staple of historical exhibitions; with roots in Holocaust research and commemoration, witness testimony has become a key mode for restoring the voice and humanity of those who suffered and for helping those who were not there identify with victims in a more deep and affective way. For bearing witness to testimony is considered an act that demands individuals to take responsibility for what they see (for example, Felman, 1992). Roger Smith has theorized this responsibility as a "pedagogy of witness" that occurs in spaces like memorial museums, where "the animation of specters … has the potential to deeply haunt the formation of contemporary consciousness and conscience" (2014: p 2). In these slave pens, because there are no living witnesses whose testimony can be shared, the figures are indeed ghost-like, appearing out of the darkness of the cells to speak directly to the visitor, who is then "given – and saddled with – agency" (Bal, 2001: p 207) and the expectation that they will take responsibility for what they have witnessed.

But in this museum, the burden of responsibility is different from Holocaust and other memorial museums that remember violence long past. As the museum's name, The Legacy Museum: From Enslavement to Mass Incarceration, suggests slavery is only part of the story that the museum tells. In fact, the museum is making an argument that slavery did not end but simply changed shape throughout American history. This is a radical departure from the work of more traditional history museums that seek to emphasize a break with the past; even the NMAAHC, despite its centering of race to the American experience, has a clear end to the historical exhibit – the election of Obama – that suggests US victory over racial injustice. The Legacy Museum's argument is one that has gained traction through books like Michelle Alexander's *The New Jim Crow* and Ava DuVernay's documentary *13th*; the museum represents the first concrete, museological representation of this argument. Thus, the room housing the main exhibit, which in its original version was very small for a museum with such a weighty topic, is divided into four sections – periods of racial injustice in American history and present – which are laid out chronologically along a main wall. This linear chronology gives an overview and to make their way through the full exhibit visitors must move back and forth through the space.

The first section, Enslavement in America, begins as the others do, with a word and number: Kidnapped: 12 million. A brief overview on the main wall uses text panels and images interspersed with short quotes that cut vertically down the wall and spill onto the floor to tell of the first evolution of enslavement in America, from the transatlantic to domestic slave trade. In one of the first indications of the connections the museum is making between past and present, a large photo shows imprisoned men in Malawi in 2011 being made to sleep "like in the middle passage." In this section one also starts to notice the use of language that will recur throughout as part of the careful construction of an argument that slavery did not end in 1865, but instead evolved into new forms that continue today. Words like "permanent status," "racial hierarchy," "hereditary," and "caste system" are reminders that slavery laid the groundwork for the racial inequality that is structured into America's institutions today.

Enslavement in America extends into the middle of the room with a focus on the selling of human beings – diaphanous pieces of fabric hang from ceiling to floor imprinted with sections of John G. Winter's slave catalogue in which he advertises "Negroes, Mules, Carts, Wagons, etc." An adjacent wall is covered by reprints of advertisements of enslaved people for sale and those asking for the return of escaped slaves, as well as ads posted by enslaved or formerly enslaved people searching for their loved ones. A triptych of touchscreens allows visitors to delve deeper into topics related to enslavement, such as the economics of slavery and its reach into all American institutions, or resistance and revolt, a common theme in other museums' portrayals of American chattel slavery (for example, Araujo, 2021). And in a small theatre in the back of this section, one of EJI's ultra-sophisticated videos (they have partnered with HBO, Google and a number of visual artists on audiovisual materials) gives an overview of enslavement in America and explains the museum's goal to "foster honest conversation about the legacy of slavery."

In this first section visitors might begin to notice the museum's striking use of color. Almost the entire exhibit is in black and white, with only some soft, terracotta orange – not unlike the weathered brick buildings that line Montgomery's once grand Dexter Avenue – breaking up the stark lines. But like everything in the museum these color choices are deliberate. White throughout the exhibit is used to represent ideas, statements, and actions by white people against racial justice, such as the advertisements for enslaved people being sold, while black is used to represent Black agency, ideas, and actions that advance racial justice, such as the ads searching for loved ones. The museum's core argument is thus given an added layer of color symbolism, reflecting the ways in which exhibit design and the forms that memory and historical narrative take in museums helps to shape their content and messages.

Winding one's way back, visitors encounter the second period: Terrorized: 9 million. In this section, the overview wall explains how, upon the end of slavery, convict leasing and then lynchings became a kind of "second slavery" and racial terror. A huge and haunting photo of one lynching sets the tone – a white crowd, including children, gathered under the feet of a hanging victim – and images of newspaper headlines announcing upcoming lynchings remind visitors that these were public spectacles, implicating thousands of white Americans. In the center of this section is a round table of touchscreens. On two sides of the table are interactive maps of the US with red dots marking counties in which lynchings were perpetrated.[6] Visitors can click on any county or state and see how many lynchings were carried out and of whom (where this information is available); some of these red dots can be clicked on for brief stories detailing the lynchings. The other two sides of the table show testimonial videos of people touched by this racial terror – families that were forced to flee, descendants whose ancestors were lynched whose pain has not disappeared with time. These testimonies help to humanize this violence and remind visitors that the consequences are ongoing. A wall of jars of soil lines the back of this section, samples collected from each county in Alabama in which there was a lynching. The jars, arranged chronologically, are a stunning range of colors and textures with the county name, the victim's name, and the date. The soil collection is part of EJI's Community Remembrance Project, in which EJI works with communities to document racial terror lynchings, collect soil from the sites, install historical markers, and ultimately "foster meaningful dialogue about race and justice."[7] In the small alcove behind the soil, a video about the Community Remembrance Project plays on one wall and on the other, a touch screen with a warning about the disturbing images shows images of lynchings, which would have circulated as postcards and souvenirs.

The museum (and memorial) is a culmination and physical, visual representation of EJI's research on lynchings in America and in some ways the third section, Segregated: 10 million, seems perfunctory – a display on civil rights that for most African American museums is central to a teleological story of overcoming injustice. But in The Legacy Museum this story is reframed and the focus is on the legal frameworks that enabled, enforced, and sustained segregation. A racial justice timeline of the Supreme Court highlights in black the decisions that have advanced racial justice and in white those that have set it back, up to the present day; there are many more decisions in white. In the middle of the section, large walls display signs from the days of segregation ("This park for white people only"), Jim Crow laws ("No whites and Blacks can play checkers together") and the commitments of politicians and other public figures to segregation ("I say segregation now, segregation tomorrow, segregation forever" – George Wallace, 1963). There are some moving videos of civil rights protests, tucked in between these stark reminders of the breadth of Jim Crow hatred, and in the back of the section a theatre plays a video about the Montgomery Bus Boycott, but these moments of relief from the relentless injustice and racism on display are too small to counter the overarching narrative. This is driven home in the museum's narrative transition from segregation to mass incarceration, which explains that the criminal justice system was an effective tool for the repression of the Civil Rights Movement and a new form of racial terror lynching.

Thus the museum's narrative brings the visitor up to the present with the fourth and final section: Incarcerated: 8 million. Having moved through slavery's evolving forms – from the transatlantic to the domestic trade, to convict leasing, racial terror, and segregation – the narrative ends with a denunciation of the present form of slavery in our criminal justice system: built upon the racialization of criminality, political emphasis on "law and order," and the War on Drugs, the criminal justice system has effectively perpetuated the US's racial caste system by disproportionately locking up people of color. A powerful documentary describes the terrifying violence of Louisiana's infamous St. Clair prison and touch screens outline the widespread reverberations of mass incarceration in the US. Underlining the depth of injustices in the criminal justice system, a wall displays reproductions of letters received by EJI from people in prison begging for help: a woman sentenced to life without parole for possession of 2.2 pounds of marijuana, begging to get out to see her children; a man sentenced to life in St. Clair for stealing a bicycle.

But the focus of this section is the simulated prison visitation room in which visitors can "talk" to incarcerated individuals. Taking a seat and reviewing the invasive list of prison rules for visitors, which leaves only to the imagination the indignities that prisoners are subject to, visitors pick up a telephone and hear the story of the prisoner on a video screen in bars before them. All of the individuals were actually locked up and their stories are heartbreaking reminders of the injustices of our prison system: a woman describes giving birth to a baby, after being raped by a prison guard, only to have the infant taken from her after less than 24 hours; a young man describes his 18 years in solitary confinement after being sentenced to life in prison at 14 years old.[8] Unlike the ghostly specters in the slave pens, these people are very much alive, telling their stories in high definition to the visitor, similarly imploring that visitors shoulder some responsibility for this injustice. But their stories of being "disposed, captive and silenced" in the prison system suggests that they might be more akin to "living ghosts" in American society (Hudson, 2017: p 93). Just as enslaved individuals were stripped of their humanity and placed in cages, so these individuals are discarded and dehumanized in the contemporary manifestation of slavery in the US.

The museum makes a small effort to end a visit on a hopeful note. Visitors walk from the main exhibit through a room with warm, orange walls lined with photos of heroes and activists in the struggle for racial justice, while music celebrating resistance plays. The room provides a bit of light, but again not enough to brighten the dark narrative of America's past. And the final corridor through which visitors exit is lined by large photographs and questions posing ethical dilemmas to visitors: a reminder about the Thirteenth amendment loophole and the question of whether slavery should be completely abolished in the US; a photo of a Confederate statue and the question of what should be done with these monuments. The corridor opens up to a few more touchscreens on which visitors are encouraged to take actions – signing petitions, finding out about volunteer opportunities in their states, and learning more about the work of EJI. But despite these efforts to offer visitors a note of hope, the overwhelming experience and message of the museum is devastating: the US is a nation built upon a foundation of racism and racial inequality so that slavery has not ended, but has only evolved to take new, less obvious but no less pernicious forms today.

"Reshaping the national conversation"[9]

The Legacy Museum envisions itself as "an engine for education about the legacy of racial inequality and for the truth and reconciliation that leads to real solutions to contemporary problems."[10] There is not a past that is more contested in the US than that of slavery and its ongoing legacies of inequality; contemporary debates over Confederate symbols, critical race theory, reparations, and Black Lives Matter remind us that the past is hardly past. Yet, a glance at other African American museums suggests that this past is most comfortably addressed in narratives that end in the uplifting triumph of the Civil Rights Movement. Slavery, segregation, lynching, and other past forms of racial violence are kept firmly in the past. Even in the NMAAHC, the past is literally buried deep underground and visitors ascend to a present filled with African American achievements. This is common to most memorial museums, such as the United States Holocaust Memorial Museum (USHMM) or 9/11 Museum, which tell narratives of very specific histories that are kept distinct from the present, in part through their representation in museum form (Sodaro, 2018).

The Legacy Museum is different; its starting point is the present. Of course, the sociological study of memory shows us that it is always the present from which we define, remember, and represent the past, but The Legacy Museum's journey through the past is one that started with EJI's work to ameliorate problems in the present. Founded in 1989 by Bryan Stevenson, EJI "is committed to ending mass incarceration and excessive punishment in the United States, to challenging racial and economic injustice, and to protecting basic human rights for the most vulnerable people in American society" (About EJI, 2021). After two decades of doing this difficult work, EJI turned to the historical project of tracing the roots of the inequality that they witnessed on a daily basis with their research on slavery and lynching. Thus, the historical story told in the museum is not relegated to a bygone era, but is the background and context for the present social problems that EJI works to overcome. This is evident in the evenly divided space of the museum into its four periods of racial injustice. Slavery and mass incarceration are linked and given equal space, reminding visitors that slavery has not been left in the past. This is also evident in the weaving of present into the past, such as the jars of soil collected today from sites of past racial terror, or the testimony of people who continue to be haunted by this violent past. It is evident in the exhibits' design, particularly in the graphic use of color, with white denoting white supremacy stretching from 400 years ago up into the contemporary era of mass incarceration. And it is particularly evident in the enslaved and incarcerated individuals who speak to the visitors, and implore them to feel an individual, personal connection to – and responsibility for – this contentious past and its memory.

In this way, the museum is not letting its (white, American) visitors off easily, but is instead presenting them with a historical account in which they are implicated. To understand this, it is helpful to turn to memory studies for insight into social relationships vis-à-vis the past. In his book, *The Implicated Subject: Beyond Victims and Perpetrators*, Michael Rothberg introduces the concept of the implicated subject to describe a relationship to historical and present injustice, oppression and violence that doesn't fit the usual, clear cut categories of victim, perpetrator and bystander: "Implicated subjects occupy positions aligned with power and privilege without being themselves direct agents of harm; they contribute to, inhabit, inherit, or benefit from regimes of domination but do not originate or control such regimes" (2019: p.1). In the US, they/we are the beneficiaries and participants in a deeply entrenched system of racist injustice, violence, and oppression. Rothberg argues that accepting this position can "open up a space for new coalitions across identities and groups" because it "draws attention to responsibilities for violence and injustice greater than most of us want to embrace and shifts questions of accountability from a discourse of guilt to a less legally and emotionally charged terrain of historical and political responsibility" (2019: p 20).

In its unflinching story of past racial oppression that directly links to today's injustices, The Legacy Museum is reminding us that most of us are implicated in and thus hold some responsibility for this contentious past and its memory. It is not a comfortable experience to visit the museum, particularly for white Americans, as it provides a stark and powerful reminder of how deeply entrenched racism and white supremacy are in our society. As I have noted earlier, the goal of memorial museums like The Legacy Museum is to change attitudes and beliefs. In this case, the challenging narrative the museum tells and the implication that it places upon its (white) visitors is meant to promote "the truth and reconciliation" that can help solve "contemporary problems." By encouraging visitors to face that which is most contested and contentious in US history and its ongoing manifestations, the hope of EJI is that the museum will move the country closer to greater equality and justice. In the words of Bryan Stevenson, "The Legacy Museum is a small but important effort to confront our nation's silence and to change the distorted narrative that too many have been taught" (The Legacy Museum, 2018). With each visit, The Legacy Museum helps to counter hegemonic historical narratives and reshape American collective memory of slavery and its lasting legacy.

Conclusion

The Legacy Museum is not a national museum and is thus freed from the expectation that national museums, such as the NMAAHC, tell an uplifting story that adheres to hegemonic American historical memory. The Legacy Museum was created by a non-profit organization and built with private funds raised from foundations and individuals, at a cost of $20 million for both the museum and memorial (Dafoe, 2018). Because it is on privately owned land, does not receive government funding, and was created and is run by EJI, it is free to tell the story that it wishes to tell, which is one of white America's implication in our contentious past. A national museum, or any museum receiving public funding, would mostly likely not be able to make such a strident argument against racial progress. In an ironic twist, however, it is located in the "Cradle of the Confederacy," in a state and city that continue to cling to the Lost Cause myth of southern glory.[11] Despite this seemingly inhospitable environment for such a museum, it appears that the museum and memorial have been powerful engines of revitalization for the depressed city of Montgomery. In the first year that the museum and memorial were open, Montgomery had 400,000 more visitors and sold 107,000 more hotel rooms than in the previous year (Schneider, 2019) and although the pandemic appears to have hit the city hard – when I visited in June 2021 the downtown felt like a ghost town – there are still many construction projects underway and many tourists in town for the museum, hopefully signaling continued revitalization.

As recent events have made clear, this is both a precarious and propitious time for challenging narratives of racial history in the US. On one hand, white nationalist hate groups proliferate, voting rights are being rolled back all over the country, and states and school districts are falling over themselves trying to ban "critical race theory" in schools, demonstrating that many, particularly on the right, are working overtime to sever the past from the present in the interest of maintaining the (white supremacist) status quo. But these frantic attempts to shut down progress towards racial justice are evidence that progress is being made and honest reckoning is starting to occur. The BLM protests of 2020, the wave of universities and other institutions acknowledging their past ties to slavery, and new momentum on reparations, including the program enacted in Evanston, IL,[12] are clear steps towards addressing the lasting legacy of slavery in the US.

All of this is happening against the backdrop of a global pandemic that has revealed and deepened inequalities and ravaged economies in the US and around the globe. Yet, even while museums were devastated by the shutdowns, they have perhaps also gained a new relevance: because cultural institutions play a significant role in engaging the public around difficult social issues and contentious memories, as society opens back up and continues to confront the changing debates around race in America, The Legacy Museum becomes ever more important. In fact, EJI is embracing this role and new potentialities with the newly reopened and much larger museum, evidencing its continued and growing significance as a cultural institution. In this post-postracial America, as understanding of the historical roots and dimensions of racism in the US collide with present systemic injustices and racial terror, it becomes less possible for the majority of the population to absolve themselves of implication and responsibility for the past. The Legacy Museum represents an important cultural space for the acknowledgment of implication and its concomitant responsibility for redressing past wrongs and reshaping a more equitable society.

Notes

[1] Research for this chapter was conducted in June 2021 at The Legacy Museum with the generous support of the Professional Staff Congress-City University of New York (PSC-CUNY) Research Award Program.

[2] There is a thriving subfield at the intersection of memory studies and heritage/tourism studies focused on dark tourism that examines this popular interest in visiting sites of death, trauma, and atrocity.

[3] For example, a recent survey found that 81 per cent of respondents find history museums "absolutely" or "somewhat trustworthy" (Dichtl, 2018).

4   There is currently a bill before Congress to make the African Burial Ground in New York a national museum, with an expanded building and a partnership with the Smithsonian National Museum of African American History and Culture.
5   That number has now gone up to 6500.
6   This map is the heart of EJI's work to document racial terror lynchings. Supported by Google, the map can also be found on their website: https://lynchinginamerica.eji.org/explore.
7   https://eji.org/projects/community-remembrance-project/
8   The young man is Ian Manuel. His story has a "happy" ending as EJI was able to get him released.
9   The Legacy Museum, 2018.
10 https://museumandmemorial.eji.org/museum
11 The Lost Cause is a fictional narrative of the past that claims that slavery was a benign institution and that the Civil War was a war over states' rights, not slavery. It reframes the Confederate cause as honorable and heroic and remains very potent today, particularly in the South (for example, Domby, 2020).
12 Evanston's new reparations program, the first in the US, is aimed at addressing the "historical harm" done to Evanston residents through "discriminatory housing policies and practices and inaction by the City" (City of Evanston, 2021). The program will distribute $10 million in housing grants to families who were discriminated against in the housing market.

References

"About EJI" (2021) Equal Justice Initiative, Available from: https://eji.org/about/ [Accessed November 3, 2021].

Anderson, B. (1991) *Imagined Communities: Reflections on the Origin and Spread of Nationalism*, New York: Verso.

Araujo, A.L. (2021) *Museums and Atlantic Slavery*, New York: Routledge.

Autry, R. (2013) "The Political Economy of Memory: The Challenges of Representing National Conflict at 'Identity-Driven' Museums," *Theory and Society* 42: 57–80.

Bal, M. (2002) *Travelling Concepts in the Humanities: A Rough Guide*, Toronto: University of Toronto Press.

Bennett, T. (1988) "The Exhibitionary Complex," *New Formations* 4: 73–102.

Blake, S. (2020) "Why the George Floyd Protests Feel Different – Lots and Lots of Mobile Video," *dot.LA*, [online] June 12, Available from: https://dot.la/george-floyd-video-2646171522.html [Accessed August 25, 2021].

Brand, A.L., Inwood, J.F. and Alderman, D. (2022) "Truth-Telling and Memory-Work in Montgomery's Co-Constituted Landscapes," *ACME: An International Journal for Critical Geographies*, 21(5): 468–483.

Bronin, S. (2020) "Op-Ed: How to Fix a National Register of Historic Places That Reflects Mostly White History," *Los Angeles Times*, [online] December 15, Available from: www.latimes.com/opinion/story/2020-12-15/historic-preservation-chicano-moratorium-national-register [Accessed August 26, 2021].

Brooms, D. (2012) "Lest We Forget: Exhibiting (and Remembering) Slavery in African-American Museums," *Journal of African American Studies* 15(4): 508–523.

Buchanan, L., Quoctrung, B. and Patel, J. (2020) "Black Lives Matter May Be the Largest Movement in US History," *The New York Times*, [online] July 3, Available from: www.nytimes.com/interactive/2020/07/03/us/george-floyd-protests-crowd-size.html [Accessed August 26, 2021].

Burns, A. (2013) *From Storefront to Monument: Tracing the Public History of the Black Museum Movement*, Amherst, MA: University of Massachusetts Press.

City of Evanston (2021) "Memorandum: Adoption of Resolution 37-R-27," March 22, Available from: https://cityofevanston.civicweb.net/document/50624/Adoption%20of%20Resolution%2037-R-27,%20Authorizing%20the.pdf?handle=E11C7B73E1B6470DA42362AB80A50C46 [Accessed November 3, 2021].

Cotter, H. (2016) "Review: The Smithsonian African American Museum Is Here at Last. And It Uplifts and Upsets," *The New York Times*, [online] September 15, Available from: www.nytimes.com/2016/09/22/arts/design/smithsonian-african-american-museum-review.html [Accessed August 27, 2021].

Dafoe, T. (2018) "A First Look Inside the New Alabama Museum Boldly Confronting Slavery and Its Brutal Legacy," *Artnet*, [online] April 26, https://news.artnet.com/art-world/legacy-museum-memorial-peace-justice-1272686 [Accessed August 27, 2021].

Dichtl, J. (2018) "Most Trust Museums as Sources of Historical Information," *American Association for State and Local History*, Available from: https://aaslh.org/most-trust-museums/ [Accessed August 27, 2021].

Domby, A. (2020) *The False Cause: Fraud, Fabrication, and White Supremacy in Confederate Memory*, Charlottesville, VA: University of Virginia Press.

Duncan, C. (1991) "The Art Museum as a Ritual of Citizenship," in I. Karp and S.D. Lavin (eds) *Exhibiting Cultures: The Poetics and Politics of Museum Display*, Washington, DC: Smithsonian Institution Press, pp 88–103.

Dwyer, O. and Alderman, D. (2008) *Civil Rights Memorials and the Geography of Memory*, Chicago, IL: Center for American Places at Columbia College.

Felman, S. (1992) "The Return of the Voice: Claude Lanzmann's Shoah," in S. Felman and D. Laub (eds) *Testimony: Crises of Witnessing in Literature, Psychoanalysis and History*, New York: Routledge, pp 204–283.

Fernandez-Kelly, P. (2020) "A Sociological Note on George Floyd's Death and the Pandemic," *Items, Social Science Research Center*, [online] June 18, Available from: https://items.ssrc.org/covid-19-and-the-social-sciences/society-after-pandemic/a-sociological-note-on-george-floyds-death-and-the-pandemic/ [Accessed August 25, 2021].

Halbwachs, M. (1992) *On Collective Memory*, Chicago, IL: University of Chicago Press.

Heany, M. (2020) "The George Floyd Protests Generated More Media Coverage than Any Protest in 50 Years," *Washington Post*, [online] July 6, Available from: www.washingtonpost.com/politics/2020/07/06/george-floyd-protests-generated-more-media-coverage-than-any-protest-50-years/ [Accessed August 25, 2021].

Hudson, M. (2017) *Ghosts, Landscapes and Social Memory*, London: Routledge.

Landsberg, A. (2018) "Post-Postracial America: On Westworld and the Smithsonian National Museum of African American History and Culture," *Cultural Politics* 14(2): 198–215.

The Legacy Museum (2018) Museum catalogue, Equal Justice Initiative.

Linenthal, E. (1995) *Preserving Memory: The Struggle to Create America's Holocaust Museum*. New York: Viking.

Linn-Tynen, E. (2020) "Reclaiming the Past as a Matter of Social Justice: African American Heritage, Representation and Identity in the United States," in V. Apaydin (ed) *Critical Perspectives on Cultural Memory and Heritage: Construction, Transformation and Destruction*, London: UCL Press, pp 255–268.

Olick, J.K. (2007) *The Politics of Regret: On Collective Memory and Historical Responsibility*, New York: Routledge.

Rothberg, M. 2019. *The Implicated Subject: Beyond Victims and Perpetrators*, Stanford, CA: Stanford University Press.

Schneider, K. (2019) "Revitalizing Montgomery as it Embraces its Past," *New York Times*, [online] May 21, Available from: www.nytimes.com/2019/05/21/business/montgomery-museums-civil-rights.html [Accessed August 26, 2021].

Schult, T. (2020) "Reshaping American Identity: The National Memorial for Peace and Justice and Its Take-Away Twin," *Liminalities* 16(5): 1–45.

Smith, R. (2014) *A Pedagogy of Witnessing: Curatorial Practice and the Pursuit of Social Justice*, Albany, NY: SUNY Press.

Sodaro, A. (2018) *Exhibiting Atrocity: Memorial Museums and the Politics of Past Violence*, New Brunswick, NJ: Rutgers University Press.

SPLC (2019) "The Year in Hate and Extremism 2019," *Southern Poverty Law Center*, [online], Available from: www.splcenter.org/year-hate-and-extremism-2019 [Accessed August 26, 2021].

Sturken, M. (2016) "The Objects That Lived: The 9/11 Museum and Material Transformation," *Memory Studies* 9(1): 13–26.

Sturken, M. (2022) *Terrorism in American Memory: Memorials, Museums, and Architecture in the Post-9/11 Era*, New York: New York University Press.

Teeger, C. and V. Vinitzky-Seroussi, V. (2007) "Controlling for Consensus: Commemorating Apartheid in South Africa," *Symbolic Interaction* 30(1): 57–78.

Torpey, J. (2006) *Making Whole What Has Been Smashed: On Reparations Politics*, Cambridge, MA: Harvard University Press.

Wagner-Pacifici, R. (1996) "Memories in the Making: The Shape of Things that Went," *Qualitative Sociology* 19(3): 301–321.

Williams, P. (2007) *Memorial Museums: The Global Rush to Commemorate Atrocities*, Oxford: Berg.

Woodley, J. (2022) "'Nothing Is Lost': Mourning and Memory at the National Memorial for Peace and Justice," *Memory Studies*, https://doi.org/10.1177/17506980221114080

Young, J. (1993) *The Texture of Memory: Holocaust Memorials and Meaning*, New Haven, CT: Yale University Press.

PART III

Genocide, Memory, and the Historicizing of Trauma

9

Remembrance and Historicization: Transformation of Individual and Collective Memory Processes in the Federal Republic of Germany

Werner Bohleber

Introduction

The Holocaust, the war of extermination and other National Socialist mass crimes brought such extreme devastation upon the world as has never been seen before and have far exceeded the bounds of conventional modes of comprehension and interpretation at work within memory, critical reflection, and historical insight. They challenge us not only to understand historically how this could have happened, but they also force us to confront a disturbing reality, to confront the horror of what happened and the suffering of the victims and the witnesses. Overcoming the extreme traumatization of people and its consequences became an unavoidable task not only for the individual survivors and their reorganization of life and of how they dealt with their past, but also for the societies affected by it. Moreover, the monstrosity of the unprecedented crimes against humanity posed new challenges to various scientific disciplines, such as history and the social sciences, but also to psychoanalysis.

The historians Jörn Rüsen (2001), Saul Friedländer (1994), and some others vehemently argue for including the concept of trauma in the theory of history. The Holocaust is a "borderline experience of history" that refuses to be integrated into a coherent pattern of interpretation. With a "sense of its own, or rather a counter-sense, the Holocaust has inscribed itself into the patterns of interpretation and orientation of the present, before these were specifically conceived in the cultural practices of historical memory" (Rüsen, 2001: p 183). The way to this understanding of the Holocaust was paved by the results of trauma research, namely that the experience of trauma for the affected person as a "catastrophic challenge to the formation of meaning" (Rüsen, 2001: p 154) only comes into effect afterwards, which the traumatized person often has to work on for a lifetime. This also explains the paradoxical fact that today Auschwitz is much more central to historical consciousness than it was in past decades.

It was not only the events of the Holocaust that had to be understood in a historically appropriate way, but also the cultural practices of remembering, how German society became aware of the Holocaust and the criminal extermination policies of National Socialism over the decades. The two were intertwined. Thus, the progress in historical research on the Holocaust and the extermination policy gave new impetus to the willingness to remember. But they also triggered new attempts at defense, through which remembering and the recognition of having been involved as perpetrators were repeatedly interrupted or distorted by relativizing justifications or defenses of guilt.

The historian Charles Maier compares the historians' dispute in 1986–88 about memory and the self-understanding of the Federal Republic to an "inhibited psychoanalytic treatment": "A history is not yet fully revealed – transference and catharsis are not yet possible" (Maier, 1988: p 196). This comparison is certainly not without reason. The decades-long social debate about an undisguised perception of the Nazi crimes, of the Holocaust and the war of extermination, led to the formation of contentious memories. Understanding them in depth requires the insights of psychoanalysis on how to deal with affect-laden memories, with feelings of fear, guilt, and shame, and with the defensive movements to protect a self-image experienced as threatened. Such memories may appear unacceptable to the individual; they are repressed, denied, encapsulated, reworked, or projectively externalized because they appear too painful to the self-image. These psychic processes play a role not only in individual memory, but also at the collective level. Moreover, psychoanalytic insights can also contribute to understanding the unconscious factors of the attraction that National Socialism and its ideology exerted on the German population, with its inherent intertwining of ideality and a radicalizing unprecedented destructivity. The traumatization of people experienced en masse as a result of the Holocaust, the policy of extermination, and other military actions is of particular importance. Their sustained psychiatric and psychoanalytical research only got underway in the 1970s. The difficulty was that one was dealing with memories that were overwhelming and psychically unmanageable. They could not be given meaning by the individual and integrated into his mental experience. Activated by associative triggers, they kept intruding uncontrollably into consciousness and coming to haunt the minds of survivors. The past thus remained present not only for the affected individuals, but it could not pass away for the affected societies either.

In the first part of my chapter, I will present the phases of the societal struggle to remember the past, with its manifold mixtures of its actualization and defending against it. This gave rise to social controversies that were ignited by the conflict between the desire for a positive national self-image and the negative memories opposing it. But all these attempts at defense were only temporarily successful. The social forces that helped historical reality to break through were stronger. But what it meant to recognize it became a question that always had to be negotiated with.

The existential quality of meaning of the Holocaust has a different signature and a different perspective for victims and perpetrators as well as for their descendants. For the victims and survivors of the Holocaust, the events had an extremely traumatizing effect. In a different way, large parts of the German population were exposed to traumatic experiences through war, bombings, flight and expulsion. The repression of one's own involvement in the Nazi regime in the postwar period and the refusal to adequately reflect on the reality of what had happened were not least due to the consequences of these traumatizations. We know from psychoanalytic research that the processing of traumatic catastrophes takes place over several generations. I will present these transgenerational consequences in a second part.

In a third and fourth part, I will discuss the specificity of the so-called "negative memory" of crimes committed or to be responsible for, and then conclude with reflections on what this implies for a German awareness of identity after the Holocaust.

The culture of commemoration in the Federal Republic of Germany

The blockade of the collective memory of the Germans in the postwar period, which is hardly understandable from today's perspective, was fed by the defense against becoming aware of one's own involvement in the Nazi regime and admitting it not only to oneself but also to others. This defense had a specific depth structure that was co-determined by the traumatic experiences of large parts of the population. They had left lasting traces in the experience and the memory of the individual and had affected social and political attitudes. Nothing was more ardently desired than a return to normality, and an individual and collective positive self-image was created by feeling like a victim of the war. The blame was placed on Hitler and a small number of major war criminals, who, however, would in no way represent the German people. This new victim awareness was a continuation of the Nazi *Volksgemeinschaft* and created a continuity of collective belonging. The real victims of the Germans did not belong to this community of victims and were studiously left out. Although the crimes committed against the Jews "in the name of the German people" were acknowledged at the official political level, the criminals remained largely faceless. A closure mentality prevailed for the most part, combined with strategies of denial, downplaying, and misleading. The reconstruction of the country and pride in the so-called economic miracle in the 1950s made it easier to avert one's gaze. In this way, a positive self-image could be maintained, normalized, and stabilized through a collective victim identity fixated on oneself. Nor should be ignored that the thinking and feelings of many people in Germany at that time were still shaped by ideological elements from National Socialist indoctrination, by anti-Semitism, racial purity thinking, and the idealization of the *Volksgemeinschaft*.

The long-lasting pathological refusal to remember and to deal with the criminal reality of the Nazi regime, but instead to seek some stabilization in a past collective sense of community, had led to a psychosocial immobilism. This socially pressing problem challenged psychoanalytic explanations. In 1967, "The Inability to Mourn" by psychoanalysts Alexander and Margarete Mitscherlich was published. The book elicited an exceptionally broad public response. The Mitscherlichs reminded the Germans of their enthusiastic and narcissistic adulation of the *Führer*, whose death robbed the nation of his representation as a collective ego ideal and resulted in a deflation of self-esteem. An impending melancholic impoverishment of the self had been warded off by a massive derealization of the Nazi past. This psychic "emergency reaction" strengthened into a rigid defensive attitude, whereby no adequate work of mourning became possible. It would have been the prerequisite to replace the old ideals, the exaggerated collective narcissism with a delusional inflation of the sense of self-awareness and to make a painful work of mourning possible.

Only the major trials of perpetrators from the *SS Einsatzgruppen* in the East and from the Auschwitz and Treblinka extermination camps in the 1960s, as well as the reports on the Eichmann trial in Jerusalem, marked a turning point in public awareness. The trials were the first genuine forays "into the heart of the matter: the annihilation of the Jews and the war of destruction in the East" (Wehler, 2008: p 21). These confrontations with the past and the debates on these issues cast new light on the conflict between the criminal nature of the Nazi state and the quest for a sustainable, identity-forming ideology that the Federal Republic as a democratic entity could convincingly espouse. This ideology was called for with increasing insistence by conservative politicians who saw the stability of democracy threatened by the unremitting references to Nazi atrocities. A slow but profound change in public and political arenas set in, and more and more a social mentality was formed that identified with the need to uncover and investigate the criminal past and was prepared to bear collective responsibility for this painful reality. "Coming to terms with the past" (*Vergangenheitsbewältigung*) became a political key word. This social change was also promoted by a modernization process that replaced the authoritarian-structured society of the 1950s with a modern civil society. It was able to initiate an internal democratization of society.

The student protest movement of 1968 radicalized and generalized the growing criticism of the unresolved past. It openly accused the entire generation of parents and especially the fathers of their involvement with Nazism. But answers to the question "What did you do under National Socialism?" remained rudimentary or met with stubborn silence. Although the real victims of the Nazi regime now came into focus, and with them the persecution and exclusion of the Jews, the discussion stopped at the point where it would have been about the active role the parent generation had played in the extermination process. This step of asking parents would have been too painful and remained more or less taboo. Instead of dealing with this conflict, many members of the 1968 generation identified with the Jews and other victims of the Nazi regime and distanced themselves from the inherited history of the perpetrators, which was thus once again repressed and continued the familial speechlessness. It took time to break through these barriers.

It was not until the TV broadcast of the American *Holocaust* series in 1979 that the Holocaust became anchored in the public awareness and made a shattering and lasting impression on people. It took the telling of individual fates to break down their refusal to empathize and their defenses against acknowledgment of the victims' suffering. People were now ready to face up to the unimaginable horrific crimes that had taken place. It was a painful learning process which also reactivated the ever-present counterforces that sought to more or less dispose of Nazi history by historicizing it and to end the period of reflection on historical-moral guilt.

An important episode in the process of these social and political debates was the 1985 speech by the highest representative of the Federal Republic, Federal President Richard von Weizsäcker, on the 40th anniversary of the end of World War II. Weizsäcker called on current Germans to acknowledge and take responsibility for the past and the "grave legacy" bequeathed to them by the generation before. He said that commemoration of these crimes is the only chance to regain the moral sovereignty without which political sovereignty would be entirely without substance. Critical remembrance of the past and of the Nazi atrocities would not explode the collective identity of the Federal Republic. Rather it must be part and parcel of its normative foundation. The Holocaust was thus recognized as a negative founding impulse of the Federal Republic.

In 1986, the so-called *Historikerstreit* (Historians' Controversy) once again initiated a broad public debate on how the Holocaust should be historically classified. It was triggered by an attempt by revisionist historians to question the singularity of the Nazi genocide by comparing it to Stalinist crimes. The highly emotional debate ultimately underlined the unique nature of the Holocaust.

The East German revolution, the fall of the Wall in 1989, and the reunification of the two German states also ended the discrediting of West German efforts to come to terms with the past by the German Democratic Republic (GDR), which had established a different memory policy. For them, National Socialism was an embodiment of capitalism. With its elimination and the establishment of an anti-fascist socialist society, National Socialism was declared overcome and there was no need for an independent coming to terms with the crimes of the Holocaust. In addition, the GDR – dictated by the Soviet Union – had taken an anti-Zionist turn and built up the state of Israel as an enemy image (Herf, 1997).

In the 1990s, Holocaust research was given new impetus by the opening of archives in Eastern Europe. Now also the killings and mass executions of Jews by the *SS Einsatzgruppen* came to the attention of the German public. In his 1996 book *Hitler's Willing Executioners*, Daniel Goldhagen demonstrated to the Germans the brutality of the shootings of Jews in the East in concrete terms and in great detail. The travelling exhibitions produced by the Hamburg Institute for Social Research in 1995 and 2001 on the crimes of the *Wehrmacht* (the regular German armed forces) destroyed the illusion that it had been only the *SS Einsatzgruppen* who committed the millions of murders in the East. The myth of the "clean" *Wehrmacht*, which would not have been involved in the Holocaust, collapsed. There were heated and sometimes enraged controversies, but eventually the German public widely accepted that the *Wehrmacht* had participated in Nazi mass crimes on a large scale during the war.

A public debate also started in the 1990s, one that lasted more than ten years, about erecting a monument in Berlin to commemorate the murdered Jews of Europe. This episode became, once again, a debate about the Germans' self-understanding. Jürgen Habermas put the problem in a nutshell:

> Do we make the self-critical memory of "Auschwitz" ... an explicit part of our political self-understanding? Do we accept the disturbing political responsibility that arises for those born later from the breach of civilization perpetrated, supported, and tolerated by Germans as an element of a fractured national identity? (Habermas, 1999: p 154)

In 2005 the memorial was inaugurated.

The change in social awareness due to the intensive debate on the history of National Socialism in the German public between 1985–2000 was probably one of the reasons that at the end of the 1990s memories of one's own experiences in the war, of flight and expulsion, and of the bombing war could increasingly be brought up and discussed in public among the German population. Another reason was that these were the experiences of people who, now 60 and 70 years old, had lived through the Nazi era and the war as children and young people. We know today that traumatic memories that have been split off come back into consciousness in old age. It was necessary to find private and public language and narratives for one's own suffering. The deep imprint of extreme violence on German society was once again expressed here, and the traumas of the individuals, which could now be spoken about and discussed as a generation-specific experience, moved one's own experience into a different context. The recognition that lay in this did not help to heal the trauma, but in many cases it did help to be able to bear it better. These public debates were not only about the memories of one's own experiences, but also about the temptation to try to relieve oneself of collective guilt by putting one's own suffering in the foreground, which gave rise to the suspicion that one's own suffering was to be set off against that of the victims.

Thus, the decades from 1960 to 2000 were a time of a "progressive restoration of remembrance" (König, 2008), in which the murder of the European Jews, despite great resistance, gradually took centerstage in the political and societal arenas. In ever new shock waves, the German public had been confronted with repudiated parts of Nazi history. As if in an upward spiral, it gradually became possible to uncover the repressed and denied past, so that the ground was taken away from the tendencies toward defensiveness and not wanting to know. In the course of this increasingly self-critical examination of Nazi history, a public reflexive culture of commemoration emerged that also included the long process of collective memory formation itself with its successive phases of reception. Historian Peter Reichel noted that it took time "before the most incomprehensible and painful core of the whole story could be publicly remembered and it became possible to face up the resulting obligation for lasting commemoration" (Reichel, Schmid, and Steinbach, 2009: p 18). As a result, new standards for the understanding of history and the culture of commemoration became established. Attempts to maintain a traditional national identity against the Nazi crimes had thus been deprived of ground. The conviction had prevailed that only the public commemoration of the Holocaust and the unrestricted remembrance of the crimes and guilt could restore moral sovereignty and stabilize a democratic reflexive identity.

Individual and social representation of traumatic memories

Until now, the focus has been on collective memory formation, whereas the interpenetration of individual and social memory processes has been left out.

From the therapeutic treatments of Holocaust survivors, of war participants, and of politically persecuted persons we know that the individual cannot succeed for himself in an idiosyncratic act to comprehend and process his overwhelming and traumatic experiences. The traumatic experience disrupts the ability to organize memory traces into mental representations and to store them in narratively communicable memories. The symbolization and integration capacity of the self breaks down in this area, causing the traumatic experience to be split off from the other mental areas. This splitting off and encapsulation initially creates a containment for a reality that cannot be coped with, which was associated with unbearable feelings of fear of annihilation, helplessness and pain. Psychologically, the splitting off of these bad experiences is initially a help, but makes their reminding representation dependent on specific conditions of an empathic environment. The core of traumatic experience, however, often eludes any communicability.

Disasters that are defined as man-made – such as Holocaust, war and political and ethnic persecution – involve specific means of de-humanization and personality destruction that are used to annihilate the victims' historical and social existence. It is beyond an individual's capacities to integrate such traumatic experiences into a narrative context that is purely personal; a social discourse is also required concerning the historical truth of the traumatic events, as well as their denial and defensive repudiation. Generally, only historical explanation and social recognition of causation and guilt will be able to restore the interpersonal context, thus opening up the possibility of finding out what actually happened at the time in an uncensored way. This is the only way that the shattered understanding of the self and the world can be regenerated. If defensive impulses predominate in society or rules of silence prevail, traumatized survivors are left alone with their experiences. Instead of drawing support from other people's understanding, they are often dominated by ideas of their own guilt which they rely upon as an explanatory principle.

A society of perpetrators: transgenerational identification processes in postwar Germany

On a scholarly and a societal level, there has been increasing realization over the past few decades that it takes time to come to terms with major traumatic disasters and to accept responsibility and guilt. It is not something that can happen in the course of one generation. More than 70 years have passed since the end of World War II. This allowed us to identify a specific transgenerational dynamic that gave the concept of generation a special meaning as a category of memory. Karl Mannheim had added to the traditional diachronic and genealogical concept of generation a synchronic dimension. According to this, a generation is a cohort related in age whose biography is shaped by the common reference point of an incisive historical event, most of which is catastrophic in character (Weigel, 2006). In psychoanalysis, the concept of generation acquired a specific status through the psychotherapeutic treatments of children of Holocaust survivors, but also of children from the perpetrator generation. Again and again, the specific attachment relationships between parents and children were described, through which unprocessed traumatizations, but also defense phenomena against guilt and responsibility were transgenerationally transmitted. Members of the second generation not only became carriers of the parental legacy, but as child survivors and as children of war they themselves were often traumatized or severely psychologically damaged, which in turn affected the third generation.

The members of the *first generation*, who were involved in National Socialism as active perpetrators or as bystanders, had created a "usable past" (Moeller, 1996), doing their best to deny their own involvement in the Nazi regime, especially as perpetrators. This required a separation of the past into pleasant and unpleasant memories, which required a considerable amount of psychic energy. However, many biographies of war participants reveal other conditions of this collective pathology. Extreme exercise of violence and traumatizing experiences of violence, other war impacts, bombings, and flight formed a biographical subtext as a mixture of experiences with a complex interrelationship of crime, war, perpetration, trauma, and memory. As we know today, emotional rigidity, derealization of the past, and repression of one's own deeds are also direct consequences of traumatization, which impairs the ability to engage reflexively with the past. Here the moral problem of guilt avoidance enhanced pathological memory processes that are traumatic in their origin. The apologetic awareness of themselves as victims that the members of the perpetrator generation have subsequently created was fed from both sources, the guilt defense and the traumatic experiences.

The *second generation* grew up in the shadow of the willful self-deception of parents who thought of, and referred to, themselves as victims. Silence about their own involvement in the Nazi regime and gaps in family biographies produced a nebulous and sometimes distorted sense of reality in their children. The family was the arena of a mysterious or murky past. Powerful unconscious forces affected the communicative exchange, so that the gaps in transmission and memory could exert a particularly uncanny effect. Social science research has shown how untold stories hidden in other family discourse have an extremely strong transgenerational effect (Bar-On and Gilad, 1992; Rosenthal, 1997). The taboo placed on the question of their parents' involvement in the Nazi era impaired the children's ability to inquire and obtain information. Inside the family itself, the offspring of the perpetrator generation sensed a kind of unspoken ban preventing them from taking an active interest in such questions, a consequence of identification with the parents' attitude, as well as an attachment based on childhood loyalty. I would like to briefly present some of these forms of identification.

1. *The child as self-object; negative identifications.* Many parents forced loyalty upon their children, amidst their own refusal to reflect upon what they had done thus preventing any genuine confrontation with their Nazi ideals; instead, they used their children to instill in them a worldview that justified themselves. Dissidence and independent-mindeness on the part of the children were shouted down, discredited in the name of stubbornly championed Nazi ideals, and categorized accordingly. Powerless to fend off these attacks, the children were unable to distinguish amongst secrecy, deception and betrayal. So as not to endanger their relationship with the parents, the children espoused a "protective attitude vis-à-vis the histories of the preceding generation" (Faimberg, 2005) and often adopted their worldview and their right-wing view of the nation.
2. *Counter-identifications.* In opposition to their compromised parents, their children turned to the victims of this generation. Many became involved in political and scientific projects that set themselves the task of researching and reconstructing the history and role of the victims. Frequently, however this counter-identification took place at the ego-ideal and superego level and did not penetrate to the deeper and earlier strata of the personality structure. The old unconscious infantile identifications with the parents remained intact. As the psychoanalytic treatments of members of this generation revealed, their unconscious emotional attachment to the internalized parental representations of their early years often outlived all subsequent arguments about their parents' involvement in National Socialism.
3. *Splitting the father image.* In the psychoanalytic treatment particularly of children of Nazi perpetrators, the early attachment to an idealized image of the father often proved to be the rock on which all efforts to come to terms with the father's (criminal) history threatened to fail. The patients protected the relationship to the father by splitting the image of him they carried within them. One part of it was the idealized father of early childhood, experienced in reality or only longed for, the other part was the compromised or criminal father, with whom, however, they wanted nothing to do.

    I would like to illustrate this with an extreme example. In an interview (Frankfurter Rundschau No.127 of 3.6.1996) the eldest son of Martin Bormann commented on his relationship to his father. The journalist had asked him about a photo of his father that was in his study. He replied that he saw his father in the photo, but not Hitler's secretary: "It does not touch me directly as a son what political errors and perhaps even political crimes my father committed in his role as head of the party chancellery and as secretary of the *Führer*." The son insisted that one must distinguish between a private person "father" and a public person "father." His inner attachment to the father brought him into conflict in the assessment of his crimes. They did not seem quite real to the son: "Maybe he even committed political crimes." He took his father's side and therefore had to ignore and deny the reality of a criminal father, which was painful and cruel for him.

In all these forms of identification, the early attachment, which had become unconscious, to a beloved authority to whom one must remain loyal, made the detachment from these parents extremely difficult. Thus, among members of the second generation, efforts to uncover concealed and warded off history were often mixed with defensive processes. The ego was repeatedly exposed to the danger of unconsciously turning into an accomplice of the parents and their attitudes perpetuating the "conspiracy of silence." It was fully acceptable to talk about the Holocaust, as long as the question of what the parents themselves had concretely done and to what extent they had participated in crimes remained taboo.

Nevertheless, the profound rupture that the Nazi past had created between the generations formed a painful thorn in the psyche of many members of the second generation. Especially in their middle and later adulthood, it was possible for some of them – often in a very painful process – to recognize and work through the psychic constellations involved, and thus to break out of the emotional clinch with their parents and achieve distance through an independent perspective. This process was in turn facilitated by a critical reflection in society on the crimes of the Nazis, and the taboos, myths, and legends they lived by. Such inquiries about the involvement of parents in the Nazi regime produced many memorial documents and also literary publications of family histories since the 1990s. But in many cases, clarification and reconstruction had been possible only in fragments, and many members of the second generation had to live with an irreconcilable ambivalence as to whether and to what extent their parents had been involved in National Socialism and its crimes.

The importance of family memory for the third and fourth generation

The members of the *third and fourth generation* no longer have any direct contact with the Nazi period, because the generation of contemporary witnesses has almost completely died out, thus, the existential concern is largely missing. Now, it is the so-called secondary experiences of this past which have mostly become embedded in the family memory. To explore them, the distinction between communicative and cultural memory (Assmann, 1992) has proven helpful.

Communicative memory is recollection exercised by living communicators of experience. It encompasses some 80 years, usually three to four generations living at the same time and forming a community of shared experience, memory, and narrative communication by way of personal exchange. One can also refer to it as "three-generation memory" that moves on as the time frame changes. *Cultural memory*, by contrast, is a collective symbolic construction and encompasses larger periods of time. It is based on media, like texts, pictures, memorials, anniversaries, and rites, which are themselves subject to social conflict and change.

In the transition from communicative to cultural or collective memory, *family memory* plays an important role. Its relationship to communicative and cultural memory is complex. On the one hand, children's individual memory is shaped by collectively transmitted cognitive knowledge, but on the other hand, it is also shaped by family memory, in which experiential knowledge is directly transmitted narratively. The family memory forms a filter through which contents of the collective memory are absorbed, manipulated, or excluded. Emotional loyalty attachments play a decisive role in these communication processes. Research has shown how the involvement of family members in the Nazi regime was reflected in family memory (Bar-On and Gilad, 1992; Brendler, 1995; Rosenthal, 1997; Welzer et al, 2002). In many cases of family communication, family history was hidden or tabooed, resulting in a derealization of the Nazi past and in fantasizing and revising the grandparents' perpetrator past. A tendency to purify and idealize one's own family members led many of the families studied to a mythicizing reworking and purification of biographies, especially of grandparents who supported and sustained the Nazi regime or – even further – participated in its crimes. However, caution should be applied to generalizing interpretations of the results of such family memory studies. We know how strong loyalty obligations can be when one does not want to put one's family in an unfavorable light. The family member is protected vis-à-vis the outside world, but secretly doubts could remain whether these presented biographical data were not reworked and whitewashed.

Remembering crime and the negative memory

Since the beginning of the new millennium, there has been increasing discussion about how the National Socialist crimes against humanity can be represented in the future. The historians Knigge and Frei (2002) argue that remembering of the Holocaust and thus of the crimes *suffered* is gradually becoming conventionalized in society, but that the formation of a social memory out of negative memories of the crimes *committed or for which one* is *responsible* has still not become the rule but remains the exception. "Negative memory" (Koselleck, 2010) must be enforced again and again, because commemoration only has a "substantially humanizing and democratizing effect … if it also includes the – painful, shameful, unsettling – memory of one's own history of injustice and crime for which one is responsible or for which one shares responsibility" (Knigge and Frei, 2002: p XI). In this way, the authors criticize the growth of a purely "victim-identified memory culture" (Jureit, 2010) that had been developing in parts of German society since the 1970s. The historian Reinhard Koselleck has paradigmatically stated that "for us as Germans there is only one possibility: The perpetrators and their deeds must be included in remembrance and not just the victims commemorated as such and alone. This is what distinguishes us from other nations" (Koselleck, 2002: p 27). He continues,

> We can only commemorate the victims we have murderously and technically produced if we have sufficient self-awareness to remember our own dead as well, and so also the perpetrators amongst our relatives, amongst our ancestors, in our own nation. This is part of the difficulty that characterizes the negativity of our memory. (2002: p 29)

He then continues,

> So *what* is to be remembered? I think the simplest answer is: to have to think the unthinkable, to learn to speak the inexpressible, and to try to imagine the unimaginable. Even as we call for this, we realize how quickly we arrive at the limits of what is possible. (2002: p 24)

Koselleck emphasizes that we must try "to transfer the inexpressible into language" (2002: p 29) because they are not experiences themselves but their representations that are passed on.

Psychoanalytically, we can shed further light on this issue. Listening to the story of Holocaust survivors means opening oneself up with one's imagination and one's feelings to the details of what the perpetrators did to them and what they had to suffer, because otherwise we do not enter into affective contact with the experience of these traumatized victims. However, vicarious experience can only ever be an approximation.

These findings from trauma research make it clear that a reminiscent recourse to secondary remembrance cannot only be about conveying knowledge, but also about opening up one's emotional perception to the abysmal nature of the crimes and the sufferings of the victims and not closing oneself off to the effect. Here, both in the individual and in societal discourse, we encounter specific defensive reactions to which we are all exposed when confronted with extreme traumatic content. They happen because we instinctively recoil from the violence, the horror, the pain and the fear of traumatic events, so as to avoid feeling these things ourselves and exposing ourselves to them in the imagination. The incisive power of these memories and the sheer horror of what has happened to the victims threatens to overwhelm the psyche of the listener and lastingly shake his psychic balance. Moreover, the images and scenes we are confronted with can have a continuing haunting character. In order to protect oneself from this and to make the situation more bearable, the listener is tempted to pre- or unconsciously turn away from the terrible reality, to partially block it out, to minimize it, or to become emotionally indifferent.

Becoming aware of these defensive tendencies and accepting them as part of our self, however, enables distance and opens a way out of this seemingly aporetic situation, which makes it possible to nevertheless open up to the history of "Auschwitz," and to keep the negative memories alive instead of protecting ourselves from them. It is a moral imperative for the German awareness of identity that this past can never be allowed to fade away. Negative commemoration, in this sense, is a "willful and deliberate self-concern," which, however, must not revolve within itself, "but should turn into political and fellow human responsibility" (Knigge, 2002: p 434).

What does all this mean for the subsequent generations and what they can learn about the Nazi atrocities and the Holocaust? Now that the generation of contemporary witnesses have more or less died out, knowledge about the Holocaust and the Nazi regime finally passes from communicative memory to cultural memory, so that we no longer have access to primary experiences and testimonies that are conveyed in direct personal contact. Mere cognitive knowledge is not sufficient. For a true appreciation of the enormity of these events, a younger generation of learners should come into contact with the horrific details of the Holocaust in their imagination without being overwhelmed by it, remaining paralyzed or refusing to remember. If this happens, then he or she remains below the threshold of an experience that is necessary to make in order to grasp the historically unique inhumanity. These psychological realities repeatedly confront pedagogical engagement with the Holocaust with the dual problem of maintaining the sensitivity of the individual, while at the same time avoiding or offsetting too great a strain on the senses. The essential thing is to keep the psychic space of the individual open to the survivor's testimony, so that the affects generated by that testimony can remain conscious, thus creating the ground for reflection on the whole issue and an exchange with others.

Helmut König (2008) reminds us that the remembrance of the Holocaust must not mutate into a commemorative religion. Spaces must be reserved for concrete narratives and reports from the appalling years when the Nazis were in power. He draws on Hannah Arendt, who emphasized that it must be a form of narrative that expresses the harshness of real experience in a sharpened and condensed way. What has happened must be truly absorbed into consciousness and acknowledged. With all truthfulness to reality, it must be clear that it is a representation and not reality. "In this way, narration creates distance and causes the listener not to freeze in horror" (König, 2008: p 634).

Negative memory and German identity after the Holocaust

National myths have an identity-securing function. They were thoroughly discredited by the Nazi regime. Negative memory took the place of an identity-forming positive myth. Germany thus occupies a special position, because no other country has subjected itself to similar remembrance work and made the signs of moral shame so visible. No kind of pride could be gained from this; on the contrary, the historical facts continue to convey a kind of negative identity (Münkler, 2009).

Family history and perpetrator history in the narrower sense can only be preserved in Germany in the mode of the "we." They remain a part of collective memory as negative memory. The remembrance of the perpetrators and the deeds, of the involvement of one's own parents and grandparents cannot be outsourced or split off. The confrontation with a history of disgrace creates in the individual a conflict with the collective "we-identity" and an ambivalence in relation to national feelings.

Research on the historical consciousness of young people indicates how they experience Nazi history as something that belongs to them in a diffuse way. As Germans, they cannot escape this historical context, but at the same time they have a desire to distance themselves, which seeks to narrow down Nazi history to a specific group of criminal people and exclude them from the national collective to which the young people feel they belong (Kölbl and Fröhlich, 2015). A large-scale scientific study of school trips to Auschwitz (Kuchler, 2021) indicated that, on the one hand, students expressed deep bewilderment and emotional shock as well as identification with the victims, while, on the other hand, they established the greatest possible distance between the Nazis of the time and themselves. When the subject of the perpetrators came up, the young people defended against a national commonality with this group of people. They sought to demonize the perpetrators and all Nazis. The fact that their own ancestors had belonged to the perpetrators and to the bystanders was something they blanked out (Kuchler, 2021: p 188). Here, too, there is a strong desire to let oneself be guided in the collective self-image by positive notions of national identity and to fade out the family connection to the Nazi past.

This issue of what a positive national identity for Germans might look like is the subject of controversial debate in the political and social sciences.

Jürgen Habermas (1990) argues for a post-nationalist political culture constantly redefining itself through its critical engagement with the past. He proposes to identify with a "constitutional patriotism" and to replace the representations of national identity that are no longer viable. He urges his fellow Germans to free themselves of diffuse notions of the nation-state and to discard those "pre-political" crutches that go by the name of nationality and community of destiny (*Schicksalsgemeinschaft*). Habermas keeps his distance from all emotional aspects of collective coexistence and relies solely on an ideal image of collective self-identification with reason (Hacke, 2008). Psychoanalytically, such a view falls short, for the idea of a nation as an "imagined community" (Anderson, 1983) is emotionally deeply rooted both in the child's development and in collective fantasies. The concepts of "motherland" and "fatherland" are reminders of this. Early notions of a large-group identity emerge in interplay with individual self-images in the third year of life and continue to develop constantly (Volkan, 1988). The devastating political abuses in 20th-century nationalism should not lead us to negate the affective significance of national belonging fantasies in general (Bohleber, 2010 for more details).

Social scientists seek to find out empirically how phenomena of a collective identity are expressed in contemporary German society. The controversial issue that remains is what forms of collective identity will assert themselves. Münkler and Hacke speak here of the necessity of a "normalization process." This process "is merely the expression of the fact that like any other political entity, the Federal Republic is dependent on its ability to develop a positive historical identity that can gradually emerge from the shadow of the Nazi past" (2009: p 29). But no matter how this process of normalization and the resulting elements of a "positive identity" is empirically filled out, the chain of generations linking the Germans of today with the perpetrators of yesterday cannot simply be broken. German society must live with its historical responsibility for the Holocaust; it remains a part of its sense of identity, which also includes obligatory positive values, such as the affirmation of human rights stated in the Basic Law of the Federal Republic and the right to asylum for politically persecuted persons.

The 2015 refugee crisis was then one of those major political and social conflicts in which this commitment was up for debate in society. Whereas in 1992 there was only a slight willingness to accept the 400,000 refugees from the Bosnian war as well as a strong defensive attitude, a change in the attitude of German society now became apparent toward the 800,000 Syrian refugees. Although fear of strangers and xenophobia were still widespread, a spontaneous willingness to accept the refugees prevailed. For older Germans, the images of the refugee columns on the Balkan route had, in the depths of their experience, updated the refugee treks of millions of Germans who had been expelled from the eastern territories in 1945.

For Chancellor Angela Merkel, as for other politicians and for large parts of the population, it was clear that no fences could be erected to regulate the influx and turn away distressed refugees. Here, too, memories of Nazi crimes, the fences of the concentration camps, and the wall of the GDR had been emotionally activated in the minds of many people. Although fierce resistance arose against the political model of a liberal German society open to the world and violence broke out, the borders remained open. For the otherwise pragmatic German chancellor, her fundamental political convictions were challenged here. She sharply demarcated herself against all forms of racism, anti-Semitism, and denial of history. Part of society was unable to cope with this policy. Fears of foreign infiltration and fears of the loss of cultural and national identity, fueled by globalization, increased. The result was a polarization of the social climate and a strengthening of the right-wing populist and in parts extreme right-wing party Alternative for Germany (AfD), which instrumentalized these fears politically. But the fundamental values of an open, liberal society that is assertively aware of its history prevailed politically in this confrontation.

Conclusion

For a long time, a collective defense against acknowledging and taking responsibility for the horrific Nazi crimes was prevalent in German society. The inability to accept historical reality was not only due to attempts to maintain a good individual and collective self-image, but was also a consequence of the traumas suffered. Different memory interests of social groups also played a role, as did the generational dynamics that unfolded between members of the perpetrator generation, their children and grandchildren. As a result, the memory culture was characterized for a long time by contentious memories, which repeatedly provoked new debates, but nevertheless made historical clarifications possible and gradually removed the ground from the tendencies towards denial and not wanting to know.

In order to understand more deeply the individual and collective conflicts that were ignited by memories, it is necessary to include not only the cognitive-rational debate about historical reality, but also the emotions involved in it. With its knowledge of affectively controlled defense processes and of the consequences of traumatic experiences, psychoanalysis could contribute to a better understanding of this long-lasting process of social enlightenment and of the memory pathologies that manifested themselves in the process.

After the long decades of international historical research on the Nazi regime, the Holocaust, and the war of extermination, with the many social controversies they set in motion and which led to a working through of memories, their results are now widely accepted. Fundamental new historical insights are probably no longer to be expected; further research serves to differentiate and deepen our knowledge (Brechtken, 2021).

But the long shadow of this past and the recurring confrontations with this "unacceptable history" do not let go of German society. The focus is now on questions of how the abysmal nature of the crimes and the immeasurable suffering of the victims can be transmitted to the memory formation of future generations in such a way that their confrontation with what happened does not get stuck in a purely cognitive transmission, but allows for an emotional perception and impact.

A positive collective self-image based on good national traditions was destroyed by the crimes of the Nazi regime and cannot be revived. There is no way back to an "emotional radiance" (Elias, 1989) of the idea of nation. The negative memory about the perpetrators and their crimes as well as about the involvement of one's own ancestors in the Nazi regime cannot be outsourced from a positive identity or purified from it and idealized. The search for a positive identity must take other paths. It helps that a serious reflection on the historical responsibility with its painful and also shameful memories does not remain inconsequential, but from within itself brings forth an impulse to human responsibility and a commitment to the basic values of a liberal and democratic culture.

References

Anderson, B. (1983) *Imagined Communities: Reflections on the Origin and Spread of Nationalism*, London: Verso.

Assmann, J. (1992) *Cultural Memory and Early Civilization. Writing, Remembrance, and Political Imagination*, Cambridge: Cambridge University Press.

Bar-On, D. and Gilad, N. (1992) "Auswirkungen des Holocaust auf drei Generationen," *Psychosozial* 51: 7–21.

Bohleber, W. (2010) *Destructiveness, Intersubjectivity, and Trauma. The Identity Crisis of Modern Psychoanalysis*, London: Karnac.

Brechtken, M. (2021) "Einleitung," in M. Brechtken (ed) *Aufarbeitung des Nationalsozialismus, Ein Kompendium*, Göttingen: Wallstein, pp 9–19.

Brendler, K. (1995) "Working through the Holocaust. Still a Task for Germany's Youth?," in R.J. Kleber, C.R. Figley, and B.P.R. Gersons (eds) *Beyond Trauma: Cultural and Societal Dynamics*, New York: Springer, pp 249–275.

Elias, N. (1989) *Studien über die Deutschen: Machtkämpfe und Habitusentwicklung im 19. und 20. Jahrhundert*, Frankfurt: Suhrkamp.

Faimberg, H. (2005) *The Telescoping of Generations: Listening to the Narcissistic Links between Generations*, London: Routledge.

Friedländer, S. (1994) "Trauma, Memory and Transference," in G. Hartman (ed) *Holocaust Remembrance: The Shapes of Memory*, Oxford: Blackwell, pp 252–263.

Habermas, J. (1990) "Nochmals: Zur Identität der Deutschen. Ein einig Volk von aufgebrachten Wirtschaftsbürgern," in J. Habermas *Die nachholende Revolution: Politische Schriften VII*, Frankfurt: Suhrkamp, pp 205–224.

Habermas, J. (1999) "Der Zeigefinger: Die Deutschen und ihr Denkmal," in *Der Denkmalstreit – das Denkmal?*, Berlin: Philo Verlagsgesellschaft, pp 153–158.

Hacke, J. (2008) "Wir-Gefühle: Repräsentationsformen kollektiver Identität bei Jürgen Habermas," *Mittelweg 36*, 17(6): 12–32.

Herf, J. (1997) *Divided Memory: The Nazi Past in the two Germanys*, Cambridge, MA: Harvard University Press.

Jureit, U. and Schneider, C. (2010) *Gefühlte Opfer: Illusionen der Vergangenheitsbewältigung*, Stuttgart: Klett-Cotta.

Knigge, V. (2002) "Statt eines Nachworts: Abschied der Erinnerung. Anmerkungen zum notwenigen Wandel der Gedenkkultur in Deutschland," in V. Knigge and N. Frei (eds) *Verbrechen erinnern: Die Auseinandersetzung mit Holocaust und Völkermord*, München: C.H. Beck, pp 423–440.

Knigge, V. and Frei, N. (eds) (2002) *Verbrechen erinnern: Die Auseinandersetzung mit Holocaust und Völkermord*, München: C.H. Beck.

Kölbl, C. and Fröhlich, A. (2015) "Geschichtsbewusstsein Intergenerationell," in G. Mey (ed) *Von Generation zu Generation: Sozial- und kulturwissenschaftliche Analysen zu Transgenerationalität*, Gießen: Psychosozial Verlag, pp 99–120.

König, H. (2008) *Politik und Gedächtnis*, Weilerswist: Velbrück Wissenschaft.

Koselleck, R. (2002) "Formen und Traditionen des negativen Gedächtnisses," in V. Knigge and N. Frei (eds) *Verbrechen erinnern. Die Auseinandersetzung mit Holocaust und Völkermord*, München: C.H. Beck, pp 21–32.

Kuchler, C. (2021) *Lernort Auschwitz. Geschichte und Rezeption schulischer Gedenkstättenfahrten 1980–2019*, Göttingen: Wallstein.

Maier, C.S. (1988) *The Unmasterable Past: History, Holocaust, and German National Identity*, Cambridge, MA: Harvard University Press.

Mitscherlich, A. and Mitscherlich, M. (1967) *The Inability to Mourn: Principles of collective behavior*, New York: Grove Press.

Moeller, R.G. (1996) "War Stories: The Search for a Usable Past in the Federal Republic of Germany," *The American Historical Review* 101: 1008–1048.

Münkler, H. (2009) *Die Deutschen und ihre Mythen,* Berlin: Rowohlt Berlin.

Münkler, H. and Hacke, J. (eds) (2009) *Wege in die neue Bundesrepublik: Politische Mythen und kollektive Selbstbilder nach 1989*, Frankfurt: Campus.

Reichel, P., Schmid, H., and Steinbach, P. (2009) *Der Nationalsozialismus – Die zweite Geschichte: Überwindung – Deutung –Erinnerung*, München: C.H. Beck.

Rosenthal, G. (ed) (1997) *Der Holocaust im Leben von drei Generationen: Familien von Überlebenden der Shoah und von Nazi-Tätern*, Gießen: Psychosozial-Verlag.

Rüsen, J. (2001) *Zerbrechende Zeit: Über den Sinn der Geschichte*, Köln: Böhlau.

Volkan, V. (1988) *The Need to have Enemies and Allies: From Clinical Practice to International Relationships*, Northvale, NJ: Aronson.

Wehler, H.U. (2008) *Deutsche Gesellschaftsgeschichte, Fünfter Band: Bundesrepublik und DDR 1949–1990*, München: C.H. Beck.

Weigel, S. (2006) *Genea-Logik. Generation, Tradition und Evolution zwischen Kultur- und Naturwissenschaften*, München: Fink.

Welzer, H., Möller, S., and Tschuggnall, K. (2002) *"Opa war kein Nazi": Nationalsozialismus und Holocaust im Familiengedächtnis*, Frankfurt: Fischer.

10

Enlisting Lived Memory: From Traumatic Silence to Authentic Witnessing

Carol A. Kidron

In one of his most seminal texts, Clifford Geertz depicts the ethnographer's search for a "thick description" – a description of lived experience "on the ground" that would capture otherwise tacit cultural meaning worlds as practiced and experienced in everyday lives (1973). Although subsequent readings of Geertz's theory have highlighted his focus on the interpretive lens of our interlocutors in the field, far less attention has been given to Geertz's assertion (long before anthropology's critical turn) that the ethnographer too must reflexively consider how scholarly discourse and personal ideological perspectives frame and therefore selectively interpret our ethnographic gaze and thick descriptions. In the spirit of Geertz's call for academic and personal self-reflexivity, in this chapter I explore the evolution of my own interpretive lens when doing field work and publishing about Holocaust memory and commemoration in Israel. I will consider the way my scholarship has been shaped by the following frames or lenses: (i) critical constructivism and hegemony theory, (ii) critical perspectives on trauma theory and potential pathologization of trauma victims and their descendants, and (iii) personal positioning as Holocaust descendant protective of survivor family "privacy," silence, and authenticity. After a brief literature review I will present vignettes illustrating three different "turns" in my scholarship each followed by a discussion of personal positioning, scholarly framing, and my resultant moral dilemmas.

Epistemological frames of Holocaust memory

Critical memory scholars have proposed that all memory is social, partial, and strategically constructed and "put to work" to amass and sustain governmental and elite power and capital (Halbwachs, 1980; Schudson, 1997). Despite the ethically loaded nature of Holocaust and Genocide memory, Holocaust memory is no exception. Holocaust commemoration and public forms of memory work are selectively instrumentalized in national ceremonies, museum exhibits, and commemorative trips to Poland. In the service of Israeli statecraft, Holocaust memory deploys embedded value-laden collective Jewish-Israeli narratives of survival and national redemption, unifying an increasingly politically homogenous, critical, and individualistic society (Bauman, 1998; Handelman, 2004). Holocaust survivors and their descendants are enlisted and/or self-constituted as carriers of authentic memory as familial and personal identity-memory work intersect and intertwine in the service of one of Israel's key grand narratives (Kidron, 2015).

However, for those who have formatively experienced everyday personal or familial Holocaust-related lived memory work, or for that matter civil religious collective national Holocaust commemoration as foundational mythic narrative, these hermeneutics of suspicion are in no way incommensurable with a profound (albeit often conflicted) commitment to Holocaust memory. To complicate matters, the resultant dilemma does not remain static – but rather is perpetually shaped by contemporary discourse and practice. With the ravages of time, as the iconic Holocaust survivor generation passes away, new commemorative practices and hierarchies of suffering emerge where holographic images of deceased survivors, descendant second-hand memory, and expert pedagogy take the place of survivors. The shift to second- and third-hand memory engenders new moral dilemmas surrounding much feared forgetting, testimonial authenticity, and identification with witnesses once or twice removed. These dilemmas are part and parcel of the wider macro recurring theme in Holocaust and Genocide studies relating to the crisis of representation and valorized remembering.

Descendants of survivors mark a particularly interesting historical shift in the politics and ethics of memory work. As potential carriers of both private and public national Holocaust memory, their personal life stories embody and potentially exemplify the ideal seamless identity work of the collectivized citizens or, alternatively, ruptures that threaten forgetting (see DeGloma, 2014). Generational differences between first, second and third generation memory work, based on distance from the founding event, changing social values, contexts, and enlistment practices provide intriguing longitudinal reflection of social stasis and change. Close readings of qualitative phenomenological data on descendant meaning worlds disclose multiple interpretive lenses, ranging from person-centered therapeutic narratives on transmitted trauma to the public national performance of valorized transmitted wounds, and finally critique of the demise of survivor authenticity and resistance to public enlistment (Kidron, 2021). Although a minority, there are even those who call for forgetting.

Despite extensive literature on the outlined processes and dilemmas, scholars have yet to examine the ways that their personal positioning, scholarly frames, and yes, even moral missions shape their representations of their interlocutors. Two perhaps contradictory key frames have been central to the professional zeitgeist of Holocaust scholars. The first is a hermeneutics of suspicion regarding the politics of Holocaust memory, a scholarly lens that is rooted primarily in Israel. In keeping with this frame, Holocaust scholars have sought to disclose the hegemony of enlistment, be it in the education system (Feldman, 2008), museums (Goldberg, 2012), ceremonies (Handelman, 1990), or trauma therapy (Kidron, 2009). For some scholars like myself, Jewish-Israeli ethnic and national heritage poses a second contradictory frame or interpretive lens and ultimately a moral dilemma, namely the potential for more personal commitment to Holocaust commemoration and the concern surrounding Holocaust forgetting to shape one's interpretation and analysis. Be it as descendants of survivors and/or citizens, critique is tempered or troubled by the valorized moral mission of commemoration and remembrance. As will be seen, one possible outcome of this dilemma is the critique of the politics of enlisted memory and its implications for future public commemoration while prioritizing private "resistant" familial memory and its reconceptualization as more privileged and authentic remembrance. The dilemma of scholars grappling with these political, ideational, and professional issues centers on whether they can totally disentangle their empirical data and analysis from their more personal orientations. As DeGloma (2014) has noted, our personal narratives as subjects are embedded in particular mnemonic eras. We each represent not only our personal subjective worlds but encapsulate the dilemmas and paradoxes of our time, including those that relate to the ethical crises of memory. Therefore, it is essential that scholars reflexively explore the way their research resonates with these personal and collective narratives.

Although anthropology for one has encouraged auto-ethnographic self-critique and reflexivity (Geertz, 1973; Ellis, Adams, and Bochner, 2011), the great majority of self-reflexive Holocaust studies have highlighted two rather reductionist perspectives and personal positions. The first is activist in nature. It involves exploring personal and politically progressive critiques regarding right-wing Zionist construction and enlistment as moral agenda. The other explores familial psychological or ideational wounded legacies as some scholars work through their scholarship to explore their selves (see Slyomovics, 2015). In both cases there has been little self-reflexive critique of the particularity and partiality of these readings of the way scholars' personal agendas frame, bias, and potentially "distort" (Schudson, 1997) scholarship. These studies have marginalized an examination of the potential for ideologically motivated distortion of data in the name of political and/or psychological self-understanding and political activism.

Holocaust descendant memory

According to the illness construct of PTSD, trauma survivors, having experienced such a rupture in the linear flow of experience, may suffer from chronic depression, repression, and numbness (Barocas and Barocas, 1973; Schwartz, Dohrenwend, and Levav, 1994). The syndrome is thought to potentially impair survivor parenting, which is described as incapable of affect and intimacy and overprotective of the child (Zilberfein, 1995). A familial "wall of silence" is said to often shroud the history of parental suffering in oppressive silence. The metaphor of the "wall of silence" signifies the absence and erasure of the genocidal past (Bar-On, 1992). The literature concludes that descendants may suffer from transgenerationally transmitted effects of PTSD, expressed in a series of maladaptive behavioral patterns and a damaged sense of self (Halik, Rosenthal, and Pattison, 1990). Although researchers in the 1990s concluded that the third generation did not suffer from the pathological effects of transmitted trauma, they called for extended examination of the potential impairment of this high-risk population (Winship and Knowles, 1996; Lazar et al, 2004). More recent findings point to higher levels of third generation transmitted trauma, lower levels of differentiation of self, and poorer family communication compared to control groups (Giladi and Bell, 2013), along with higher levels of anxiety in situations of collective danger (Hoffman and Shrira, 2017). Globalizing this pathologizing trend, maladaptive third, fourth, and even fifth generation transmitted trauma have been reported in studies of descendants of Ukrainian genocide (1932–33) (Bezo and Maggi, 2018) and mental health responses in Japan after the 2011 Fukushima nuclear disaster (Palgi et al, 2012). According to the therapeutic paradigm that emphasizes "completing the story," the survivor and descendants are called on to undergo talk therapy to excavate the repressed past, breaching the wall of silence and completing "unfinished mourning" within a therapeutic framework (Dasberg, 1992: p 45). Talk therapy in therapeutic settings and public forms of testimony and commemoration aim to liberate the silenced past, transforming it into voice.

This therapeutic perspective on the healing potential of talk therapy has interfaced with and amplified the emancipatory practice of cultivating the testimonial voice of subjugated victims worldwide as part of ethnic and national politics of identity and memory (Pupavac, 2001). The therapeutic and political aspects of this practice reinforce one another dialectically, as the vocalization of previously silent or silenced pasts is considered not only individually healing but also socio-politically redemptive for the ethnic/ national collective (Leys, 1996). As critically outlined by Shaw (2007) and Fassin (2008), testimonial voice has been epistemically constructed in the social sciences, the humanities, and in popular cultural representations of post-conflict and post-colonial contexts as essential components of truth telling considered to facilitate peace and reconciliation. Individual and/or familial memories of victimhood that remain silent have been conceptualized as markers of surviving violent regimes, political silencing, violent non-volitional rupture, and the failure of humanist entrepreneurs to bear witness and document the past (Fassin, 2008). With silence as the battleground of a moral crusade in humanist organizational and academic circles, failures to verbalize painful pasts become highly charged and contested objects of research.

Constituting Israeli descendant identity, memory and testimonial voice

In contrast to second generation Holocaust descendants who claim to carry the burden of memory primarily in the private sphere and who resist public forms of commemoration (Kidron, 2009), the great majority of third generation descendants (grandchildren of survivors) highlight the centrality of public school-based collective memory practices and public media representations of the Holocaust as constructing their identities (Kidron, 2015). Mobilization of the third generation begins as early as the 4th grade when pupils are asked to prepare a family tree singling out the third generation who will use their trees to "show and tell" their special link to the Holocaust past. The next stage of third generation construction/mobilization begins in the 11th or 12th grade when they join school organized (nationwide) commemorative trips to sites of Holocaust atrocity in Eastern Europe. Although both third generation and non-third generation youth join these trips, third generation are asked to give public testimony to their grandparental survivor past in pre-trip preparation workshops, during the trip and in post-trip school-wide Holocaust ceremonies (Kidron, 2015).

Approximately 55 per cent of Israeli high school children (between the ages of 16–18) have travelled to Poland on trips organized by the national education ministry (and customized by their school curriculum planners) to learn about the Holocaust first-hand. Although the first pedagogic trips to Poland set out in the mid-1960s, ruptured diplomatic relations between Poland and Israel soon led to a 20-year hiatus, with high school visits renewed only in 1983. Pedagogic experts (Keren, 2000) assert that the trip aims to transform school children into witnesses of the scourge that is the

Polish death-world so that they may appreciate the critical importance of the revival of a strong Jewish Israel and explore the remnants of the now lost legacy of Jewish Diasporic culture. Balberg-Rothenstreich (2004) explains that school programs encourage the exclusive commemorative role of third generation so that they may simultaneously act as their grandparents' messengers in a victorious return to the site of survival and as the group's mediators to the distant survivor past primarily for those who do not have a familial connection to the Holocaust. The process of transforming third generation pupils into mediators entails constitutive practices unfolding incrementally throughout the pre-trip, trip, and post-trip periods. Third generation students are asked to present familial Holocaust legacies to their class during the trip and in post-trip discussions. Some trips include customized third generation visits to the surviving remnants of descendants' familial homes or hiding places where they become memory guides/brokers for the group in their own right. Feldman (2008) critiques the trip as a pedagogic ritual in the arsenal of the State's civil religion, aimed to socialize new generations of nationalist Jewish-Zionist Israeli citizens equipped with a xenophobic Holocaust historical frame with which to make meaningful their future army service and socio-political choices and worldview. In response to a growing multivocality of ideological positions in Israeli society and critical voices in academia, the past two decades have witnessed a more diverse and balanced ideological framing of trips to Poland, including a more humanist perspective as well as the emergence of organized trips for adults. However, this diversity has not altered the core ritual components, including the witnessing of survivor testimonies at sites of atrocity, visits to third generation ancestral sites, and third generation "testimony" in school upon their return home.

Although scholars highlight the primacy of pedagogic construction and the ways that third generation representatives are given the task of emancipating silenced "voices," they also depict a recursive looping back to the memories of the domestic formation of silence which authenticates the status of the third generation as carriers of trauma and memory while emotively invigorating their voice. Others claim the primacy and authenticity of silence over voice critiquing public enlistment of familial memory. Aiming to examine and move beyond the unilinear relationship between silence and voice, this chapter presents accounts of third generation descendants as they reflexively depict the multidirectional and mutually qualifying trajectories between testimonial voice in the public Israeli domain and Holocaust-related silence in the domestic familial domain.

Briefly stated, as the survivor generation passes away the question of carrier status and hierarchies of suffering take on new urgency. For many, these are no longer philosophical academic debates, but urgent and meaningful questions of social and historical identity.

Personal interpretive lenses: three analytical and moral turns

My first salvage mission at a support group for Holocaust descendants
My first research project was undertaken towards my MA degree and sections of my thesis were later published (Kidron, 2003). I undertook participant observation at a support group for the second generation in Israel analyzing group-based mechanisms and resultant processes of identity construction. I proposed and concluded that the support group agenda presented by facilitators framed identity-memory work that would ultimately constitute carriers of familial and potentially collective Holocaust memory. Although participants joined the group in the hope of understanding the long-term emotional impact of survivor parenting on their adult sense of self, I claimed that group narration processes entailing core scenarios of intergenerational trauma transmission re-emplotted their childhood memories, pathologizing and enlisting the second generation as wounded carriers of memory. Developed in later research and publications, the wounds of trauma transmission were conceptualized in the group as both constituting descendants who could be survivors in their own right, obviating the need for existential experience of Holocaust suffering. Although in the beginning of the support group process descendants resisted pathologization claiming they were not suffering from transmitted trauma, facilitator monologues framed emotional wounds as an inevitable and permanent "burden" to be carried by the second generation and almost intentionally transmitted to a third generation. The facilitator presented the final group agenda as follows:

> It is our last session – so we must ask *what is next – where do we go from here*? If we look back at the year and sessions we have discussed the different difficulties and problems we have *in common* as children of survivors … if I sum up the general feelings expressed here we see *we all carry a very heavy burden with us that we cannot get rid of. We carry it in all aspects of our lives and it affects all aspects of our life.* What do we do with it? How do we integrate it into our life? What do we do so that we can continue as separate individuals with our own lives without the burden destroying our lives and *what do we do with our children – the next generation. We want them to know and feel the burden but how can we transmit it to them and still let them separate from us.*

Rather than seeking coping skills or healing, and seemingly in response to the group agenda, the participants accept, narratively reenact and internalize the future scenario of the irrevocable burden and transmission of the burden and in the process they continue to constitute themselves as carriers of Holocaust memory. Referring to the intergenerational effects of trauma and the resultant descendant profile, one veteran participant describes the burden as follows:

> This is my second series in the group. I just want to say that everything that was said touches a familiar chord. One thing that is really important for me to understand, as a second-generation survivor, is *what I am doing to my kids … transmitting* to my children … there must be *patterns of unconscious behavior creating a third generation who will continue to carry the burden.*

The most striking aspect of this narration is the certainty with which the participant notes the inevitability that his behavior patterns, the scars of descendant historical trauma, have created a third generation that will continue to carry the traumatic past. Another participant completed the emergent profile of the third generation descendant by highlighting the burden of memory and testimony:

> I have come to terms with my burden and my *responsibility to preserve their memories,* even if it means I have this *split personality, their past and my present.* I know it isn't fair to *turn them into a third generation* but my children will have to *learn to carry this burden* of mine, for *all those* who died and *can no longer tell their story.*

In this narration, the second generation descendant appears to come to terms with the burden, and eloquently describes the copresence of the traumatic past and present within the descendant self. Referring to the descendant's mnemonic-moral mission, she asserts that the second generation and their children must carry the weight of contemporality and fulfil the role of carriers of Holocaust memory not only as inevitable psychic familial process but as moral obligation to all those who died. The emphasis of the depiction of the third generation has shifted away from the psychological realm of individual scars and memory work, into the collective realm of obligation to perpetuate not only the personal-familial trauma and loss but to tell the collective story of "*all those* who died."

Self-reflexive commentary

When seeking to isolate my interpretive lenses, I believe the most dominant lens is hermeneutic suspicion. The organization is presented as constructing carriers of memory while ultimately pathologizing them and enlisting them. Although, perhaps ironically, this was never my intended analytical frame, I was perpetually aware that the allure of my research depended not upon an apolitical and universal analysis of support group processes of identity construction but rather upon a critique of state-supported commemorative-therapeutic projects in service of Holocaust memory. In early presentations of my work, I insisted I was concerned solely with person-centered constitution and memory work, asking how might participants begin a construction process (eight sessions) convinced they were merely troubled by the familial past and complete the process as suffering from an illness construct – transmitted trauma – while vowing to transmit the construct in the name of preserving Holocaust memory. Yet I cannot deny that I was aware that a more political frame entailed symbolic and ultimately professional capital. I eventually integrated macro political questions in my publications and public lectures, although they always remained secondary relative to the discursive construction of identity.

This early nexus between personal academic and non-academic agendas and local discourse generated my second moral dilemma: was my work fueling the kind of political critique that was both unintended and at that time unsupported, and therefore was I complicit and had I lost agency over my work? Moreover, my own personal Zionist perspectives were inseparable from the more traditional and less critical view of the Holocaust as the epitome of anti-semitism that necessitated the founding of the Jewish State. Although I believe all critical Holocaust scholars must consider how they grapple with the topic that is most certainly cosmologically "holy" while at the same time professionally deconstructing their data when necessary, these two dilemmas, my loss of agency over the key implications of my work as well as its political afterlife that conflicted with my own moral universe, combined to make for an extremely trying experience.

The research outlined here was also my first experience of "salvage anthropology." At this early stage of my career I truly blindly believed I was protecting the private intimate world of personal and familial memory from intervention. I admit that I filtered out all positive experiences that may have been had by participants and was not entirely concerned with the fact that there were few interviews to evaluate to what degree my co-participants were consciously choosing enlistment or as I had believed were unequipped to understand how their identities were being altered in the name of therapeutic salutogenics. My claim (repeated in every conference talk) was that had the organization stated upfront a disclaimer of sorts – please be aware that all support groups, or for that matter all social interaction, entail transformation of self – then perhaps I would have said the agent has chosen to take the risk of enlistment in the name of self-exploration and communal belonging. Ultimately it would take another three years to the completion of my doctorate to understand that in postmodern contexts my second generation interlocutors would later exchange Holocaust carrier status for any number of multiple constructed and self-constructed identities in the name of self-examination, and only I perhaps took their identity work so very seriously as hegemonic intervention of a passive self. This, of course, cannot be understood in isolation from the very complex professional zeitgeist of sociological and anthropological Foucauldian hermeneutics of suspicion and critique of nation building – the taken for granted grand truths that were foundational in my graduate education.

After this dilemma, and perhaps in response, I found myself presenting two new yet no less contradictory agendas. On the one hand, I sought out the pre-enlisted private sphere where I might find those who resist construction, who in a Marxian sense do not have false consciousness. Here I was still enamored with a hermeneutics of suspicion yet aimed to find those who in today's terms were "woke." I hoped to find descendants who were critical, reflexive, and aware of enlistment or merely protective of their privacy and some kind of intimate familial experience as a negation or corrective to public commemoration. But at the same time I admit I became aware during my first interviews that I was seeking resonance with my own personal experience as second generation descendant and there was an intuitive reason behind my insistence on "privacy" to perform familial Holocaust memory, which might also explain my moral mission to promote a more agentic position vis-à-vis institutional commemoration. As I describe in my work on survivor family silence (Kidron 2009), I began this second phase after an initial methodological crisis in the field. My second generation interlocutors responded "nothing" to a very factual opening question about what they know about their parents' Holocaust past until finally one descendant disclosed her taken for granted experience of the silent embodied presence of the Holocaust in the everyday domestic life world. This response totally altered my questions and my agenda. I began the interview with a question regarding the presence of the past in everyday life that was lived in Halbwachs and Nora's sense in its own right.

Although organically grounded, my findings validated my resistance to public enlistment. Descendants were very much enthralled and embedded within their personal and familial emotional meaning worlds relating to their parents' Holocaust survival and its legacy. Second generation descendants were not constituted by therapeutic discourse's trauma theory, nor were they products of the Israeli national crisis of Holocaust representation – quite the contrary. Public Holocaust narratives marginalized the familial and personal in favor of mythic heroic and resistant ghetto fighter narratives. The incommensurability of the familial legacies of the great majority of second generation Holocaust descendants and the national narratives that represented the Holocaust permitted for the lived experience of silent embodied memory "off the grid" of national public discourse and practice. For example, when telling me about the presence of the Holocaust in her home, Michelle proudly showed me a tablespoon. I stared at the spoon, wondering why she is showing it to me in the middle of the interview. She tells me, smiling, "This was my mother's spoon." Still confused, I respond noncommittally, "Really." Realizing I do not understand, she explains, "This was my mother's spoon in Auschwitz. This is what she ate with, you know THE SOUP." Attempting to restore my professional composure despite my surprise, I ask her where the spoon is kept in her parent's home, thinking to myself that it must be in some closed cabinet for safekeeping. She explains with a broader smile, "It was in the kitchen, in the drawer, with the other utensils ... we ate with it. My mother fed me my morning oatmeal with it."

Enmeshed in the everyday sensuous life of the household, the spoon enables the taken for granted lived experience of the Holocaust past via the embodiment of relations of love and caring. I asked Michelle how she understands her mother's choice to keep the spoon in use at home rather than donate it to the national Holocaust museum. She replies, "Look, she won, she survived with that spoon. Every time she fed me or my sister she probably said to herself, 'Hah, I won – not only didn't I die, but this spoon that kept me alive is now feeding my children.'" The spoon's everyday mundane material functionality allows it to perform in "its relational force or will" in the home precisely so that the family may routinely reenact the relief of hunger, nurturance, and survival. They are "living" with and through the Holocaust, and, in this way, surviving the Holocaust becomes perhaps the most tacit and "present" experience of the body enacted between mother and child, becoming the most basic and life-giving of "transmissions." Thus, rather being displayed in museums – frozen sites of memory, the spoon remains woven into the daily practices of the home so that it may perpetually inscribe in the lived body (Merleau-Ponty, 1962) the sensual experience of survival. Materially constituted and sustained embodied memories of survival, tightly interwoven in the everyday domestic social milieu, depict what Nora (1989) and Halbwachs (1980) term "lived memory."

Israeli and global Holocaust scholarship in the social sciences, forever critical of nation building and its civil mythology, has focused entirely upon the instrumentalization of the Holocaust and even the marginalization of passive forms of survival. Yet most interestingly, much of this scholarship has failed to examine the lived experience of these passive survivors – the interesting alternative micro-mechanisms of memory work that take place in their lives. Again, the academic zeitgeist enlisted its own axioms, out of tune with everyday lives of Jewish adult Israelis. As new bedfellows, trauma theory and post-colonial theory would call upon the anthropology of memory to liberate the nationally silenced passive sheep to the slaughter and emotionally wounded victims of intergenerational transmission – to tell their stories, not for the nation but for agentic healing and self-discovery.

It is here, at a new discursive crossroad, that I found myself conflicted once again. As part of the academic community, I was most certainly familiar with trauma theory and post-colonial theory and could not deny that survivors and descendants were in fact silent and emotionally wounded. Yet, as clarified, my personal and professional experience pointed to *emotional resilience*, and my doctoral data disclosed an alternative domestic form of silent embodied memory work that was at once not self-perceived as pathogenic and most certainly not "silenced" by public discourse. Silent memory work was in fact the platform or mechanism of authentic commemoration whereas the national engineered narratives of public voice were presented as suspect of ultimately "silencing" subjective lived experience. In great contrast to my dilemma during my first academic trajectory outlined, my second trajectory allowed for a far more robust and grounded critique of public discourse – both therapeutic and mnemonic – claiming that I had discovered a lacuna in memory studies and Holocaust studies that in fact discursively "silenced" nonverbal forms of lived memory.

Although I cannot deny that I continued to perceive my research as a salvage mission of private familial memory, in this second turn there was far more data to legitimate my claims. I could gradually focus upon the bottom-up lived experiences of what the field provided and not my battle against the hermeneutics of Israeli Holocaust memory or national enlistment. This time around my interlocutors most powerfully stated – without the "selective distortions" of my interpretive lens – that their private embodied memory obviated any need or interest in public forms of memory and that public memory remained a form of Holocaust representation that served political and national needs that would forever present the past through changing ideational collective prisms rather than as resonant with their survivor parents' experience. Those in the minority who would choose to do memory work in the public sphere sought forgotten history or professional capital as carriers of memory, yet they would forever insist upon the gap between lived private memory and public commemoration.

Although I could confidently trace the gap between private and public memory, empirically grounding the distinction between avowed descendant emotional vulnerability and the pathologizing construct of transmitted trauma would present a greater challenge. Although colleagues in psychology and psychiatry would support my critique of transmitted trauma as distinct from the psychosocial effects of survivor parenting, my interlocutors' accounts of Holocaust-related permanent emotional "scratch" (Kidron et al, 2019) or wound problematized my position. Echoing my work in the support group, again I became self-critical, questioning whether I was in denial about the depth and breadth of descendant emotional distress. Here again it was precisely the personal dilemma of facing my "demon" of depathologization that triggered a new round of interviews. Here, too, contemporary discourse played a critical role as my new self-critique occurred precisely during the height of the scholarly turn surrounding resilience. I therefore began to question whether, just as descendant Holocaust memory called for a deconstruction of the lived experience of silence in the private sphere, perhaps transmitted embodied Holocaust memory would in some way uniquely alter the phenomenology of psychological wellbeing, emotional vulnerability, and distress. My findings ultimately pointed to what my colleagues and I termed *descendant resilient vulnerability*. Descendants chose to perpetuate their emotional vulnerability as what they recounted was a "badge of honor." Ironically my descendant interlocutors accepted their carrier status, which I critiqued in trajectory number one – this time seemingly without the institutional construction/enlistment. As Holocaust presence was valorized as central to familial remembrance of the atrocity and its victims, emotional distress would be a non-pathological marker of remembrance and vulnerability would have to persist in the face of potential wellness and forgetting. Here of course one would have to ask, in what way had public and often political narratives of Holocaust commemoration constituted descendant commitment to resilient vulnerability? Although accounts of early formative moments of parent-child interaction that constituted vulnerability pointed to the potential of disentangling the experience from public discourse, construction theorists would correctly claim that there would be no way to unravel private and public mnemonic construction processes.

The third trajectory – third generation memory work in the public sphere

In 2015, I returned to the phenomenological experience of descendants, both second and third generation (grandchildren of survivors), in the public sphere. Three discursive shifts contributed to second generation involvement in public forms of commemoration:

1. Late modern interest in heritage/genealogy and in particular in roots trips.
2. Increased acceptance of therapeutic discourse and popularized coaching in the Israeli middle class which triggered public identity work previously considered self-serving and frivolous by the Israeli "ideal collectivist self" (Yankellevich, 2020).
3. Anxiety surrounding the approaching demise of the survivor generation triggering new attempts to access familial historical knowledge before it was too late.

Despite activity in the public sphere, second generation descendants became temporary consumers of public knowledge while still resisting testimonial practices. My assumption was that, in great contrast, the third generation would take on the testimonial role their parents had rejected. I hypothesized that whereas second generation parents undertook personal and familial memory work in niches of domesticity in the public sphere (Kidron, 2013) and remained collectively silent and resistant to public testimony, coveting the "authenticity" of silence after experiencing first-hand survivor embodied transmission, the third generation, more distanced experientially from survivor grandparents and constructed in the school system to become carriers, would be committed only to public performative "dead memory" (Nora, 1989).

Surprisingly I discovered that there were third generation descendants who would begin their journey as products of construction in the public sphere only to loop back to the private sphere seeking out early childhood phenomenological traces of grandparent and parent embodied transmission to validate their authenticity and position themselves higher on the hierarchy of Holocaust suffering (Kidron, 2021). My research on the third generation would therefore emerge in two very different phases: in the first phase, I had the great fortune to receive constructive criticism from the editor of the special issue in *History and Memory* (see White, 2000) pointing out that my repeated references to hegemonic enlistment of a second or third generation were in fact a strawman's argument as no one doubted the politics of memory in nation building/maintenance and this was not a novel contribution. He pointed out that I was reducing complex private-public relations to a simplistic interaction between the engineers of memory and their supposedly top-down constructed carriers of national memory. Just as my work on private memory sought out and disclosed new non-binary experiences of silence and voice, here too I was encouraged to reexamine the motivations and experience of the enlisted as agentic co-engineers of memory and the hegemonic institutional brokers as facilitators providing a platform for those families and individuals seeking traces of their heritage unavailable in the private sphere. Returning to my data, I did in fact disclose an agentic cooperation – almost a *symbiotic* and not parasitic relationship between descendants and commemorative institutions. However, at this first stage (Kidron, 2015), although I acknowledged second generation agency, I continued to portray the third generation as passive and unreflexive pawns in the Israeli school system, where the only individual agentic voice to be heard would be critique of their previously silent parents – again speaking the narrative of hegemonic construction of vocal public witnesses.

In the second phase of this trajectory – again motivated by constructively critical colleagues during work on a paper for another special issue this time in *History and Anthropology* (Kidron, 2021) – I returned to data from my dissertation on voices of reflexive and non-enlisted or self-critical enlisted third generation descendants. Again using the wrong interpretive lens, I had previously selectively "ignored" this material as unrepresentative of the majority voice. To my good fortune, I began to collect new data only to discover the way the third generation, ten years after their trips to Poland, is embedded in a new social and discursive context in which the survivor generation is dwindling (and with them the lived experience of Holocaust legacies) and growing left-wing critique of trips to Poland raise new moral questions regarding national Holocaust memory. These young descendants spoke of public enlistment on trips to Poland as activating renewed emotive memories of intimate and private Holocaust transmission in their formative years at home with survivor grandparents and second generation parents. For example, Miriam recounts: "In Poland you reach some sort of climax, from the intensity, the shock, and when it connects to your personal history … it connects in insane levels of intensity, you become so emotional, you have to share your experience and vent, and you act in ways that you would not recognize yourself." Tamara provides a glimpse of intimate recollections triggered on her trip to Poland: "I had watched my mother light the memorial candle on Holocaust Remembrance Day. She didn't say a word but the depth of her emotion … I guess those things effect you – they get transmitted somehow."

The trip to Poland activates and amplifies childhood experiential emotional hooks present prior to pedagogic construction processes. Learning to give voice to familial legacies on school trips to Poland mobilizes formative silence which ultimately merges with and energizes voice. Both silence and voice are qualified by these multidirectional trajectories.

Processing the data, I understood that a third generation hybridity – encapsulating both private emotive experience and public carrier status – grants descendants a self-perceived more privileged national role. They would claim a new form of authenticity that is contingent upon both lived memories of survivor grandparenting and Holocaust pedagogic "training" in sites of atrocity where they discover their authentic voice. Only this hybrid mnemonic experience would be capable of defying the ever growing temporal and existential gap between the present and the Holocaust past. Sharona asserts:

> "Yes, we have to make a contribution to commemoration, because we are more connected when we come from 'there' [survivor families or perhaps … Holocaust]. When it's a story that's yours, it's easier for people to identify with it when it's a personal story. Obviously if someone comes and tells a story that's theoretical, learned in the library or in a museum … it's not the same as when I would say I'm a survivor, it's much more close to home, more accessible."

By referring to herself as a survivor whose transmitted tale is "close to home" Sharona voices not only her sense of authenticity, but "territoriality" and ownership over the Holocaust chronotope and the story it engenders.

Ironically, hybrid third generation descendants who perceive themselves as both products of the public and private sphere and desperately in search of authentic embodied childhood memory allow me to return at least half way to my previous intellectual and ethical comfort zone prioritizing the private sphere as essential site of authentic Holocaust presence. The recursive loop back from public to private permits once again for a romanticized view of authentic childhood embodied transmissions and domestic lived memory while paying lip service – albeit this time more sincerely – to public national memory and the role of collective carriers of memory.

This final trajectory has raised new moral dilemmas. As my intellectual interest and novel epistemological contribution as a scholar remains focused on lived memory, as either resistant to public memory or apathetic towards it, to what extent am I (still) distorting, in Schudson's (1997) terms, descendant accounts to highlight their loop back to the private domain – and more importantly the dependence of authentic and therefore effective public memory work on personal or private memory work? With the passing of the survivor generation – I myself "have to move on" and face the question – how relevant and viable is the issue of authenticity when the second generation are in their 60s and early 70s? This of course relates to very sensitive issues of facing one's own generational shortened trajectory. Third generation pathologization of their parents called upon a reconsideration of my past depathologization of the second generation – again calling into question my salvage mission.

Discussion

This chapter has attempted to lay bare a self-reflexive and self-critical account of the way subjective/personal moralistic scholarly and extremely personal positions shape our empirical and analytical lens. I believe the presentation of my trajectories, and ultimately two-decades long history of my work on descendant Holocaust legacies, may provide a number of useful insights into the micro and macro politics of memory and memory scholarship and perhaps more importantly into the way the politics of memory can never be disentangled from formative ideational (and yes, ideological) and emotive moral missions. Emergent dilemmas stem from the incommensurability of two permanently entangled positions – a Gramcian and Foucauldian politics of memory that would forever deconstruct national collective memory and the construction of carriers of memory on the one hand, and ideological commitments to collective Holocaust remembrance and yes authentic public witnessing on the other. As social and national contexts prepare for the demise of the first generation, even the most late modern nihilist resists full-blown betrayal if not of Jewish collective memory then of our cultural forebears. I would propose that this dilemma points to the limits of sociological hermeneutics of suspicion and calls for a more profound sociology of lived and yes moral meaning-making (see Mizrahi, 2016) where our formative ethical life worlds take priority over scholarly deconstructive moral missions and resist the deconstruction of meanings (that for good or bad) have made us who we are.

However my continued, almost fetishized attempt to liberate the private sphere from the grips of public intervention and enlistment goes beyond, I believe, philosophical or political sociological theory or critique. If my work forever traces and concludes that all analytical roads (second, third and even public testimonial carriers) lead back home to silent moments of emotive Holocaust transmission, while never quite letting go of the directive of public remembrance, I would have to ask what for me as an anthropologist of memory remains to be resolved. My work has in fact shown domestic, private resilience, agency, and strategic enlistment of the public sphere, and yes even the failure of a third generation descendant who has yet to "return home" to his "real" Holocaust past. My answer would be two-fold. First, on a purely theoretical level, I believe I continue to prioritize lived memory and its ultimate marginalization vis-à-vis public commemoration as I and my colleagues have yet to fully decipher or perhaps make a case for memory as the lived and embodied re-presence of the past. I would venture to say that survivors of atrocities and social suffering and their descendants intuitively "know" that memory – whether we use the banal term authentic or not – is the phenomenological experience of being there, of being in the past while in the present. This lived presence of the past will forever be at odds with public and politicized discourses/narratives about the past. What we in my view incorrectly term collective memory or remembrance is in fact only our way to put the rewritten past to work to constitute the future in the image of politically desirable narratives. Whether examining therapeutic discourses on transmitted trauma or pedagogically constituted testimonies in Poland, both forms of "memory" are rewritten narratives in service of troubled selfhood, institutional capital, and national domestic policy.

Second, if we are to sustain moral integrity pertaining to the personal and collective value of remembrance in the form of genocide prevention or pedagogy towards universal human empathy in the face of suffering (and ultimately perhaps conflict prevention), then we would have to carefully monitor the gap between the historical and phenomenological experience of survivor suffering as our bench mark for prevention and the more political instrumentalized uses and abuses of suffering framing what often appear (or are disguised) as no less valuable moral agendas. If this were to be my perspective, I would have to come to terms with my mnemonic activism and remain self-critical of salvage missions I claim to be ethically problematic. I would also have to come to terms with the incommensurability of Holocaust memory and Holocaust commemoration and most painfully perhaps accept that when the last survivor dies, lived memory and emotive and embodied interaction will have to evolve in keeping with its context – becoming dependent upon holographic images of survivors, descendant witnesses trained and renarrativized by institutional memory brokers, or digitized and animated historical archives. Alternatively, we might relinquish our particular ties to ancestral ethnic lived suffering and interact and empathize with the lived memories of contemporary victims – once again one of the more ethical lessons of many survivors' and descendants' lived Holocaust memory.

References

Balberg-Rothenstreich, A. (2004) "A Pedagogic and Humanist Journey or Fashionable Coming of Age Trip? Fifteen Years of Youth Trips to Poland," *New Directions* 10: 158–167. (Hebrew).

Bar-On, D. (1992) "Israeli and German Students Encounter the Holocaust through a Group Process: 'Working Through' and 'Partial Relevance,'" *International Journal of Group Tensions* 22: 81–118.

Barocas, H.A. and Barocas, C. (1973) "Manifestations of Concentration Camp Effects on the Second Generation," *American Journal of Psychiatry* 130(7): 820–821.

Bauman, Z. (1998) "Hereditary Victimhood: The Holocaust's Life as a Ghost," *Tikkun* 13: 33–38.

Bezo, B. and Maggi, S. (2018) "Intergenerational Perceptions of Mass Trauma's Impact on Physical Health and Well-being," *Psychological Trauma: Theory, Research, Practice, and Policy* 10(1): 87–94.

Dasberg, H. (1992) "The Unfinished Story of Trauma as a Paradigm for Psychotherapists: A Review and some Empirical Findings on Paradigms and Prejudices," *Israel Journal of Psychiatry and Related Sciences* 29(1): 44–60.

DeGloma, T. (2014) *Seeing the Light: The Social Logic of Personal Discovery*. Chicago, IL: University of Chicago Press.

Ellis, C., Adams, T.E., and Bochner, A.P. (2011) "Autoethnography: An Overview," *Historical social research* 36(4): 273–290.

Fassin, D. (2008) "Humanitarian Politics of Testimony: Subjectification through Trauma in the Israeli-Palestinian Conflict," *Cultural Anthropology* 23(3): 531–558.

Feldman, J. (2008) *Above the Death Pits, Beneath the Flag: Youth Voyages to Holocaust Poland and Israeli National Identity*. New York: Berghahn.

Geertz, C. (1973) *The Interpretation of Cultures: Selected Essays*. New York: Basic Books.

Giladi, L. and Bell, T.S. (2013) "Protective Factors for Intergenerational Transmission of Trauma Among Second and Third Generation Holocaust Survivors," *Psychological Trauma: Theory, Research, Practice, and Policy* 5(4): 384–391.

Goldberg, A. (2012) "The Jewish Narrative in the Yad Vashem Global Museum," *Journal of Genocide Research* 14(2): 187–213.

Halbwachs, M. (1980) *The Collective Memory*. New York: Harper Colophon.

Halik, V., Rosenthal, D.A. and Pattison, P.E. (1990) "Intergenerational Effects of the Holocaust: Patterns of Engagement in the Mother-Daughter Relationship," *Family Process* 29(3): 325–339.

Handelman, D. (1990) *Models and Mirrors: Towards an Anthropology of Public Events*. Cambridge: Cambridge University Press.

Handelman, D. (2004) *Nationalism and the Israeli State: Bureaucratic Logic in Public Events*. Oxford: Berg.

Hoffman, Y. and Shrira, A. (2017) "Shadows of the Past and Threats of the Future: ISIS Anxiety Among Grandchildren of Holocaust Survivors," Psychiatry Research 253: 220–225.

Keren, N. (2000) "Teaching the Holocaust in Israel," *Internationale Schulbuchforschung* 22(1): 95–108.

Kidron, C.A. (2003) "Surviving a Distant Past: A Case Study of the Cultural Construction of Trauma Descendant Identity," *Ethos* 31(4): 513–544.

Kidron, C.A. (2009) "Toward an Ethnography of Silence: The Lived Presence of the Past in the Everyday Lives of Holocaust Trauma Descendants in Israel," *Current Anthropology* 50(1): 5–27.

Kidron, C.A. (2013) "Being There Together: Dark Family Tourism and the Emotive Experience of Co-Presence in the Holocaust Past," *Annals of Tourism Research* 41: 175–194.

Kidron, C.A. (2015) "Survivor Family Memory at Sites of Holocaust Remembrance: Institutional Enlistment or Family Agency?," *History & Memory* 27(2): 45–73.

Kidron, C.A. (2021) "Emancipatory Voice and the Recursivity of Authentic Silence: Holocaust Descendant Accounts of the Multidirectional Dialectic between Silence and Voice," *History and Anthropology* 32(4): 442–461.

Kidron, C.A., Kotliar, D.M., and Kirmayer, L.J. (2019) "Transmitted Trauma as Badge of Honor: Phenomenological Experiences of Holocaust Descendant Resilient Vulnerability," *Social Science and Medicine* 239: 112524.

Lazar, A., Chaitin, J., Gross, T. and Baron, D. (2004) "Jewish Israeli Teenagers, National Identity and the Lessons of the Holocaust," *Holocaust and Genocide Studies* 18: 188–204.

Leys, R. (1996) "Traumatic Cures: Shell Shock, Janet and the Question of Memory," in P. Antze and M. Lambek (eds) *Tense Past: Cultural Essays in Trauma and Memory.*, New York: Routledge, pp 103–145.

Merleau-Ponty, M. (1962) *The Phenomenology of Perception*. London: Routledge and Kegan Paul.

Mizrachi, N. (2016) "Sociology in the Garden: Beyond the Liberal Grammar of Contemporary Sociology," *Israel Studies Review* 31: 1–30.

Nora, P. (1989) "Between Memory and History," *Representations* 26: 7–25.

Palgi, Y., Ben-Ezra, M., Or, A., Dubiner, Y., Baruch, E., Soffer, Y. and Shrira, A. (2012) "Mental Health and Disaster Related Attitudes among Japanese after the 2011 Fukushima Nuclear Disaster," *Journal of Psychiatric Research* 46(5): 688–690.

Pupavac, V. (2004) "Psychosocial Interventions and the Demoralization of Humanitarianism," *Journal of Biosocial Science* 36(4): 491–504.

Schudson, M. (1997) "Dynamics of Distortion in Collective Memory," in D.L. Schacter (ed) *How Minds, Brains and Societies Reconstruct the Past*, Harvard, MA: Harvard University Press, pp 346–351.

Schwartz, S., Dohrenwend, B.P., and Levav, I. (1994) "Nongenetic Familial Transmission of Psychiatric Disorders? Evidence from Children of Holocaust Survivors," *Journal of Health and Social Behavior* 35: 385–402.

Shaw, R. (2007) "Memory Frictions: Localizing the Truth and Reconciliation Commission in Sierra Leone," *International Journal of Transitional Justice* 1: 183–207.

Slyomovics, S. (2014) *How to Accept German Reparations*. Philadelphia, PA: University of Pennsylvania Press.

White, G.M. (2000) "Emotional Remembering: The Pragmatics of National Memory," *Ethos* 27(4): 505–529.

Winship, G. and Knowles, J. (1996) "The Transgenerational Impact of Cultural Trauma: Linking Phenomena in Treatment of Third Generation Survivors of the Holocaust," *British Journal of Psychotherapy* 13(2): 259–266.

Yankellevich, A. (2020) "Running to Stay in the Same Place? Personal Development Work and the Production of Neoliberal Subjectivity among Israel's Last Republican Generation," in E. Bell, S. Gog, A. Simionca, and S. Taylot (eds) *Spirituality, Organization and Neoliberalism,* Northampton, MA: Edward Elgar Publishing, pp 27–45.

Zilberfein, F. (1995) "Children of Holocaust Survivors: Separation Obstacles, Attachments and Anxiety," in J. Lemberger (ed) *A Global Perspective on Working with Holocaust Survivors and the Second Generation*, Jerusalem: JDC-Brookdale Institute and Amcha, pp 413–422.

11

Changing Memories of the Shoah in Post-Communist Countries: New Memories and Conflicts

Selma Leydesdorff

Memory is never static, but rather a construction embedded in changing personal, social, and temporal settings. Memory is never neutral, and reflects the interaction between personal and dominant collective memories. When a political culture changes, recollections and collective memories become contested, and new ones become dominant and come to the fore. This is clearly visible when we look at the "new" histories in the post-communist world, where the surge of commemorative work that highlights the World War II-era victimization of citizens by communist forces is driven by agents with nationalist ideologies and agendas competing with the memories of the Shoah. These form part of the mnemonic tensions in many places throughout Europe which seek to identify victims and perpetrators and their histories and focus on their own particular sufferings; they want to be recognized. Their arguments reveal how nationalist ideologies can conflict with widely accepted versions of history. The result is a political effort to monopolize victimhood, and an appeal to the West to take suffering under communism more seriously. It is a renewed nationalist narrative that celebrates a past that is replete with struggles for freedom and pride, one that has been viciously suppressed for decades. The new view can be imposed by the state or a dominant political group, and any resistance to its acceptance can be punished, since the new regimes are typically undemocratic and intolerant of opposing views. In this chapter, I discuss some important cases and show how history has become politicized.

Nationalism, pride, and shame about the past have created new historical canons and destroyed old ones. Historical research is subordinated to the forces of politics that seek to remember or to forget. This is most acute in Russia, where an assault against the NGO *Memorial* and the kind of research being done there tries to silence the counter-histories of historians who listen to stories of oppression, persecution, murder, and the sad lives of the millions who were sent to the Gulag. *Memorial* has excavated a shameful past which is not embraced by those who want a positive history of Russian heroism that celebrates the fight against the Nazis without mentioning the communist terror. *Memorial* has created an enormous archive, and participants are actively interviewing everywhere in Russia, even deep in Siberia. With their huge amount of evidence, they present a challenge to the government that opposes openness about an atrocious past. Continuing lawsuits are a sign of the fervent wish of the authorities to prevent the crimes of the Stalin era and the aggressive policies thereafter from being uncovered and made public.

These politics also hinder a pluralist attitude where the past can be contradictory. Only one "correct" view can exist. This is also the case outside Russia. I do not mean to suggest that all the historians I mention in this chapter are directly under threat, but in many places the tension between nationalist and internationalist interest in shaping historical vision has damaged the freedom of academic historical research and its recognition. The result is the creation of new countermemories and narratives that support national interests. History is thus being used by those who have the authority and political support to alter in the context of official educational curriculum or the materials presented in museums in the name of promoting what is considered a more "modern" approach to the past. The word "modern" is used to hide this agenda when it actually advances a nationalist view.

Changing collective memories and the mnemonic battle

In his pioneering work, Maurice Halbwachs (1925) argued that we reconstruct our past using our mental images of the present. As the present changes, memory also changes. He addressed this phenomenon in his work on collective memory, which established him as a major figure in the history of sociology. The idea that memory is shaped by social and political conditions, and by time, was also pursued by Tony Judt (2005) in his magnum opus *Postwar* in which he reflected in his "Epilogue" on the memory of the Holocaust/Shoah in Western Europe.[1] He argued that the history of the massive collaboration with the Germans by Europeans during World War II in occupied territories in the West has been veiled by emotional resistance and feelings of guilt. Indeed, people did not want to hear such shameful stories, and shared the public opinion that the whole nation had been anti-Nazi. It took decades before there was space in which to doubt this assumption, and by now the historical consensus about interpretation of the past has been broken. Admitting collaboration with the Nazis has become unavoidable, especially after the book *Vichy France and the Jews* by Marrus and Paxton was published in 1981. This book provoked a fierce debate, among historians and in public opinion, about the extent of collaboration, one that ultimately led to widespread agreement that collaboration was common throughout Europe.

According to Judt, the result of the debate was, up to that point in time, to be a victim seemed a Jewish prerogative; but new groups, like German victims, also claimed victimhood and wanted recognition and compensation for their sufferings. Jean-Michel Chaumont (2010) has asserted that the outcome of the resulting new attitude to the war and its trauma was a real battle for victimhood claimed by several groups. Of course, that the Jews were not the only victims is undeniable. Nevertheless, even though there were numerous cases with ample justification, many claims of victimhood were driven by self-interest, an effort to receive compensation, or by imaginary phantasies with no basis in evidence.

In the former communist world, the memory-story has always been different from the historical canon that was taught in schools in Western Europe. After the demise of communism, new nationalist histories have claimed that their own particular groups, or the populations of their countries, were also victims of the atrocities committed by communism, sometimes equating their fate with the sufferings of the Jews under Nazism. In fact, some politicians have asserted that the population of several former Soviet countries like Hungary survived two genocides, and thus experienced more violence than did the Jews, who "survived only one." I refer to the stories about the past in the large area of land extending from the Baltics down to the Ukraine, called *Bloodlands* by Timothy Snyder (2010), where people were killed and tortured on an immense scale. These lands have been a battlefield with ever-changing borders, and have been dominated by the totalitarian regimes of both communism and Nazism, which have now been replaced by nationalist regimes. At the same time, the political changes since the fall of communism have destabilized memorial cultures.[2]

The Great Patriotic War: an imposed and dominant Stalinist interpretation of the 20th century

From the end of World War II until the demise of the Soviet empire, only one dominant discourse about the past was permitted by the authorities in countries that were part of the communist world. In its newspeak, the correct and only acceptable way to frame that past was as a war in which countless *innocent Soviet citizens* were murdered by *fascist hordes*. In fact, the name assigned to the defense of Russia was the "Great Patriotic War," and it celebrated the heroism of the resistance against the German invaders. According to this view of history, the loss of millions of people was wholly the loss of *Soviet citizens*. In other words, no distinctions were made among the different nationalities living in the territory, where traditionally many cultures and nationalities had lived, and in which many different histories of the past existed. The reality that people had a particular identity with their own history was suppressed. In addition, every initiative to demonstrate an alternative cultural heritage or an alternative local political life in theatres, youth organizations, and memory was forbidden.

The past was "Russified," which meant for instance that the history of the Jews, or a special place for the various itineraries of people living in Baltic countries or the people of the Caucasus, no longer existed. Moreover, although it was a framework implemented by the Soviet Union, it became the only permissible way to talk and write in other countries of communist Europe. Of course, according to this view, oppression under Stalinism did "not exist," and research on suffering under Stalin was and remains severely impaired (FIDH, 2021).

The dominant discourse prescribed how people had to interpret and tell history, as well as how they had to adapt their own personal stories. It shocked me while doing my research on Sobibor, one of the major deathcamps in Eastern Poland, to discover how often the survivors I interviewed struggled with a past where in the official language Jews had become mere *Soviet citizens*, which they had never been in reality. They had never really belonged to the Russian nation. For instance, the leader of the uprising of the destruction camp Sobibor in 1943, Sasha Pechersky, was permitted to talk about the war when he returned from the Nazi-camp and the partisan unit he had joined to his town Rostov on Don in 1945 (Leydesdorff, 2017). Yet although he was a public speaker, he was forbidden to talk about what had happened to him as a Jew, or about the fate of other Jews in Sobibor or in other concentration camps. I have described his ensuing loneliness in my book about him and how his life ended in depression and despair. I also interviewed Aleksei Waitsen in Ryazan (east of Moscow), who told me that after the war there was no one to talk to about Sobibor.[3] He, too, was left alone with his memories. Later, he could sometimes relate them to other survivors, but only to them specifically and only after he had managed to locate them. When I asked him if he could talk about the camp, he replied, "I never mentioned the camp." I could hardly believe it, and asked him: "To nobody?" His answer was: "No." He did not even discuss his experiences with his wife. It was not acceptable to talk about the fate of Jews. And there was no one to talk to about it, since his family had been murdered, he said. He repeated, "I confessed to nobody that I was in a camp."[4] I carefully checked the word he used, "confessed," which is a remarkable choice in that it connotes a feeling of deep shame and/or personal guilt. Yet that is the expression he used.

Competing memories: victims in the West and the East – who suffered more?

In Europe, two memories compete as rivals in the struggle for dominance: in the West, the Holocaust/Shoah dominates; and in the former communist world, the memory of communist oppression and the invasion by the Nazis are more important, which refers to the random murder of local populations and not only Jews. The European Union, while expanding to the East, was committed to integrating the history of communist oppression into the existing story of the Shoah, and to creating one common memory as part of the effort to integrate the two parts of the European community culturally.

It is self-evident that, in all the countries of Europe, people remember an atrocious past during World War II and relate in personal ways to the misery of their larger families, parents, and grandparents. Moreover, they do so in various ways. Many believe they were affected worse than others. The arguments I raise in this chapter are grounded on the foundational notion that it does not make sense to argue that one has suffered more than someone else. This perspective stems from my personal background as the child of two parents who were imprisoned for a long period of time: my mother was in several German concentration camps (among them Auschwitz); while my father suffered from the atrocities that the Japanese committed in the Netherlands East Indies, and he was also an inmate of the Japanese world of concentration camps. During my childhood, there was an ever-present confusion and competition between my mother and father about who had been worse off. That they both suffered in different and horrific ways was, for me, more than sufficient.

Inspired by the lessons of my personal life and my career as a historian, I am convinced that no one should compare sufferings; it does not make sense to create a hierarchy of sorrow at a personal or national level, and to argue about whose fate was worse. It is urgent to look for the existence of options other than claiming an exclusive victimhood, and to investigate how we can remember and integrate the histories of both parts of Europe. However, right-wing populists in the post-communist countries have created new narratives about the past which are mostly nationalist and sometimes intertwined with religion, and which have both absorbed and resisted existing accounts of what people experienced. This new nationalist narrative of the past, which is frequently anti-Semitic, merges with an uncomfortable feeling that Jewish suffering has received too much attention. Such protagonists of neo-nationalism firmly claim their own central place in historical memory. Creating and using these one-sided accounts, they establish "imagined communities" where the "other" is excluded from the community (Anderson, 1983).

The old language of victimhood has become part of a new canon and a new language in which some take symbolic revenge for the perceived absence of their particular community from memory. In other words, victimhood is part of the search for a non-communist identity. Many who search for this post-communist standpoint claim an identity which is supported by narrated (spoken) biographies and autobiographies and opposes more traditional means of preservation in written texts that, until then, had indeed been stifled or manipulated (Ebenshade, 1995). They counter the official discourse that served as the guardian of a past that erased their particular history, resisting it with the memories told by individuals whose stories bring to light and illuminate once-obscured and now mobilized memories (Konrád, 1982: p 75).

Who is the victim of what? Can a victim also be a perpetrator?

Modern political disputes over victimhood are spurred by a search for a collective new non-communist identity, which has formed the basis for a newly canonized collective memory (Ochman, 2013). Within the new narratives of the past, some advance one step further: their focus on their own fate denies the misery of others. This attitude has become a core part of all nationalist right-wing movements in the whole of European politics, and is also taken up by the far right in Western Europe. This vision is hostile to whatever does not belong to the new canonized history, and is tightly intertwined with both modern anti-semitism and the denial of the fate of the Jews. In addition, such a one-sided paradigm ignores the fact that victims can also have been perpetrators. For instance, the population of the Baltic states suffered profoundly under communism; however, we also know that many joined the Nazis and helped to kill an enormous number of Jews. In this way, they also became true victimizers. In the end, in the post-communist world, the memory of the Shoah was weaker than people's experienced history of communist oppression. Their story was more concerned with the recent suffering under communist domination, which would become an integral paradigm that powerful actors have used to erase other aspects of history and reinterpret the past.

In fact, peoples and nations would reframe history for their own purposes (Onken, 2007). Because countries looking for "new" accepted narratives created their own narratives, and because the new histories were more ideological and political than historical, an escalation of memory wars has occurred, one in which Russia with its "great patriotic war" has been on the defensive. This revision of history is still evolving rapidly: commissions (often highly political) have been installed to revise and evaluate history, polemics have become normal, and even legal means are employed to impose revisions. Nationalist histories are also integrated into the language of new nationalist movements and politics, which strongly desire the heroization of a particular country, and new legislation is passed accordingly. I cautiously generalize about these phenomena, despite the fact that the amount of evidence is massive and ever-increasing, and is written in many languages.

Still, one can understand why the dominance of the framework of the Holocaust/Shoah had less appeal for the inhabitants of the post-Soviet world. The memory of suffering under communism was and is a more pressing part of their mental world (Zombory, 2017). Memory then became more politicized, and with the rise of new nationalist parties memory was utilized to construct narratives based on the trauma of a recent past that was replete with pain and rage. Shame and pride are guiding the new views of the past and overruling alternative versions that are dominant elsewhere.

Polish nationalism and the destabilization of memory: "down with the pedagogy of shame"

The most fierce and bitter battle of memory concerns two major museums in Poland. The Polish government has intervened in this conflict to support the way that they want the Polish population to remember their past (Garbowski, 2015). In Gdansk, the construction of a museum was a new initiative. The aim of its exhibition was to acknowledge that different and opposing visions of the past should be acknowledged and taken seriously. The goal was to create a place that would let people listen to stories both from the West and from the East.

Attacks on the museum started in 2007 in reaction to an article published in a Polish newspaper which argued that the narratives told in the museum in Gdansk about World War II did not give due credit to the Polish nation. The article contended that the West should learn from what happened in Poland, and visitors should become cognizant of how much the Polish nation had suffered. It was asserted that, in the West, it was largely unknown how brutal the German occupation, the Soviet aggression against Poland, the annexation of the Baltics, and the Polish Ukrainian conflict had been. Supposedly, there was no knowledge of the number of Poles who were Soviet causalities.

During the ensuing debate the voices of a competing victim became louder, which added to the confusion in the debate and worsened the mnemonic chaos. The Center Against Expulsions, which is affiliated with the powerful German Federation of Expellees (Bund der Heimatvertriebenen) that represents the interests of 12 million Germans affected by the outcome of the war and the ensuing massive deportations and killing of Germans, attempted to focus attention on the ways in which Germans had also suffered during the war and how they were expelled from Poland. Their narratives were unacceptable to the Polish government and to most of the public opinion. The idea that Germans could be victims existed beyond even the realm of Polish imagination; Germans could only be perpetrators, so it was argued. The argument advanced by Polish government forces destabilized the notion of victimhood advanced by the German Federation of Expellees and hindered their effort to remind the existing Polish memorial culture that other people had also suffered, even the perpetrators. The reaction was an official nationalistic counterview which imposed a lens through which everyone had to agree that it was the Polish population who suffered the most while suffering under and resisting both Nazism and communism.

Russia versus Poland about Katyń, Hungary 1956 and Czechia 1968: the struggle for freedom

The year 1989, when the Soviets withdrew and the Berlin Wall fell, is of course a monumental year in the history of the former Soviet-dominated countries. In several places, however, other dates are relatively more crucial. In fact, the demise of communism is remembered in a variety of ways (James et al, 2015). Some memories are more persistent than others. Many oppose the dominant historical view that has been imposed. In fact, any debate on the past of Poland is dominated by the Katyń massacre and the negative view of Russia as the heirs to those who systematically hid an evident truth. Polish public opinion correctly demands the right to accuse the Russians of being the perpetrators of the massacre.

The Katyń massacre was a mass murder of nearly 20,000 officers of the Polish army carried out by the NKVD (the "People's Commissariat for Internal Affairs," that is, the Soviet secret police) in April and May 1940. Of the total killed, about 8,000 were officers imprisoned during the 1939 invasion; another 6,000 were police officers; and the remaining 8,000 were what the Soviets described as "landowners, saboteurs, factory owners, lawyers, officials, and priests." The Soviets denied that it was they who had done the killing, and instead accused the Germans. Ever since, the two nations have contentiously disagreed about blame for Katyń. There are also many more instances of betrayal and murder of Poles by Russians which the Russians try to obscure. For example, in 1944, the Russians stood on the bank of the river Vistula on the outskirts of Warsaw and did not intervene while the Nazis murdered the Polish resistance directed by the "Home Army" (A.K.). This happened close by and they could have intervened. But Katyń is more central to any debate and justifies Polish nationalism. This has become a permanent reason for tension between the two states and their public opinions. There have been no serious developments of the argument and both parties have stood firm.

Poles were definitely victims of communism as well as Nazism. However, this should not obscure the fact that many Poles killed Jews, and did not need Germans to do so. In addition, it is also the case that many Polish communists were Jewish and condoned the anti-semitism of the Soviets. I will return to these "truths" and the ensuing resentment when I write about the memory of Sobibor.

Today, Polish historical writing is expected to be in opposition to the Soviet version of the Katyń massacre (Etkind at al., 2012); whereas, in Russia, the "Katyń lie," according to which the killing was caused by the atrocity of the Germans, is still widely accepted (Chrobacynski and Trojanski, 2016). Although Russians have acknowledged Soviet responsibility in the past, the Russian authorities, acting on an order from the local prosecutor's office, recently removed plaques commemorating victims of the Terror and the Polish officers executed by the NKVD in 1940, while the Soviet Union was still collaborating with Nazi Germany. This removal may have been a regional initiative, but it is very much in line with Russia's aggressive attempts under President Vladimir Putin to obfuscate or rewrite the darkest pages of Soviet history.

As the fall of communism in 1989 does not universally constitute a major turning point in all national and local histories, other moments have a more prominent place in the public arena and are considered more important and more particular to certain nations. In Hungary, for instance, a major turning point occurred in 1956, in which a massive uprising was brutally suppressed by the Soviet army; and in the Czech Republic such a moment is 1968, when the ruling communist party failed to reform society and the country was invaded by the Soviet army. Indeed, for Hungary and the Czech Republic, and for many other countries, the most defining moments of memory are national and, while recognizing the importance of the fall of communism, those of 1989 are less commonly invoked.

One or diverging visions of history? Trouble in and with the museum

The proposed director of the new Gdansk museum, Pawel Machcewicz, opted to conserve the memory of World War II from all perspectives. When he was appointed, he wanted to show that perspectives of the past can be different and contradictory. He wanted to confront western visions of history with Polish visions and with the old communist history. However, he was immediately accused of promoting a European identity distinct from a Polish identity and hostile to the country. The original idea of the creation of a Gdansk museum had been supported by Donald Tusk, who became president of Poland in 2007 and later served as president of the European

Union from 2014–19. Tusk was aware that the collective memory in the West was markedly different from the post-communist memory in the East. He also knew that the integration of these memories, which he deemed necessary, could only occur if collective knowledge existed. The right-nationalist wing, however, managed to win the debate with its rhetoric, and Tusk left for European politics.

Ultimately the Gdansk museum, which had cherished all kinds of modern and beautiful ideas about how to present and understand history, was monopolized by nationalist policies (Muller, 2010, 2017), and none of the enlightened ways of explaining history could be implemented. In his book, the former director, Pawel Machcewicz (2017), provided a detailed account of the direct involvement of the government in its effort to control history and to transform the interpretation of the war into a nationalist narrative. For him and his staff, it was crucial to present a complicated and textured vision of Polish history that was not one-sided. In this way, they hoped to reinforce pro-democratic feelings in the country and beyond. I will return to this narrative in the final part of this chapter, when I describe what occurred regarding the museum of Sobibor.

Earlier debates: history and national pride

Disagreement about the past is not new in Poland. A fierce debate ignited following the publication in 2012 of *Neighbors: The Destruction of the Jewish Community in Jedwabne, Poland*, written by Jan T. Gross, who described how on "One day, in July 1941, half of the population of a small east European town murdered the other half--some 1,600 men, women and children." This massacre took place in Jedwabne, in north-eastern Poland. Up until the publication of this book, historians had blamed the massacre on the Nazis. Gross, however, claimed that the Nazis' participation in, and responsibility for, these crimes had been exaggerated. In fact, he argued, a virulent Polish anti-Semitism was unleashed by the German occupation. As a consequence of his writing, he received many serious death threats. He was also forbidden to talk any longer about "Polish" camps because, it was asserted, all the camps were German. In fact, it is still illegal for historians to call the camps in Poland "Polish," since of course they were German, and it is also forbidden to discuss the ways in which the Polish Home Army (the *Armia Krajowa*, or A.K.) represented a mortal danger for those Jews who escaped the concentration camps in Polish territory (Zimmerman, 2020). The A.K. certainly resisted the Germans, and were victims of persecution by the Nazis; but these victims also created their own victims: the Jews.

Another example of the suppression of historical memory in Poland is the dispute about the nomination of a new head of the Jewish museum, during which the government refused to accept Darius Stola. The ruling Law and

Justice party (PiS) wanted to frame the exhibition to portray the country's victimhood and heroism. The aim of the PiS was to persuade Western audiences that Poles overwhelmingly assisted Jews during the Holocaust. The reality, however, was that while many Jews were saved, many were also denounced or killed by Poles. Stola had been responsible for an exhibition to remember a 1968 anti-Jewish campaign orchestrated by the then-communist government. According to the PiS, the exhibition presented a distorted image of the Poles, since it also showed the anti-Semitic attitude of the ruling communist party and of many other Poles (Gross, 2007). This was bad for the image of Poland. Stola had been chosen by a selection committee for a second term as director, but the Minister of Culture refused to confirm him and sign the appointment. The organizer of the 1968 exhibition could not hold such an important position.

"Down with the pedagogy of shame" was one of the buzz phrases of the campaign against Stola's policies, which stood for diversity and openness. Stola's detractors wanted to show only proud heroes. They demanded that Poles must stop apologizing for their alleged sins, foremost among them their cooperation with the Nazis in exterminating European Jewry. The government pressured Stola to resign. Stola refused, but his contract was set to expire at the end of February 2019, and the government did not want him reappointed. As a compromise, a search for a new director began. The committee chose Stola again, and the country's Minister of Culture, Piotr Gliński, was formally required to reappoint Stola. He did not, however, and the world-renowned museum was left without a director. In 2020, to end this Warsaw-Jewish museum impasse, Stola agreed to step down from his post.

Stola described his decision as being motivated by a pragmatic concern for the museum's future. At the same time, he accused Minister Gliński of "justifying his refusal with false pretexts." To rationalize his position, Gliński had accused Stola of "pursuing very aggressive politics" which "damaged the institution." He also claimed that the director refused to agree to the organization of a conference dedicated to Lech Kaczyński, the deceased Polish president and twin brother of the ruling party leader Jarosław Kaczyński.

In 2021, another major scandal occurred which again revealed the precariousness of historical discourse in a country where there is no agreement about the past. Two well-known historians, Jan Grabowoski and Barbara Engelkin, were forced to write public apologies to an elderly woman, Filomena Lesczyńska, for the alleged dissemination of "inexact" information about the attitude of her uncle during the German occupation of Poland. He had been the mayor of a small village not far from Bialystok, and was accused of being responsible for the killing of Jews hiding in a forest. She was supported by a foundation with close connections to the government whose mission is to defend the image and reputation of Poland (Kula and

Lyon-Caen, 2021).[5] Their nationalist pride aims at new kind of historical narrative in which politics has replaced the search for a multivocal history, and where lies have supplanted the truth. In fact, forced public apologies have been relatively common in the region for decades, since they were part of the communist policies.

The Baltic answer to Soviet oppression: nationalism ignoring the fate of the Russian population

The three Baltic states, Estonia, Latvia, and Lithuania, lost their independence at the beginning of World War II. They became part of the Soviet Union until the Nazi invasion of 1941. During the Nazi occupation, many inhabitants considered the territory to have been liberated from the communist yoke, which ended when the Red Army reconquered the three Baltic states. After the war they again became part of the Soviet Union until 1991, when they became independent. There were, in fact, numerous reasons to think that independence would bring liberation after years of communist oppression. After independence, and even earlier, in the 1980s, there was a surge in projects of life stories in Estonia (Köresaar and Jõesalu, 2016). Memories would reveal "another" and different history, and interviewing started on a mass scale. From the beginning, there was an emphasis on the collection of existing stories which would add to the history of the nation.

Starting in 2000, the major Estonian Museum of Occupation published a questionnaire that focused on suffering and resistance during the Soviet period. These themes, of course, did not cover all of daily life. More importantly, positive feelings about the Soviet times were not noted, and perhaps not tolerated. Furthermore, Russians were not involved in several studies despite the fact that, as of 2011, 38.5 per cent of Tallinn's population were ethnic Russians and 46.7 per cent in other places (in Latvia 25 per cent, in Lithuania 5.8 per cent). The history of the Russians living in Estonian territory was omitted because of "differences between the mnemonic practices of the different ethnic groups," as it was worded (Köresaar and Jõesalu, 2016: p 53). The result is an absence of positive stories about the history of Estonian Russians, and this has sometimes produced tense situations. The main narrative of the Museum of Occupation is that the Estonian nation is a victim of World War II (Wulf, 2008; Kopecek, 2013). Estonians are portrayed as helpless victims of Soviet violence or as soldiers "forced" by the 1940–41 Soviet occupation to collaborate with the Germans in order to defend their homeland (Kaljund, 2020). Absent from this history are more than a dozen Nazi concentration camps that were located in Estonia and guarded by Estonians. This active collaboration should have been included.

The dominant Latvian story similarly stresses the victimhood of the nation and a denial of Latvian complicity in the crimes perpetrated against Jews. Latvian policemen assisted with the deportations and killing of Jews, and 90 per cent of the Jews living in Latvia were murdered. In this case as well, for a long period of time only the Soviet narrative was sanctioned, according to which Soviet citizens were killed by Nazi barbarians. Against this new narrative of Latvian victims and heroes, some modern Latvian historians have argued that many Jews were part of the Soviet administration and had welcomed the Red Army in 1940. The killing of Jews during the Holocaust/Shoah is not denied, but rather justified and overshadowed by the accusation of collaboration with the Soviets (Zisere, 2013).

Likewise, the nationalist turn in Lithuania, the third Baltic state, is very clear.[6] Moreover, in Lithuanian historical discourse there is hardly any interest in Jewish life prior to the Holocaust/Shoah. People seem to have forgotten that Vilnius, the capital, was a major center of Jewish thought. Jewish culture and thinking, preserved, and shared by magnificent libraries and places of study, have disappeared, and consequently have been forgotten. Also, hardly any research is conducted about the issue of why so many Lithuanians followed the Germans, and why following the Germans did not solely constitute resistance against communism but ended with the persecution of Jews. On the contrary, those Jews who resisted Lithuanian collaborators and killed them are accused of murder.

The politics of collaboration and pride: Hungary

A special case and example of this mnemonic lens that accentuates communist oppression is "The House of Terror" in Budapest, Hungary, commemorating persecutions under communism.[7] It is the institute *par excellence* that uses the template of the Holocaust/Shoah to frame the story of victims of communism (Zombory, 2020). Indeed, the exposition resembles a display of Holocaust memories. A closer examination, however, reveals that it constitutes sophisticated propaganda for a confused nationalist reckoning with a troubled communist past. In Hungary, the right-wing populist party, Fidesz, has become stronger since the elections of 2010. Its foundation is the popular anti-communist and anti-Russian feelings in the country. The Nazis and the Russians have both occupied Hungary. Its consequences and the resultant ensuing oppression have long been discussed as if they were not linked and did not experience mutual interaction (Petö, 2017).

Hungarians have a difficult past: the alliance between Hungary and the Axis Powers in 1940 kept the majority of the Jews of Hungary "safe" until 1944, while in 1941 "foreign nationals" were sent to the Ukraine, where they were killed. More killing of Jews and more expulsions followed in the years to come. When the Germans entered the country in 1944, they did not encounter much resistance. In fact, they were even invited in by the country's leader, Miklós Horthy, who had previously fostered anti-Semitism. The Nazis wanted 100,000 Jews for "work," which was an exchange agreement made by the Nazis with Horthy so that he could remain in power. In fact, Horthy decided to send the workers' families as well, and delivered 437,000 Jews to the Nazis. In six weeks, half a million Jews were killed. The Hungarian government, the Gendarmes, and local authorities organized the transport to the camps.

Later that year, the Germans took over the government and deposed Horthy. From that moment, the fascist Arrow Cross Party ruled, and committed atrocious crimes, including the random killing of Roma and Jews. It should not be forgotten, however, that thousands of Jews were killed before the Germans entered the country. According to present Hungarian historiography, the Germans and the Russians were both guilty of murdering Jews, assisted by the Arrow Cross Party which did "not represent the Hungarian nation." In this way, the Holocaust/Shoah was reframed to advance a nationalist claim that the Hungarian nation actively opposed the Nazis. The argument that was advanced is that Nazism and communism were foreign totalitarian forces, and hostile to a Hungarian political tradition. This nationalist pride led to the mythology of a "double occupation" which made all Hungarians victims of the two totalitarian regimes, while Hungarian responsibility for the deaths of thousands of foreign and non-foreign Jews was obscured. Furthermore, the more power Fidesz obtained, the more the memorial culture was reshaped and history was transformed into political propaganda. Fidesz laid hold of the press and television and could take advantage of the existing deeply-rooted prejudices against Jews. Sociological research shows that between 2003 and 2009, 9–14 per cent of Hungarians felt emotionally uneasy about Jews. This percentage would increase to over 20 per cent in the years 2010 and 2011 (Kovács, 2019). The American Jew, George Soros, has become a national symbol of the anti-semitic attack mounted by the right. Anti-Jewish symbols and language are ubiquitous in Hungary, and they are supported by nationalist historical narratives.

A museum in Sobibor

As I have previously carried out research on Sobibor, the awful destruction camp in Eastern Poland, I wanted to know if and how much the Polish nationalist debate would influence the message of the museum that is under construction. Sobibor was part of Operation Reinhard, the name given to the construction of three camps (Belzec, Sobibor, and Treblinka) built with the murder of Jews as their only purpose. I was curious about this case because my grandparents were murdered there. I wondered why for a long time the uprising of 1943 was not part of any collective memory. I think this has changed; there are now movies and there is literature. I myself wait for the moment when I can add a stone with the names of my grandparents to the "Lane of Memory." I have also been incredulous and incensed that the Polish members of the steering committee have at that time been able to remove Russian members from their ranks. This is an egregious injustice: so many Russians were killed there, and the Sobibor uprising (1943) was orchestrated by Russians. Now, while writing this chapter in 2022 during the war in Ukraine, I realize that Russian participation would have been dangerous since this kind of participation is part of the official policy and would have been part of a recognition of criminal politics. Reacting to their removal from the museum committee, Russians have promoted a filmed celebration of the heroism of this uprising with a heavy accent on the fate of the Russian soldiers.[8] The government also intervened in this memorial culture, and in 2018 a railroad line between Moscow and Rostov on Don, named after Alexander Pechersky,[9] the leader of the uprising, was initiated "to mark the 75th anniversary of the heroic rebellion at the Sobibor death camp."[10] Political diplomacy between Russia and Israel dominates the Russian effort to pose a counter history.

Many of those involved in the institution of the Sobibor museum admit that what is occurring has very little to do with the writing of history, but concerns only the interpretation of history. Representatives of the Netherlands, who have been active participants on the board, have insisted that Sobibor should particularly include a place to remember individuals, as is done in Auschwitz, where in Birkenau there is a place for the mourning of individuals who lost their lives. Therefore, the names of people who suffered and were killed in Sobibor should also be memorialized, honored, and remembered. In Belzec as in Treblinka, only first names are provided, constituting a form of anonymity. In Belzec, there were fewer survivors and names are not known, whereas about Sobibor, where there were more survivors, we know many names. The Dutch administration has kept up in a remarkable way and noted who was deported in trains to the east. The Netherlands is active in the museum project, since one-third of Dutch Jewry were murdered in Sobibor. I was told that Poles do not want a memory culture that consists of individual names, but desire a more collective memorialization. In fact, they want a collective story about the three camps. Although it is rarely acknowledged, collective remembering facilitates the creation of collective narratives that can be manipulated. On the other hand, "we descendants" only want the names of our family members who were killed to be publicly memorialized. Much important archaeological research is done on the site, but no such work has offered an answer to the question of how we should most truthfully remember.[11]

Can we remember together?

Earlier I raised the problem of the integration of diverse and seemingly contradictory memories. The objective of integration has failed, and is bound to fail increasingly in the future as long as nationalism continues to dominate the narratives of the past. The fight against nationalist abuse of history can seem hopeless. Many new narratives of history will continue to arise which are not based on serious historical research but crafted to support national pride and honor. Unfortunately, this is a clear tendency. It brings with it lies, exclusions, compulsion, and violence. In contrast, some people exhibit magnificent power and resilience towards the expression and protection of a more sincere history.

In order to enable an honest exchange, we in the West need to develop more knowledge about, and sensitivity to, the mass killings that occurred under communism. Often, however, people who want to study violence under communism are accused of denying "The uniqueness of the Shoah." However, this framework of contention is problematic. Fully acknowledging the sorrow of the other, and understanding it, is altogether different from denial.

One could argue that one should not only look at changes in knowledge, but instead at how such changes are governed. What is designated as the truth does not exist in a vacuum outside of the influence of power, but is a part of politics, and each society develops its own discourse for distinguishing between true and false statements. Indeed, actors create and develop discourses that compete with each other in creating their versions of the truth. This "truth" should be more pluriform and democratic. There should be an open debate, where many and even contradictory voices are audible. We need to cultivate a complex and a multifaceted view that allows memory projects to be rooted in compassion, tolerance for contradiction, and inclusivity. Any hierarchy of suffering should be abandoned.

The contradictions in these new histories should become an integral part of a public discourse, and no image of the past should be appropriated as a new standard canon or by politics. The issue of the conflict about European memory shows that victims can also have been perpetrators. We can see that to be the case only if we dare to widen our interpretation. Our task as historians is to contest the abuse of images of the historical past and to enforce pluralism, while acknowledging the tension between our personal, local, national, and other interests. Such a change is possible.

Notes

[1] There is an endless debate about whether to use the word Holocaust or the word Shoah. See Michman (2021).

2   A good example is Bartov (2018) which describes in a micro-history the changing position of one particular town and the shifting frontiers.
3   Interview at USHMM made by author in Ryazan (March 21 and March 22, 2010). There is not yet a number.
4   Alexsy Wajcen (March 21, and March 22, 2010) in Ryazan, Interview in USHMM, Washington, DC.
5   I give here this French article which refers to a lot of Polish material.
6   See also Lapierre (1993) and Lemée (2018).
7   Pető, A. (2019) "The Lost and Found Library," *Memory at Stake* 9: 72–82.
8   See the movie by Konstatin Khabensky, in which the Russian government has invested money and propaganda. The documentary, which presents graphic images of what happened there, was made under the auspices of the Ministry of Propaganda, which worked together with the Israeli Ministry of Propaganda.
9   Between the capital Moscow and Rostov on Don where Pechersky lived.
10 Quoted from source that is currently blocked out due to the Russian war in Ukraine.
11 I am grateful to Doede Sijtsma, working on Polish German reconciliation, and Krzysztof Weyher of the Dutch embassy in Warsaw. In talking with them, I realized that the contrast between individual memorialization and collective memory is a way to circumscribe opposing objectives. I am curious to see the end result. The museum of Sobibor is a satellite of the museum of Majdanek, where the director is appointed by the state.

Acknowledgments

I am grateful to Andrea Pető from Hungary, Andras Kovaćs from Hungary, Anna Muller from the University of Michigan (a former inhabitant of Gdańsk), and Muriel Blaive from Prague.

References

Anderson, B. (1983) *Imagined Communities, Reflections on the Origin and Spread of Nationalism*, London: Verso.
Barov, O. (2018) *Anatomy of a Genocide: The Life and Death of a Town Called Buczacz*, New York: Simon and Schuster.
Chaumont, J.M. (2010) *La concurrence des victimes*, Paris: La Decouverte.
Chrobaczynski, J., and Trojanski, P. (2016) "Auschwitz and Katyn in Political Bondage: The Process of Shaping Memory in Communist Poland," in M. Pakier and J. Wawrzyniak (eds) *Memory and Change in Europe, Eastern Perspectives*, New York: Berghahn, pp 246–264.
Ebenshade, R. (1995) "Remember to Forget: Memory, History, National Identity in Postwar East-Central Europe," *Representations* 49: 72–96.
Etkind, A., Finnin R., Blacker, U., Fedor, J., Lewis, S., Mälksoo, M., and Mroz, M. (2012) *Remembering Katyn*, Cambridge: Polity.
FIDH (2021) "Crimes against History."
Garbowski, G. (2015) "Historical Memory and Debate in Poland and Central Europe: A Review Essay," *The Polish Review* 60(1): 97–110.
Gross, J.T. (2007) *Fear: Anti-semitism in Poland after Auschwitz*, New York: Random House.

Gross, J.T. (2011) *Neighbors: The Destruction of the Jewish Community in Jedwabne, Poland*, Princeton, NJ: Princeton University Press.

Halbwachs, M. (1925) *Les cadres sociaux de la mémoire*, Paris: Les Presses Universitaires de France.

James, M, Blaive, M., Hudek M., Saunders, A., and Tsyszka, S. (2015) "1989 After 1989: Remembering the End of State Socialism in East-Central Europe," in M. Kopecek and P. Wciślik (eds) *Thinking through Transition: Liberal Democracy, Authoritarian Pasts, and Intellectual History in East Central Europe After 1989*, Budapest: Central European University Press, pp 463–504.

Judt, T. (2005) *Postwar: A History of Europe since 1945*, New York: Penguin.

Kaljund, L. (2020) "Between Occupation and Freedoms: Memory, Narrative and Practice at Vabamu in Tallinn, Estonia," in Stephen M. Norrris (ed) *Museums of Communism: New Memory Sites in Central and Eastern Europe*, Bloomington, IL: Indiana University Press, pp 401–425.

Konrád, G. (1982) *The Loser*, New York: HBJ.

Kopeček, M. (2013) *Past in the Making: Historical Revisionism in Central Europe after 1989*, Budapest: Central European University Press.

Köresaar, E., and Jõesalu, K. (2016) "Post-Soviet Memories and 'Memory Shifts' in Estonia," *Oral History* 22: 47–58.

Kovács, A. (2019) "Postkommunistischer Antisemitismus: Alt und neu. Der Fall Ungarn," in Ch. Heilbronn, D. Rabinovici, and N. Sznaider (eds) *Neuer Antisemitismus? Fortsetzung einer globalen Debatte*, Frankfurt: Suhrkamp Verlag, pp 276–309.

Kula., A. and Lyon-Caen, J. (2021) "Le juge, la nièce et les historiens," *La Vie des Idées*, June 2021: 1–9.

Lapierre, N. (1993) *Le Silence de la Mémoire. A la recherche des Juifs de Plock*, Paris: Plon.

Lemée, C. (2018) "History-memory of Litvak Yiddish spaces after the Holocaust. Between worlds of life and worlds of assassination," *Ethnologie française* 18: 225–242.

Leydesdorff, S. (2017) *Sasha Pechersky, Holocaust Hero, Sobibor Resistance Leader, and Hostage of History*, New York: Routledge.

Machcewicz, P. (2017) *Der umkämpfte Krieg. Dat Museum des Zweiten Weltkriegs in Danzig, Entstehumng und Streit*, Krakow: Znak Horyzont.

Marrus, M. and Paxton, R. (1981) *Vichy France and the Jews*, Stanford, CA: Stanford University Press.

Michman, D. (2021) "Why Is the Shoah Called 'the Shoah' or 'the Holocaust'? On the History of the Terminology for the Nazi Anti-Jewish Campaign," *The Journal of Holocaust Research* 35(4): 233–256.

Muller, A. (2010) "Objects Have the Power to Tell History," *Krytyka Poliyczna and European Alternatives* 4: November 4.

Muller, A. (2017) "War, Dialogue and Overcoming the Past," *The Public Historian* 39(3): 85–95.

Ochman, E. (2013) *Post-Communist Poland: Contested Pasts and Future Identities*, London: Routledge.

Onken E.C. (2007) "The Politics of Finding Historical Truth: Reviewing Baltic History Commissions and Their Work," *Journal of Baltic Studies* 38(1): 109–116.

Petö, A. (2017) "Revisionist Histories, 'Future memories': Far-Right Memorialization Practices in Hungary," *European Politics and Society* 18(1): 41–51.

Snyder, T. (2010) *Bloodlands: Europe between Hitler and Stalin*, New York: Basic Books.

Wulf, M. (2008) "The Struggle for Official Recognition of 'Displaced' Group Memories in Post-Soviet Estonia," in M. Kopeček (ed) *Past in the Making: Historical Revisionism in Central Europe after 1989*, Budapest: Central European University, pp 221–238.

Zimmerman J.D. (2020) "The Polish Underground Home Army (A.K.) and the Jews: What Postwar Jewish Testimonies and Wartime Documents Reveal," *East European Politics and Societies* 34(1): 194–220.

Zisere, B. (2013) "The Transformation of Holocaust memory in Post-Soviet Latvia," in J.P. Himka and J.B. Michlic (eds) *Bringing the Dark Past to the Light, The reception of the Holocaust in Postcommunist Europe*, Lincoln, NB: University of Nebraska Press, pp 300–319.

Zombory, M. (2017) "The Birth of the Memory of Communism: Memorial Museums in Europe," *Nationalities Papers* 45(6): 1028–1946.

Zombory M. (2020) "Visualizing Revisionism: Europeanized Anticommunism at the House of Terror Museum in Budapest," in S.M. Norris (ed) *Museums of Communism, New Memory Sites in Central and Eastern Europe*, Bloomington, IN: Indiana University Press, pp 46–78.

12

How Difficult Pasts Complicate the Present: Comparative Analysis of the Genocides in Western Armenia and Rwanda

Jacob Caponi and Fatma Müge Göçek

Introduction

The 20th century was marked by collective violence throughout the world. Two cases cumulating within "the Age of Genocide," the 1915 Armenian Genocide and the 1994 Genocide Against the Tutsi, are rarely analyzed together, even though such a comparative analysis reveals patterns in the social architecture of collective violence.[1] In this chapter, we focus on identifying such repertoires of violence and power that emerge through systemic critical comparison by juxtaposing the two genocides on three empirical parameters of genocide memory production, specifically in terms of the (i) *concept* (of genocide); (ii) *agency* (of social actors involved in genocide); and (iii) *narration* (of the larger context of genocide, especially in the post-genocidal phase). This critical comparison captures the process of violence unfolding from the origins through to today by assessing the relevance of time and space across the three parameters. Such critical comparison reveals two significant insights regarding the post-genocidal phase. First, the temporal and spatial boundaries of genocide expand beyond the initial collective physical destruction in the short-term to a long-term process of boundary making around trust, accountability, memory-making, and forgetting. Second, contentiousness located in the post-genocide phase actually originates throughout the process of genocide, only to develop into a contentious narrative thereafter.

In summary then, through our interpretive lens, we argue genocidal processes are contentious because of the inherent difficulties in the initial formulation, execution, and narration of genocide. In doing so, we hopefully provide some insight in response to Hinton's (2012) question: "Why, we need to ask, are certain cases forgotten, remembered, recognized, or even intentionally hidden or written out of history?" To address the contentious memories of genocide, we develop an expanded historical lens to show how multiple factors influence the definition of genocidal acts and processes as they unfold through time.

In what follows, we lay out how our interpretive lens shifts the analysis of genocide as a singular act to a relational process pertaining to the concept of genocide, the agency of social actors, and the temporal and spatial historical context. In the second half of the chapter, we apply our cases to illustrate how contentious memory is integral throughout the process of genocide. By *concept*, we refer to the meanings that define genocide, such as its extremeness, illegality, collective nature, and the degree of violence, and we explore how contention exists from the start through ambiguities that emerge in public discourse, especially due to issues of secrecy and accountability. Contentious memory does not evolve only in the aftermath of genocide, but contention is entangled throughout the process of conceptualizing genocide. *Agency* is concerned with social actors who attempt to maximize their power as they set the boundaries of violence within parameters that are determined temporally and spatially at two levels: the *experiential level* that specifically focuses on the standpoints of social actors on the ground, and the *educational level* that specifically focuses on of the standpoints of "knowledge entrepreneurs" who "shape and spread their group's definition of social reality to wider audiences" and "seek to manipulate, intensify, mobilize, or alter knowledge repertoires of carrier groups with which they are associated" (Savelsberg, 2021: p 3). Focusing on the third parameter, *narration*, we consider how actors give meaning to collective violence by embedding it in a macro-historical timeline. Specifically, the public narration of genocide develops with attention to four often temporally linear, historical macro-episodes, each of which is a matter of contention in its own right. These include: (i) colonization, (ii) nation-state formation, (iii) internal polarization, and (iv) post-genocidal (re)narration. As powerful social actors define these historical episodes, they work to abrogate claims about their accountability for acts of physical violence. Such abrogation emerges through *the perversion of social reality* on the one side and *subversion of social justice* on the other.[2]

In the process, some social actors not only project their destructive intent onto others, but they then move on further to fully obfuscate their own acts of collective violence. Their controversial public stand in turn naturalizes and normalizes the collective violence of regimes in power, thereby reproducing power over time.[3]

Re-embedding collective violence into modernity

After the French Revolution, scholars relied on modern assumptions about the universality of human experience and history to explain the social world. The nation-state, progressing in linear temporality within a confined, sovereign space, evolved as the political unit of analysis. From the vantage point of Western hegemony, assumptions about the universality of the nation appear rational because they hold historical development as invariable across time and space (Steinmetz, 2007). From within this framework of history, the Holocaust is presented as the most horrific event of the 20th century, representing a "moral universalism" in relation to other genocides which then turn into "particularities" (Alexander, 2012). Yet, a global historical sociological analysis reveals collective violence is not a rare break in humanity, but instead the underbelly of modernity itself. Collective violence, and thus attempts to make the collective memory of such episodes, are thus relevant in different spaces and times, at both national and transnational levels (Simko, 2020). In order to better understand how processes of power and control in our contemporary context shape efforts to make, define, and remember acts of collective violence, scholars must engage in a critical "re-embedding" of imperialism and colonialism into social theories (Go, 2020; Hammer, 2020).[4]

This critical correction to social theory suggests that the two sociological practices of binary thinking (such as perpetrator/victim, good/evil; true/false, and so on) and universalization (that is, accepting the invariability of time, space, and interaction) are inadequate in explaining collective violence and memory. In other words, the behaviors of social actors on the ground in various contexts are dynamic throughout different episodes of collective violence, as opposed to categorically fixed throughout time and space (Luft, 2015; Rothberg, 2019). Furthermore, participation in collective violence unveils modernity's paradox of abstraction as the rational human must forget rational thinking and view the other person as an "abstract thing/object" which is no longer human (Bauman, 2007). In this way, contemporary civil discourse relies on abstraction for nation building (that is, silencing historical events in national narratives) and to explain irrational behavior which is a threat to the nation-state (such as "terrorism") (Zubrzycki and Woźny, 2020). However, by re-embedding analyses of historical collective violence into our social theories, we are able to empirically articulate abstract concepts as repertoires of power and control that explain the nature of social interaction in particular societies.

This discussion of the European project of modernity emphasizes the inadequacy of initial theories based on universalism where their silenced empirical foundation is solely limited to the Western European experience. In order to overcome this limitation, we introduce the critical study of the experience of the extreme collective violence across time and space. We specifically reconceptualize the three factors of *concept*, *agency*, and *narration* with the critical insight that these do not stay universally static across time and space but transform in particular patterns that emerge when one investigates these three factors.

Concept (genocide)

The very concept of genocide – how we understand it as an event or episode in the world – is often contentious. To narrow down genocide to a bounded event, or as a solely collective behavior, overlooks the significance of emotions and therefore patterns of meaning formation within society at large. The centering of rationality produced "valuable, but sometimes limited kinds of theories" which sideline conflict and contentious events resulting in deaths and mourning (Otele, Gandolfo, and Galai, 2021: p 5). Instead, an understanding of genocide as an ongoing process of extreme collective violence must include discussions of ongoing behavior, evolving and contentious memory, and trauma alongside one another. The reframing of genocide as "a process" thereby empirically (and critically) contextualizes the concept across time and space.[5]

The intellectual conception of genocide traces back to Raphael Lemkin's legal intervention in the aftermath of the Holocaust. Based on the catastrophe of violence against the Jews, Lemkin not only came up with the publicly accepted definition of genocide, but the United Nations' Convention on the Prevention and Punishment of the Crime of Genocide ([1948]1951) legitimized the concept in praxis as well (Lemkin, 1944; Hinton, 2012). Focusing on the formation of the phenomenon of genocide in relation to the Armenian and Rwandan cases reveals the limitations of the formal and universal legal definition of genocide and calls our attention to the significance of the intersection of time and power. That is, the relationship between when the collective violence takes place and who can be held accountable for genocide via international law may limit our understanding of how such acts of collective violence unfold over historical time and project into the future.

Lemkin (1953) describes genocide as "a rare crime of great magnitude," but this assumption of rarity relies on Western notions of acceptable violence. After the Civil Rights Congress charged the United States with genocide at the 1951 United Nations meeting, Lemkin decried the statement saying, "by no stretch of imagination can one discover in the United States an intent or plan to exterminate the Negro population" which illustrates Lemkin's outright denial that violence against Black people, including colonialism, could be defined as genocide (Lemkin, 1953; see also Samudzi, 2020). The top-down application of genocide by the international community thus allows state officials to encode and control repertoires of ongoing targeted violence as somehow less than genocidal while bottom-up approaches to naming genocide are squashed by "official" standards. To address this contention, we argue for a relational approach to genocide where social boundaries and violence are the focus of analysis rather than exceptional cases of genocide as "static entities" (Sweet, 2020).

A relational approach to the sociology of genocide not only analyses public, legal boundaries of the concept, but also hones in on collective violence that social actors silence in the public sphere. According to this perspective, the meanings of legal definitions are sociologically constructed via the interactions of individuals, institutions, and ideology while other definitions are denied. The various boundaries around naming collective violence as genocide should not be of surprise as time progresses; yet even in cases where the word genocide is applied, the international community falls short in ensuring accountability.

Agency (social actors)

Bringing in the agency of social actors highlights the recent methodological shift from top-down formal structural and political processes of action to bottom-up informal interpretive processes of voice. Different social actors are continuously added to an expanded analytic framework seeking to better analyze and disentangle the contentious memory-making process such as memoir writers (Göçek, 2015), survivors of gender-based violence (Fox, 2021), and co-witnesses (Kacandes, 2022). These additions expand the analytic boundaries of extreme collective violence by bringing in new social actors and critically studying the manner in which they shape the definitions of contentious historical episodes. The concepts of the "co-witness" and "knowledge entrepreneurs" call our attention to the fact that social actors who are not physically involved in actions of genocide can nevertheless be involved in critically analyzing and defining the process of violence. This analytic framework expands our understanding of agency to include various social actors, specifically academics, who analyze the process (Brown and Malone, 2004; Hammer, 2020; Savelsberg, 2021; Kacandes, 2022).

Another aspect of Enlightenment thinking, in addition to false universality, that becomes relevant in this context is the false objectivity of the knowledge entrepreneur, a construction undermined by critical theorist Jürgen Habermas's analysis of knowledge and human interests. Habermas (1971) demonstrates how social sciences become weaponized by politics as some scholars accept, normalize, and naturalize their standpoint to the exclusion of local actors. As Brown and Malone (2004: p 110) argue, for instance:

> Scientists speak in two different linguistic registers. One is a personal narrative that speaks of emerging knowledge claims, using strategies

that are rhetorical and political. The other is the public and technical language of scientific objects, another rhetoric that presents itself as antirhetorical and apolitical, a language that represents scientific discoveries in objective and rational terms ... [they not only participate in] the politics of personal persuasion ... [but also] engage in a politics of impersonal persuasion, presenting scientific research as purely rational and logical.

Hence it is imperative for knowledge entrepreneurs to engage in critical self-reflexivity in order to capture that which is overlooked due to alleged objectivity.

Narration (context)

Narration in turn refers to the ways that some social actors interpret and reinterpret extreme collective violence, packaging it into story form with context, plot, and moral. With regard to the Armenian Genocide and the 1994 Genocide Against the Tutsi, which bookend the 20th century, four historical episodes where power and knowledge intersect in distinct ways to interpret violence are vital to the narratives actors create about genocide: *imperial colonization, nation-state formation, internal polarization culminating in genocide*, and *post-genocidal (re)narration*.[6] Each of these historical episodes is central to the ways actors come to comprehend genocide as an act of collective violence that evolves through time, is rooted in the past, and reaches toward the future. For instance, Jarvis (2021: p 11) notes:

> In Algeria it is common and not the least bit controversial to refer to French colonization as a genocide – it would be provocative, in fact, to deny this. There, the revolutionary narrative is openly and ritually celebrated as the birth of a sovereign nation emerging from the night of colonial terror.

During the 20th century, the West enacted colonialism and imperialism throughout the world. Nation-state formation then occurred, especially in the aftermath of World War II, as colonized people sought independence from Western rule. Following the Holocaust, memory production unfolded primarily within the bounds of the nation-state, but more recently scholars highlight the fact that "even isolationist ideologies in such a world demand acknowledgment of other nations and a conscious effort to define one's own cultural space against, or in relation to, that of another" (O'Brien, 2021: p 13). Nationalism thus acts as a polarizing force as it leads states to adopt certain narratives of violence as official, marginalizing and excluding others in the process, especially those of minorities not recognized in the body politic. While official narratives may treat genocides as isolated and bounded acts, we must consider how our understanding of such acts of collective violence can be situated in a historical timeline, allowing narrators to root violence in history.

Finally, post-genocidal (re)narration occurs when those excluded from the body politic increasingly question nationalist silences and historical exclusions. Such subversive actors challenge official accounts and definitions. This is especially significant since "[t]he kinds of imagination and memory that are kept alive by writing, publishing, circulating, and interpreting literary texts have also created clandestine space for decolonial contestation that foments rather than neutralizes rebellion against the authority of the state" (Jarvis, 2021: p 173). This pattern also captures the resistance to the hegemonic official memory through the concept of "cultural memory" which is a form of "remembrance amongst social groups that manifests itself in multiple forms and relies upon acts of narration ... [that involve] a consideration of why and how we remember what we remember – and, on the other hand, why and how we forget" (Frawley, 2021: pp 5–6, 18).

Considering this character of conflicting memories, the process of dealing with contentious memories has potential to "encourage dialogue and enhance democratic politics" (Toth, 2022: p 6). Our goal, then, is to expand analyses and discussions of contentious memory in line with the aims of this volume. In summary, the introduction of *concept*, *agency*, and *narration* expands the analytic boundaries of extreme collective violence to include genocide as a process that is shaped/reshaped by social actors who interpret this process under larger historical patterns.

Part I: Difficult conceptual formation – ambiguities within the phenomenon of genocide

Focusing on the formation of the phenomenon of genocide in relation to the Armenian and Rwandan cases reveals the significance of the intersection of time and power. That is, the relationship between the temporality of physical violence and the application of "genocide" within conversations of accountability. Additionally, the tension between conception and praxis evolves globally and nationally as the pursuit of nation building relies on collective memory.

Intersection of time and power

The 1915 Armenian Genocide predates the genocide definition; still, many argue that not only do the adverse conditions in especially 1915–17 qualify what happened as genocide, but the Allied Powers led by Great Britain also identified what took place as the first crime against humanity. The fact that the Turkish state and society still deny that what occurred was genocide demonstrates the significance of the interaction of time and power in the formation of the phenomenon. The Turkish state denies the attribution on two grounds: first, since what happened predates the 1948 enactment of international genocide law, they claim the term cannot be employed ex-post facto. Second, the Turkish state then contends that it was Western powers that forced such a term onto the violence that occurred during World War I as "collateral damage," and they did so in order to legitimate their subsequent invasion of the Ottoman Empire. While this dispute originates in World War I, Turkish state and society continue to contest the definition of the episode which they attribute to the imposition of Western norms and values to censor the stability and sovereignty of the Turkish Republic today. This continuity of dispute over meaning illustrates the intersection of time and power in generating knowledge.

The 1994 Genocide Against the Tutsi in Rwanda falls instead on the other side of the temporal spectrum, post-dating the formation of the concept of genocide. Still, it also exhibits the significance of the intersection of power and time, albeit in a different formulation. The politics of naming the collective violence in Rwanda is both highlighted and hidden by scholars and diplomats. The Rwandan government insists that naming the "Genocide Against Tutsi" is necessary to highlight Tutsi as the victim while those opposing the official naming claim the title silences the experiences of non-Tutsi harmed in the collective violence (Jessee, 2017; Mwambari, 2020; Fox, 2021). The ongoing discussion on the politics of naming reveals contention between knowledge entrepreneurs and political actors, a contention which continues to evolve through time.

Intersection of theory and praxis

The tensions created by the discrepancy between time and power map onto and are exacerbated by another intersection, this time between theory and praxis. This intersection partially explains the degree of polarization and contention as the involved social actors are decontextualized from what happened on the ground and as a consequence, neatly divided into "victims and perpetrators." This is why, despite the international community's abjection to genocide, the naming of such atrocities is often met with political hurdles which are related to the victim-perpetrator binary of mutually exclusive groups by which some group is deserving of justice and another group is deserving of ridicule (Zubrzycki and Woźny, 2020).

A critical and comparative study of genocides can strengthen our understanding of mass violence, power, and contentious memory through analyzing repertoires of violence and control. Such an analytic framework de-centers the Holocaust as the universal case of genocide and instead rethinks the concept of genocide through comparison (Hinton, 2012). This is not to deny the reality of the Holocaust's destruction, but our hope is to achieve further understanding how genocide unfolds through repertoires of contention. As we illustrate, social actors manipulate accountability through collective memory processes by reinforcing a victim-perpetrator binary as a form of legitimacy. Respective leaders of a violent period remain unaccountable and subsequently whitewash and portray themselves as innocent leaders moving past the social ills of their predecessors. In the case of Rwanda, *not* naming the 1994 Genocide Against the Tutsi as genocide creates tensions in solidifying the narrative of Tutsi people as victims. In the case of Turkey, naming the Armenian Genocide as *genocide* creates tensions as Turkish leaders can only fall on the "perpetrator" realm of the binary and thus become illegitimate leaders. While our cases are at the opposing ends of the 20th century, the repertoires used to avoid accountability follow a similar pattern in the aftermath of violence.

Prevention of genocide requires analyzing the patterns of planning, execution, and aftermath. The linear temporality of our cases is different, but the periodization within temporality is where we observe the meaning-making process of collective memorialization. The periodization reveals how contemporary Turkey and Rwanda utilize collective memory as a tool for nation building and for the avoidance of accountability.

Part II: Difficult social actor negotiation – diverging standpoints in practice

Social reality emerges out of the intersection of knowledge and experience. Yet, our definitions of historical truth have systematically favored knowledge (read experts) over experience (read lay people). This is, we argue, due to the parameters of Western modernity within which both the Armenian and Rwandan genocides are embedded.

For instance, in relation to experience, Western modernity operates under an erroneous imaginary of universality to normalize and naturalize the experience of the hegemonic class as if it represented the entire class structure.[7] In doing so, Enlightenment thinking silences and erases the voices of all social groups marginalized by the hegemonic class. When applied to the specific cases of the collective violence inherent in both Armenian and Rwandan genocides, this translates into normalizing and naturalizing the standpoints of those in power, namely the perpetrators at the expense of the victims – as defined in the context of one point in time. This may also explain why reconciliation committees that are supposed to treat perpetrators and victims with equity end up serving the needs of the perpetrators at the expense of the victims (Crocker, 2000; Gutmann and Thompson, 2000).

Western modernity also privileges publicly visible social behavior at the expense of, on the one side, what occurs in the private sphere and, on the other, abstract categories such as thoughts, narratives, and ideologies. Such privileging is especially contentious in the case of the collective violence embedded in the Armenian and Rwandan genocides because removal of the private sphere effectively erases the violence from the public gaze. Since those who generate knowledge about such events, such as scholars and public intellectuals, have primary access to and are constrained by the public sphere, their standpoints unconsciously privilege the interests of social actors who remain dominant in the public sphere.

Variable experience

In relation to the history of collective violence, there are often two standpoints that emerge out of who had power to monopolize violence at whose expense, namely perpetrators and victims, in addition to the majority of bystanders. Theoretically, all those who do not fall into this binarism of victim and perpetrator make up the bystanders Hannah Arendt (1963) identified as crucial in escalating or containing the collective violence. In the case of the Armenian Genocide, it was the ruling members of the Union and Progress government established at this particular juncture that comprised the experience of the perpetrators. Even though Armenian subjects of the empire have been defined as the primary victims, recent research has revealed the inclusion among the victims of other social groups such as Greeks, Chaldeans, Arabs and Assyrians.[8] In Rwanda, the mere categories of "Hutu" and "Tutsi" reformulate over time and through power from class identities to ethnic identities; to present-day experiences relational to the genocide, but categories outlawed via the constitution. To assign a static, moral value to these categories would require assumptions about time, space, and related meaning.

History does not operate through binarisms – today's perpetrators can turn into future victims. As a consequence, it may be prescient to treat all involved parties neutrally as social groups that assume different roles in the collective violence over time. The Union and Progress members who were the main perpetrators during the Armenian Genocide became persecuted themselves in the 1926 alleged assassination attempt against Mustafa Kemal and during the 1925–27 Independence Tribunals that hanged people without giving them any legal recourse to question the death verdicts against them. Empirically then, the social groups of Union and Progress members as well as Armenians need to be analyzed through time and across space to capture the variation in their roles across the spectrum of violence.

Variable knowledge

Even though public intellectuals, thinkers, state officials, and officers and journalists all contribute to the generation of knowledge, we focus in this particular discussion on the knowledge of social science scholars regarding the collective violence of the Armenian and Rwandan genocides. Since the inherent violence is publicly marginalized, erased, or obfuscated, it is hard for scholars to access knowledge regarding the violence from official documents, reports, and even newspapers in the public sphere. Genocides systematically subvert or destroy all sites of collective violence and subversive knowledge production. When possible, such as in Rwanda, oral histories offer a great deal of insight. Oral tradition is not only culturally significant, but political leaders before and during the genocide denied schooling to the Tutsi, creating barriers to reading and writing (Jessee, 2017). However, there remain many individuals who are too traumatized to publicly discuss the violence (Fox, 2021). Courageous memoirs detailing the atrocities encountered are an additional way for stories to be told. Many survivors from the Armenian Genocide remain marginalized in the literature due to the lack of public recognition, but social groups such as Greeks, Jews, Assyrians, and Chaldeans, as well as those of Turkish officials and officers, also experienced the genocide and lived long enough to turn it into knowledge. It is therefore imperative to investigate the memoirs of "other" social groups.

Since the discussion in memoirs of such collective violence often extends all the way to the present, it is crucial to draw the sample of memoirs widely at first, then form a subset of only those that discuss all instances of collective violence. In this manner, one can empirically locate not only the members of all social groups (instead of narrowing the categories down to victim/perpetrator/bystander) in relation to the collective violence under question, but also gain a longitudinal perspective regarding how these social roles change over time and across space. In summary, then, knowledge generated by social groups on genocides vary across time and space, making their interpretation challenging not only contemporaneously, but across time as well.

Part III: Difficult contextualization – (re)narrating genocide through subversion

Repertoires of violence and power are repurposed with regard to four periods: (i) colonization, (ii) nation-state formation, (iii) internal polarization leading to genocide, and (iv) post-genocidal (re)narration. With our expanded historical lens, we view each of these periods as historical episodes marked by power dynamics that are relevant to the meaning of genocide, on the one hand, and periods that are incorporated into the contentious memories and accounts of genocide, on the other. The first three periods are briefly discussed for historical context while the later period is elaborated upon with greater attention later. Powerful actors define and use each of these periods to remove accountability and obtain legitimacy. Thus, for instance, in the post-genocidal (re)narration, contemporary Turkey fails to acknowledge the genocide in hopes of a gradual "forgetting." In Rwanda, collective memory is impressed onto individuals to emphasize the harms of colonial influence and violence against the Tutsi while silencing any violence of the current government. The periodizations are often observed as rifts in political control, but the repertoires of power- and meaning-making illustrate how those in power maintain control through repeated tactics (Tilly, 2006).

Chrétien (2003: p 37) warns against the "double trap" in writing about history where a "liberal" history suggests peace in pre-colonial periods and a "radical" history overemphasizes the beginning of colonialism and imperialism, overlooking far too often the significance of pre-colonial histories. There is therefore a need for a critical approach to how macro processes at different periods frame collective violence, gradually escalating in genocide and its contentious aftermath. The initial comparison of Ottoman and Rwandan colonization by the West reveal a significant difference in the nature of outside intervention: while Ottoman colonization is initiated by the Ottoman rulers to reach the new modern standards by which Western Europe starts to dominate the world, the Rwandan colonization is not only initiated by the West, but it entails direct economic, political, and cultural intervention by which Western colonizers reconfigure the local social structure, removing agency from colonized Rwandans. However, the historical processes and their impact are similar through the alteration of social structures. Notably, the resulting nationalism and polarization through violent exclusion sets the necessary conditions for genocide and post-genocidal narration.

Colonization

In both cases, boundary making and identity formation rely on Western assumptions of modernity. The Ottoman rulers start to systematically adopt Western goods, institutions, and ideas from the early 18th century onward (Göçek, 1987). It first commences with reforming the military institution to prevent increasing Ottoman defeats in front of Western armies. New military education entails year-round training where the local military units maintained by provincial governors gradually become centralized into academies and military units in major Ottoman cities. Financing these endeavors changes the land tenure system from in kind to cash payment, gradually privatizing all agricultural lands. It is also as a consequence of these transformations that the communal subjects of the empire gradually turn into private citizens as they redefine their identities through nationalism, becoming public participants in the imagined community of the nation (Anderson, 1983).

German and Belgian colonialists redefined identity in Rwanda. While the German colonists did institute an ethnic component in referring to the

Hutu and Tutsi identities, which were socio-economically defined before colonialism, it was Belgian colonialists who were even more egregious in repurposing the Hutu and Tutsi identities as "legitimate" ethnic groups. Belgians also reorganized the political infrastructure of Rwanda, igniting political power struggles for decades to come. Using the "Hamitic myth," which likened Tutsi to Northern Africans and thus Europeans based on pseudo-science phrenology, the Tutsi were considered by Belgians as migrants from descendants of "Caucasians" unlike other ethnic groups. This social stratification of ethnic difference was going to be crucial for political leaders who cleverly repurposed ethnicized ideology when orchestrating the genocide (Des Forges, 1999).

Nation-state formation

As countries become indirectly or directly colonized by Western modernity, their norms, values, and social structure alter in ways that privilege reason over religious belief, individual rights over communal privileges, and a new imagined national identity and belonging alongside the exclusion from the nation. It is this polarization that consequently will tear the moral fabric of respect and mutual trust across identity divides, leading in turn to collective destruction.

Hierarchies of citizenship are re-formulated from colonialism to nation building as access to the public sphere is restricted and the enactment of the private sphere is enforced. Ottoman modernization reaches a new stage with the access to power of the Young Turk reformers in 1908, a political process that not only destroys the empire eventually but leads the military contingent within to fight an independence struggle leading to the establishment of the Turkish Republic in 1923. In the Ottoman context, the Young Turks, as their name indicates, start privileging Turkish ethnic and racial identity over the broad Ottoman imperial one. It is during their reign that population surveys start to mark how the ethnicities of the empire are distributed, especially in comparison to the Turks, in an attempt to recruit more Turks to the parliament instead of religious minorities.

In the process of gaining independence during 1950s Rwanda, political parties were not solely bound by ethnic identity, but the ensuing Hutu government promoted the myth of the Tutsi as foreign to ostracize them under the same pseudo-racial conception used by colonial rule. Under the rule of President Kayibanda, a transition in power between the Tutsi and the Hutu allowed Hutu to then have full access to governmental positions, education, and other employment opportunities at the expense of the Tutsi. It was then that the Hutus further restricted Tutsi access to the public and private sectors in the name of "ethnic rebalancing" and short periods of violence included the massacres of Tutsi. General Juvénal Habyarimana initiated a successful coup in 1973 by which he declared "to end ethnic division and regional favoritism and to restore national unity," but the reality of Habyarimana's regime is the institutionalized violence against Tutsi (Straus, 2006: pp 190–191).

Internal polarization to genocide

As both countries start to redefine their populace in new terms to guarantee them direct political representation in parliament, those social groups deciding who belongs and does not belong to the nation start expending more power over others. Eventually, those who are defined as not belonging to the body politic on various grounds not only become increasingly marginalized, but the new nation-state first protects them individually as citizens, abrogating their communal privileges. Then, the nation-state withdraws all legal protection from these minorities, leaving them open to full abuse during genocide.

With regard to the Armenian Genocide, the attempts of the Young Turks to create a common Ottoman identity instead of an ethnic Turkish one failed as many social groups like the Greeks, Bulgarians, Bosnians, Arabs, and Armenians tried to establish their own nation-states. The combination of great Ottoman military losses on all imperial fronts and the Western European protection of Ottoman religious minorities, especially Christians, quickly polarized local relations. Since the Muslim Turks had the additional advantage of being able to carry arms at all times and the religious minorities did not, the early years of World War I provided the context to execute the genocidal project against the Armenians who rightfully claimed Anatolia as their ancestral lands. First stigmatizing them as "traitors," the Ottoman Turkish officials and officers belonging to the Union and Progress party then systematically destroyed Armenian communities throughout the empire through forced migration, massacres, and plunder. Although this genocidal destruction briefly stopped at the end of the World War in 1918, it did nevertheless continue until the beginning of the Turkish Republic in 1923. The official narrative denying the genocide starts to emerge coevally with the execution of the genocide, a process that continues to this day.

Alternatively, Rwanda experienced several "triggering events" leading up to and coinciding with the 1990–1994 Civil War and subsequently the 1994 Genocide against the Tutsi. Habyarimana's regime spread falsified accounts of the Rwandan Patriotic Front (RPF), a Tutsi-led rebel group formed by exiles in Uganda, and declared Tutsi as the enemy of Rwanda. The decades of dehumanization institutionalized by Hutu-led governments manifested into mobilization tactics consisting of stocking up on machetes and other weapons, training the *Interahmwe* (an MRND youth-group turned militia), and delivering propaganda on radios around the country to prepare for "self-defense" (Des Forges, 1999). The Tutsi were no longer seen as an ethnic group within Rwanda, but instead dehumanized into an abstract evil. International actors continuously ignored warnings by individuals on the ground in Rwanda about ongoing violence, and on April 6, 1994, Habyarimana's plane was shot down. To this day, the assailants are unknown, but the plane crash is identified as a catalyst of the 1994 Genocide Against the Tutsi because political leaders immediately blamed the Tutsi (Nyseth Brehm and Fox, 2017). In the hours and days after the plane crash, Tutsi and others associated with Tutsi people were raped, tortured, and killed in public and private, including in churches that once harbored the Tutsi during earlier periods of killing. In around 100 days, estimates of those killed in the genocide range from 800,000 to over 1 million (Des Forges, 1999; Nyseth Brehm, 2017). Largely on their own accord, the RPF declared victory on July 4, 1994 and began rebuilding the nation on ideals of unity and reconciliation.

Post-genocidal (re)narration

The aftermath of the genocide is a century-long process in the case of the Armenian Genocide and nearly three decades in the case of Rwanda; yet, both cases continue the process of (re)narration and (re)interpretation. In the case of the Ottoman Empire that then became a Turkish Republic, denial of the genocide became institutionalized as the former perpetrators became its new heroic leaders. The ensuing official narrative whitewashed the crimes Turkish officers and officials committed against humanity by destroying the empire's Armenian communities, thereby evading punishment. In the case of Rwanda, the victims of the genocide lead the government under the RPF whose violence immediately after the genocide and contemporary political oppression practices are silenced to avoid accountability and maintain legitimacy.

This abrogation of accountability in both cases necessitates two narrative strategies, perversion of social reality on the one side and subversion of social justice on the other. We take up Rothberg's (2019: p 16) concept of *implicated subjects* and consider how "historical violence and ongoing inequities demand a more differentiated analysis than that afforded by a collapse of beneficiaries into perpetrators." *Implicated subjects* are situated within dynamic structures of power over time and space, and a binary of perpetrator-victim is insufficient for complex, intersecting periods of violence. In theorizing domestic violence Sweet (2020: p 932) argues a relational approach to knowledge production exposes "facile binaries and power-laden boundaries." Theorizing collective violence also requires a similar approach as public-private binaries valued by Western modernity drive repertoires of power and control. For example, post-genocide government leaders repurpose Western rhetoric such as the "War on Terror" to label political opposition as "terrorists."

A bottom-up, relational approach prioritizes knowledge at the boundaries by considering the experiences, knowledge, and identities of people at the margins of power. This approach considers the public-private divide as socially constructed and instead dissolves public-private into relational interactions rather than separate entities. As such, the perpetrator-victim binary is revealed as oversimplified over time and space when dynamics of violence, too, are relational. Yet, while focusing on *implicated subjects* problematizes mainstream ideas of justice and accountability by expanding our understandings of social actors as having dynamic and even contradictory identities and behaviors, our goal in this chapter is to highlight how connections among long-distance legacies create solidarity projects around the world (Rothberg, 2019).

Post-genocidal Ottoman Empire and Turkish Republic (1923–present)

Establishing a new republic on the ashes of an empire enabled the Turkish perpetrator elite to erase the imperial past, arguing that the new Turkey was strictly going to focus on the future. All collective violence that occurred before 1923 was marginalized as pre-history, thereby erasing the claims of especially the Greeks, Armenians, and Kurds who also rightfully claimed large regions of the empire as their ancestral lands to no avail. Crucial in this process was the 1928 alphabet reform whereby all Turkish citizens were forced to switch from Arabic to Latin script, effectively severing the connection of all Turks to their own imperial history. The new centralized knowledge created by the new educational institutions of the republic systematically altered historical reality by minimizing the violence of the Turks while maximizing the sedition of all imperial groups. Likewise, the national judiciary privileged the national interests of the state before those of its citizens, especially those "minority" citizens who were now treated as foreigners on their own ancestral lands.

Post-genocidal Rwanda (1995–present)

Within the first decade after the genocide, scholars reported a sense of "collective amnesia" with regard to how violence evolves. The creation of a national memory takes time, as is evident in other societies with difficult pasts, and eventually the institutional memory-making process through *Ingando* (re-education camps), national commemoration practices, and transitional justice *Gacaca* courts cured "collective amnesia" with blame on the Hutu "bad governance" and colonialism (Nyseth Brehm and Fox, 2017).

However, the transformation of collective amnesia into collective coping and blaming does not occur equally among Rwandans. Those who have not "healed" from rape and other traumas suffered during the genocide, and individuals who have not admitted culpability based on the national collective memory, are sidelined in the national reconciliation process (Jessee, 2017; Fox, 2021). The idea of citizens being Rwandan-first sidelines the experiences of *implicated subjects* and minority identities in the name of unity and reconciliation. Again, a comparative genocide analysis illustrates this is not unique to Rwanda, but instead a commonality for nations making sense of conflict and mass violence. Scholars and human rights activists continue to keep watchful eyes on the Rwandan government, but as knowledge entrepreneurs, their interpretive analysis must also be analyzed.

Conclusion: Collective memory and contentious meaning-making

Post-genocidal periods become contentious through the three difficult processes of conceptual formation, social actor negotiation, and narration. Problematizing the victim-perpetrator binary, Zubrzycki and Woźny (2020) discover nations with complex histories around violence struggle to especially recognize the collective violence enacted against others. Indeed, in our comparative case, Turkey refuses to acknowledge the concept of genocide as the Armenian Genocide overlaps with World War I, the dissolution of the Ottoman Empire, and Young Turks eventually establishing nationhood. In Rwanda, violence through colonialism and Hutu-led governments, referred to as "bad governments," are at the forefront of collective memory with regard to how the 1994 Genocide Against the Tutsi evolved. The emphasis on defining the current government as "good" carries with it the inherent assumption that they are unable to commit violence.

The selection of these two cases evolved from our own "interpretive lens" which acknowledges dynamic meaning-making via the interactions of individuals and institutions "as they shift over time and place" (Naples, 2003: p 84). Our standpoints (the first author as a white American scholar using feminist theory and a critical genocide studies lens, and the second author using the same lens, but this time as an ethnic Turk that categorically belongs to the social group of perpetrators) are important to acknowledge as points of power in knowledge making, but superficial recognition of one's privilege is not equivalent to reflexivity (Rothberg, 2019: p 19). As Sweet (2020: p 941) argues, reflexivity is neither the addition of multiple viewpoints nor standpoints, but the process of reflexivity "requires attending to how and when alternative forms of knowledge may be *better*" (emphasis in original). In the context of contentious post-genocide memory, reliance on top-down analyses privilege oversimplified binaries and "official" narratives of collective violence while alternative sites of knowledge are silenced and/or ignored and privileged hegemonic ideologies persist (Fox, 2021).

Collective violence and contentious meaning-making continue when ahistorical accounts of accountability place blame on one group while absolving all others. Instead, we argue for an analysis of collective violence which identifies how implicated actors navigate accountability over time and space. For the cases of genocide in Western Armenia and Rwanda, four periods illustrate how various actors renegotiate accountability and legitimacy: (i) colonization, (ii) nation-state formation, (iii) internal polarization leading to genocide, and (iv) post-genocidal (re)narration. These historical periods interact to structure the contentious post-genocidal process: colonization takes away accountability from colonized people; nation-state formation provides accountability only to those who do not have power previously; and internal polarization before genocide is marked with the institutionalization of violence and how social actors engage in genocide construction at a particular junction, emphasizing in the process how meanings around genocide are shaped. Finally, post-genocidal (re)narration is where the ambiguity of the boundaries of genocide are exposed. The public exercise of collective violence is formally perverted by refusing acknowledgment and privileging denial. Informally, the abrogation of acknowledgment undermines accountability and, with it, social justice.

As sociologists, our "task is to place actors' logics within the power structures they conceal" (Bourdieu and Wacquant, 1992: p 251; Sweet, 2020). Our goal in using reflexivity and a critical genocide studies framework is to build a theory which is exportable to other contexts and cases to reach a better understanding of the knowledge construction process of genocide, and to do so in order to predict and prevent further occurrences of contentious, collective violence. In conclusion, addressing contentious memory must especially focus on accountability as it is ultimately what separates acknowledgment from denial.

Notes

[1] Samantha Power (2002) coined the 20th century as the Age of Genocide to highlight the numerous atrocities and resulting political reluctance to invoke the word genocide.

[2] It is significant to note that we dismiss the victim-bystander-perpetrator triad, focusing instead on "implicated subjects" in comparative genocide studies (Rothberg, 2019).

[3] When genocide is hierarchically assigned as "the crime of all crimes," leaders of post-genocide nations take advantage of their ability to push the boundaries of what harms against society are allowed – targeting journalists, forced disappearances, oppressive laws, policies restricting criticism, and so on.

[4] In following Hammer (2020: p 4) who suggests re-embedding social theorizing in colonial histories, we further suggest a re-embedding of genocide and other forms of collective violence to "better understand the processes that shape our sense of we-ness but may lie outside our assumed analytic focus."

[5] See Navaro-Yashin et al (2021: pp 10–11) who wrote: "in addressing and emphasizing the endurance of violence, we follow the lead of scholars of the Armenian genocide and the Palestinian Nakba who have studied them as 'ongoing' (Salamanca et al, 2012;

Ekmekçioğlu, 2016; Suciyan, 2016) … To say that violence is ongoing is to highlight the way violence leaves wounds that are traceable even in sites where evidence has been quite effectively effaced. It is to argue that violence comes back, that it returns and resumes, or that it haunts politics, materialities, and subjectivities forever. To insist that violence is 'ongoing' is to open the field for the study of violence in the many guises and shapes it takes, both human and nonhuman, in the aftermath of atrocities. To suggest that violence is 'ongoing' is to question the very rubric of 'aftermath' itself. It is to ask whether there really is an after to violence."

6 These four categories refer to how power and knowledge intersect in relation to political rule, an intersection that impacts the contemporaneous definition of genocide differently. They emerged from Göçek's analysis of collective violence in Ottoman and Turkish history, a sociological analysis covering approximately 220 years from the onset of modernity in 1789 to the conclusion of the study in 2009. Collective violence initially emerged as a concept with the colonization of the Ottoman Empire through the adoption of the Western conception of collective violence located in the public sphere. The nation-state formation process that ensued redefined such collective violence in terms of group identities; these group identities became polarized within the binary framework of Western modernity leading to the collective violence that was, for the first time in human history, termed genocide. The final stage of post genocidal renarration was enacted by the Turkish state that categorically denied the term and imposed this 'official' denial onto the populace. Only recently have scholars started to question this conceptualization of genocide denial in Turkey (Göçek, 2015: Introduction).

7 It is the interaction of the ruling class with state and civil society that enables a class to become hegemonic (Gramsci, 1971: pp 545–546).

8 Note the similarity to the Holocaust where the Nazi government decimated "homosexuals," priests, leftists, and the Roma in addition to the Jews, thereby destroying all that was "different" and "the other."

References

Alexander, J.C. (2012) *Trauma: A Social Theory*, Malden, MA: Polity Press.
Anderson, B. (1983) *Imagined Communities: Reflections on the Origin and Spread of Nationalism*, London: Verso.
Arendt, H. (1963) *Eichmann in Jerusalem: A Report on the Banality of Evil* (2006 edition), New York: Penguin Books.
Bauman, Z. (2007) *Modernity and the Holocaust*, Cambridge: Polity Press.
Bourdieu, P. and Wacquant, L.J.D. (1992) *An Invitation to Reflexive Sociology*, Chicago, IL: University of Chicago Press.
Brown, R.H. and Malone, E.L. (2004) "Reason, Politics, and the Politics of Truth: How Science is Both Autonomous and Dependent," *Sociological Theory* 22(1): 106–122.
Chrétien, J.P. (2003) *The Great Lakes of Africa: Two Thousand Years of History*, New York: Zone Books.
Crocker, D.A. (2000) "Truth Commissions, Transitional Justice, and Civil Society," in R.I. Rotberg and D.F. Thompson (eds) *Truth v. Justice*, Princeton, NJ: Princeton University Press, pp 99–121.

Des Forges, A. (1999) *"Leave None to Tell the Story": Genocide in Rwanda*, New York: Human Rights Watch.

Ekmekçioğlu, L. (2016) *Recovering Armenia: The Limits of Belonging in Post-Genocide Turkey*, Stanford, CA: Stanford University Press.

Fox, N. (2021) *After Genocide: Memory and Reconciliation in Rwanda*, Madison, WI: University of Wisconsin Press.

Frawley, O. (ed) (2021) *Women and the Decade of Commemorations, Irish Culture, Memory, Place*, Bloomington, IN: Indiana University Press.

Go, J. (2020) "Race, Empire, and Epistemic Exclusion: Or the Structures of Sociological Thought," *Sociological Theory* 38(2): 79–100.

Göçek, F.M. (1987) *East Encounters West: France and the Ottoman Empire in the Eighteenth Century*, New York: Oxford University Press.

Göçek, F.M. (2015) *Denial of Violence: Ottoman Past, Turkish Present, and Collective Violence against the Armenians, 1789–2009*, New York: Oxford University Press.

Gramsci, A. (1971) *Selections from the Prison Notebooks of Antonio Gramsci*. Translated and edited by Q. Hoare, and G. Nowell-Smith, New York: International Publishers Co.

Gutmann, A. and Thompson, D. (2000) "The Moral Foundations of Truth Commissions," in R.I. Rotberg and D.F. Thompson (eds) *Truth v. Justice*, Princeton, NJ: Princeton University Press, pp 22–44.

Habermas, J. (1971) *Knowledge and Human Interests*, Boston, MA: Beacon Press.

Hammer, R. (2020) "Decolonizing the Civil Sphere: The Politics of Difference, Imperial Erasures, and Theorizing from History," *Sociological Theory* 38(2): 101–121.

Hinton, A.L. (2012) "Critical Genocide Studies," *Genocide Studies and Prevention* 7(1): 4–15.

Jarvis, J. (2021) *Decolonizing Memory: Algeria and the Politics of Testimony*, Durham, NC: Duke University Press.

Jessee, E. (2017) *Negotiating Genocide in Rwanda: The Politics of History*, Glasgow: Palgrave Macmillan.

Kacandes, I. (2022) *On Being Adjacent to Historical Violence*, Boston, MA De Gruyter.

Lemkin, R. (1944) *Axis Rule in Occupied Europe: Laws of Occupation, Analysis of Government, Proposals for Redress*, Concord, NH: Carnegie Endowment for International Peace.

Lemkin, R. (1953) "Nature of Genocide: Confusion with Discrimination against Individuals Seen," *New York Times*, [online] June 14, Available from: www.nytimes.com/1953/06/14/archives/nature-of-genocide-confusion-with-discrimination-against.html [Accessed December 14, 2021].

Luft, A. (2015) "Toward a Dynamic Theory of Action at the Micro Level of Genocide: Killing, Desistance, and Saving in 1994 Rwanda," *Sociological Theory* 33(2): 148–172.

Mwambari, D. (2020) "Emergence of Post-Genocide Collective Memory in Rwanda's International Relations," in E. Nyaga Muji, D. Mwambari, and A. Ylönen (eds) *Beyond History: African Agency in Development, Diplomacy, and Conflict Resolution*, London: Rowman & Littlefield, pp 119–134.

Naples, N.A. (2003) *Feminism and Method: Ethnography, Discourse Analysis, and Activist Research*, New York: Routledge.

Navaro-Yashin, Y., Biner, Z. Ö., Bieberstein, A. von, Altuğ, S. (eds) (2021) *Reverberations: Violence Across Time and Space* (1st edition), Philadelphia, PA: University of Pennsylvania Press.

Nyseth Brehm, H. (2017) "Subnational Determinants of Killing in Rwanda," *Criminology* 55(1): 5–31.

Nyseth Brehm, H. and Fox, N. (2017) "Narrating Genocide: Time, Memory, and Blame," *Sociological Forum* 32(1): 116–137.

O'Brien, S. (2021) *Trauma and Fictions of the "War on Terror": Disrupting Memory*, New York: Routledge.

Otele, O., Gandolfo, L., and Galai, Y. (eds) (2021) *Post-Conflict Memorialization: Missing Memorials, Absent Bodies*, Cham: Springer International Publishing.

Power, S. (2002) *A Problem from Hell: America and the Age of Genocide*, New York: Basic Books.

Rothberg, M. (2019) *The Implicated Subject: Beyond Victims and Perpetrator*, Stanford, CA: Stanford University Press.

Salamanca, O.J., Qato, M., Rabie, K., and Samour, S. (2012) "Past is Present: Settler Colonialism in Palestine," *Settler Colonial Studies* 2(1): 1–8.

Samudzi, Z. (2020) "Paradox of Recognition: Genocide and Colonialism," *Postmodern Culture* 31(1).

Savelsberg, J.J. (2021) *Knowing about Genocide: Armenian Suffering and Epistemic Struggles*, Oakland, CA: University of California Press.

Simko, C. (2020) "Marking Time in Memorials and Museums of Terror: Temporality and Cultural Trauma," *Sociological Theory* 38(1): 51–77.

Steinmetz, G. (2007) "Scientific Authority and the Transition to Post-Fordism: The Plausibility of Positivism in US Sociology since 1945," in G. Steinmetz (ed) *The Politics of Method in the Human Sciences: Positivism and Its Epistemological Others*, Durham, NC: Duke University Press, pp 167–169.

Straus, S. (2006) *The Order of Genocide: Race, Power, and War in Rwanda*, Ithaca, NY: Cornell University Press.

Suciyan, T. (2016) *The Armenians in Modern Turkey: Post-Genocide Society, Politics and History*, London: I.B. Tauris.

Sweet, P.L. (2020) "Who Knows? Reflexivity in Feminist Standpoint Theory and Bourdieu," *Gender & Society* 34(6): 922–950.

Tilly, C. (2006) *Regimes and Repertoires*, Chicago, IL: University of Chicago Press.

Toth, M. (2022) *European Memory and Conflicting Visions of the Past, Memory Politics and Transitional Justice*, Cham: Springer International Publishing.

Zubrzycki, G. and Woźny, A. (2020) "The Comparative Politics of Collective Memory," *Annual Review of Sociology* 46: 175–194.

13

Conclusion: Memory and the Social Dynamics of Conflict and Contention: Interpretive Lenses for New Cases and Controversies

Janet Jacobs and Thomas DeGloma

For over a century, scholars, writers, artists, and thinkers have been interested in and fascinated by the artifacts and meanings of memory. The quest to know and understand how memories are created, how they are coded and retained or lost, and how they shape identity and a sense of self is foundational to both psychological and sociological theory. While the tendency among many scholars and scholarly traditions has been to consider memory as an individual and personal domain, the notion that memory can also have a social, that is, collective component, was first articulated by Émile Durkheim ([1912] 2001) in the *Elementary Forms of Religious Life*. In that classic text, Durkheim describes the way in which group rituals and symbol systems represent the sacred in society and provide the means by which ancestral memory is transmitted across generations. Within this Durkeheimian paradigm, ritual cultures establish the social means and interactive contexts through which collective identity and a shared past is re-inscribed into social consciousness.

Following Durkheim's initial insights on ritualized memory as a distinctly social phenomenon, his student Maurice Halbwachs ([1952] 1992) laid the groundwork for the study of memory as a collective phenomenon and an element of social life. In *The Social Frameworks of Memory*, Halbwachs provides a sociological approach that links our understanding and experience of individual or personal memory to the social realm, and to collective meanings. He writes:

> it is in society that people normally acquire their memories. It is also in society that they recall, recognize, and localize their memories. …

It is in this sense that there exists a collective memory and social frameworks for memory; it is to the degree that our individual thought places itself in these frameworks and participates in this memory that it is capable of the act of recollection. ([1952] 1992: p 38)

Both in *The Social Frameworks of Memory* ([1952] 1992) and another text, *The Legendary Topography of the Gospels in the Holy Land* ([1941] 1992), Halbwachs elaborates on the role that myths, narratives, and symbol systems play in the transmission of memory, particularly as social structures such as the family, religion, and class relations inform the preservation and dissemination of remembrances of the past. It is also in these works that Halbwachs identifies the importance of landmarks, social locations, and iconography as social sites of memory.

As Halbwachs's work grew more influential in the late 20th century, research on social, cultural, and collective memory became foundational for contemporary understandings of national and group identity. Such research has reinforced the notion that holding a shared vision of the past is essential to group solidarity; and because group solidarity is often embedded in difficult remembrances, researchers have increasingly focused their analytic lenses on the social processes involved with remembering difficult and painful pasts (see Wagner-Pacifici and Schwartz, 1991; Vinitzky-Seroussi, 2002; Olick, 2007). Within this growing and increasingly complex field, the study of memorialization, especially of violent conflicts, mass traumas, and oppressive histories, has become a particularly significant and rich area of analysis. Among the numerous scholars who are grappling with the meaning of memorialization, Jeffrey C. Alexander (2004) suggests that, in remembering histories of genocide, social actors often seek to create a better and more just world. Describing the importance of Holocaust museums as a model for public commemoration, Alexander writes:

It seems clear that such memorializations aim to create structures that dramatize the tragedy of the Holocaust and provide opportunities for contemporaries, now so far removed from the original scene, powerfully to reexperience it. … In each Holocaust Museum, the fate of the Jews functions as a metaphorical bridge to the treatment of other ethnic, religious, and racial minorities. The aim is manifestly not to "promote" the Holocaust as an important event in earlier historical time, but to contribute to the possibilities of pluralism and justice in the world of today. (2004: p 257)

In this powerful and provocative discussion, Alexander returns to the themes that were first articulated by Halbwachs, reminding us that collective memory is, after all, a social and cultural construction, the significance of which lies in the ways that collective visions of the past, including traumas, are preserved, expressed, and reinvented with particular consequences for an understanding of the present and future.

In addition to Alexander, other scholars have also turned to the study of contentious and difficult memory as a social and political phenomenon. Such scholars have highlighted themes of forgetting and remembering within the political discourse with regard to difficult and painful issues and experiences. In particular, Alon Confino's (2006) work addresses the various meanings that the study of memory brings to interpretations of history. Confino contends that because social frames of memory are embedded in the politics of culture and history, collective representations cannot be understood apart from the social relations of power which control the technologies of memory and that mediate historical events for the larger society. Within Confino's paradigm, collective memory thus becomes a contentious space in which issues of power and powerlessness, along with visibility and invisibility, problematize the meaning systems of memorialization.

In keeping with Alexander's and Confino's approaches, as well as those of several other scholars, the studies presented in this volume have offered new and important perspectives on contentious memory and the attending phenomenon of counter-memorialization. As discussed in our introduction to this volume, the production of countermemories is most frequently associated with "the views of marginalized individuals or groups" (Zerubavel, 1995: p 11) whose voices and histories have been silenced or erased. Grounded in the work of Foucault (1971, 1977) and Barthes (1980), countermemories offer an alternative perspective on the past in which the lives and experiences of the forgotten and/or subjugated are reclaimed (Tello, 2022). As an expression of memory and memorialization, countermemory has been conceptualized through art, text, monumentalization, and through subversive acts that symbolize resistance and bring new meaning to the process of remembering. To this end, James Young (1992) points to the abstract imagery of countermemorials in Germany which, by example, tell a compelling story of the missing Jews of Europe.

Following Young, the emergence of countermemories in other postgenocide societies has also been analyzed. In Sarajevo, for example, a sculpture of canned beef has been identified as a counter-memorial that satirizes the international communities' aid to a starving and besieged city (Sheftel, 2012). Anna Sheftel's (2012) study of this counter-monument suggests that this form of remembering captures "Bosnian dark humour … as very powerful criticism of both the Bosnian past and present" (2012: p 147). In a very different approach to countermemory, activists in Hungary have turned to the more traditional tropes of persecution, tragedy, and suffering to commemorate the complicity of Hungary in the genocide of World War II. Through text, photographs, and memorabilia, Hungarian activists have created a grassroots counter-memorial highlighting Hungary's official collaboration in the destruction of European Jewry, a narrative that has been suppressed by the contemporary nationalist government (Eross, 2016). Turning to Rwanda, Janet Jacobs (2017) explores countermemory from the perspective of victim representation in memorial culture. Drawing on the tensions surrounding the remembrance of rape as an act of genocide, Jacobs considers the need to break the silence surrounding sexual assault in warfare while simultaneously preserving the dignity of victims. Here she argues that counter-memorials convey the responsibility to remember, with care and sensitivity, those whose bodies have been brutalized and exploited (2017). Turning to contemporary research on the United States, scholars such as Ron Eyerman (2001), Susan Neiman (2019), and others have begun to unpack the contentious memories surrounding the meanings of slavery and the history of racism.

Building on these and other foundational studies of contentious memory, the authors in this volume have furthered our understanding of the ways that social memory intersects with power and how processes of memorialization are often steeped in social contention. In Part I, the authors grappled with generational memory, social context, gender, and hate as focal points for mnemonic tensions. To this end, Edna Lomsky-Feder has examined memories among Israeli war veterans, exploring the ways in which motifs of honor and heroism assume new meanings across generations as memorialization shifts with changing political and social frameworks. Nicole Fox then considered the memory of victimized women in Rwanda. Developing a multifaceted feminist perspective, Fox analyzed how the memory of gendered violence during genocide is often suppressed or silenced, a pattern of memorialization that reproduces relationships of power which are contentious and transcend the boundaries of memorial culture.

Shifting to the history of social movements, Roberto Vélez-Vélez considered the importance of individual remembrances (collected memory) in shaping the movement to close the US navy base on the island of Vieques in Puerto Rico. Vélez-Vélez persuasively argued that personal memories form the core of a collective memory out of which social movements are born and resistance is mobilized. Finally, Gary Alan Fine, Christopher Robertson, and Cal Abbo considered the significance of contentious reputations in the 2016 US presidential campaign. Focusing on collective memories that originate out of social perceptions of an individual's past, these authors illustrate the ways in which strong emotions such as hate are galvanized through political processes that draw sharp distinctions between good and evil in a polarized and tension-filled political landscape. Taken together, the chapters in Part I outline valuable interpretive lenses that consider how personal memories provide a mode or form of mnemonic contestation, highlighting tensions between personal and collective visions of the past.

Turning to Part II, the authors examined memorial motifs through varied lenses that bring into focus issues of slavery, race, or immigration/deportation. Accordingly, Sofya Aptekar focused on deported US veterans whose autobiographical memories reveal the tensions between the memory of a stigmatized identity (deportee) and the memory of honor and citizenship (veteran), and how these frames of remembrance are in contention with one another. In this analysis, Aptekar highlighted the use of memory to remedy social injustice as the dishonored veterans engage in the creation of countermemories that challenge the dominant narrative of the veterans' deportation, exclusion, and vilification. Following this discussion, Claire Whitlinger's chapter drew on the commemorative history of the 1964 murders of civil rights workers in Mississippi. To illuminate the importance of intergroup and interracial collaboration in overcoming the tensions of the past, she provided a comparative analysis between two mnemonic time frames (1989 and 2004) in which this painful history is reimagined and retold. The changes that occur in the 2004 (40th) commemoration of the murders reflect the emergence of a strong countermemory through shared storytelling, revealing two important dimensions of remembrance: commemoration as an act of protest and commemoration as a path towards social justice. Finally, this section closes with Amy Sodaro's exploration of the memorialization of the brutality of slavery. Through an investigation of The Legacy Museum: From Slavery to Mass Incarceration in Montgomery Alabama, Sodaro has interrogated the use and misuse of memory and the ways in which power functions to control the representations of a shameful and violent past. Sodaro compared The Legacy Museum to the Smithsonian National Museum of African American History and Culture, the former funded by a non-profit organization and the latter by the US government. In linking funding to the politics of memory, she argued persuasively that The Legacy Museum is "free" to tell a more complete story of slavery that disrupts the hegemonic narrative in which both the histories and continuities of cruelty and atrocity have been traditionally ignored and/or erased.

Finally, the scholars featured in Part III approached memory from varying yet interrelated points of view. The first two chapters by Werner Bohleber and Carol Kidron respectively considered the intergenerational transmission of trauma. The third chapter by Selma Leydesdorff took a comprehensive view of the new generational histories that are emerging across the post-communist European landscape; and in the last chapter, Jacob Caponi and Fatma Müge Göçek offered a historical perspective on the power dynamics of memory across time and diverse cultural landscapes. To begin, Bohleber adopted a psychoanalytic perspective to explain and understand how emotion-based memories (guilt, shame, and fear) are passed down from one generation to the next within post war German families. In particular, he elaborated on the processes by which families communicate a confluence of remembrances that lay the foundation for the emergence of collective memory among successor generations who seek to uncover the repressed histories of their families and of their nation. Following Bohleber, Kidron also looks to successor generations to better understand the construction of survivor identities through time and history. In her work, Kidron contends that second and third generation Holocaust descendants assume the moral responsibility for preserving and transmitting the past to future generations. This responsibility, while psychologically challenging, illuminates the resiliency of children and grandchildren of Holocaust survivors and the complexity of their identity formation.

Turning to Selma Leydesdorff's chapter on eastern European memory tropes, her analysis highlights the mnemonic tensions that have come to define the meaning of victimhood within various nationalist agendas. In countries such as Poland, Hungary, and Russia, national remembrance focuses on the memorialization of communist perpetrators and victimized citizens, obscuring the history of Holocaust atrocities and Nazi complicity within these countries' pasts. Bringing a personal and deeply passionate perspective to her analysis, Leydesdorff considers the shifting politics of Eastern Europe in which "new histories" are blurring the boundaries of memory between the genocide of World War II and the communist oppression that followed the defeat of Germany.

In the final chapter Jacob Caponi and Fatma Müge Göçek have taken a broad view of genocide through a comparison of the Armenian Genocide of 1915 and the 1994 genocide in Rwanda. Although each period of violence is rooted in specific histories and geographies, Caponi and Göçek reveal the layers of contention that are at the core of genocidal conflict and thus persist in the collective memories that are re-remembered and reconstructed in the aftermath of violence. In this regard, they explore the ways in which social and political relations of power underlie the interpretive frameworks that are brought to bear on defining and memorializing genocide, as powerful actors seek to control the narratives and knowledge of difficult pasts.

Given the diverse collection of insightful work in this volume, it is clear that the study of contentious memory has become an important area of research for our understandings of mass trauma and political and social upheaval, both past and present. Across these chapters, the contributors suggest that there are numerous and highly significant ways in which individuals, societies, nations, and cultures reveal or reframe histories of collective suffering and shame. Elaborating the social frameworks of memory that were first theorized by Durkheim and Hawlbachs, the research presented here furthers our understanding of contentious memory and mnemonic conflict, illuminating histories of racism, sexism, anti-Semitism, xenophobia, and political oppression that inform the evolution of countermemory and fractured collective recollections.

As a multifaceted resource for scholars who wish to probe the social and political relations of memorialization, this volume helps us to consider how memory continues to be shaped, used, and abused; and how memory can also serve as a force for change and social justice. While each of the authors have focused on a particular case or group of cases, we encourage readers to use these varied perspectives to examine and consider new cases of contentious memory. As we look to the violence that currently impacts groups such as the Uyghurs in China, the Tigrayans in Ethiopia, and the Rohingya in Myanmar, we can see how collective memories are already being managed, navigated, and forcefully controlled. It is our hope that the scholarship in this book will provide new interpretive lenses and pathways to exploring and making visible the multiple frames of memory and mnemonic controversy that in time will come to define these as well as other terrible pasts.

References

Alexander, J.C. (2004) "On the Social Construction of Moral Universals: The 'Holocaust' from War Crime to Trauma Drama," in J.C. Alexander, R. Eyerman, B. Giesen, N.J. Smelser, and P. Sztompka (eds) *Cultural Trauma and Collective Identity*. Berkeley, CA: University of California Press, pp 196–263.

Barthes, R. (1980) *Camera Lucida: Reflections on Photography*, New York: Farrar, Straus, and Giroux.

Confino, A. (2006) *Germany as a Culture of Remembrance: Promises and Limits of Writing History*, Chapel Hill, NC: University of North Carolina Press.

Durkheim, E. ([1912] 2001) *The Elementary Forms of Religious Life*, New York: Oxford University Press.

Erőss, A. (2016) "'In Memory of Victims': Monument and Counter-monument in Liberty Square, Budapest," *Hungarian Geographical Bulletin* 65(3): 237–254.

Eyerman, R. (2001) *Cultural Trauma: Slavery and the Formation of African American Identity*, Cambridge: Cambridge University Press.

Foucault, M. ([1971] 1988) "Nietzsche, Genealogy, History," in J.D. Faubion (ed) *Aesthetics, Method, and Epistemology* (vol. 2), London: Penguin, pp 369–391.

Foucault, M. (1977) *Language, Counter-Memory, Practice: Selected Essays and Interviews*, Ithaca, NY: Cornell University Press.

Halbwachs, M. ([1941] 1992) "The Legendary Topography of the Gospels in the Holy Land," in L.A. Coser (ed) *On Collective Memory*, Chicago, IL: University of Chicago Press, pp 193–235.

Halbwachs, M. ([1952] 1992) "The Social Frameworks of Memory," in L.A. Coser (ed) *On Collective Memory*, Chicago, IL: University of Chicago Press, pp 37–189.

Jacobs, J. (2017) "The Memorial at Srebrenica: Gender and the Social Meanings of Collective Memory in Bosnia-Herzegovina," *Memory Studies* 10(4): 423–439.

Neiman, S. (2019) *Learning from the Germans: Race and the Memory of Evil*, New York: Farrar, Straus, and Giroux.

Olick, J.K. (2007) *The Politics of Regret: On Collective Memory and Historical Responsibility*, New York: Routledge.

Sheftel, A. (2012) "'Monument to the International Community, From the Grateful Citizens of Sarajevo': Dark Humour as Counter-memory in Post-conflict Bosnia-Herzegovina," *Memory Studies* 5(2): 145–164.

Tello, V. (2022) "Counter-memory and And-and: Aesthetics and Temporalities for Living Together," *Memory Studies* 15(2): 390–401.

Vinitzky-Seroussi, V. (2002) "Commemorating a Difficult Past: Yitzhak Rabin's Memorials," *American Sociological Review* 67(1): 30–51.

Wagner-Pacifici, R. and Schwartz, B. (1991) "The Vietnam Veterans Memorial: Commemorating a Difficult Past," *American Journal of Sociology* 97(2): 376–420.

Young, J.E. (1992) "The Counter-Monument: Memory against Itself in Germany Today," *Critical Inquiry* 18(2): 267–296.

Zerubavel, Y. (1995) *Recovered Roots: Collective Memory and the Making of Israeli National Tradition*, Chicago, IL: University of Chicago Press.

Index

References to endnotes show both the page number and the note number (170n4).

A

Abbott, A. 137
Abramsky, S. 99
accountability 100, 167, 237, 240, 244, 246, 250–251, 253
Aderet, O. 37
African American Museum Project 159
African Americans
  history of 157–158
  museums 157–159, 164, 166
  and racial inequality 115
African Burial Ground 158, 170n4
Agam, I. 33
agents of memory 8, 93, 138, 148
aggravated felonies 114–115, 128
Aguilera, C. 20n3
Akayesu, J.P. 62n6
Alexander, J.C. 259–260
Alexander, M. 162
Allied Powers 242
Allport, G. 143, 144
Alternative for Germany (AfD) 193
American Greatness 103–104
Anacostia Museum 158
ancestral ethnic lived suffering 214
ancestral memories 258
Anderson, K. 98
anti-Semitism 180, 193, 205, 221, 222, 225–227, 230
apartheid archives, ignorance of Black women's experiences of violence in 51
Arab–Israeli conflict 37
Arbery, A. 154
Arendt, H. 190, 245
Armenian Genocide (1915) 19, 236, 239, 252, 263
  collective violence 244–245
  internal polarization to 249–250
  narration of 241
  post-genocidal (re)narration 250
  theory–praxis interaction 244

time–power intersection 242
variable experience 245
variable knowledge 246
see also Genocide Against the Tutsi in Rwanda (1994)
Arrow Cross Party 230
As if There Was No War (Lomsky-Feder) 30, 31, 32
Association of African American Museums 157
attribution error 93–94
Auschwitz 178, 180, 190, 191, 207, 231
authenticity 101, 130, 197, 198–199, 202, 210–212
autobiographical memories 8–11, 15, 38, 262
  of deported veterans 113–114, 116, 122, 126, 127, 129–130
  sexual and gender base violence 50, 52
Autry, R. 158

B

Badilla, M. 20n3
Baker, R. 98
Balberg-Rothenstreich, A. 202
Baltic states
  answer to Soviet oppression 228–229
  killing of Jews with Nazis 222
  suffering under communism 222
Barajas, H. 116–118, 120, 126
Becker, H. 138
Belgian colonialists 247–248
Ben-Ari, E. 43
Biden, J. 91, 106, 107
binary thinking 238
biographical memory, use and abuse of 93
Black Lives Matter 154, 155, 166, 169
body politic 242, 249
body-shaming 103
Bohleber, W. 17

INDEX

Bosnia 260
 genocidal rape survivors 58–59
 war refugees 192
Breaking the Silence 38, 41–43
Brown, R.H. 240–241
burden
 irrevocable and transmission of 203–204
 of memory and testimony 204
Bush, G.H.W. 91
Bush, G.W. 99, 106, 158
bystanders 17, 18, 90, 167, 185, 191, 245

C

Caldwell, B.C. 115
Campbell, R. 60
Carter, J. 91
Center Against Expulsions 223
ceremonial occasions 120
certificates, as proof for service in military 119, 120, 123
Chaidez, G. 120
Chaney, J. 16, 134
Charlottesville Unite the Right rally 160
Chaumont, J.-M. 219
Chrétien, J.P. 247
citizenship hierarchies 248
civil and human rights education bill 135, 139, 140–141
civil rights workers murder in Mississippi 134, 262
 commemorations *see* commemorations
 justice for 145–146
Claremont Review of Books 90
Clinton, B. 91, 93, 94, 95, 106
 see also Clinton, W.J.
Clinton, H. 93–94, 96
 hatred for 95, 101–105
 reputations 91
 sexualizing 103
 and Trump, presidential battle between 15, 89
Clinton, W.J. 90
 see also Clinton, B.
Cockburn, A. 98
Coles, J. 62n11
collaborative remembering 6
collected memories 50–51, 61n1, 148, 261
collective amnesia 251–252
collective identity 5, 18, 144, 146, 147, 181, 192, 258
collective memories 5, 8–9, 50, 51, 56, 61n1, 81, 148, 259, 264
 changing, and mnemonic battle 218–219
 gendered dynamics of 49
 national 212
 of personal pasts 15
 and social memories 55
collective remembering and forgetting 21n8

collective violence 236, 250, 251, 252–253, 254n6
 genocides *see* genocides
 politics of naming 243
 re-embedding into modernity 238–242
 and variable experience 245
 and variable knowledge 246
colonization 237, 241, 246, 247–248, 253, 254n6
Comité Pro-Rescate y Desarrollo de Vieques 72
commemorations 16, 50, 55, 135, 189
 banal projects 138
 and murder of civil rights workers in Mississippi 262
 of 1989 (twenty-fifth anniversary commemoration) 16, 135, 141–142, 144–145, 147, 262
 of 2004 (fortieth anniversary commemoration) 16, 134, 135, 138–147, 262
 collective 16
 consequences of 136
 as events, conceptualization of 136–138
 gendered dynamics of 49
 in Germany 179–183
 of Holocaust 156
 large-scale 135, 137, 146
 negative 190
 outcomes, and interactional dynamics 143–146
 planning process 145, 147
 as products of memory movement 147–148
 of racial violence 148
 smaller-scale 137
 and social change 135
 and social identities 148
 using memorial museums 157
Committee of Colored Citizens 159
communicative memory 188, 190
communist oppression 219, 221, 222, 228, 229, 232, 263
concealment practice 33
confederate symbols and memorials 1, 2, 3, 20n2, 160, 166
Confino, A. 260
Connolly, K. 59
contentious meaning-making 253
contentious memories 2, 237, 260, 263–264
 collective memories, in American politics 90
 and conflicts 4–6
 at the fall of the Soviet Union 93
 and memorial museums 155–157
 memory-making process 240
 social foundations of 5–11
Correa, J. 123–124
Coser, L. 93
counterfactual analysis 136, 139–141, 147
counter-identification 186
counter-memorialization 260
counter-memorials 260–261

countermemories 8, 51, 113–114, 122, 127–130, 137, 260, 262
  see also veterans, deported
co-witnesses 240
cultural discourses 29, 36, 43–44
cultural memory 188, 190, 242
cultural trauma 21n8, 50
Czech Republic 19, 20n3, 225

D

Daphna-Tekoah, Sh. 38
defensive reactions 189–190
DeGloma, T. 8, 122, 199
della Porta, D. 137
Deported Veterans Support Houses 15, 113, 114, 116, 117
descendants 18
  descendant resilient vulnerability 209
  Holocaust see Holocaust
  of survivors 198
  of Ukrainian genocide 200
Durkheim, É. 258
DuVernay, A. 162–163
Dworkin, A. 49

E

Eichmann trial in Jerusalem 180
Eisenhower, D. 91
Elementary Forms of Religious Life (Durkheim) 258
Emanuel African Methodist Episcopal Church incident 1, 2
emotional energy, intense 15, 91
emotional labor 52, 59–61
emotional loyalty attachments 188
emotional resilience 208
emotional restraint 33
emotion-based memories 262
Engelkin, B. 227
Epstein, J. 99–100
Equal Justice Initiative (EJI) 160, 161, 163–169, 165
  Community Remembrance Project 164
  see also Legacy Museum, The: From Slavery to Mass Incarceration
Espiritu, Y.L. 124, 129
Estonia 228
  see also Baltic States
European Union 221
Evanston 169, 170n12
expropriations 74, 75–77, 80, 84, 85n3
Eyerman, R. 261

F

facilitators framed identity-memory work 203
fake news 93
Falleti, T. 142
family memory 18–19, 187–188

Fassin, D. 201
father image, splitting 187
fear 17, 33, 81, 82, 83, 123, 134, 159, 178, 184, 190, 192–193
Feldman, J. 202
Fernandez-Kelly, P. 154
Fidesz party 229, 230
Fields, J.A., Jr 20n2
films 38, 142–145
First Intifada 35
Floyd, G. 1, 154
forgetting 9, 11, 51, 198–199, 209, 236, 247, 260
Foucauldian politics of memory 212
4Ds campaign 72
Freedom Rides 2
Frei, N. 188
French Revolution 238
Fried, C. 99
Friedersdorf, C. 101
Friedländer, S. 177
Fujii, L.A. 58

G

Gable, P. 96
Garcia, J.M. 130n2
Garcia camp 69, 77–78, 85n3
Gates, H.L. 102
Gdansk museum 223, 225, 226
Geertz, C. 197
genocidal rape 57, 58–59, 62n6
Genocide Against the Tutsi in Rwanda (1994) 14, 19, 51, 236, 241, 243–250, 252, 263
genocides 17, 20
  agency (social actors) 236–238, 240–141, 242, 243
  ambiguities within 242–244
  concept of 237, 239–240
  diverging standpoints in practice 244–246
  Genocide Against the Tutsi in Rwanda (1994) 19, 236, 241, 243–250, 252
  internal polarization leading to 249–250, 253, 254n6
  narration (context) 237, 241–242
  post genocidal renarration 250–251, 253, 254n6
  (re)narrating through subversion 246–252
  see also Armenian Genocide (1915); collective violence
German Federation of Expellees 223–224
Germans
  blockade of the collective memory in the postwar period 179
  identity after the Holocaust 191–193
  real victims of 180, 181
  see also Nazis
Germany 178
  colonialism 247–248

INDEX

commemorations in 179–183
constitutional patriotism 192
countermemorials in 260–261
defensive reactions in 189–190
economic miracle 180
National Socialism 178, 181–183, 185, 186, 187
transgenerational identification processes in 184–187
see also Holocaust
Gitlin, T. 103
Gliński, P. 227
Göçek, F.M. 254n6
Goldberg, M. 102
Goldhagen, D. 182
Goodman, A. 16, 134
Gould, S.J. 139
Grabowoski, J. 227
Gramcian politics of memory 212
Great Patriotic War 219–221
Griffin, L. 140
Gross, J.T. 226
group identities 50, 192, 254n6, 259
group narration processes 203
group rituals 258
group solidarity 8, 259
guilt 17, 19, 35, 38, 115, 167–168, 178, 181, 183–185, 218, 221, 230
Gulf War 37

H

Habermas, J. 182, 192, 240
Habyarimana, J. 248–250
Hacke, J. 192
Halbwachs, M. 5, 92, 207, 218, 258
Hamburg Institute for Social Research 182
Hammer, R. 253n4
Harel-Shalev, A. 38
harm and injury, memories of 121–122
Harris, F. 84
Heise, D. 140
Herblock (cartoonist) 89, 94
hermeneutic suspicion 204
heroic discourse 44, 45
Heyer, H. 20n2
Hinton, A.L. 237
Hiss, A. 95
Historikerstreit (Historians' Controversy) 181–182
history, and national pride 226
Hitler, A. 99, 179
Holocaust 17–18, 49, 177–178, 193, 238
  commemorations 199
  descendants, memory of 200
  embodied memories of survival 206, 207, 208
  first generation 185, 212
  fourth generation descendants 187–188
  hybrid third generation descendants 211–212
  Israeli descendant identity, memory and testimonial voice 201
  memory, epistemological frames of 198
  pedagogic engagement 190, 198, 201–202, 211, 213
  politics of memory 199
  public debate on 181–182, 183
  second generation descendants 185, 201, 204, 209
  sensual experience of survival 207
  third generation descendants 187–188, 201, 202, 204
Holocaust series 181
Holocaust/Shoah 218, 221, 223, 229, 230
Horthy, M. 230
"House of Terror, The" 229
Hungary 19, 219, 225, 229–230, 260–261, 263
Hutu 61n2, 245, 248–249, 251, 252

I

identities 11, 205
  child as self-object; negative identifications 186
  positive 194
  pre-established 92
  social 148
  as veterans 117, 118, 121
Immigrant Legal Resource Center 114
implicated subjects 167, 250, 251–252, 253n2
"Inability to Mourn, The" 180
Interahmwe 249
intergroup relations, maintenance of 143–144
interpretative approaches 11–13
Iran 52
Israeli militarism 13, 261
  cultural discourses 29, 36, 43–44
  dynamic and influenced memories of soldiers 44
  heroic discourse 44, 45
  interpretive paradigm research 31
  media, and traumatic discourse 37
  Nahal Battalion combatants 39
  1948 War of Independence 13, 30, 33, 34, 36, 39, 44
  occupied territories *see* occupied territories, Israel militarism
  perpetrators' trauma 38
  personal memories of soldiers 29, 30, 35, 40, 44–45
  policing civilians and combating terrorist cells 36
  psychological discourses 34
  public discourse 36–37
  resilience discourses 40, 45
  restraining discourses 43
  silencing mechanism *see* silencing mechanisms
  soldiers as victims 32

and trauma *see* trauma
unshared memories of soldiers 44
Yom Kippur War (1973 War) 13, 29, 30–39, 42, 44
Israeli war veterans *see* Israeli militarism

J

Jacobs, J. 261
Japan, post-Fukushima nuclear disaster 200
Jarvis, J. 241
Jasper, J. 144
Jedwabne massacre 226
Jewish museum 226–227
Jones, A. 103
Judt, T. 218, 219

K

Kaczyński, J. 227
Kaczyński, L. 227
Kaner, R. 41
Katyń massacre 224–225
Kemal, M. 245
Khabensky, K. 233n9
Kidron, C.A. 45n2
Killen, E.R. 16, 135, 139, 140–141
Kimeldorf, H. 137
Kipnis, L. 105
Knigge, V. 188
knowledge entrepreneurs 237, 240–241, 243
König, H. 190–191
Koselleck, R. 189
Ku Klux Klan 134

L

Lalami, L. 99
Landsberg, A. 155
Latinx people 115, 118, 123, 125
Latvia 228–229
  see also Baltic states
Law and Justice party (PiS) 226–227
Lee, R.E., statue of 160
Legacy Museum, The: From Slavery to Mass Incarceration 16, 155, 159–169, 262
  color symbolism 164
  Enslavement in America section 163–164
  final corridor 166
  Incarcerated section 165–166
  non-national museum 168
  Segregated section 164–165
  Terrorized period section 164
Legendary Topography of the Gospels in the Holy Land, The (Halbwachs) 259
Lemkin, R. 239
Lesczyńska, F. 227
Limbaugh, R. 94
Linenthal, E. 157
Lithuania 228–229
  see also Baltic states

lived memories 207
  of contemporary victim 214
  Holocaust *see* Holocaust
London, H. 102–103
Lost Cause myth 168, 170n11
Luker, K. 130
Lynching Memorial *see* National Memorial to Peace and Justice

M

Machcewicz, P. 225–226
Mahoney, J. 142
Maier, C. 178
Malone, E.L. 240–241
Manekin, D. 33
Mannheim, K. 184
Manuel, I. 170n8
Marrus , M. 219
McCarthy, K. 125–126
McEwan, C. 51
memoir writers 240
memoirs 156, 246
memorial museums 16, 155, 162, 168, 225–226
  commemorations using 157
  and contentious memories 155–157
  impact of pandemic on 169
  Legacy Museum, The *see* Legacy Museum, The: From Slavery to Mass Incarceration
  national 168
  national conversation, reshaping 166–168
  National September 11 Memorial Museum 157
  in Poland 223
  in Sobibor 230–231
  United States Holocaust Memorial Museum (USHMM) 155, 157, 166
  see also museums
memorialization 14, 49, 52, 55, 56, 231, 233n11, 244, 259–260, 261, 262, 263, 264
memory boom 155–156, 158
memory movements 16, 134, 137–138, 147–148
memory-making 61, 93, 236, 240, 251
Merkel, A. 193
meta-data 58
Mexican drug cartels 124
Meyer, R. 137
military presence
  bombing, as a living trauma 80–83
  and expropriations 74, 75–77, 80, 84, 85n3
  impact of 69–70
  mnemonic signifiers 70, 74–76, 78, 80, 81, 83, 85
  and mobilization 70–71, 82, 84
  remembrance of 74
  soldiers versus civilians 77–80
Mill, J.S. 141
misremembering 9

INDEX

Mississippi Burning (film) 142, 145
Mississippi Truth Project 16, 135, 139, 140, 141
Mitscherlich, A. 180
Mitscherlich, M. 180
mnemonic authority 7, 50, 114, 122–123
mnemonic battles 3, 10, 19, 138, 218–219
mnemonic capacity 21n7, 142
mnemonic communities 6–7, 30, 81, 84
mnemonic denial 9, 18, 134, 135, 180, 184, 193, 222, 229, 239, 250, 253, 254n6
mnemonic discovery 9
mnemonic entrepreneurs 7, 50, 138
mnemonic selectivity 9
mnemonic solidarity 5, 7
mnemonic supremacy 50–51
mnemonic tensions 122–126
Montgomery 161–162, 168
  see also Legacy Museum, The: From Slavery to Mass Incarceration
moral considerations, absence of 35–36
moral entrepreneurs 138
moral injury 38
MOVE 142–143
Münkler, H. 192
Museum of Occupation, Estonian 228
museums
  African American 157–159, 164, 166
  Anacostia Museum 158
  Gdansk museum 223, 225, 226
  Museum of Occupation, Estonian 228
  9/11 Museum 155, 166
  Reut Museum 39
  Smithsonian National Museum of American History 158
  Smithsonian National Museum of African American History and Culture (NMAAHC) 158–159, 170n4, 262
  see also memorial museums

N

Najmabadi, A. 52
narration 259
  and mobilization 70–71
  and relocation and migration 77
  significance of 70
NATAL (the Israel Trauma and Resiliency Center) 37, 38
Nation, The 103
nation building, and civil discourse 238
National Memorial to Peace and Justice 16, 155, 160
National Museum for African American History and Culture (NMAAHC) 158–159, 162, 166, 168
National September 11 Memorial Museum 157
National Socialism 178, 181–183, 185, 186, 187

nationalism 155, 156, 160, 192, 218, 223–228, 232, 241–242
nation-state formation 241, 248–249, 253, 254n6
Navaro-Yashin, Y. 253n5
Nazis 17–18, 218
  and Baltic states 222
  invasion by 221
  regime 193
  Volksgemeinschaft 179
  see also Holocaust
negative memories 189–190, 194
  and German identity after the Holocaust 191–193
  and social memory 188–189
Neighbors: The Destruction of the Jewish Community in Jedwabne, Poland (Gross) 226
Neiman, S. 261
Neshoba County 134, 135, 142, 145–147
  see also commemorations
Netherlands, the 231
New Jim Crow, The (Alexander) 162
New York Historical Society 158
New York Times 90, 95–98, 100, 102
Newsome Bass, B 1–2, 3
NGO Memorial 218
¡*Ni una bomba más!* 73, 81, 84
9/11 Museum 155, 166
Nixon, R. 90, 91, 93, 94–95, 100, 106
NKVD 224, 225
non-communist identity 222
non-traumatic battle reaction 39
Nora, P. 206, 207
normalization processes 192
Nyseth, H. 53

O

Obama, B. 94, 100, 106–107, 159
Obermann, K. 95, 98
occupied territories, Israel militarism
  activity in 36
  combat experiences, avoiding speaking of 33
  policing operations in 44
  terror attacks and Palestinian uprisings in 37
Olick, J.K. 148
Operation Reinhard 230
Ottoman colonization 247
Ottoman Empire, and Turkish Republic 251
Ottoman modernization 248–249

P

Palestinians–Israelis relations 36
Palin, S. 99
parasocial interaction 91, 97
Paxton, R. 219
Pechersky, S. 220
pedagogic construction 201–202, 211, 213
perpetrators
  trauma of 38
  as victims 245

perpetrator–victim binary 251
personal injuries, historicization of 17
personal memories 8, 11, 14, 15, 18, 29, 30, 35, 40, 44–45, 70, 130, 261
personal narratives 121, 122–123, 199
personal positions 197, 199, 212
Pettigrew, T. 144
Philadelphia 134
Philadelphia Coalition 134–135, 146–147
Poland 198, 201–202, 211, 263
  disagreement about the past 226
  and Germany 226, 227
  Home Army (A.K.) 224, 226
  and Israel 201
  Jedwabne massacre 226
  and Katyń massacre 224–225
  Law and Justice party (PiS) 226–227
  museums 223, 225, 226
  nationalism and destabilization of memory 223–228
  nationalism of 223–228
  pedagogic trips to 201, 210–211, 213
  and Russia 224–225
  Sobibor 220, 225, 226, 230–231, 233n11
political hatred
  artistic representation, of public disdain 89, 94, 102
  and emotions 91
  and partisans 89–95, 97, 99, 106
  and reputations 89–95, 99, 105, 107
  see also Clinton, H.; Trump, D.; United States 2016 presidential election
political loathing 90, 91, 92, 96
political violence
  women's experiences during 51
politicized memory 223
Polletta, F. 72
post-genocidal renarration 250–251, 253, 254n6
post-traumatic stress disorder (PTSD) 41, 45, 200
Power, S. 253n1
power dynamics of memory 14, 15, 246, 262–263
pride 1, 34, 117, 158, 180, 191, 217–218, 223, 226, 228, 229–230, 232
primary signifiers 75
Prince, J. 145
prison system, injustices of 165–166
private memory 208, 210, 212
protests, as events 137
public apologies, forced 228
public disdain 89, 94, 102, 105

R

Rajiva, M. 58
rape 60
  genocidal 57, 58–59, 62n6
  of Zo Hnahthlak people 52
reflexivity 12, 199, 252–253

refugee crisis (2015) 192
refugee research, memory in 129
regret, politics of 156
Řehořová, I 20n3
Reichel, P. 183
Reilly, R.C. 59
remembrance 11
  of crime and the negative memory 188–191
  cultural practices 178
  progressive restoration 183
  secondary 189
  social process of 74
reparations
  new momentum on 169
  new program 170n12
  politics 156
reputations 91, 93, 106
rescue behavior 53–54
Resisim 40–41
responsibility, moral 35, 263
resultant descendant profile 204
Reut Museum 39
Ricoeur, P. 21n9
right to speak, monitoring of 42
ritualized memories 258
Roof, D. 1, 2–3
Roosevelt, F.D. 90
Rotem, N. 39
Rothberg, M. 167–168
Rüsen, J. 177
Russia 231, 263
  Great Patriotic War 220
  heroism in 218
  and Israel 231
  versus Poland 224–225
Rwanda 261
  Civil War (1990–1994) 249
  colonization of 247
  genocide in *see* Genocide Against the Tutsi in Rwanda (1994)
  memory of victimized women in 261
  national memorials in 51
  post-genocidal 251–252
Rwandan Patriotic Front (RPF) 249, 250

S

St. Louise, S.P. 119–120
Sanes, D. 14, 72–73, 77, 81, 84
Sarajevo 260
Schicksalsgemeinschaft 192
Schudson, M. 212
Schwerner, M. 16, 134
secondary experiences, of the past 187
secondary signifiers 75, 77, 80
self 11
self-examination 205
self-reflexivity 199, 204–209
Sewell, W. 136, 137, 141, 147

sexual and gender-based violence (SGBV) 51, 53–54
sexual violence 52, 57, 261
shame about the past 218, 223
shared experiences 5, 57–59, 81
Shaw, R. 201
Sheftel, A. 260
Shoah 19, 217, 221, 222, 232
  see also Holocaust/Shoah
silence 185, 200
  among the generation of combatants 34
  individual silences and social silences 59
  institutionalization of 50
  listening to 61
  past silences and contemporary inequalities 50–52
  replacing 9
  sanctions against those who break 43
  sexual violence, in Somalia 51
  sharing experiences through 57–59
  of survivor family 206
  "wall of silence" 200
silencing mechanisms 42–43
  around military violence 42
  authorizing violence 42–43
  monitoring the right to speak 42
  sanctions against those who break the silence 43
Skocpol, T. 141
slavery 161–162, 262
  institutions acknowledging their past ties to 169
  memorial museums *see* memorial museums
Smith, R. 162
Snyder, T. 219
Sobibor 220, 225, 226, 230–231, 233n11
social actors
  and public remembrance 50, 53
social appropriation 84
social forces, impact of 6
Social Frameworks of Memory, The (Halbwachs) 258–259
social memory, and negative memories 188–189
social movements, as mnemonic agents 71
social relationships, and memory studies 167
social revolutions 141
soldiers
  versus civilians 77–80
Soros, G. 230
South Carolina 2
SS Einsatzgruppen 180, 182
Stalinism 220
Stevenson, B. 160, 161, 167–168
Stola, D. 226, 227
stress continuities 10
stress discontinuities 10
student protest movement (1968) 181
subversive semiotics 2

survivor identities 263
Sweet, P.L. 250, 252
symbol systems 258–259

T

Takševa, T. 58
talk therapy 58, 200
Tang, E. 124
task force 144–146, 147
Taylor, B. 154
testimonies 10, 18, 42, 50, 201
theory–praxis intersection 243–144
13th (documentary) 163
Thomas, J.M. 123–124
Till, E. 159
Time magazine 98
time–power intersection 242–143
transitional justice 56, 61–62n4
trauma 10–11, 30, 52, 58, 81
  collective traumas, historicization of 17
  discourse 31–32, 43
  individual and social representation of 183–184
  intergenerational effects of 203
  intergenerational transmission of 262
  mass 263
  normalized 30, 40–42, 45
  of the perpetrator 44
  and resilience 36–40
  secondary 60
  secondary/vicarious 59
  in the theory of history 177
  transmitted 200, 208–209
  traumatized voices, in public sphere 39
  varied meaning among generations of soldiers 44
Treblinka 180, 230, 231
Trump, D. 91, 93–94, 103, 155, 159–160
  hatred for 94–97
  and Hillary Clinton, presidential battle between 15, 89
  and Kenya 100–101
  as master of greed 97–100
  reputation 91
Trump, I. 98
Trump Derangement Syndrome 99–100, 105
trust, importance of 56
Tubin, D. 33
Turkey 242–243, 244, 246–247, 248, 249, 251, 252, 254n6
Tusk, D. 225–226
Tutsi 61n2, 248
  see also Genocide Against the Tutsi in Rwanda (1994)

U

United States
  Civil Rights Movement 2–3, 135, 158, 161, 165, 166

criminal justice system 16, 115, 126, 160, 161, 165
despised president 93, 101, 107
hegemony 16, 115–116, 129, 156, 168, 210
non-US-citizens in armed forces 114
prison system, injustices of 165–166
race and memory in museums 157–160
racial history, challenging narratives of 169
United States 2016 presidential election 90–91
contentious reputations in campaign 261
United States Holocaust Memorial Museum (USHMM) 155, 157, 166

V

"Valley of Tears" series 37
variable experience 245
variable knowledge 245–246
veteran identity 123
through material objects 117–118
on US-facing social media 118–119
veterans, deported 15, 113, 262
aggravated felonies 114–115, 128
autobiographical memories 113–114, 116, 122, 126, 127, 130
banished veteran, construction of 117–122
certificates, as proof for service in military 119, 120, 123
commitment to the US military and the United States 125
countermemories 113–114, 122, 127–130, 137
criminality of 123, 125–126
deaths of 120
and emphasis on the US flag 121
and the government 122
honorable discharge, proof of 119
immigrants 114–115, 116, 118, 121, 123–125, 127–130
interpretative approaches 126–129
in Mexico 115
naturalization 114, 115, 116, 117, 124, 125
past, nature of 124
photographs of deportees as service members 119–120
provisions within the mass deportation apparatus 114
sharing of their memories of military service 121
and substance use 121, 125
Veterans Day 121
Veterans for Peace in Tijuana 116
Vichy France and the Jews (Marrus and Paxton) 219
victim-identified memory culture 189
victimization 19
victim–perpetrator binary 252
victims 217
of military violence 42–43

as perpetrators 222–223
politics of victimhood 19
within various nationalist agendas 263
in the West versus the East 221–222
Vieques 14, 69, 74, 75, 77–78, 80–82, 84, 85
military presence in *see* military presence
Vieques Movement 69–73
Vilnius 229
Voegeli, W. 101
Volksgemeinschaft 180
von Weizsäcker, R. 181

W

Waitsen, A. 220
War on Drugs 124
warfare
of extermination 193
normalization of 31
remembrances, personal version of 43–44
sexual assault in 261
warrior ethos 30, 33, 34, 36, 40
see also Israeli militarism; veterans, deported
Washington Post 96
Weber, M. 139
Wehrmacht 182
Welch, B. 104
William Winter Institute for Racial Reconciliation 142
Winter, John G. 163
Womack, L. 105
women
in apartheid archives 51
Bosnian genocidal rape survivors 58–59
as cardinal actors and voices of resistance 79
experiences during genocide 14
experiences during political violence 51
including women and stories of 51, 53–54
memorial space, absence of 57–58
in public memorialization 55
rescue behavior of 53–54
rescuers 54
testimonies from 42
trauma, recognition of 38–39
see also silence
World Health Organization 62n10
World War II 19, 219
Woźny, A. 252

Y

Yom Kippur War (1973 War) 13, 29, 30–39, 42, 44
Yoneyama, L. 129
Young, J. 260
Young Turks 248, 252

Z

Zionist combatants 35
Zo Hnahthlak people, mass rape of 52
Zubrzycki, G. 252

www.ingramcontent.com/pod-product-compliance
Lightning Source LLC
Chambersburg PA
CBHW051530020426
42333CB00016B/1867